Understanding Ethnic Violence

This book seeks to identify the motivations of individual perpetrators of ethnic violence. The work develops four models, labeled Fear, Hatred, Resentment, and Rage, gleaned from existing social science literatures.

The empirical chapters apply these four models to important events of ethnic conflict in Eastern Europe, from the 1905 Russian Revolution to the collapse of Yugoslavia in the 1990s. Each historical chapter generates questions about the timing and target of ethnic violence. The four models are then applied to the case, to learn which does the best job of explaining the observed patterns of ethnic conflict.

The findings challenge conventional wisdom, in that the Resentment narrative, centered on a sense of unjust group status, provides the best fit for a variety of cases. While Fear, Hatred, and Rage do motivate hostile actions, Resentment pervasively appears to inflame ethnic animosity and drive outcomes in the timing and pattern of action.

Roger D. Petersen is Associate Professor of Political Science at the Massachusetts Institute of Technology. He has done fieldwork in Lithuania and Kosovo and has published *Resistance and Rebellion: Lessons from Eastern Europe* with Cambridge University Press in 2001. He has published articles in the *Journal of Politics* and *European Journal of Sociology*. Petersen is also co-editor (with John Bowen) of *Critical Comparisons in Politics and Culture* (Cambridge University Press, 1999).

Cambridge Studies in Comparative Politics

General Editor
Margaret Levi   *University of Washington, Seattle*

Assistant General Editor
Stephen Hanson   *University of Washington, Seattle*

Associate Editors
Robert H. Bates   *Harvard University*
Peter Hall   *Harvard University*
Stephen Hanson   *University of Washington, Seattle*
Peter Lange   *Duke University*
Helen Milner   *Columbia University*
Frances Rosenbluth   *Yale University*
Susan Stokes   *University of Chicago*
Sidney Tarrow   *Cornell University*

Other Books in the Series

Continued on page following Index

Understanding Ethnic Violence

FEAR, HATRED, AND RESENTMENT IN TWENTIETH-CENTURY EASTERN EUROPE

ROGER D. PETERSEN

Massachusetts Institute of Technology

 CAMBRIDGE
UNIVERSITY PRESS

CAMBRIDGE UNIVERSITY PRESS
Cambridge, New York, Melbourne, Madrid, Cape Town,
Singapore, São Paulo, Delhi, Tokyo, Mexico City

Cambridge University Press
32 Avenue of the Americas, New York, NY 10013-2473, USA

www.cambridge.org
Information on this title: www.cambridge.org/9780521007740

First published 2002
Reprinted 2004, 2006, 2008, 2009, 2011

A *catalog record for this publication is available from the British Library.*

Library of Congress Cataloging in Publication Data

Petersen, Roger Dale, 1959–
Understanding ethnic violence : fear, hatred, and resentment in twentieth-century
Eastern Europe / Roger D. Petersen.
  p.   cm. – (Cambridge studies in comparative politics)
Includes bibliographical references and index.
ISBN 0-521-80986-X – ISBN 0-521-00774-7 (pb.)
1. Ethnic conflict – Europe, Eastern – History– 20th century.   2. Europe, Eastern – Ethnic
relations – History – 20th century.   I. Title.   II. Series.
DJK26. P48   2002
305.8′00947′0904 – dc21   2002017403

ISBN 978-0-521-80986-3 Hardback
ISBN 978-0-521-00774-0 Paperback

For my parents

Contents

Preface

The motivation for this book comes from a simple intuition: Emotion is an essential part of human nature and has something to do with ethnic violence and conflict. When I began this project, many of my fellow political scientists greeted this intuition with indifference. Some were even hostile. This reaction convinced me that a book on emotions and ethnic violence was worth doing. I believe that most political scientists share an understanding that emotions must have something to do with ethnic violence. I also believe that they neglect the role of emotion because it seems too amorphous and lies outside the dominant paradigms of the field. This book is an effort to show that the essential role of emotion in ethnic violence can be captured systematically and that emotion and rationality are not always irreconcilable forces that require completely separate modes of analysis. In fact, as I point out in the text, assumptions about the importance of emotion already exist implicitly in many of the most widely known theories of social science.

This book was also driven by a substantive question: What micro-mechanisms were involved in producing the homogenization of Eastern Europe during the twentieth century? While the actions of the Germans and Soviets were clearly critical in producing this overall outcome, there were many events in which neighbor attacked neighbor without much direction by outside forces. These events have been crucial in polarizing populations and destroying the conditions for ethnic heterogeneity. Furthermore, these events provide opportunities to isolate and understand the mechanisms driving individuals toward participation in ethnic violence. It is my hope that this book will appeal to both social scientists working on ethnic violence at large and area specialists focusing on Eastern Europe.

In an important way, this book continues in the vein of a previous work. In *Resistance and Rebellion: Lessons from Eastern Europe* (Cambridge University Press, 2001), I identified sequences of mechanisms leading to sustained violent resistance against powerful regimes. One of the main goals in that project was the identification of normative mechanisms and their operation within community networks. In rebellion against the strong, I argued that an understanding of these community-level norms holds the key to explaining variation in the organization of violence. In this book, I continue to study a nonrational (but not necessarily irrational) mechanism and its role in producing violence. Here, the focus is mainly on mechanisms motivating perpetrators of ethnic violence, usually violence against minorities. For this phenomenon, I argue that emotional mechanisms, rather than norms, help explain variation in target and timing.

While I applied for no funding for this project, I received considerable support in other ways. Going back to 1995, I have presented versions and sections of this book at the Center for Slavic Studies at the University of California at Berkeley, the Olin Center for Strategic Studies at Harvard University, the Department of Politics at New York University, the Harriman Institute at Columbia University, the Public Choice Annual Conference, the Association for the Study of Nationalities annual conference, Wilder House at the University of Chicago, the German-American Frontiers of Social Science Conference, and the Political Science Department at the Massachusetts Institute of Technology, among other forums.

The most important source of support came from graduate students at Washington University in St. Louis. While teaching in the Political Science Department, I led an informal group of students doing research on Eastern and Central Europe. Two chapters of this book directly result from this interaction. John Ginkel is the author of Chapter 7, "The Reconstruction of Independent States." Beth Wilner is the author of Chapter 9, "Czechoslovakia, 1848–1998." Andrea Gates helped in researching Chapter 5; her German language skills were crucial in developing that section. Andrew Duttlinger was also part of the group. I benefited greatly from their insights and their friendship.

There were two reviewers for Cambridge University Press. I would like to thank the anonymous reviewer, but I would like to especially acknowledge the other reviewer, Donald Horowitz. He will be able to recognize several major junctures in the book where I took his advice. The book is much improved because of his detailed suggestions. Jon Elster's input, as well as his personal support, has shaped this project. His own work on emotion has significantly influenced this book.

At Cambridge University Press, I thank Lewis Bateman, Senior Editor of Political Science, and his assistant Lauren Levin. Jennifer Carey did an outstanding job as copy editor. I would also like to thank Margaret Levi, the general editor for the Cambridge Studies in Comparative Politics series, for her interest in and support of this work. Many outstanding scholars have published in the Cambridge Studies in Comparative Politics series and I am proud to now be among them.

Above all, I thank my wife, Daniela Stojanovic, for both personal inspiration and intellectual criticism and insight.

1

Introduction

In September 1999, Richard Holbrooke attributed Bosnia's postwar problems to the existence of evil influences: "The forces of darkness – separatists, racists, war criminals, and crooks – are still there, continuing their efforts to keep the people in the dark ages."[1] Holbrooke implies that the modern age will eliminate, or should eliminate, these retrograde causes of ethnic conflict. This book approaches the persistence of ethnic conflict from a different set of assumptions. It treats the motivation to participate in or support ethnic violence and discrimination as inherent in human nature. Until we realize that the capacity to commit ethnic violence lies within all of us we are in danger of constantly being surprised at the emergence of forces from the "the dark ages." Furthermore, we will remain unable to develop the most effective constraints and preventions.

This work will develop four stories, or models, each describing a process motivating individuals to commit violent or punitive actions against ethnic others. Each of these stories will be based on a single emotion that underlies a theory or set of theories commonly found in the social science literature on ethnic conflict. The Fear[2] story is distilled from the security dilemma theories of international relations; Hatred builds on the "ancient hatreds" view often found in journalistic accounts; Resentment develops concepts from social psychology that concentrate on consciousness of group status; Rage is extracted primarily from psychological theories linking frustration and aggression. Each of these emotion-

---

[1] *New York Times*, September 14, 1999.
[2] I will use capital letters to designate the specific construct used here and a small letter when referring to the emotion in general or as used by others.

1

based explanations specifies a sequence linking observable structural change, belief formation, emotion, and action. In effect, each is a narrative of a social process that tells how individuals treat information, how the saliency of one goal becomes heightened, and how ethnic violence or discriminatory actions result. Crucially, each of these emotion-based narratives predicts a different pattern in the timing and targets of action.

These are not the only four emotions relevant to ethnic conflict, nor is emotion always the most important factor in igniting ethnic hostility. Clearly, there are dozens of factors that can influence the outbreak and intensity of ethnic animosity. The central question here, though, is why individual human beings commit acts, sometimes brutal and humiliating acts, against other individual human beings of a different ethnic category. This is a microlevel phenomenon that requires an assessment of motivation. These four emotions, more than most others, build on existing literatures and conventional wisdoms regarding this motivation.

This theoretical approach is employed to understand the patterns and puzzles of ethnic conflict in twentieth century Eastern Europe. The cases, described shortly, cover a wide expanse of time and space stretching from the 1905 Russian Revolution to the collapse of Yugoslavia in the 1990s. Several empirical chapters apply the four stories – Fear, Hatred, Rage, and Resentment – to important events, or nonevents, of ethnic conflict in the region. Each chapter assesses the fit of each story, tests its predictions, and generates discussion. By the end of the volume, the reader will see that certain emotional mechanisms have motivated ethnic conflict more than others. In particular, the Resentment narrative, centered on a belief and sense of unjust group status, provides the best predictive and descriptive fit toward a variety of cases of ethnic conflict in Eastern Europe. While an emotion-based account cannot explain every case, and while Fear and Hatred motivate hostile ethnic actions in some situations, Resentment pervasively appears to inflame ethnic animosity and drive outcomes in the timing and patterns of action.

Why Emotion?

In order to explain patterns of ethnic violence in Eastern Europe's modern period, both motivation and constraint must be understood. Of these two forces, the issue of motivation is more puzzling, if not more crucial, in understanding the events of Eastern Europe. The primary purpose of an emotion-based approach is to compare and assess different motivations.[3] As outlined in detail in the next chapter, emotions are mechanisms – recognizable individual-level causal forces – that work to change the level of saliency of desires. It is assumed that almost all individuals strongly and commonly desire a few basic things: safety, wealth, and status or self-esteem. Emotions alert the individual to heighten the pursuit of one basic desire above others to meet the demands of changing conditions. For example, fear orients the individual to take actions, fight or flight, to meet a threat. Metaphorically, an emotion acts like a "switch" – it creates compulsions to meet one environmental demand above all others.[4]

This conception of emotion helps solve several problems. First, it challenges the assumption of the stability of preferences that underlies many social science treatments of ethnic conflict. This simplifying assumption is too simple in regard to ethnic conflict. The same individual may be compelled to participate in ethnic violence for multiple reasons. Sometimes status concerns drive the action, sometimes safety concerns, and sometimes hatred captures an individual. Emotion helps explain how and when one concern becomes dominant and, in some cases, all consuming.

Second, emotion helps explain the essentialization of identities that underlies ethnic conflict. While identities are multiple and malleable, identities can crystallize when one is in the grasp of a powerful emotion. Eastern Europe, especially in the first half of the century, was a diverse area with a complex history. Religion, language, traditions, customs, institutions, political affilitation, and personal factors were all capable of influencing the actions of any given individual in different situations. Despite multiple sources of identity, perpetrators of ethnic violence arrive at the same basic essentializing sequence: "I am a member of X, he is a member of Y, and members of Y should be targeted for violence."[5] Each emotion-based narrative provides an explanation of how, in the face of social complexity and fluidity, such a brutal simplicity comes to frame outlooks and motivate action.

---

[3] As will become evident, I am not using the term *emotion* in common psychological and biological senses.

[4] Robert P. Abelson has used this term to discuss changes between instrumental and expressive modes of motivation and behavior. See "The Secret Existence of Expressive Behavior" in Jeffrey Friedman, ed., *The Rational Choice Controversy: Economic Models of Politics Reconsidered* (New Haven, CT: Yale University Press, 1996), pp. 25–36.

[5] The approach here necessarily reifies groups. The project tries to understand the motivation of perpetrators of *ethnic* violence and such perpetrators, by definition, reify group identities.

Third, and related to the preceding points, emotion helps explain the spontaneous yet directed and purposeful nature of many critical violent events in Eastern Europe. How does a collective body, such as a violent mob, come to act as a coherent unit in terms of specifying an ethnic target? Emotion can coordinate motivations and effectively point a legion of individuals in one particular direction.[6] Emotion can substitute for leadership. The social sciences have long struggled to explain the aggregation of behavior among a loosely connected set of individuals. The emotion-based narratives show how common experiences provide a collective understanding of the "justness" of violence and the specification of a target.

While a multitude of passages could be used to illustrate these points, here I will employ only three, all from the same region. In *Land Without Justice*, Milovan Djilas describes a Montenegrin attack on the local Muslim population that he witnessed as a youth. After the shooting death and subsequent funeral of a local Montenegrin clan chieftan, the previously feuding Montenegrin clansmen turned as one on the local Muslims. I quote at length:

Immediately after Bosko's burial, without any special consultation, the Poljani, and others with them, took their concealed weapons and marched on the Moslems. Half of them were unarmed, but weapons were not necessary. The Moslem population against whom they were marching was unarmed, and most were not warlike, except those that lived along the former border, most of whom had moved farther into the interior in 1912 or 1918. The Montenegrins were not particularly well organized. They placed themselves, quite spontaneously, under the command of former officers, now pensioned, who they had brought along and urged into the lead.

Never was there such a campaign, nor could one even imagine that this was hidden in what is called the national soul. The plundering of 1918 was an innocent game in comparison with this. The majority of crusaders were themselves later ashamed of what happened and what they had done. But – they did it. My father, too, who was not particularly given to cruelty, at least not more than any other Montenegrin, never liked to talk about it. He felt shame for having taken part in those events, like a drunkard who sobers up after committing a crime . . .

As soon as the regular army appeared, the lawless mob realized that the matter was serious and immediately withdrew. After that the Moslem villages slowly withered. The Moslems of that region began to migrate to Turkey, selling their lands for a trifle. The district of Sahovici, and in part, also, of Bijelo Polje, were emptied, partly as the result of the massacre and partly from fear. The Moslems were replaced by Montenegrin settlers.

---

[6] For this particular point, I will be building on Donald Horowitz's recent work, *The Deadly Ethnic Riot* (Berkeley: University of California Press, 2001). Horowitz has found a selective targeting phenomenon in a wide variety of cases, see especially Chapter 4.

The affair produced general horror, even among most of those who had carried it out. My older brother and I were shocked and horrified. We blamed Father for being one of the leaders of the mob. He himself later used to say that he had always imagined the raid was intended only to kill a few Moslem chiefs. Expressing abhorrence at the crimes, Father nevertheless saw in it all something that my brother and I neither would or could see – an inevitable war of annihilation, begun long ago, between two faiths. Both were fated to swim in blood, and only the stronger would remain on top.[7]

The passage exemplifies several key aspects of Eastern European violence that will arise in the following chapters. First, leadership is superfluous; the mob did not need to be organized or directed. In fact, pensioned military officers were "urged into the lead." While every mob has individuals in front, it does not necessarily follow that these individuals have created the mob. Social scientists should not assume that participants are ignorant dupes of elites. Whether masses are manipulated or not is an empirical question.

Second, the passage indicates that seemingly average people were motivated to commit violence that they later regretted. Djilas describes his father as "not particularly given to cruelty." Rather, he was seized by something like inebriation. The assumption of stability of preferences has little explanatory power for this phenomenon. The concept of emotion developed here, by providing a theory of preference change, tries to explain how an ordinary man like Djilas' father can be motivated to attack his ethnically distinct neighbors. How can we explain behavior that is later regretted?

Third, the event described clearly created an essentialization of identity. Before Boskovic's killing, the primary conflict in the area involved feuding between Montenegrin clans. After the Boskovic burial, the Montenegrins were operating under a frame in which only the Montenegrin and "Moslem" identities were meaningful.

The passage highlights several additional aspects of ethnic violence that will be witnessed repeatedly in the empirical chapters. The action occurred in the absence of constraints. When the regular army appeared, the mob dispersed. Much of the worst ethnic violence in Eastern Europe has occurred in periods of state collapse. The lack of constraint is essential, but it is only one part of the story. While Eastern Europe has witnessed

---

[7] Milovan Djilas, *Land Without Justice* (New York: Harcourt, Brace, and Co., 1958), pp. 206–08.

several periods of collapse of empire and state, multiple rounds of occupation and reoccupation, and numerous instances of wartime chaos, violent ethnic outbreaks have not always occurred. Also, when violence did occur, different groups became targets at different times. Furthermore, the social and political impact of this brief period of violence was immense. The events of a few days cleared an entire region of its Muslim population. Brief pogromlike actions have reordered the political and social landscape of the entire Eastern European region, not just the Balkans. The substantive chapters will illustrate this calamitous violence in the Baltic and Czechoslovakia as well as the Balkans. Finally, notice that the participants were not responding to any threat. Their victims were not warlike.

Ivo Andric provides a similar description of how the "wild beast" emerges in the absence of constraint to wipe out the complexity of social and economic life. Andric described the sudden violence that erupted in Visegrad in 1914:

The people were now divided into the persecuted and those who persecuted them. That wild beast, which lives in man and does not dare to show itself until the barriers of law and custom have been removed, was now set free. The signal was given, the barriers were down. As has so often happened in the history of man, permission was tacitly granted for acts of violence and plunder, even for murder, if they were carried out in the name of higher interests, according to established rules, and against a limited number of men of a particular type and belief. . . . In a few minutes, the business quarter, based on centuries of tradition, was wiped out. It is true that there had always been concealed enmities and jealousies and religious intolerance, coarseness and cruelty, but there had also been courage and fellowship and a feeling for measure and order, which restrained these instincts within the limits of the supportable and, in the end, calmed them down and submitted them to the general interest of life in common. Men who had been leaders in the commercial quarter for forty years vanished overnight as if they had all died suddenly, together with the habits, customs, and institutions which they represented.[8]

As the cases frequently show, the collapse of constraints is often accompanied by a tacit understanding regarding a "proper" target of violence – the "wild beast is set free" but only to act against people "of a particular type and belief." Even in the absence of leadership and direction, Eastern Europe's violence has seldom been random. Emotion, similarly experi-

---

[8] Quoted in Peter Maass, *Love Thy Neighbor: A Story of War* (New York: Alfred Knopf, 1996), p. 11.

enced by a mass of people, can provide the basis for a common understanding that an ethnically distinct group is an enemy deserving some form of attack or punishment. The results can be devastating and permanent. In contrast to the events described in the previous passages, outsiders often play the crucial role in initiating the violence. In the Eastern European cases, discussed in this book, however, significant numbers of the local population have been ready followers. Tone Bringa, a Scandanavian anthropologist and author of *Being Muslim the Bosnian Way*, makes the following observation regarding the Muslim-Croat village in Bosnia where she did her field work:

In the end what was so painful to most Muslim villagers and to many of their Croat neighbors was that the attackers were not only 'outsiders.' When HVO started shelling and killing Muslims and burning their houses in the village, some of the Muslims' Catholic Croat neighbors joined in, although the attack had been planned and initiated by people far from the village. Starting out as a war waged by outsiders it developed into one where neighbor was pitted against neighbor after the familiar person next door had been made into a depersonalized alien, a member of the enemy ranks.[9]

Although outside forces came in and fired the first shots, neighbors soon attacked neighbors. Old acquaintances became "depersonalized aliens" in a classic case of ethnic essentialization. As in the two previous examples, communal violence forever changed the face of Bringa's village: Nearly every Muslim house had been destroyed. In a short period of time, a harmonious, mixed village became homogenized through violence. It is unlikely that most refugees will return. While Croatian politicians and paramilitaries may have benefited from this savagery, the question of individual motivation remains at the heart of this event.

In these examples, individuals willingly participated in violence against a depersonalized ethnic target. By comparing the fit of four narratives, the empirical chapters examine the processes that triggered the emotional mechanisms behind these types of actions.

The Plan of the Book

The book consists of two main parts and a conclusion. Making up Chapters 2–4, Part One develops theory. Chapter 2 outlines the general features of an

---

[9] Tone Bringa, *Being Muslim the Bosnian Way* (Princeton, NJ: Princeton University Press, 1995), p. xvi.

emotions-based approach to ethnic conflict. The third and fourth chapters expand on the logic and intellectual heritage of the four stories: Fear, Hatred, Resentment, and Rage. The reader will find that many diverse strands of the ethnic conflict literature possess commonalities in their treatment of motivation. To a significant degree, the four emotion-based models are a distillation of the existing literatures and are not new in themselves.

Part Two, the comparative section, strives to accomplish two goals. First, it seeks to explain puzzling variation in ethnic conflict within fairly narrow ranges of time and space. In this work, explanation means identification of a causal mechanism linking individual perpetrators to their actions against a specific ethnic target at a specific time. For instance, one section will ask why, in similar situations of near chaos, Ukrainians primarily attacked Poles in 1939 but Jews in 1941. Fear, Hatred, Resentment, and Rage are considered in turn. The leading contenders, in this case Rage and Resentment, are then discussed in more detail. Second, comparisons are made across time and space in an effort to understand the changing prevalence of one mechanism versus another. In other words, does one model explain ethnic conflict best in the interwar years but have little predictive or descriptive power in the post-Communist era? Do certain models lose their explanatory power with modernization?

In developing the comparative agenda of the book, the periodization found as follows guided the selection of cases. There are six distinct periods, each marked by changes in state stability and policy, as well as differences in the amount and type of violence. In effect, these periods distinguish the broad context within which the emotional mechanisms operate. Two types of change, modernization and war, most prominently define the critical contours. Since the early or mid-nineteenth century, Eastern Europe has undergone a slow process of modernization. This slow structural process has been punctured at several junctures by rapid upheavals, the most wrenching being the two world wars and the collapse of Communism. Ethnic violence has occurred mainly during these periods of upheaval when state power collapsed. In between these periods of relative anarchy, the state often established discriminatory ethnic policies. Within this general history, the following periods serve as useful referents:[10]

Period One: The Modernization of the Multinational Empire. Needing to compete with other states, the multinational empires that covered Eastern

---

[10] This classification fits the history of the Russian and Austro-Hungarian Empires better than the Balkan states and the Ottoman Empire.

Europe required educated populations and a mass army. Thus, the state extended its reach through education, conscription, and standardization of language policies. These policies produced contact among members of the empire that had previously lived in relative rural seclusion. Here is Ernest Gellner's well-known story of Ruritania and Megalomania. The policies of the modernizing multinational empire were often ethnically discriminatory. For instance, the Russian Empire installed linguistic Russification policies for an extended period and developed and expanded ethnically skewed bureaucracies and military ranks. On the other hand, relatively little ethnic violence occurred during this period of state stability.

Period Two: World War One and the Collapse of Empire. With the disintegration of the state, constraints evaporated and violence often erupted. Incipient states battled the forces of the old order to establish political boundaries. This violence, on the whole, was often "ethnic" only in an ambiguous sense. The battles were often colored with political overtones, rather than ethnic ones. However, the period did witness pogromlike attacks and the settling of ethnic scores.

Period Three: Interwar Nationalizing States. The newly born nation-states established ethnically discriminatory policies, sometimes highly discriminatory policies. Here, Rogers Brubaker's distinction between *polity-upgrading nationalism* and *polity-seeking nationalism* is apt. In the latter, permeating the first two periods of this categorization, the nation focuses on gaining a state; in the former, applicable to the third period, the nation uses the state and its institutions to establish its dominance. As Brubaker sums up:

A nationalizing state, I have suggested, is one understood to be the state *of* and *for* a particular ethnocultural 'core nation' whose language, culture, demographic position, economic welfare, and political hegemony must be promoted and protected by the state. The key elements here are (1) the sense of 'ownership' of the state by a particular ethnocultural nation that is conceived as distinct from the citizenry or permanent resident population as a whole, and (2) the 'remedial' or compensatory project of using state power to promote the core nation's specific (and heretofore inadequately served) interests.[11]

As an exemplar, Brubaker describes interwar Poland, one of the most heterogeneous states in Europe. Using different tactics toward each

---

[11] Rogers Brubaker, *Nationalism Reframed: Nationhood and the National Question in the New Europe* (Cambridge: Cambridge University Press, 1996), pp. 103–04.

minority, the Poles developed institutional measures to create a "Poland for Poles." Germans were the target of language policy (reduction of the number of German language schools from 1,250 in 1921–22 to 60 in 1937–38) and land reform (the expropriation of "alien" landlords);[12] Jews were not hired in the civil service or administration; Ukrainians and Belorussians were not even recognized as distinct peoples.

Again, with the presence of a functioning state, ethnic violence, with some notable exceptions, was uncommon.

Period Four: The Time of Occupations and War. Caught between Hitler and Stalin, the region underwent a series of occupations and endured a period of violence unparalleled in the history of Europe. Much of the northern part of the region went through multiple shocks. The Baltic states and much of Poland were occupied first by the Soviet Union, then by the Germans, and then again, at the end of the war, by the Soviets once more. While most of the deaths were the result of the Soviet-German war or German extermination policies, a large number of episodes of interethnic violence occurred during the transition periods between occupations. In these brief periods of anarchy, violence was unambiguously ethnic in nature and, perhaps more arguably, mass in character. Moreover, there was enormous variation in the nature of this violence. Violence occured in some regions but not others; different groups were targets in different regions.

Period Five: Communist Rule. With Moscow in control of most of the region, a period of relative ethnic calm held. The mass extermination of Jews, the mass expulsions of Germans, and the changing of boundaries reshaped and greatly homogenized the ethnic makeup of the region. Still, Communist policies would set the stage for the next period of upheaval, especially in Yugoslavia.

Period Six: The Collapse of Communism. Again, states collapsed producing considerable variation in outcomes. The Baltic states remained peaceful, but varied in the content of their ethnic institutions. Czechs and Slovaks parted peacefully, while the component peoples of former Yugoslavia killed each other in unambiguously ethnic warfare.

The comparative section consists of six chapters. The first four form one unit examining violence and discrimination in the Baltics across the entire twentieth century. The third chapter concentrates on Period One and the 1905 Russian Revolution; the following chapter looks at the pat-

[12] Brubaker discusses policy toward the Germans in *Nationalism Reframed*, pp. 86–93.

terns of ethnic violence during the third and fourth periods focusing mainly on chaotic situations accompanying the shifting Soviet and German occupations. The fifth chapter, written by John Ginkel, examines the post-Communist era centering on the different citizenship and language policies among the Baltic states. The sixth chapter then steps back and explores the pattern of ethnic conflict in the Baltics across the entire century.

The fifth chapter, written by Beth Wilner, investigates variation in ethnic conflict in the Czech and Slovak regions over several periods. This chapter serves two purposes. It allows productive comparison with the Baltic chapters and addresses a more specific puzzle. How did the Czech nation, portrayed as one of the most tolerant and impassive in Europe, end up with one of the most homogeneous populations on the continent? What role did ethnic conflict and violence play in this process?

The sixth chapter examines Yugoslavia during the fifth and sixth periods. How did the catastrophe occur and what role did mass-based emotion play in it? Why didn't modernity prevent the brutality that occurred there? This chapter leads into the conclusion.

The concluding chapter of the book summarizes the findings and provides discussion. The chapter begins with a review of the six empirical chapters. What have we learned about ethnic conflict? What are the benefits of an emotion-based approach in explaining variation across a sizable number of cases and a sweeping time period? The second subsection addresses major methodological challenges and issues. Building from the Yugoslavia chapter, the question of the role of elites in creating and manipulating emotions arises. Has the modernization and urbanization of Eastern Europe, that is, the broad structural changes that have occurred there, produced and shaped the observed paths to ethnic conflict? Or has the variation in these paths been so riotous that no such consistent linkage can be found? The book concludes with a discussion of prevention. What have we learned that can be applied to the political and social institutions developing today in Eastern Europe? What are the possibilities for outside intervention?

What This Book Is and Is Not About

Based on a wide range of social science literature, this book tells four emotion-centered accounts of ethnic violence. The work then employs the comparative method across a broad expanse of time and space to test each account's plausibility and prevalence. Although I am a political scientist, this book is by no means a standard work in that field. To a large extent, this book is not about politics. The work here operates primarily at the individual and macrostructural levels. Emotions are individual level mechanisms. The book seeks to understand the prevalence of these individual level mechanisms within the sweeping changes wrought by modernization, state formation, and state collapse – the forces that create the divisions in the periodization above. Politics generally occur in the intermediate levels – politics is the stuff of parties, leaders, institutions, and laws. In one sense, the book's explanatory success will be an indication that politics do not matter as much as many might think. On the other hand, the book's explanatory shortcomings will provide evidence of the power of agency and politics.

The book is mostly concerned with ethnic conflict and violence, not its absence, among groups that have lived together peacefully. In trying to isolate how emotional mechanisms operate, the most insightful periods are those when constraints collapse and individuals can choose to commit violence, or abstain from it, against a range of targets. In this situation, a variety of outcomes are possible – violence or no violence, target X rather than target Y, and so on. Such variation is necessary for social scientific and comparative analysis. Furthermore, without the clouding features of legal constraint, clear ethnic motivations often become the primary force driving behavior.

The book is less concerned with how populations have collaborated in the ethnic cleansing projects of occupying powers such as the Nazis and the Soviets. In these cases, new layers of incentive and constraint cloud the picture. Furthermore, there is little variation in ethnic target – the occupier chooses the target, the native population can only decide how much to go along with it. Even that choice may be heavily constrained. While the ideological or racial policies of the Soviets and the National Socialists were of immeasurable importance in shaping the ethnic map of Eastern Europe, the focus here lies in isolating the mechanisms which pitted one neighbor against another.

In previous work, I addressed the puzzle of how "weaker" peoples manage to maintain violent resistance against "stronger" peoples.[13] The primary cases involved Lithuanian rebellion against the Soviets in 1940–41

---

[13] Roger Petersen, *Resistance and Rebellion: Lessons from Eastern Europe* (Cambridge: Cambridge University Press, 2001).

and 1945–50, as well as other anti-Soviet and anti-Nazi cases. In that previous work, I specified several important mechanisms – social norms, focal points, rational calculation, and emotions – and showed how sequences of these mechanisms work to produce sustained violence against powerful regimes. While emotional mechanisms played a role in explaining outcomes in those cases, social norms played a greater role. When the weak confront the strong, the central question involves risk. I argued that norms shape the way individuals confront risk.

In the present work on ethnic violence, the primary puzzle concerns violence of "stronger" peoples against "weaker" ones. In the empirical sections, the reader will encounter Lithuanian and Ukrainian violence against Jews, Czech mob action against Germans, and Serb mayhem against Bosnians and Albanians, among other cases. The perpetrators in these cases, in stark contrast to my earlier work on anti-Soviet and anti-Nazi resistance, did not usually face significant risks. In these cases, the puzzle rotates around motivation rather than risk reduction. It may be disturbing, but the following pages will show perpetrators who, at least at the time, *wanted* to commit violence against an ethnically distinct target. How did they come to want to commit these actions? This is the central question of this book. The basic answer involves emotion – a mechanism that explains a shift in motivation.

PART I

Theory

2

An Emotion-Based Approach to
Ethnic Conflict

Although theories of ethnic conflict are rarely emotion based, most of them implicitly utilize some conception of emotion to answer the question of individual motivation.[1] Convincing theories of ethnic conflict must provide some answer to the puzzling question of why any individual would go out and beat, humiliate, or discriminate against another human being. In Eastern Europe, the substantive basis of this work, neighbors have engaged in grotesque acts of violence against their ethnically different neighbors. Why? As Donald Horowitz has argued, explaining the motivation for such action must go beyond ambition to antipathy, past incentives to passion.[2]

Defining Emotion

Emotion is a mechanism that triggers action to satisfy a pressing concern. An emotion operates to meet situational challenges in two ways: (1) An emotion raises the saliency of one desire/concern over others; in other

---

[1] Walker Connor, for example, *Ethnonationalism: The Quest for Understanding* (Princeton: Princeton University Press, 1994) is well known for his emphasis on the psychological bases of nationalism and ethnic conflict, but has no such theory. Some authors have written emotion-based works about the causes of international wars, a violent but very different phenomenon than the one at hand. See for example, Thomas J. Scheff, *Bloody Revenge: Emotions, Nationalism, and War* (Boulder, CO: Westview Press, 1994). Also, Stuart Kaufman, *Modern Hatreds: The Symbolic Politics of War* (Cornell University Press, 2001), provides an extensive treatment of emotion and its effect on ethnic violence. I will refer to this work later in this chapter.

[2] Horowitz makes such claims in both *Ethnic Groups in Conflict* (Berkeley: University of California Press, 1985) and *The Deadly Ethnic Riot* (Berkeley: University of California Press, 2001).

17

words, emotion helps select among competing desires.[3] (2) An emotion heightens both cognitive and physical capabilities necessary to respond to the situational challenge.[4] Consider the following example. A man desiring safety, wealth, and self-esteem is walking in a dark wood. All of a sudden, he hears a strange animal noise and becomes afraid. The emotion of fear sweeps over him. Fear pumps adrenalin into his body or produces an instinctive threatening pose that serves to frighten the animal off. Fear (the emotion) acted as a mechanism (an individual level, recognizable pattern) to cause action (fight/flight) to meet a pressing concern (safety). The view here follows Frijda in emphasizing emotions as changes in "action readiness" to satisfy "concerns."[5] Frijda differentiates between "surface concerns" that are connected with the values of a particular human environment and the concerns hard wired in the species' constitution, although the former must derive from the latter to a great extent.[6] To meet these concerns, the individual possesses a repertoire of activation and deactivation mechanisms that change action readiness. These mechanisms are the emotions.[7] They change readiness physically and cognitively, they alert the individual to modify relationships in the environment. In this view, the defining element of emotion is the associated "action tendency."[8] Frijda provides examples of alertness, anger, and craving:

---

[3] For a related view, see Ronald DeSousa, *The Rationality of Emotion* (Cambridge, MA: MIT Press, 1987).

[4] Emotion theorists often discuss emotion in terms of six features: arousal, intentionality, cognitive antecedents, valence, action tendency, and expression. The first statement is related to intentionality. The second statement incorporates arousal, expression, and action tendency. Action tendency is explicitly discussed as follows. The question of cognitive antecedents is crucial to the distinction between Rage and the other three emotions and forms a large part of the discussion in the latter pages of this chapter. Valence is not particularly relevant since all of these emotions possess a negative sign. For a brief summary statement of these six elements, see Jon Elster, "Rationality and the Emotions" *The Economic Journal*, 106 (1996): 1386–88. Elster's larger treatment is found in *Alchemies of the Mind: Rationality and the Emotions* (Cambridge: Cambridge University Press, 1999).

[5] Nico H. Frijda, *The Emotions* (Cambridge: Cambridge University Press, 1987).

[6] Ibid., p. 466.

[7] For a broader discussion of social mechanisms, see Peter Hedstrom and Richard Swedberg, eds., *Social Mechanisms: An Analytical Approach to Social Theory* (Cambridge: Cambridge University Press, 1998).

[8] There is a long history of viewing emotion in terms of action tendency. In the sixteenth century, Juan Luis Vives saw emotion as a faculty that allowed individuals to seek good and avoid evil. Hobbes wrote of appetites and aversions in much the same vein. In the twentieth century, Frijda is preceded by Magda B. Arnold *Emotion and Personality* (New York: Columbia University Press, 1960) and followed by Andrew Ortony, Gerald Clore, and Allan Collins, *The Cognitive Structure of Emotions* (Cambridge: Cambridge University

There is a discrepancy or mismatch that initiates the program; decrease in the discrepancy guides and terminates the behavior. . . . If, for instance, the situation is seen as an unfamiliar one, action tendency is generated for actions removing that unfamiliarity: alertness, scanning the environment. If the situation is one that blocks freedom of action, action tendency emerges that aims toward removing that obstruction: anger. If mismatch consists of something desirable not possessed, action tendency is toward possession: craving or desire.[9]

Fear, Hatred, and Resentment are discussed in terms of action tendencies that prepare the individual to change the environment. Rage must be treated differently.

In a closely related point, *many, but not all, emotions are instrumental.*[10] Emotion drives the individual to reach a recognizable goal. Fear is instrumental because it produces actions that directly meet a pressing concern in the form of a threat. While most might recognize the possibility that fear is instrumental, they assume that other emotions, like hatred and resentment, are noninstrumental, if not clearly dysfunctional. In this volume, Fear, Hatred, and Resentment are treated in the same way – as processes centered on an emotional mechanism facilitating individual action to satisfy an identified desire/concern. Fear prepares the individual to satisfy safety concerns; Hatred prepares the individual to act on historical grievance; Resentment prepares the individual to address status/self-esteem discrepancies. Rage, in contrast, posits an emotion that often drives the individual toward self-destructive actions. With Rage, the emotion still addresses pressing concerns, but those concerns are emanating from frustration or a troubled personality. In this case, emotion directs the individual toward actions that may relieve internalized frustration or the problems of a conflicted personality. Given their source, however, Rage often produces cognitive distortions that can lead to irrelevant or counterproductive actions (such as searching for scapegoats). A primary benefit of the emotional approach is that it can accomodate both instrumental and noninstrumental action.

Press, 1988). In the latter work, the authors have differences with Frijda on the issue of treating emotion as action tendency (see p. 11, for example). Still, the similarities in usage outweigh the differences.

[9] Frijda, *The Emotions* pp. 76–77.

[10] Summing up a common view from emotion theory, David D. Franks and Viktor Gecas write that in the face of enormous complexity emotion "allows us to decide what is worth thinking about and what is relevant and irrelevant once we start thinking." See "Current Issues in Emotion Studies and Introduction to Chapters" in David D. Franks and Viktor Gecas, eds., *Social Perspectives on Emotion* (Greenwich, CT: JAI Press, 1992).

Emotion is a mechanism that explains shifts in motivation.[11] Note that in the example of the man in the woods, the emotion worked to automatically raise the saliency of one desire, safety, over others such as self-esteem or wealth. Here is one of the key benefits of an emotion-based theory of ethnic conflict. A multiplicity of motivations drive individuals to participate in ethnic violence. While economists might plausibly assume that unitary actors (individuals or firms) maximize profits and legislative scholars can acceptably assume that politicians work to maximize chances for reelection, analysts of ethnic conflict are generally more cautious in assuming one fundamental utility consistently driving the actions of perpetrators of ethnic violence. Not only are there multiple plausible motivations at work, but the same individual may be driven to commit ethnic violence by different motivations at different times. The participant in ethnic violence may be acting on revenge at one particular moment, on the desire to help preempt attack on his or her own group at another time, and the wish to "put members of another group in their place" in yet another situation. The emotion mechanism is based on an idea that one desire tends to become dominant and overriding in certain situations. An appropriate metaphor is that of a "switch."[12] Multiple desires are all seen as important, but extremely difficult to compare, or to order, in any general sense.[13]

Emotion produces shifts in motivation by mediating between cognition and desire. There is considerable psychological evidence to show that emotion

---

[11] For similar treatments, see Stuart Kaufman, *Modern Hatreds* and Susan Fiske and Shelley Taylor, *Social Cognition*, Second Edition (New York: McGraw-Hill, 1991), p. 456. Note that I am largely avoiding the issue of preference change or adaptive preferences. I am simply positing that emotion helps the individual select an action by heightening one desire among a short list that cannot be convincingly ordered. On the issue of preference change, see Jon Elster, *Sour Grapes: Studies in the Subversion of Rationality* (Cambridge: Cambridge University Press, 1983).

[12] In line with Andric's "wild beast" and Djilas' "inebriation," Paul Ekman writes about "emotional wildfires," emotions that produce uncontrollable desires. See Paul Ekman, *Telling Lies* (New York: Norton, 1992).

[13] There is another feature of emotions worthy of mention that I am less sure about: *Emotion is a mechanism that can switch concerns from the egocentric to the collective.* One of the fundamental questions underlying any type of ethnic political behavior asks why an individual would sacrifice or act on behalf of a group (or against another group). There may be a constellation of emotional mechanisms that help link the individual to the collective. For instance, a cognition of danger leads to the emotion of fear, the cognition that others in one's identifiable ethnic group also feel a similar fear then leads to a second emotion (that needs to be identified) that increases solidarity and changes the focus to the welfare of the collective.

affects cognition and cognition affects emotion.[14] However, in terms of the present analysis of ethnic conflict, cognition is treated as prior in the causal sequence for Fear, Hatred, and Resentment.[15] Along with many socially oriented theorists, the present approach sees emotion primarily as "thought that becomes embodied because of the intensity with which it is laced with personal self-relevancy."[16] Beliefs about threat lead to fears; beliefs about status inconsistency lead to resentments; beliefs about history and vengeance lead to hatreds. The treatment of Fear, Hatred, and Resentment mirrors that of Ortony, Clore, and Collins (1988) who write: "Our claims about the structure of individual emotions are always along the lines that *if* an individual conceptualizes a situation in a certain kind of way, *then* the potential for a particular type of emotion exists."[17] There are three elements at hand: (1) the situation, (2) the conceptualization, (3) the emotion. In most instances, all three are occurring almost simultaneously, but for the instrumental emotions in this study they are treated sequentially in the order just provided. It is the first element of this sequence, the situation, that provides the link to the structural half of the "independent variable" of many theories of ethnic conflict.

Several theories of ethnic conflict see structural changes as the engine that leads to ethnic conflict. These structural changes can also be seen as the situations that initiate the cognitive-emotive sequence. As outlined in the introductory chapter, in Eastern Europe two types of structural change produced radically different situations in terms of power and status

---

[14] For a more extensive discussion see Cheshire Calhoun, "Cognitive Emotions?" in C. Calhoun and R. C. Solomon, eds., *What is an Emotion: Classical Readings in Philosophical Psychology* (New York: Oxford University Press, 1984), pp. 327–42. For an eloquent argument for the inseparability of emotion and cognition, see Francis F. Seeburger, "Blind Sight and Brute Feeling: The Divorce of Cognition From Emotion" *Social Perspectives on Emotion* 1 (1992): 47–60.

[15] Rage critically reverses the order. With Rage, emotion affects cognition in several identifiable and important ways. This relationship is treated extensively below.

[16] This quote is from the discussion of emotion and cognition found in David D. Franks and Viktor Gecas, "Current Issues in Emotion Studies" in David D. Franks and Viktor Gecas, eds., *Social Perspectives on Emotion: A Research Annual* (Greenwich, CT: JAI Press, 1992), p. 8. Claire Armon-Jones points out that while emotion is dependent upon cognition, cognitions do not constitute emotion because the same belief could produce two different emotions. See Claire Armon-Jones, "The Thesis of Constructionism" in Rom Harre, ed., *The Social Construction of Emotions* (New York: Basil Blackwell, 1986), pp. 41–42.

[17] This statement mirrors that of Ortony et al., *The Cognitive Structure of Emotions* p. 2.

21

relations among ethnic groups. First, the forces of modernization – literacy, urbanization, the expansion of the state – worked to form ethnic groups, as well as to produce an acute awareness of which groups were strong and weak, which were high status and which were low status. Second were the abrupt structural shocks that accompanied a century of war, occupation, and the collapse of empires. Indeed, in a few short days the power and status position of groups could radically change. For example, Baltic states switched political realms three times within a very short period. They went from independence to Soviet rule during 1940–41, then to German occupation, and finally back to Soviet domination. With each change, power and status relations among groups shifted.

Emotion results from structural change through the intervening processes of conceptualization and evaluation, perhaps better signified by the term *belief-formation*. When individuals come to believe that the new situation has produced some type of discrepancy among groups, or has produced a perceived threat from another group, an emotion results that generates a change in the saliency of a particular desire. In the example above, the individual's fear of an animal attack heightened the concern for safety. In turn, the emotion generated action tendencies to meet that desire. In regard to ethnic conflict, the sequence of events is roughly the same. Structural change produces information that is processed into beliefs that in turn, and almost inevitably, create emotions and tendencies toward certain actions. The process is summarized in Figure 2.1.

As indicated by Figure 2.1, the emotion, once generated, produces feedback effects on information and belief. For the instrumental emotions, the beliefs that have already been formed become reinforced. For example, once one is in the grip of Fear, reports about danger and threat will crowd out other information. When one is in the clutch of Resentment, indicators of group status constantly infiltrate one's thoughts. Under Hatred, long dormant historical "facts" come to dominate thinking and discussion. For Fear, Hatred, and Resentment information is selected in order to meet the elevated goal. Unlike the noninstrumental Rage, however, emotion only acts to select the information that is most relevant to the elevated goal. In the instrumental paths, emotion impacts cognition through a feedback loop. In Rage, emotion dominates and distorts cognition.

The following two chapters break down three major views of ethnic conflict (Fear, Hatred, Resentment) into the components of this diagram. What kind of structual change starts the process? What are the assumptions about the beliefs that arise from the structural change? How do these

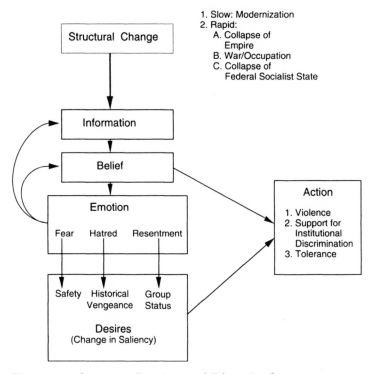

Figure 2.1   Structures, Emotions, and Ethnic Conflict

beliefs lead to emotions and changes in saliency of desires? These are the elements that separate competing theories of ethnic conflict.

Action

The primary dependent variable is ethnic violence. The empirical chapters identify puzzles involving variation in targets and timing of violence. The quality of the violence is also relevant because the nature of violence can often help distinguish among competing explanations. When a religious figure, rather than a political figure, is singled out at a particular time as a target of violence, certain inferences about the perpetrator's motivation may be made. To emphasize a point made earlier, the project is especially focused on violent actions occurring between neighboring ethnic groups during periods of state collapse. The effects of emotion are most stark in these often brief but crucial periods. Isolating the affects of

23

emotion can be best accomplished by studying periods when the myriad of normal constraints has been lifted.[18]

It is also important to emphasize that the project is not focused on actions directed from outside the region by foreign powers. It is not interested in violence entirely directed by the Soviets or Nazis, for example.

At various points the analysis will shift to institutional discrimination (the focus of Chapter 7, for example). Hopefully this shift will allow for a broader view of the effects of emotion on ethnic politics without detracting from the main goal – explaining variation in ethnic violence.

Predictions

Each instrumental path sees an observable structural change generating an emotional mechanism that in turn heightens the saliency of a desire (safety, vengeance, status) that promotes ethnic violence and conflict. It should be emphasized that the structural changes originating the process are readily observable and their presence or absence varies among cases. The linkages between structure and emotion prevent simply finding evidence of the emotion we seek and attaching it as an explanation of the conflict. Breaking down each of the competing theories in this way facilitates the creation of a testable hypothesis.

Each of these theories produces competing predictions of the *timing* of conflict and the *target* of violence and/or discrimination. Due to the assumption of instrumentality (underlying Fear, Hatred, and Resentment), emotion identifies the target as the group that stands in the way of achieving a blocked desire. The nature of the structural change predicts when another group is likely to be perceived as blocking the desire. The respective hypotheses are straightforward. The next chapters show how these hypotheses were distilled from well-known literatures and how they can predict discrimination and toleration as well as violence. Here, hypotheses for each of the three instrumental emotions are given in their most stark and violence-oriented forms:

---

[18] Not all emotions lead to action. Claire Armon-Jones has listed four conditions qualifying emotions as capable of motivating an agent. These conditions include the conviction of belief, the vividness of the cognitions, the intensity of the attitudes underlying the emotion, and the emotion's consuming nature. See Armon-Jones, "The Thesis of Constructionism" p. 49. The violent and semianarchic conditions underlying many of the cases in this book exhibit these four conditions and are an excellent laboratory to study how emotions lead to action.

Fear Structural changes such as the collapse or weakening of the political center eliminate institutional constraints and guarantees to produce a situation characterized as anarchy or emerging anarchy. Under these conditions, Fear heightens the desire for security. *The target of ethnic violence will be the group that is the biggest threat.* The theory is not supported if the target of attack is not a threat.

Hatred ("Ancient Hatred") Structural changes such as the collapse of the center eliminate constraints and produce an opportunity to commit aggression against other groups. *The target of ethnic violence will be the group that has frequently been attacked with similar justification over an extended time period.* If the target has not been a frequently attacked ethnic group, or if the target is attacked with a completely new justification, then the hypothesis is not supported.

Resentment Structural changes such as the collapse or weakening of the center and/or occupation rearrange ethnic status hierarchies by changing sovereignty relations, composition of political positions and police, and other features such as language policy. *The predicted ethnic target will be the group perceived as farthest up the ethnic status hierarchy that can be most surely subordinated through violence.* If the target group is lower on the ethnic status hierarchy, then Resentment is not supported. If the target group is higher on an ethnic hierarchy but cannot have its position reduced through ethnic violence, then Resentment does not apply. If two possible target groups are higher on an ethnic hierarchy and either one or the other can be brought to a subordinate position, and if the lower group is the target, then Resentment *alone* is not a sufficient explanation. The choice of a suboptimal target would need to be explained in conjunction with another theory (possibly Hatred or Rage) or simply by another theory.

Note that these motivations are not mutually exclusive. Many cases may be "overdetermined" in that multiple motivations are driving the outbreak of ethnic violence. For instance, as shown in the empirical material on Yugoslavia, both Fear and Resentment produce accurate descriptions and predictions for certain events in Croatia and Bosnia.

Indicators

Indicators of threat potential, status hierarchy, and "hated group" are necessary to test these three competing theories.

Ethnic status hierarchy can be linked to observable indicators such as sovereignty, language policy, political position holding, composition of the forceholders. This is not a case of post hoc theory development in the sense that some vague form of resentment is found for any observed ethnic conflict. The structural changes, the indicators of repositionings of ethnic hierarchy, and the conflicts themselves are all observable.

"Hated group" tries to capture the meaning of the "ancient hatred" argument. The same foe is again fought for the same reasons. There has to be a significant history of actual attacks or outright conflict to make such a designation. Here, the target need not really be "ancient" – a consistent history of similar types of attacks against the same ethnic group over several generations can qualify the target as "long hated." The key question is whether the history of interethnic relations has created roles and identities that individuals take on during periods when constraints have been lifted.

For Fear, threat potential requires assessment of the ability of the ethnic group to inflict significant *physical* damage against other groups. Both mobilizational potential and vulnerability of one's group to attack are relevant factors. The former concerns organization while the latter involves geography and demographics.[19]

The Instrumental Emotions and Related Hypotheses in Historical Context

This study links the theoretical ideas of emotion, developed in this chapter, to the history of Eastern Europe, periodized in the preceding chapter. Figure 2.2 illustrates how the two can be brought together.

The numbers and the vertical orderings within the figure represent the indicators described in the preceding section. The vertical order of groups represents relative position on the ethnic status hierarchy which is pegged to observable indicators such as language policy, staffing in the military and police, staffing in the bureaucracy, and land redistribution policy. The numbers themselves represent each group's relative regional abilities to mobilize force – their threat potential. Within each hierarchy, X stands for the empirical power or occupier. A number with X attached represents an

---

[19] Perhaps the best outline of indicators relevant to the Fear narrative is found in Barry Posen, "The Security Dilemma and Ethnic Conflict" *Survival* 35 (1993): 27–47. I will return to Posen's argument in Chapter 4.

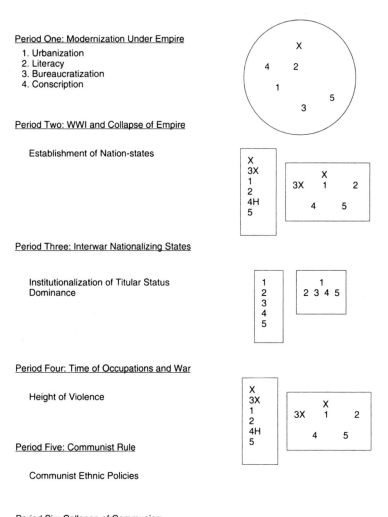

Period One: Modernization Under Empire

1. Urbanization
2. Literacy
3. Bureaucratization
4. Conscription

Period Two: WWI and Collapse of Empire

Establishment of Nation-states

Period Three: Interwar Nationalizing States

Institutionalization of Titular Status
Dominance

Period Four: Time of Occupations and War

Height of Violence

Period Five: Communist Rule

Communist Ethnic Policies

Period Six: Collapse of Communism

Institutional Change and Violence

Figure 2.2   Predicting Targets in Historical Context

ethnic group favored or associated with the empire or occupying power. The letter H represents a group that is in a relationship of "ancient hatred" with the most powerful regional group in the hierarchy.

Starting with the circle at the top, the period of the modernizing empire, the various groups are shown without a clearly perceived ethnic

27

hierarchy. During this period, modernization creates a perception of ethnic hierarchy, represented by a straightened vertical ordering. The two boxes following from modernization represent two possible examples of hierarchy. The box on the left shows a hierarchy in which the group associated with the empire or occupier is dominant, followed by the "collaborating" group, followed by the regionally most powerful group, the second most regionally powerful group, the fourth most powerful group (which is the "ancient enemy" of Group 1), and finally the fifth most regionally powerful group.

Notice that there is an overall historical pattern. First, modernization produces the development of group consciousness of status and power hierarchy. Then this hierarchy is reordered at multiple junctures and in multiple ways throughout the century. The pattern in Figure 2.2 shows the power and status hierarchies lining up during the interwar period and then being shaken back to a more mixed pattern by occupation and war. As the empirical studies will show, this was a common pattern, although not all cases followed it to the same extent. Crucially, different countries modernized at different rates and developed a strong sense of ethnic hierarchy at different times. In some cases, this sense of ethnic hierarchy was strong during the period of empire, in other cases, this sense only developed during the interwar period with the policies of the new state. The general pattern in Figure 2.2 forms a useful heuristic that shows how variation tended to develop within the region.

As laid out above, Fear, Hatred, and Resentment predict different targets of violence or discrimination if the empire or occupier collapses. In other words, each predicts a different pattern of targets of violent action in Periods Two, Four, and Six. In Periods Three and Five, times of relative stability, the focus is mainly on institutional changes. If the situation is accurately depicted by the left hand box of Period Two, Fear predicts that Group 1 will attack the greatest threat. Assuming that the power of X has vanished, the predicted action would be 1 against 2. Hatred predicts that given the collapse of constraints, the regionally dominant group, Number 1, would attack 4H, its ancient foe. Resentment predicts that the target would be the group farthest up the ethnic hierarchy that can be subordinated through violence. If X has fled, the predicted target would be 3X.

If the ordering was X, 2XH, 1, 3, 4, 5, a single causal explanation for ethnic conflict could not be determined due to problems of overdetermination. Fear would predict conflict between the two contenders most able to inflict damage against one another: 1 and 2. Hatred would predict violence against the ancient foe: 1 against 2. Resentment would predict violence or discrimination against groups farther up the hierarchy: again, 1 and 2.

The hierarchy shown on the right hand side of Period Two exhibits another form of overdetermination. With the collapse of X, Fear clearly predicts conflict among 1 and 2, but Resentment's prediction is more problematic. Resentment holds that violence/conflict will be targeted against the group farthest up the hierarchy that *can* be brought down through this action. Thus, Resentment predicts attack on 2 if possible, but conflict with 3X if 2 is too powerful to bring down through violence. In this case, Groups 1 and 2 might form an alliance to dominate the system. These forces might be separated by a careful analysis of the conflict.

Challenges and Objections: A Comparison with Alternative Approaches

This section confronts four fundamental challenges to the emotions-based approach. I will list these challenges in order before addressing them at length.

1. What about noninstrumental emotions stressed by the psychological literature?
2. How is the emotions-based approach better than a rational choice approach?
3. Don't elites possess the ability to create these emotions? Doesn't the approach, with its structural emphasis, ignore the role of human agency?
4. Why not, for the sake of parsimony, simply link structure and action without the complications involved with emotion?

Noninstrumental Emotions

Because instrumental emotions are all based on one dominant concern, their definition is relatively straightforward. Fear prepares the individual to take action to reduce dangers in the environment; Hatred prepares the individual to attack previously identified enemies; Resentment prepares the individual to rectify perceived imbalances in group status hierarchies. With each of these emotions, the dominant concern is tied to some readily observable structural change that is external to the individual. For each of these three emotions, cognitive processes are considered to be able to direct action toward a target that is the source of the concern. With these emotions, there is a coherent flow among structure, cognition, the emotional mechanism, and the timing and target of action.

Not all emotions are instrumental. Furthermore, in contrast to Fear, Hatred, and Resentment, emotion may precede cognition. What if an individual simply wishes to lash out? Fear, Hatred, and Resentment all envision a desire to lash out, but it is a desire linked to a specific source and embedded in a specific context of group relations. What if such a desire arises from general or multiple sources and without a clear direction for action? An emotion heightening a desire to simply lash out would clearly be noninstrumental, even in the sense of relieving psychological tensions. In fact, if the target of aggression is not related to the conditions that created frustration, the negative emotions may continue, or perhaps only temporarily subside. For example, if one kicks the dog after a bad day at work, the frustration may or may not be temporarily relieved. On the other hand, frustration may increase if the dog requires a veterinarian while the problems at work remain. Rather than helping to solve problems, the emotion might deflect the individual from confronting and solving the most pressing concerns.

Despite being noninstrumental, an emotion-based path capturing the essential features of "lashing out" can be modeled by rearranging the elements found in Fear, Hatred, and Resentment. For want of a better term, I label the path found in Figure 2.3 as Rage. In effect, an individual in the grasp of Rage is seeking an outlet for his or her frustration and is looking to take it out on someone, or perhaps even anyone.

Following the links in Figure 2.3, a source generates an emotion that heightens the desire to lash out above any more specific goal. The key feature in this path is that emotion precedes cognition. Building on several strands of social psychology, when emotion precedes cognition, distortions in information collection and belief formation may occur. Most critically, the emotion may distort the way targets are identified. The strong urge to commit violence creates a need to process available information in such a way to find an enemy (victim) and justify violence against that target. One or more of a diverse set of psychological mechanisms (for example, projection and attribution) may come into play to help with this task. With these targeting mechanisms at work, it is likely that some targets will be displaced or substitute targets rather than direct targets. That is, if the

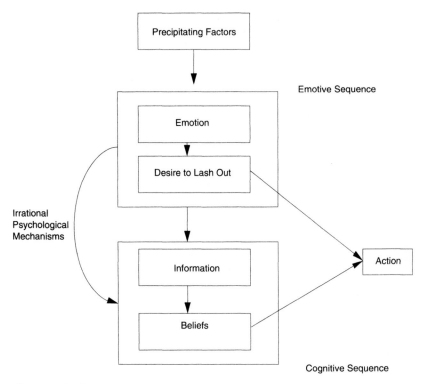

Figure 2.3   Rage

group that is the source of frustration is unavailable for attack, another group will be found to substitute for it.

Given these comments, Rage can be distinguished from the instrumental emotions on the following criteria:

a. Cognitive distortions in the selection of targets
b. The existence of clear substitute targets
c. Incoherent justifications for violence
d. Difficulty in identifying a specific source beginning the process

The purpose of this book is to explain how emotions motivate individuals to commit ethnic violence. The nature of those emotions, whether they are instrumental or noninstrumental, is of critical importance. The purpose of creating Rage is to develop a noninstrumental path to ethnic violence that can be compared to the instrumental paths and distinguished from them. Many social science theories of violence, if not necessarily

31

ethnic violence, rotate around an assumption that individuals are compelled to lash out. Specific theories often concentrate on parts of the Rage path – some on cognitive distortions, others on the precipitating factors initiating the process. Rage is a general form, an umbrella concept, meant to encompass this range of theories. Certainly, not all of the four characteristics listed above are common to every theory fitting Rage: however, the presence of one or several indicates a process leading to ethnic violence that fundamentally differs from the instrumental paths. I will address the theoretical foundations and application of this explanation in more detail in Chapter 4.

The Rational Choice Alternative

Rational choice provides a clear alternative mechanism to explain shifting actions: rational, maximizing behavior. Thus, the individual can be assigned one stable preference structure (for example, safety > revenge > self-esteem) and action can be predicted from the nature of constraints and incentives. If safety is not at issue, then the individual may commit ethnic violence in order to gain the secondary goal of revenge. Rational choice provides an explanation with reference to information and beliefs about conditions and their change, it needs no reference to emotion.

For several reasons, rational choice is difficult to apply toward participation in ethnic conflict. First, there is the obvious problem related to collective action. Any act by an individual against a large group, in this case an ethnic group, is inherently irrational in the Olsonian sense. One individual's action will not change the power or status position of an ethnic group. With their model of calculation, rational choice theorists must explain why an individual participates in group action with public goods characteristics. If violence against a weaker minority group is a public good, members of many societies seem more than happy to assume the private costs necessary to supply it.

In many instances, rational choice arguments have been stretched to include a value, a selective incentive, for "enjoyment,"[20] or for "partici-

---

[20] Edward Banfield's "Rioting for Fun and Profit" comes to mind here. While I am addressing the "fun" side of Banfield's work here, there have been recent attempts to reduce ethnic conflict to a matter of profit. See in particular, John Mueller, "The Banality of 'Ethnic War'" *International Security* 25 (Summer 2000): 42–70. Mueller, in one of his two examples, reduces the 1990s Yugoslav wars to a matter of thugs and soccer hooligans who participate primarily for the selective incentives involved with looting.

pation,"[21] but this type of selective incentive only leads back to the question of emotion. The "benefit" of this participation makes no sense without reference to emotion. Why does an individual value participation for its own sake? It is impossible to answer this question without reference to love or hate or sense of fulfillment or some other emotional factor.[22] Given this, one must wonder about the conceptual worth of assigning, for example, a hate-filled action a certain participatory "utility" or "value" when the emotion of hate itself is the driving and determinative force (not to mention the conceptual difficulties of such a task). In short, emotions should not be treated as costs. For events of ethnic conflict, the emotional mechanism provides an appropriate alternative to the logic of collective action.

Furthermore, rational choice relies on certain consistency requirements regarding preferences. Two are most fundamental. As in the example above, the agent's choices must be rank ordered. Second, the preferences must be transitive. Underlying these specific consistency requirements is a more general assumption that preferences are stable.

How realistically can preferences relating to ethnic violence and discrimination be rank ordered? Economists regularly order preferences regarding material satisfactions. However, it is one thing to assume that individuals prefer ten dollars today to twenty dollars a year from now, or to draw a curve regarding the trade-offs between guns and butter, and quite another to make assumptions about the relative values of such disparate desires as revenge, safety, and self-esteem. The emotion-based approach does not need to create these dubious rank-orderings. Emotions create a sense of urgency, they dramatically raise the salience of a particular desire, they explain compulsion. The trade-offs between revenge and self-esteem, for example, cannot be realistically calculated or represented with an indifference curve. In rational choice, the stability of preferences is a *simplifying* assumption. Most practitioners of rational choice would probably agree that this simplification is not always useful for every type of human behavior.

---

[21] In their treatment of collective action in protests against nuclear power, Muller and Opp develop a whole list of selective incentives including "fun," "participation," and so on. See Edward Muller and Karl-Dieter Opp, "Rational Choice and Rebellious Collective Action" *American Political Science Review* 80 (1986): 472–87.

[22] As Donald Horowitz notes in his massive study of ethnic riots, "Whatever leaders may plan, the plans would not come to fruition if the rioters did not find the festive infliction of suffering and degradation thoroughly satisfying. No hidden logic of costs and benefits can explain the violence *tout court*." *The Deadly Ethnic Riot*, p. 123.

Finally, as many observers have noted, rational choice has produced its most useful insights in iterative situations or under stable institutional environments. For many of the following cases, the opposite conditions held. The most violent of ethnic conflicts have occurred in periods of state collapse; the conditions under Soviet and Nazi occupations were often historically unique. When addressing discrimination, the relevant question is the creation of new intolerant institutions rather than the functioning of existing and stable institutions. In general, both supporters and critics of rational choice theory agree with this view concerning the conditions appropriate for rational choice methodology. For example, one notable proponent of rational choice, George Tsebelis, has summarized, "actions taken in noniterative situations by individual decision makers (such as in crisis situations) are not necessarily well-suited for rational choice predictions."[23]

Structure versus Agency: The Role of Elites

Perhaps the most obvious objection to the present emotions-based approach is its inattention to the role of elites. Aren't these emotions constructed and manipulated by elites for their own ends? Doesn't the approach above ignore politics?

Clearly, elites can influence the course of ethnic relations in several ways. Referring back to the links in Figure 2.1, elites can control information through their grip on the media.[24] They can shape beliefs through clever framing of the situation.[25] Elites can appeal to norms as well.[26] With

---

[23] On the antirational choice side, see Donald Green and Ian Shapiro, *Pathologies of Rational Choice: A Critique of Applications in Political Science* (New Haven, CT: Yale University Press, 1994). George Tsebelis makes this statement in *Nested Games: Rational Choice in Comparative Politics* (Berkeley: University of California Press, 1990), p. 38.

[24] For an extensive discussion of the role of the media, see Jack Snyder and Karen Ballentine, "Nationalism and Marketplace of Ideas" *International Security* 21 (Fall 1996): 5–40. Also see Jack Snyder, *From Voting to Violence: Democratization and Nationalist Violence* (New York: W. W. Norton and Company, 2000), especially Chapter 2, "Nationalist Elite Persuasion in Democratizing States."

[25] Norman Schofield believes that the nexus of comparative politics and rational choice theory lies in this shaping of beliefs. The existence of common belief, as shaped by political leaders, helps determine which of multiple possible equilibria will be selected. See Norman Schofield, "Constitutional Political Economy: On the Possibility of Combining Rational Choice Theory and Comparative Politics" *Annual Review of Political Science* 3 (2000): 277–303.

[26] On the appeal to norms, see Russell Hardin, *One for All: The Logic of Group Conflict* (Princeton, NJ: Princeton University Press, 1995) and Paul Stern, "Why Do Individuals Sacrifice for Their Nations?" *Political Psychology* 16 (1995): 217–36.

reference to nationalist myths and constant reminders of past and present victimizations, elites can inflame and intensify the emotions themselves.

It is correct to state that the emotion-based approach links structural change and mass behavior without direct reference to elites and their efforts to shape the path of ethnic conflict.[27] This omission is justified for both methodological and empirical reasons. The goal of the present approach is to lay down clear, systematic narratives of social process to serve as baselines for comparison. While elites may influence the course of events, that influence is difficult to treat systematically.[28] Demagoguery is more of an art than a science. To try to incorporate the numerous ways elites might enter into the course of ethnic conflict would entail an unacceptable loss of clarity and parsimony. I am trying to tell clear stories about the path to ethnic conflict, narratives that are generalizable across the entire century. These narratives may not apply: In fact, I expect that this approach may be inapplicable for certain cases. By discerning when and why the present approach fails we will be better positioned to understand the role of influences that it omits. It is better to be clear and wrong than unclear.

In an important sense, the emotions-based approach is a test of the influence of elites. If this structural and mass-oriented approach is able to identify patterns of ethnic conflict, then the critical explanatory role of elite strategy and influence must be questioned. Elites must then be seen as responding to structural change and mass emotion rather than shaping it. Clearly, the influences go both ways, but it is an important matter to determine which direction is dominant. Here lies the question of structure and agency, one of the major methodological dividing points in the social sciences.[29] Moreover, this distinction is central when asking how, and whether, ethnic conflict can be prevented. For if there are social processes with their own progressions and dynamics, then we must ask whether it is wise, or possible, to intervene to change or deflect the course of that progression. The discussion of "prevention" assumes that humans can create political institutions that can positively shape the course of social interactions. Creating institutions that are divorced from "broad social processes" may have unintended, counterproductive, and possibly deadly, results.

---

[27] See comments on this issue in the first chapter.

[28] In *From Voting to Violence*, for example, Jack Snyder systematically addresses the conditions that favor the success of demagoguery more than the nature of demagoguery itself.

[29] On this issue, see William Sewell, "A Theory of Structure: Duality, Agency, and Transformation" *American Journal of Sociology* 98(1) (1992): 1–29.

Through the identification of similar processes or mechanisms in diverse cases, the study of ethnic conflict will become more of a science with the attendant implications for interventions. On the other hand, the failure to identify common processes and mechanisms will also produce a valuable insight – that the study of ethnic conflict should not be a science, that interventions must be more of an art applied differently to every case. At this juncture in time, this basic question has still not been settled in the scholarly field of ethnic conflict studies. I will return to these issues both in the conclusions and in the last substantive chapter, which discusses the role of Milosevic, Karadzic, and others in precipitating ethnic violence in Yugoslavia.

As mentioned in the introductory chapter, the elite-led approach must be questioned on empirical grounds as well. In several instances of ethnic violence in Eastern Europe, it is difficult to identify leaders. This difficulty clearly presents itself during the wartime years when Soviet and Nazi regimes often eliminated local leadership through deportation and death. In other cases, leaders might be present, but it is difficult to attribute ethnic violence to their actions.[30] Again, elite manipulation can occur, but it cannot be assumed to be the primary influence.

Finally, I am in agreement with the following indignant view: "Portraying millions of individuals in many societies as mindless robots who can easily be duped into assuming fictitious identities and sacrificing their own and others' lives for the purposes of a small group of skillful self-serving manipulators represents an extremely simplistic and condescending view."[31] One senses that the portrayal of events as elite led is well intentioned. It reduces the responsibility of the mass of perpetrators by placing blame on a few evil leaders. Good intentions have little to do with social science, however.

Structural Alternatives

The inclusion of structure in Figure 2.1 immediately raises the question of the purpose of bringing the messy subject of emotion into the study at all. Why not eliminate the middle box above and simply link structural

[30] See, for example, Gordon Bardos, "Balkan History, Madeleine's War, and NATO's Kosovo" *The Harriman Review* 13 (April 2001): 36–51. See p. 40 in particular.
[31] Ivelin Sardamov, "Ethnic Warriors: Ethnicity and Genocide in the Balkans" Paper presented at the Fourth Annual Convention of the Association of Nationalities, Columbia University, New York, April 15–17, 1999.

changes to increased chances of ethnic conflict? The reason is straight-forward. The primary goal here is to know why individuals participate in acts of violence against people with whom they have lived in relative harmony for considerable lengths of time. The linkage between structure and conflict does not tell us why because it cannot identify a microlevel causal mechanism. The *mechanisms* and motivations linking structural change and ethnic conflict are found in the emotions.[32]

Furthermore, a particular structural change may produce multiple mechanisms that increase the chances of ethnic conflict. Sometimes, ethnic conflict may result from Fear *or* Hatred *or* Resentment, but other times multiple emotions, all tending toward higher conflict, may be present. Fine-grained, mechanism-based explanations specify when single mecha-nisms are at work and when cases are overdetermined. Without this level of knowledge, the analyst may attribute too much causal weight to a single variable.[33]

There is one more crucial reason to go beyond the structural variable and carefully examine the links between information, belief, and emotion. While Fear, Hatred, and Resentment all assume a similar causal relation-ship among these three elements, Rage holds that this path is affected by certain psychological mechanisms operating within the path. Therefore, examining the power and coherence of the Rage argument requires study-ing the relationship among and between these links. It is necessary to examine the available cases to see if the operation of information, belief, and emotion resembles the relatively straightforward path of Fear, Hatred, and Resentment or the more twisted paths of Rage.

Summary

Emotions are the mechanisms that heighten the saliency of a particular concern. They act as a "switch" among a set of basic desires. In the case of instrumental emotion, certain observable structural conditions and changes can be used to predict when the emotion is likely to be triggered.

---

[32] Elsewhere, I have discussed the relationship between mechanism and structure at length. See Roger Petersen, "Structure and Mechanism in Comparisons" in John Bowen and Roger Petersen, eds., *Critical Comparisons in Politics and Culture* (Cambridge: Cambridge University Press, 1999). For another view, see Arthur Stinchcombe, "On the Conditions of Fruitfulness of Theorizing about Mechanisms in Social Science" *Philosophy of the Social Sciences* 21 (1991): 367–88.

[33] I will make this argument about Fear.

The emotions-based approach concentrates on individual motivations. Many factors are important in generating ethnic violence and discrimination, but motivation is certainly one of the most fundamental. Assumptions about motivation underlie most, if not all, social science treatments of the topic. Even lawyers, with a somewhat different approach, must establish some motive if they are going to successfully convict an indictee of a violent or discriminatory crime.

The emotions-based approach is a mass (vs. elite) approach. The everyday interactions of the bulk of the population and the emotional content of those experiences is assumed to constrain elites as well as provide opportunities for rapid and violent mobilization. As many cases will show, little leadership seems to be necessary for ethnic violence.

The emotions-based approach posits a realistic and complex actor, one motivated by both instrumental and noninstrumental emotions. The approach conceives an actor that can be motivated by group-based concerns. In the emotions-based approach, the individual cares about multiple aspects – safety, status, vengeance.

The emotions-based approach specifies a mechanism and allows for prediction. It also provides a certain descriptive realism. Human beings are undeniably emotional, especially when commiting violence or discrimination against other human beings. To try to incorporate emotion into a study carries certain costs, but to eliminate emotion from study involves the loss of realism. Indeed, humans are both the most emotional and the most rational of all beings.[34] Francis Seeburger supports the marriage of emotion and rationality in vivid fashion:

Something more than merely strange has happened to the very idea of "reason" or "logic" when a character such as Mr. Spock of *Star Trek*, whose Vulcan heritage requires him to restrict himself to judgements wholly free of emotion, is presented as the paradigm of "rationality." It is no accident that Spock's struggles to confine himself to such affectless cognitions invariably end in comic failure. Someone who could succeed in such a thing would be, not a thoroughly rational being, but a psychotic. In interviews given shortly before his execution, Ted Bundy appears to reflect just such a defect. He strikes us as someone who has mastered all the right formulas, in effect, but does not really have any understanding of their inner meaning, someone who could never penetrate through the letter to the spirit. This is precisely what emotion permits.[35]

[34] For an early and forceful discussion of this point see, D. O. Hebb and W. R. Thompson, "Emotion and Society" in Leon Bramson and George Goethals, eds., *War: Studies from Psychology, Sociology and Anthropology* (New York: Basic Books, 1968), pp. 45–64.
[35] Seeburger, "Blind Sight and Brute Feeling" p. 55.

This chapter has laid out basic definitions and processes. The next two chapters expand on each emotion through conceptual clarification, connection of the basic hypothesis to the ethnic conflict literature, and, in some cases, additional hypotheses.

3

Resentment

Resentment: Structural changes such as the collapse or weakening of the center and/or occupation rearrange ethnic status hierarchies by changing sovereignty relations, composition of political positions and police, and other features such as language policy. *The predicted ethnic target will be the group perceived as farthest up the ethnic status hierarchy that can be most surely subordinated through ethnic/national violence.* If the target group is lower on the ethnic status hierarchy, then the theory of Resentment is not supported. If the target group is higher on an ethnic hierarchy but cannot have its position reduced through ethnic violence, then Resentment does not apply. If two possible target groups are higher on an ethnic hierarchy and either one or the other can be brought to a subordinate position, and if the lower group is the target, then Resentment *alone* is not a sufficient explanation. The choice of a suboptimal target would need to be explained in conjunction with another theory (possibly Hatred or Rage) or simply by another theory.

Resentment stems from the perception that one's group is located in an unwarranted subordinate position on a status hierarchy.[1] The concept hinges on the linkage between group status and individual esteem. Human beings are motivated by a desire for esteem. The concept of Resentment is much more specific than this general desire for group-based esteem, though. Here, Resentment is the feeling of being *politically* dominated by

---

[1] For discussions of ethnic conflict in ranked versus unranked systems, see Donald Horowitz, *Ethnic Groups in Conflict* (Berkeley: University of California Press, 1985). Chapters 3 and 4 have greatly influenced the present work. Also see T. David Mason, "The Ethnic Dimension of Civil Violence in the Post Cold War Era: Structural Configurations and Rational Choices" Paper presented at the Annual Meeting of the American Political Science Association, New York, September 1–4, 1994.

a group that has no right to be in a superior position. It is the everyday experience of these perceived status relations that breeds the emotion. The concept assumes that social relations are usually tinged with overtones of domination/subordination, that humans tend to think in terms of group-based hierarchies, that these hierarchies are reordered through structural changes. Crucially, the Resentment narrative holds that individuals believe these hierarchies can be reordered through violence and discriminatory policies.

This chapter details the Resentment narrative twice. The first run goes over each link from Figure 2.1 citing the intellectual background supporting the connections in the causal chain. The second run covers the historical progression found in Figure 2.2 indicating which periods should have witnessed the highest prevalence of Resentment. The chapter concludes with a discussion of the linkage between Resentment and macro theories of nationalism. In effect, I will argue, Resentment provides important but unspecified microfoundations of Ernest Gellner's structural theory of nationalism.

Microlevel Links in the Resentment Narrative

Structure and Information

Structure is a difficult concept to grasp.[2] Here, structure refers to relationships among the state and ethnic groups in terms of force and status. The strength of the state and its monopoly on force is one key structural element. The relative abilities of ethnic groups to mobilize force (their balance of power) in the absence of a state monopoly is another. Resentment is tied to structures of status relations. In the day to day operation of government, members of ethnic groups become aware of whose group is "on top" and who is "below." Status, at its core, involves an element of dominance and subordination. It is a question of who gives orders and who takes them, whose language is spoken, and whose symbols predominate. While status can be complex, status relations among ethnic groups are generally tied to the following indicators:

1. The language of day to day government
2. The composition of the bureaucracy

[2] For a discussion of definitional difficulties, see William Sewell, "A Theory of Structure: Duality, Agency, and Transformation" *American Journal of Sociology* 98(1) (1992): 1–29.

3. The composition of the police
4. The composition of the officer corps
5. Symbols such as street names
6. Redistribution of land

Some ethnic groups may be wealthier than others, but when they are forced to speak the language of others in everyday business, when they are under the eye of ethnically different police, when they cannot advance in the ranks of the state bureaucracy or the military, when land is redistributed to favor another group, then they occupy a lower level on the status hierarchy.

Structural change can affect these status relations in two important ways. First, slow changes wrought by modernization create an awareness of status relations. Modernizing states must rationalize their operations through use of a common language. These expanding states must also penetrate into formerly isolated communities to educate skilled workers, levy taxes, and conscript soldiers. All of these structurally induced activities serve to show which group is "on top" and which group is "on the bottom." Everyone comes to know the ethnicity of officers, whose language must be used, who is allowed to carry guns, the background of military officers and the police, and so on. Moreover, under modernization, the process works in two directions: Information is produced not only through state penetration of the countryside, but by the process of urbanization as peasants from the overpopulated countryside flood into the cities. Increased contact with other groups automatically produces new information. Some of that information usually indicates that business and bureaucracy are controlled by other groups and conducted in other languages.

A second form of information, again especially relevant to Eastern Europe, is less direct. Modernization brings literacy to large masses of peasants and former peasants. Individuals who identified only with their clan or their region soon discover that others speak their language and are subject to the same experiences. With literacy comes a wealth of new group-oriented information. The ability to form an "imagined community," as Benedict Anderson has so aptly phrased it, creates the ability to identify with an ethnic/linguistic group and experience the "real" emotions that stem from knowledge that one's group occupies a subordinate position on an ethnic hierarchy.

The slow structural changes of modernization produce new information necessary for the perception of ethnic hierarchy. A second type of structural change is equally or more important for the subject here. Rapid structural changes accompanying empire, war, occupation, and empire and state collapse also produce information, often blatant and dramatic information, that lets everyone know which group is "on top." For example, occupiers often staff the new police force and key positions in the bureaucracy from what they consider a "loyal" ethnic group. Language and educational policy may shift as well.

Information and Beliefs

Following the next step in Figure 2.1, new information concerning the status of one's group invariably leads to a belief about the justice of that status. If a mismatch occurs between reality and the conception of a "just" hierarchy, the emotion of Resentment is activated. With Resentment, beliefs are not formulated through the distorted lens of elite manipulated information, but rather developed through a comparative, esteem-sensitive, and group-based process. During such a process, the belief in hierarchy and a focus on its elements of domination/subordination are inevitable. At least this is the finding of a considerable variety of social scientists. Perhaps most familiar to political scientists, the work of Donald Horowitz relies on observations centered on group-based comparison and group status. In his massive study of ethnic conflict in the developing world, *Ethnic Groups in Conflict*,[3] Horowitz finds that group comparison is a nearly universal phenomenon. Furthermore, these comparisons often produce the sense of domination and subordination that defines hierarchy. After citing examples from Nigeria, Sri Lanka, Lebanon, Uganda, Kenya, Zambia, and many other states, Horowitz concludes: "Everywhere the word *domination* was heard. Everywhere it was equated with political control. Everywhere it was a question of who were 'the real owners of the country' and of who would rule over whom."[4] Horowitz employs a "positional psychology" fundamentally similar to Resentment in that "people or groups situated in a similar position 'respond in an appreciably similar way.'"[5]

---

[3] Donald Horowitz, *Ethnic Groups in Conflict*, particularly Chapter 4, "Group Comparison and Sources of Conflict" and the section in Chapter 5 entitled "Political Domination."
[4] Ibid., p. 189.
[5] Ibid., p. 184. The internal quotes are a reference to Erving Goffman's *Stigma: Notes on the Management of Spoiled Identity* (Englewood Cliffs, NJ: Prentice Hall, 1963), p. 130. In a more recent paper, after reviewing the literature on sociality and ethnicity, Horowitz concludes that "Members of ethnic groups seem to partake of all of these tendencies to cleave,

Leon Festinger, the inspiration of much of Tajfels's work, showed how the competitive spirit influencing the comparison process can result in hierarchy.[6] For both Festinger and the Bristol school, social comparisons are an absolute necessity for the creation and sustenance of the self.[7]

Social Dominance Theory, a psychological approach associated with the work of James Sidanius, is much more emphatic and explicit on the issue of hierarchy.[8] In fact, Sidanius and his collaborators hold that "all human societies are inherently group-based hierarchies and inherently oppressive."[9] Sidanius and Felicia Pratto's empirical work certainly supports the idea that individuals perceive social hierarchies. In 1989, Sidanius and Pratto sampled 723 UCLA undergraduates and asked them to rate five ethnic groups on a one (very low status) to seven (very high status) scale.

---

compare, specify inventories of putative collective qualities, seek a favorable evaluation, manifest ingroup bias, exaggerate contrasts with outgroups, and sacrifice for collective interests." See "Structure and Strategy in Ethnic Conflict" Paper prepared for the Annual World Bank Conference on Development Economics, Washington DC, April 20–21, 1998.

[6] Leon Festinger, "A Theory of Social Comparison Processes" *Human Relations* 7 (1954): 117–40.

[7] On some fundamental points, the symbolic interactionist school associated with George Herbert Mead can be seen as a forerunner of both Tajfel and Festinger. Mead emphasized that "it is impossible to conceive of a self arising outside of social experience." One of Mead's more famous statements holds that "A person who is saying something is saying to himself what he says to others; otherwise he does not know what he is talking about." In effect, conversation and communication involve two simultaneous processes: the creation of the self and the creation of an image of the self to the others. If we agree with Tajfel that an individual has a need to have a positive social identity, then the individual must say positive things about himself to others. Of course, the necessity of saying positive things about one's self in a society that is ethnically stratified may involve, or require, statements creating or supporting hierarchy. Mead's work goes beyond the scope of the present book. See George Herbert Mead, *Mind, Self, and Society* (Chicago: Chicago University Press, 1934).

[8] James Sidanius, "The Psychology of Group Conflict: A Social Dominance Perspective" in Shanto Iyengar and William J. McGuire, eds., *Explorations in Political Psychology* (Durham, NC: Duke University Press, 1993), pp. 183–219. Social Dominance Theory deals not only with ethnic and racial groups but also with gender. For a study that compares the gender aspect across Australia, Sweden, the United States, and Russia see Jim Sidanius, Felicia Pratto, and Diana Brief, "Group Dominance and the Political Psychology of Gender: A Cross-Cultural Comparison" *Political Psychology* 16(2) (1995): 381–96. Also see James Sidanius and Felicia Pratto, *Social Dominance: An Intergroup Theory of Social Hierarchy and Oppression* (Cambridge: Cambridge University Press, 1999) and Felicia Pratto, James Sidanius, Lisa Stallworth, and Malle, "Social Dominance Orientation: A Personality Variable Predicting Social and Political Attitudes" *Journal of Personality and Social Psychology* 67 (1994): 741–63.

[9] Sidanius, "The Psychology of Group Conflict and the Dynamics of Opression" p. 196.

44

African Americans, Latino Americans, Asian Americans, and Euro Americans all saw whites at the top of the hierarchy; moreover, the mean value for each group's rating was nearly identical – about 6.4. Each group rated Asians as second on the status scale; remarkably, all four groups produced a mean score of about 4.8. Likewise, the mean rating for Black status was also very similar, ranging from 3.0 to 3.4.[10]

Clearly, these data show a remarkably high level of consensus in perception of status. In the United States, a clear status hierarchy exists. Whites are at the top, Asians are in the middle, and Blacks, Latinos, and Arabs reside farther down the status ladder. All groups held a similar perception of this order. Sidanius and Pratto replicated the study fours years later and came up with similar findings.[11] The United States is supposedly a mobile and egalitarian nation, yet its citizens form highly consensual beliefs about group status hierarchies. The same phenomenon will be seen in the Eastern European case studies found in the empirical chapters of this volume.

Belief, Emotion, and Desire

Why should an *individual* emotionally react to the status position of his or her *group*? Resentment is built on the assumption that individuals care deeply about group status. Group-based goals can be linked to the individual's need for esteem. The appraisal of self, however, is only done comparatively, and when one's everyday experience is permeated by an ethnic/linguistic reality, comparison is likely to be done with groups as a basic point of reference. There are three connected points – individuals desire esteem; individuals identify with groups; therefore, individuals want to feel that their group is esteemed. The importance of high esteem is recognized by most psychologists.[12] This need seems like common sense, it is difficult to imagine that an individual would not desire esteem. It is the individual identification with groups that is more of a mystery.

The ease with which individuals identify with groups is striking. Perhaps Henri Tajfel and his associates, sometimes referred to as

---

[10] These figures are summarized by Sidanius and Pratto (1999), Figure 2.3, p. 53.
[11] Ibid., p. 53.
[12] Freud saw positive self-esteem as protection for the ego against anxiety. Others have explicitly placed the drive for self-esteem as the dominant motive of human life. See E. Becker, *The Birth and Death of Meaning* (London: Penguin Books, 1971).

the Bristol school, have conducted the most cited research on group identification.[13] In one set of experiments, subjects were divided into groups on the most flimsy criteria (style of estimating dots on a page, preferring one picture over another). No actual contact among members ever takes place. Then these subjects were asked to allocate points on a pay-off matrix to in-group and out-group members. The matrix contained a range of pay-offs that included maximum fairness as well as maximum in-group favoritism. Although no previous history of contact among subjects existed, nor any history of a group based on the created trivial difference, subjects chose a strategy of in-group favoritism over fairness in every trial of the test. These "minimal group paradigm" tests have been run in England, Germany, Switzerland, the United States, New Zealand, and Hong Kong with similar findings. The absence of in-group favoritism has not yet been found in any culture.[14] Furthermore, the Bristol school ran tests giving subjects the option to either maximize the absolute gains of the in-group or to maximize the difference in return among the in-group and the out-group. Subjects consistently chose to maximize group difference at the cost of lowering in-group profit. The experiments clearly provide evidence of a human tendency to form groups and to act to establish the advantage of their group relative to other groups.

There are several explanations for this finding. Following the reasoning above, Tajfel and the Bristol school centered their explanation around a drive to achieve positive social identity. Cognitive categories based on race or ethnicity serve to simplify a highly complex world; however, once established these categories take on a life of their own. The individual comes to accept the category assigned by the social system. The category then becomes a vehicle for esteem.

Other psychological theories pick up on the human imperative to find positive social identities and defend them, some highlighting the necessity of esteem even more prominently. The core concept of Identification Theory, as formulated by William Bloom, holds that:

In order to achieve psychological security, every individual possesses an inherent drive to internalise – to identify with – the behaviour, mores and attitudes of significant figures in her/his social environment; i.e. people actively seek identity.

[13] For a summary, see Michael Billig, *Social Psychology and Intergroup Relations* (London: Academic Press, 1976), pp. 343–52.
[14] See Sidanius, "The Psychology of Group Conflict" p. 189.

Moreover, every human being has an inherent drive to enhance and to protect the identifications he or she has made; i.e. people actively seek to enhance and protect identity.[15]

Following Erik Erikson, Bloom's Identification Theory holds that identity formation is crucial for psychic survival. Following Freud and Herbert Mead, Bloom proposes that identification begins as "a psycho-biological imperative based in the earliest infantile need to survive."[16] While the vulnerable infant has no choice but to identify with parents, Bloom, focusing on the development of nationalism, points out that identity formation and defense takes place throughout adulthood as well and will likely involve larger social groups such as the ethnic group and the nation. Crucially, shared group identifications often develop in response to changing historical circumstances.

Yet, other social scientists have looked beyond the need for positive social identity to more "hard-wired" sources.[17] Psychological theories based in evolutionary theory hypothesize that the ubiquity of identification has been created in the competition among gene pools. As survival is awarded to the species most able to avoid death and successfully reproduce, sometimes the best genes for this battle produce sharper teeth or protective coloration. Some social scientists, on the other hand, emphasize the utility of genes producing "social" weapons such as reciprocal altruism, nepotism, and other group-centric behaviors.[18] If a species is genetically "hard-wired" to help and protect its own, then the chances of its survival and reproduction may be greatly enhanced. Seen in this light, the universal tendency toward in-group identification and favoritism seen in the Bristol school experiments is hypothesized to be an inbred mechanism working to maximize fitness. It is worthwhile to note that all of the scholars mentioned above see identification processes as fundamental for survival and most basic to human existence. While Mead and Tajfel see identification as oriented toward individual survival, the evolutionists see identity formation in terms of species survival.

---

[15] William Bloom, *Personal Identity, National Identity, and International Relations* (Cambridge: Cambridge University Press, 1990).

[16] Ibid., p. 50.

[17] See the collection of essays found in Vernon Reynolds, Vincent Fagler, and Ian Vine, eds. *The Sociobiology of Ethnocentrism: Evolutionary Dimensions of Xenophobia, Discrimination, Racism, and Nationalism* (Athens: University of Georgia Press, 1986).

[18] See the general work of Pierre Van den Berghe, especially *The Ethnic Phenomenon* (New York: Elsevier, 1981).

The exact reason or reasons why individuals so easily identify with groups remains largely a matter of speculation beyond the present capacity of science. Yet, the empirical evidence supports the assumption. Recent studies have found that collective deprivation, rather than individual deprivation, is the best predictor of willingness to participate in collective action.[19]

It is important to keep in mind that this concern for group status is treated as only one among multiple individual interests; it forms the basis for hypotheses. I would only emphasize that the exclusion of group status concerns, rather than their inclusion among a set of plausible concerns, would seem to require more in the way of justification.

Desires and Violent Action

There is one final link to be considered. What is the evidence that positive in-group appraisal must involve negative out-group appraisal and even out-group denigration? What triggers individuals to beat or discriminate against an "other," in pursuit of a collective goal of "just" group status?

Again, several types of evidence support the general relationship between esteem and out-group denigration. There are dozens of anthropological, psychological, and sociobiological studies establishing the common phenomenom of ethnocentrism, a concept involving out-group denigration. To cite one study already mentioned, the Bristol school found that positive social identity of one's own group required that some other groups must be seen as less positive.[20] Social dominance theory, also discussed previously, posits mechanisms of hierarchical maintenance and reordering similar to those of Resentment: An integral element of social dominance theory posits an "out of place principle" – violence is most likely when a subordinate group has "stepped out of place."[21] Social dominance theory sees state institutions as inevitably discriminatory: "The

---

[19] Marilyn Brewer, "The Social Self: On Being the Same and Different at the Same Time" *Personality and Social Psychology Bulletin* 7(5) (1991): 475–82.

[20] For an extensive review of the literature on ethnocentrism, see John M. G. van der Dennen, "Ethnocentrism and In-group/Out-group Differentiation: A Review and Interpretation of the Literature" in Vernon Reynolds et al., eds., *The Sociobiology of Ethnocentrism: Evolutionary Dimensions of Xenophobia, Discrimination, Racism, and Nationalism* pp. 1–47.

[21] Sidanius, "The Psychology of Group Conflict" p. 199.

legal and criminal justice system will be one of the major instruments used in establishing and maintaining the hierarchical caste system."[22]

While psychology presents experimental and theoretical work on ethnocentrism and social dominance, political anthropology provides some of the most vivid evidence for the pervasiveness of status-based violence. James Scott provides broad and cross-cultural support for an ubiquitous desire for group reversal, the collective nature of this desire, and the utility of violence in establishing reversal. In *Domination and the Arts of Resistance*, Scott shows how subordinate groups develop hidden transcripts ("offstage" discourses versus the public discourses that are the stuff of historical record) that allow for the maintenance of personal dignity and self-worth. These discourses develop from actual day-to-day experiences of subordination and the near-automatic responses that result from common humiliations. Scott argues for the rather mundane origins of the hidden transcript: "Who, having suffered an indignity – especially in public – at the hand of someone in power or authority over us, has not rehearsed an imaginary speech he wishes he had given or intends to give at the next opportunity?"[23]

Scott has identified a common origin of the emotion of Resentment. For our purposes, we wish to know what happens when individuals of an entire ethnic group perceive unjust subordination, when large numbers of an entire ethnic group compose speeches and form hidden transcripts. Scott provides a possible answer:

An individual who is affronted may develop a personal fantasy of revenge and confrontation, but when the insult is but a variant of the affronts suffered systematically by a whole race, class, or strata, then the fantasy can become a collective cultural product. Whatever the form it assumes – offstage parody, dreams of violent revenge, millenial visions of a world turned upside down – this collective hidden transcript is essential to any dynamic view of power relations.[24]

Although Scott is most concerned with the hidden transcripts of long-term subordinate groups, formerly dominant groups newly out of power will have a rich hidden transcript as well. As we will see in the case studies, this transcript will contain dreams of violent revenge and visions of a world

---

[22] Ibid., p. 201.

[23] James C. Scott, *Domination and the Arts of Resistance* (New Haven, CT: Yale University Press, 1990), p. 8.

[24] Ibid., p. 9.

turned upside down (or more accurately in the case of Resentment, dreams of an upside-down world turned right-side up).[25]

Scott also provides examples showing the utility of public violence in quickly and clearly destroying the root feelings of Resentment. Perhaps his mention of the 1910 Johnson-Jeffries fight most vividly establishes this point:

Whenever a rare event legitimately allowed the black community to vicariously and publicly savor the physical victory of a black man over a white man, that event became an epoch-making one in folk memory. The fight between Jack Johnson and Jim Jeffries (the "White Hope") in 1910 and Joe Louis's subsequent career, which was aided by instant radio transmission of the fights, were indelible moments of reversal and revenge for the black community. "When Johnson battered a white man (Jeffries) to his knees, he was the symbolic black man taking out his revenge on all whites for a lifetime of indignities."[26]

Throughout *Domination and the Arts of Resistance*, Scott underlines two of the essential claims of the present work: First, domination and hierarchy are essential parts of most social systems; second, day-to-day experiences of subordination (emotion) can lead to powerful collectively held desires for changes and reversal of group status. Finally, Scott's cultural analysis of the thinking of subordinate groups concurs with the essential view of Resentment put forth here: "Fantasy life among dominated groups is also likely to take the form of *schadenfreunde*: Joy at the misfortunes of others."[27]

Finally, Donald Horowitz's recent study of hundreds of ethnic riots provides empirical support for the employment of violence as a tool to "teach them a lesson." Horowitz describes a similar phenomenon occurring in Russia, East Saint Louis, Delhi, Detroit, Sri Lanka, Nigeria, Malaysia, and other locations around the world.[28]

Scholars of ethnocentrism, social dominance theorists, political anthropologists, not to mention figures such as Frantz Fanon,[29] all posit a plau-

---

[25] In my work on the development of Lithuanian resistance to Soviet rule during 1940–41, I extensively detail this hidden transcript. See Roger Petersen, *Resistance and Rebellion: Lessons from Eastern Europe* (Cambridge: Cambridge University Press, 2001).

[26] Scott, *Domination and the Arts of Resistance* p. 41. Scott's quote is from Al-Tony Gilmore, *Bad Nigger!: The National Impact of Jack Johnson* (Port Washington, NJ: Kennikat Press, 1975), p. 5.

[27] Ibid., p. 41.

[28] Horowitz, *The Deadly Ethnic Riot* pp. 368–70.

[29] Frantz Fanon urged colonized peoples to purge themselves of deprecating self-images through the use of violence. See *Wretched of the Earth* (Paris: Maspero, 1961).

sible link between violence and status change. As the emotion theorist Nico Frijda has observed, "cruelty provides the most unambiguous proof of power over someone else. One fully controls the victim's most inner feelings."[30] Status is largely a matter of these inner feelings – an unspoken knowledge of dominance. Violence and cruelty can, with swiftness and devastation, establish new status realities.

Summary of Resentment and Additional Hypotheses

Resentment is the intense feeling that status relations are unjust combined with the belief that something can be done about it. As with Fear and Hatred, Resentment is instrumental in the sense that it alerts and compels the individual to take action toward a pressing concern.

Three points should be emphasized. First, as developed here, the Resentment argument is about a political, not economic, sense of subordination.[31] The relevant indicators are political positions, military positions, the legal status of language, and the laws of citizenship. The fundamental reasoning holds that the motivation to commit violence stems from the grinding experiences of small but numerous face-to-face humiliations.[32]

Second, a sense of subordination does not always breed Resentment. Under certain structural conditions, individuals accept a subordinate status as "just"; under other structural conditions, the emotion will follow and heighten chances for ethnically based violence and discrimination. The broadest outlines of crucial conditions follow commonsense. A sense of injustice is likely to form when a majority perceives its position as "below" a minority (when the language of the minority is the language of state and

---

[30] Nico Frijda, "Lex Talionis: On Vengeance" in Stephanie H. M. van Goozen, Nanne E. Van de Poll, and Joseph A Sergeant, eds. *Emotions: Essays on Emotion Theory* (Hillsdale, NJ: Lawrence Erlbaum Associates, 1994), p. 280.

[31] In his 1985 study of ethnic conflict, Donald Horowitz also weights politically based resentments as more important than economically based ones. He writes: "(E)thnic groups with a strong position in trade and commerce have been the victims of mass violence. But the available evidence suggests it is a distortion to attribute these attacks to economic resentment. What emerges from the data with much greater frequency is political resentment against the groups so attacked." Horowitz reiterates this finding in his more recent work *The Deadly Ethnic Riot* p. 5.

[32] James Kellas sees this type of face-to-face contact as the root of "cultural deprivation," certainly a concept related to Resentment. See James G. Kellas, *The Politics of Nationalism and Ethnicity* (New York: St. Martin's Press, 1991), p. 69.

education, when minorities hold disproportionate numbers of political positions, and so on). Of course, the majority has to come to think of itself in terms of being a majority, a process again linked to structural change and the information it produces. Perhaps most importantly, a belief of injustice results from status reversals. After having been on the top of an ethnic hierarchy, most groups come to see their dominant status as part of a natural order.

Third, aggression is more likely *when it is able* to reorder the status hierarchy in a desired direction. This point is critical. Resentment-based aggression will not be targeted against groups that are perceived as lower on the ethnic hierarchy. Likewise, small or less powerful groups will not value aggression because such a strategy will probably not be effective. Here, beliefs about the possibility of aggression affect the intensity of emotion.

Fourth, picking up on the last point, Resentment will vary in intensity. If the perception of status hierarchy is weak, beliefs of injustice and corresponding emotion of Resentment are unlikely to follow. If the perception of status hierarchy is deep and well-established, reversals are very likely to create Resentment – and the desire to rapidly reestablish the former hierarchy.

Given these points, several additional hypotheses can be formed. As opposed to the general hypotheses listed in the beginning of the chapter, these more specific hypotheses incorporate intensity of Resentment.

3a. Status reversal creates the highest intensity of Resentment and produces the highest likelihood of *violent* conflict. Status reversal results when a more regionally powerful group in an established hierarchy is dislodged from its position and placed below a less powerful group.

3b. When Resentment develops from gradually changing perceptions created by slower structural processes such as modernization, the emotion is less intense and the conflict is most likely to develop in nonviolent institutional forms.

Finally, some hypotheses can be formed concerning situations favoring cooperation among ethnic groups.

3c. If the hierarchy among groups is not clearly established, *cooperation* among them is likely, at least until a hierarchy is formed.

If there is a low perception of hierarchy, then there will be a correspondingly low intensity of Resentment. In this case, cooperation is more likely simply due to an absence of Resentment.

3d. If in the period immediately after dislodging the empirical or occupying regime the remaining groups are of relatively equal status and power, then *cooperation* is more likely.

If no group perceives itself as deserving dominance, the possibilities for experiencing Resentment are lowered and cooperation (and equality) are raised.

Macrolevel Application: Resentment and Eastern European Ethnic Conflict

The previous section explained how Resentment motivates individuals to participate in ethnic violence. As discussed in the introduction, one of the goals of this work is to link individual level mechanisms to broader macrostructural changes. This task requires linking explanation of individual motivation to the historical periodization previously outlined. During which periods should we expect to see Resentment as the driving force behind ethnic violence in Eastern Europe?

Resentment should motivate violence in periods when ethnic hierarchies are established and strong, when dominant groups within these hierarchies experience status reversals, and when a collapse of constraints allows violence to become a feasible and effective option. Resentment should motivate support for institutional discrimination (institutional dominance) rather than violence when members of a group develop an awareness of status inconsistency during a period when a functioning and stable state exists. In this situation, dominance is sought by shaping the nature of the state rather than through violence.

We should not expect to witness the path of Resentment during Period One. Resentment's foundation is the widespread perception of status hierarchy. Given a lack of modernization, rurality, and illiteracy, such a perception was not widespread. Period Two is the era of World War I and the collapse of empires. In terms of Resentment, the period would seem to be the most ambiguous – states collapsed, but most of the East European societies emerging from the rubble did not possess established hierarchies. According to hypotheses 3b, 3c, and 3d, Period Three should see Resentment produce either institutional discrimination against minorities

53

or cooperation among ethnic minorities depending upon the strength of hierarchy and the status ordering among groups. After the fall of the Russian, Austro-Hungarian, and Ottoman Empires, rural regional majorities found themselves in charge of states. Resentment, if operative, would drive these majorities to establish their dominant position through biased staffing policies in the police, military, and bureaucracy. The majority would establish their own language as the official language and make their own group's symbols synonymous with those of the state. However, if no clear status hierarchy was in place, either due to never being established (3c) or an ambiguous ordering among roughly equal groups (3d), then Resentment would not form. Cooperation, at least in the short run, would be likely. Importantly, without an established ethnic hierarchy, violence would not be predicted. Resentment should be most intense, and more likely lead to violence after strong perceptions of ethnic hierarchy have been established and reversed.

Ethnic hierarchies were well-established by Period Four. If the policies of the successive German and Soviet occupations changed these established orders in a way to place formerly dominant groups in subordinate positions, we should expect intense Resentment. In periods of occupier retreat, with the constraints off, we should expect intense violence to reestablish the previous ethnic hierarchy.

In Period Five, with most of the region in the grip of powerful Communist regimes, we should expect little violence. Furthermore, the elimination of the Jewish and German minorities and other population movements greatly reduced the complexity of ethnic relations. With fewer ethnic groups, fewer groups could be "out of place" on any ethnic hierarchy. Populational homogenization greatly reduces the risk of Resentment.

In Period Six, with the constraints of powerful states again collapsing, Resentment could be expected to surface in regions where regional majorities did not clearly dominate status positions. Again, violent ethnic conflict, as well as institutional discrimination, could be predicted in those areas.

Resentment can also be tied to the most outstanding feature of modern Eastern European history: the formation of nearly homogeneous nation-states. Twenty-odd nation-states now stand on the territory of three former multinational empires. These states are politically dominated by one linguistically defined nation. From one of the most heterogeneous states in Europe, Poland today is nearly entirely Polish. Interwar Czechoslovakia, ethnically intermixed in the interwar period to a great degree, has disintegrated into two homogenized states. The dominant nation, in almost every case, comprised the rural majority of the region in the late nineteenth century. Most of these nation-states have gone through a process of ethnic homogenization. In most of these states, ethnic violence and ethnic discrimination have been important tools in both establishing, or reestablishing, independence of a nation-state and in homogenizing the state. Istvan Deak summarized this phenomenon in the following passage:

The establishment of East European nation-states has been the most spectacular political change on the European continent in the last 150-odd years, and the only one to prove lasting. Consider the fact that in 1848 there was not a single truly independent nation-state in the region, and in 1914 only a few minor independent nation-states, all of them in the Balkans! Since that time, however, East European nation-states have multiplied rapidly.[33]

Rural regional majorities have been the great victors of twentieth century Eastern Europe. First, they threw off their imperial overlords, then they subordinated, or eliminated urban minorities. Deak again succinctly summarizes the effects of the peasants' triumph:

Rather than leading to liberation, they resulted in ever-increasing oppression of ethnic minorities. Furthermore, they hastened the native populations' conquest of the cities, which in Eastern Europe had been customarily inhabited by alien elements. I dare say even, with some obvious exaggeration, that all these revolutions aggravated xenophobia and hostility of the countryside to an alien, Westernized, and culturally more developed city. Only when seen in this light can the East European revolutions be called successful, for whereas 100 or 150 years ago most inhabitants of East European cities spoke languages and represented cultures other than those of the rural population, today there exist no such differences between country and city.[34]

Resentment provides a micronarrative explaining why rural masses participated in ethnic conflict during the past century. During modernization, regional majorities came into contact with the larger world through literacy, the growth of state bureaucracy, universal education, and conscription. They learned that they were second class citizens – and some resented it. When granted an opportunity, sections of this disgruntled rural population, led by the newly educated patriots described by Miroslav Hroch, set up states. The policies of these states reflected the majority's drive for

---

[33] Istvan Deak, "The Rise and Triumph of the East European Nation-State" *In Depth: A Journal for Values in Public Policy* 2 (1992): 77–95.
[34] Ibid., p. 82.

status and recognition, and dominance. Resentment fueled policies that drove minorities into subordinate positions. In periods when status reversals occurred, for instance during the series of occupations of the Second World War, Resentment provided the motivation for violence that would recreate the "just" order among groups.

This story should be familiar to students of nationalism. Its opening stages are a version of Ernest Gellner's famous tale of the Ruritanians found in *Nations and Nationalism*.[35] Resentment, as I argue immediately as follows, provides one of the key microlevel mechanisms implicit in Gellner's argument.

Resentment and Gellner's Ruritanians

Gellner's argument can be easily related to Figure 2.1. The very opening lines of *Nations and Nationalism* link belief (principle), emotion (sentiment), and action (movement):

Nationalism is primarily a political principle, which holds that the political and national unit should be congruent.

Nationalism as a sentiment, or as a movement, can best be defined in terms of this principle. Nationalist *sentiment* is the feeling of anger aroused by the violation of this principle, or the feeling of satisfaction aroused by its fulfillment. A nationalist *movement* is one actuated by sentiment of this kind.[36]

As with Resentment, an individual belief in an unjust situation produces an emotion that helps trigger an action. As with the emotional approach, Gellner ties the formation and intensity of the belief to structural change. His story of the Ruritanians living in the empire of Megalomania captures the essence of Period One in the categorization above. In his abstracted story of structural modernization, Gellner discussed how the Ruritanians left the countryside to enter into the cities of the Megalomanian Empire. While some assimilated, for many, this migration, and the accompanying expansion and bureaucratization of the state, produced "very concrete experiences" in which individuals "soon learned the difference between dealing with a co-national, one understanding and sympathizing with their culture, and someone hostile to it."[37] The discrepancies between the Ruritanians' own life and the ethnically distinct administrators of the

---

[35] Ernest Gellner, *Nations and Nationalism* (Ithaca: Cornell University Press, 1983). The tale of the Ruritanians is found on pp. 58–62.
[36] Ibid., p. 1.   [37] Ibid., p. 61.

Empire of Megalomania became more and more clear and less and less acceptable. In the end, Gellner concludes, "In our Ruritanian case, nationalism was explained in terms of an economically and politically disadvantaged population, able to distinguish itself culturally, and thus impelled towards the nationalist option."[38]

In effect, the Ruritanians, through modernization, developed a sense of an unjust status hierarchy. They developed, for Gellner, a "nationalist sentiment" that fueled nationalist movements. Clearly, this structurally formed and mass experienced force was more important than elite ideology. In fact, the role of ideology and ideologists is very small: "Their precise doctrines are hardly worth analyzing. We seem to be in the presence of a phenomenon which springs directly and inevitably from basic changes in our shared social condition, from changes in the overall relation between society, culture, and polity."[39] The process and emergence of nationalist movements also had little to do with rational choices of elites[40] and little to do with deep-seated and mysterious psychological forces. Common people experienced the forces of broad structural change and were "impelled towards the nationalist option."

But what precisely was the force that "impelled" the Ruritanians toward action? Gellner, operating at a historical/structural level and interested in nationalism as a broad phenomenon, is not particularly inclined to specify the force or the mechanisms that so "impelled" the Ruritanians. As David Laitin and Mark Beissinger have clearly pointed out, Gellner's theory suffers from its lack of specific microlevel mechanisms.[41] Both argue that some calibration of micro and macro stories is needed to avoid the functionalism inherent in Gellner's work. In fact, Gellner chose only to speculate in very general terms on the emotions and motivations of Ruritanian nationalists:

Subjectively, one must suppose that they had the motives and feelings which are so vigorously expressed in the literature of the national revival. They deplored the

[38] Ibid., p. 108.   [39] Ibid., p. 124.
[40] See Gellner, *Nations and Nationalism* pp. 60–62.
[41] David Laitin has also attempted to specify implicit micromechanisms in Gellner's theory. Laitin accuses Gellner of a type of reification that gives "human attributes to unspecified globs of humanity or territory." See David Laitin, "Nationalism and Language: A Post-Soviet Perspective" in John A. Hall, ed., *The State of the Nation: Ernest Gellner and the Theory of Nationalism* (Cambridge: Cambridge University Press, 1998), pp. 135–57. The quote is on p. 137. In the same volume, Mark Beissinger makes much the same point in "Nationalisms that Bark and Nationalisms that Bite: Ernest Gellner and the Substantiation of Nations" pp. 169–90.

squalor and neglect of their home valleys, while yet also seeing the rustic virtues still to be found in them; they deplored the discrimination to which their co-nationals were subject, and the alienation from their native culture to which they were doomed in the proletarian suburbs of the industrial towns.[42]

Resentment brings out Gellner's implicit views. As Beissinger notes, "Like Marxism without a theory of revolution, Gellner's theory provides no coherent vision of how nationalism works its way into the realm of substantive human action."[43] The concept of Resentment gives the sentiments of Gellner's Ruritanians an explicit form, helps build hypotheses to be tested on important phenomena of more restricted scope, such as variation in timing of ethnic violence and target of violence.[44] To further quote Beissinger, "Without a mechanism tying broad social forces to concrete human action, Gellner's ideas can never really be subjected to a rigorous empirical test."[45] Resentment aims to provide that mechanism.[46] The cases that follow provide at least an exploratory test.

Resentment and Brubaker's Nationalizing State

While Gellner's work primarily addresses nationalism during the first and second eras of the introductory chapter's periodization, Rogers Brubaker's conception of "nationalizing states" describes discriminatory actions of the

---

[42] Gellner, *Nations and Nationalism* p. 60.

[43] Beissinger, "Nationalisms that Bark" p. 170.

[44] Another of the most widely read theorists of nationalism, Eric Hobsbawm, also builds on Gellner's story of the Ruritanians and also sees a form of resentment as central to nationalism. Hosbawm writes, " All that was required for the entry of nationalism into politics was that groups of men and women who saw themselves, in whatever manner, as Ruritanians, or were so seen by others, should become ready to listen to the argument that their discontents were in some way caused by the inferior treatment (often undeniable) of Ruritanians by, or compared with, other nationalities, or by a non-Ruritanian state or ruling class." See Eric Hobsbawm, *Nations and Nationalism since the 1780s: Programme, Myth, Reality* (Cambridge: Cambridge University Press, 1990), p. 109.

[45] Ibid., p. 170.

[46] I am not the first to link Gellner's theory to the emotions involved with a perception of second class citizenship. Nicos Mouzelis asserts that Gellner spells out mechanisms linking the development of nationalist idiom with the emotions that come with failure to acquire that idiom. Mouzelis writes, "These mechanisms are related to the fact that people who fail or refuse to acquire such a nationalist idiom feel frustrated, disadvantaged, second-class citizens." See Mouzelis, "Ernest Gellner's Theory of Nationalism: Some Definitional and Methodological Issues" in John A. Hall, ed., *The State of the Nation* pp. 158–65. The quote is from p. 161. Also, in the same volume, John Hall argues that Gellner has made it clear that "humiliation rather than material self-interest provides the heart of his theory." See John A. Hall, "Introduction" pp. 1–20. I am quoting from p. 11.

third period, the interwar period. Brubaker distinguishes between *polity-upgrading nationalism* and *polity-seeking nationalism*. In the latter, Gellner's primary focus, the nation establishes a state; in the former, the nation uses the state and its institutions to establish its dominance. As Rogers Brubaker aptly describes, nationalizing states employ the discriminatory institutional measures: educational policy, language policy, staffing of the military and bureaucracy, and redistribution of land to ethnic conationals. As Brubaker sums up:

A nationalizing state, I have suggested, is one understood to be the state *of* and *for* a particular ethnocultural "core nation" whose language, culture, demographic position, economic welfare, and political hegemony must be promoted and protected by the state. The key elements here are (1) the sense of "ownership" of the state by a particular ethnocultural nation that is conceived as distinct from the citizenry or permanent resident population as a whole, and (2) the "remedial" or compensatory project of using state power to promote the core nation's specific (and heretofore inadequately served) interests.[47]

As discussed in the introduction, Brubaker describes how the interwar Polish state developed differentiated policies toward its various minorities, especially in the areas of language, schools, and employment in the civil service.

Again, and similarly to Gellner, Brubaker does not well specify any underlying force driving the policies of the nationalizing state. What he does provide is a definition of nationalism that is, like Gellner's, similar to Resentment. Like Gellner, Brubaker begins his chapter on the nationalizing states of the interwar period with a definition of nationalism that contains reference to emotion:

Nationalism can be understood as a form of remedial political action. It addresses an allegedly deficient or "pathological" condition and proposes to remedy it. The discourse that frames, and in part constitutes, nationalist political action – and the subdiscursive sentiments which nationalist political stances seek to mobilize and evoke – can be conceived as a set of variations on a single core lament: that the identity and interests of a putative nation are not properly expressed or realized in political institutions, practices, or policies.[48]

Brubaker identifies a "single core lament" – the identity of the nation is not expressed in the state's political institutions. More specific to the

---

[47] Rogers Brubaker, *Nationalism Reframed: Nationhood and the National Question in the New Europe* (Cambridge: Cambridge University Press, 1996), pp. 103–04.
[48] Brubaker, *Nationalism Reframed* p. 79.

concern here, Brubaker's single core lament can be seen as the belief that the majority ethnic group of the new states, in almost every case the former rural regional majority, did not clearly occupy the dominant position in the status hierarchy. The nationalizing state, in addressing the demands of the "single core lament" engaged in discriminatory policies in order to subordinate other ethnic groups. Although Brubaker does not explicitly say so, the "single core lament" appears to be a widely held emotion formed from a belief about the justness of a status hierarchy. The "lament" heightens perception of group status and drives certain group-oriented actions. Brubaker's micro story again would seem to link belief, emotion, and action to explain ethnic outcomes.

It is not difficult to see a common motivation running through these nationalisms and the different periods in which they played out. The same emotional force driving the Ruritanians in the first period would seem to again be at play in the interwar period. In both periods, members of the preponderant regional majority seem driven to take actions that will establish status dominance.

Despite his convincing description of the nationalizing state, Brubaker does not attempt to specify the motivations behind this type of discriminatory state. *Why* do the peoples of Eastern Europe seek dominance? What is behind the drive to "correct" the political position of the majority group? Brubaker implies, I believe, that the nationalizing nature of Eastern Europe states is based on ideas or "understandings" concerning the appropriate role of the state. Here, the "single core lament" is treated as an emotion rather than as an idea. It forms the basis of one competing emotion-based hypothesis concerning ethnic violence and conflict. In fundamental ways, Resentment specifies the core psychological-emotional nature of the "single core lament," links it to structural change (rather than ideology), and attempts to draw out its more nuanced implications. While Brubaker is basically concerned with the overall institutional changes, the general "remedial political action" wrought by the nationalizing state, the focus here is on specifying when the "single core lament" will translate into action, when it varies in intensity, and when it might be overridden by other mass emotions such as Fear and Hatred.

Summary

The concept of Resentment is in no way original. Its micro story is built upon a wide variety of social science literatures. Its macro story has much in common with some of the best known theories of nationalism.[49] This work's contribution lies in its effort to make its essence comparable to that of competing explanations. Resentment takes a form that is capable of hypothesizing the targets of ethnic violence and punitive discrimination at specific historical junctures. As opposed to the general forms found in macro theories, the actions of actual human beings can be assessed in confirming or disconfirming whether this motivation drove certain outcomes. There is clearly an intuition among a variety of social scientists that status concerns often drive ethnic conflict. Resentment specifies that intuition and tries to bring it into the realm of social science.

---

[49] Liah Greenfeld's work could also have been discussed at length here. See *Nationalism: Five Roads to Modernity* (Cambridge, MA: Harvard University Press, 1992). Greenfeld links nationalism to what she terms *"ressentiment"* – a psychological state resulting from suppressed feelings of envy and hatred (existential envy) and the impossibility of satisfying these feelings (p. 15)." In certain cases, this psychological state generates the creative power essential in the development of national identity. "Wherever it existed it fostered particularistic pride and xenophobia, providing emotional nourishment for the nascent national sentiment and sustaining it whenever it faltered (p. 16)." Similar to the present work, Greenfeld sees structural roots of *ressentiment* in the comparability between the subject and object of envy and the inability to achieve equality. The scope and purpose of Greenfeld's work is much different than the present work, however. She is most concerned with the development of national identity and the ideational properties of nationalism.

4

Fear, Hatred, and Rage

Resentment tells one story of how individuals come to participate in ethnic conflict. It is a story that seems especially suited to Eastern Europe. In that region, a coherent narrative can be told of how the status concerns of modernizing rural majorities compelled them to commit violence and support discriminatory policies in order to clearly establish a dominant position within the nation-state. But a coherent and compelling narrative does not necessarily mean that things actually happened that way. This chapter develops three alternative narratives of social processes capable of producing ethnic conflict. As was the case with Resentment, each narrative distills an account of individual motivation from well-known theories. In combination, these four paths to ethnic conflict cover the thrust, if not the nuances, of a wide range of the social science literature on ethnic strife. As with Resentment, each narrative describes a process predicting the timing and target of ethnic violence. The strength and coherence of these competing narratives is compared and tested in the empirical chapters.

Hatred: "Ancient Hatreds"

Hatred: Structural changes such as the collapse of the center eliminate constraints and produce an opportunity to commit aggression against other groups. *The target of ethnic violence will be the group that has frequently been attacked with similar justification over a lengthy time period.* If the target has not been a long hated or frequently attacked ethnic group, or if the target is attacked with a completely new justification, then the logic is not supported.

Most academics dismiss the "ancient hatreds" argument. They show how violent interethnic "histories" are often fabrications, inventions that serve the interests of rabble-rousing elites. If "ancient hatreds" means a hatred that has produced constant uninterrupted ethnic warfare, or an obsessive hatred consuming the daily thoughts of great masses of people, then the "ancient hatreds" argument deserves to be readily dismissed. However, if hatred is conceived as a historically formed "schema" that guides action in some situations, then the conception should be taken more seriously.

Hatred as a Cultural Schema

The concept of a cultural schema is aptly explicated by Sherry Ortner:

In effect, the cultural schema has been moved by an actor from an external to an internal position, from an abstract model of deeds done by ancient heroes and ritual participants to a personal program for understanding what is happening to one right now, and for acting upon it . . . there is a distance between actors' selves and their cultural models, in the sense that not all of a culture's repertoire of symbolic frames make sense to all actors at all times.[1]

The schema is an external, abstract model that *sometimes* informs a personal program for understanding and action. An ethnic hatred is defined by an antagonism against a group as an object; the antagonism is focused on purported innate characteristics of the opposing group. The two concepts of schema and hatred can be linked. Schemas can contain fairly constant representations of the innate nature of other ethnic groups. Some of these representations may be of a very negative nature. A culture possesses, as Ortner suggests, a repertoire of symbolic frames. At any given point a particular schema, although constantly existing as part of a repertoire, will not be guiding a large number of the ethnocultural group. However, the external model is always available for activation. Here is the basis for a more realistic view of "ancient" hatred. The innate negative features of an ethnic group may persist, almost indefinitely, within a cultural schema, but the emotive force of that schema is only seldom activated. Most of the time, individuals go about their business without the schema working to heighten any concern or guide any action. But the possibility always exists.[2]

---

[1] Sherry B. Ortner, "Patterns of History: Cultural Schemas in the Foundings of Sherpa Religious Institutions" in Emiko Ohnuki-Tierney, ed., *Culture Through Time: Anthropological Approaches* (Stanford, CA: Stanford University Press, 1990), p. 89.

[2] A primary debating point among social science disciplines concerns the "distance between the actors' selves and their cultural models." Those using a "thin rational view" posit an

This fact produces the constant, "ancient," quality that is so often sensed by journalists and travelers.[3]

The conception of cultural schema also addresses the nature of action that the emotion triggers. The schema provides a "script" that may specify the action to be taken. In effect, a historically and culturally formed schema embodies a liturgy and the actions are specific rituals within that liturgy. When a schema is activated, the violent and humiliating actions of one's ancestors may serve as rituals to be repeated.

Hatred, like the other instrumental emotions addressed in this project, attempts to tell a coherent story linking observable structural change, belief formation, emotion, and action. Emotions heighten basic concerns and, for some individuals, "switch on" certain desires in the manner of compulsion. Hatred heightens the desire for historically framed violence. As the state collapses or transforms, symbolic frames shift as well. The contest over certain territories, a contest long suppressed by the state and dormant in the minds of most citizens, resurrects the latent schema. The absence of state constraints, or perhaps state-encouraged opportunities, produces the belief that now is the time to act. The schema identifies the innate aggressive and unjust characteristics of "ancient" enemies, the hateful characteristics, the former violent and oppressive interactions. It becomes time "to take back what is ours," time to "settle old scores." This is the emotion of Hatred.

If Hatred is based on the existence of certain schemas, then the schema should also shape individual actions. These actions, in turn, should help us distinguish when Hatred is operative. Given the relatively unchanging scripts and rituals embodied in the schema, the justification for action should be the same across historical periods. The same innate qualities of

---

actor whose more immediate and personal economic or political goals dominate the murkier culture frame and push its significance to the background. Along this line of thinking, culture is more likely to be viewed as a resource than an unconscious constraint. Following this view, culture might help produce a set of roles, but the individual is relatively free to choose among them. Others scholars see the cultural frame as heavily constraining, or even programming, the individual's choices. Roles are not chosen, but rather accepted. Ortner takes an intermediate position where "actors may internalize a schema under certain conditions and thus may be constrained by its forms, but under other conditions may reestablish a distance between themselves and the schema." Ortner, "Patterns of History" p. 84.

[3] Rebecca West, *Black Lamb and Grey Falcon; A Journey through Yugoslavia* (New York: Penguin Books, 1995) and Robert Kaplan, *Balkan Ghosts: A Journey Through History* (New York: St. Martin's Press, 1993) provide compelling travelogues along these lines.

the target group should be taken as the reason for violence and discriminatory actions. Secondly, the acts of violence and humiliation, the acts of vengeance, should possess ritualistic qualities. In sum, Hatred predicts action against a historical target, one identified in a well-known schema. Hatred also predicts that violence will be justified in a similar manner across time periods and that the action will also appear similar across time periods.

Comments on the Plausibility of Hatred

Hatred, as formulated here, need not reach into "ancient" times. All that is needed is enough time and tradition to establish a coherent schema. In the Balkans, for example, schemas and their emotionally laden roles may not have been created in "ancient" times, but rather formed or reinforced from the more recent period of state formation. In his conclusions, the author of the 1913 Carnegie Endowment Inquiry on the Balkan Wars saw the nature of those brutal ethnic battles as setting down precedent and patterns that might later be activated. Here the analogy is one of biology and disease. Hatred is a virus that lies dormant within the ethnic group or nation, but one that can emerge with predictable effects:

Reference has already been made to the reflex psychological effect of these crimes against justice and humanity. The matter becomes serious when we think of it as something which the nations have absorbed into their very life, – a sort of virus which, through the ordinary channels of circulation, has infected the entire body politic. Here we can focus on the whole matter, – the fearful economic waste, the untimely death of no small part of the population, a volume of terror and pain which can be only partially, at least, conceived and estimated, and the collective national consciousness of greater crimes than history has recorded. This is a fearful legacy to be left to future generations. . . . Events, however revolting, are soon forgotten by the outside world and it is the inner consciousness of moral deterioration and in the loss of self-respect that the nations will chiefly suffer.[4]

It might be easy to dismiss this 1913 report except for the fact that the very quality of ethnic violence in the Balkans during both the Second

---

[4] *The Other Balkan Wars* (Carnegie Endowment for International Peace, 1993), p. 269. This volume reprints the *Report of the International Commission to Inquire into the Causes and Conduct of the Balkan Wars* (Carnegie Endowment for Peace, Division of Intercourse and Education, Publication No. 4, Washington DC, 1914).

World War and the 1990s is, at least on the surface, so strikingly similar to that described in detail in the Carnegie report.[5]

Second, as it is worth emphasizing and repeating, the emotion does not necessarily dominate, or even enter into, most of everyday life. For any culture, multiple schemas exist. Only with a particular change in structural and political realities will one of these multiple schemas emerge to motivate violent action.[6] At this juncture, I am by and large passing over the critical question of how these schemas emerge. Elites no doubt have incentives to raise one particular schema to the forefront of group consciousness. On the other hand, given an existence of multiple elite factions, we often see competing elites promoting competing schemas. Thus, violence-oriented schemas often compete with peace-oriented schemas. The question is which of these competing schemas will win out. One particular schema might win out because of the brilliance of a demagogue. However, one historical schema may dominate because it resonates with the emerging political situation. An elite may not be manipulating the situation as much as going along with, or simply exacerbating, the flow of events. At this point, the work adopts this latter view. I will come back to this question in the concluding chapters.

Third, Hatred, like Resentment and Fear, is instrumental in that it facilitates the accomplishment of a certain goal. It may be a goal that most humans find repulsive or incomprehensible, but that is not the point. As some emotion theorists point out, hatred catalyzes action in more than one way. Claire Armon-Jones writes:

The functional role of 'hatred' in these cases can be located not only in its special affective role vindicating the agent's commitment to those values which are alleged

---

[5] In *The Deadly Ethnic Riot* (Berkeley: University of California Press, 2001), Donald Horowitz describes the persistence of historically framed schemas among his own large data set. He comes to the following conclusion: "The resurrection of traditional practices during the course of rioting is supporting evidence for the role of historical memory in violent behavior" (p. 157).

[6] I have addressed this issue at length in a previous work. See the ninth chapter of *Resistance and Rebellion: Lessons from Eastern Europe* (Cambridge: Cambridge University Press, 2001). In that chapter, I discussed how political events in January 1991 in Vilnius, Lithuania unfolded in such a way as to produce a recognizable schema that motivated some individuals to participate in dangerous forms of protest. In this earlier work, the emergence of a schema was tied to a reworking of rational behavior. Individuals who recognized a historical schema derived a benefit from performing a paradigmatic role that helped to offset the costs and risks of protest. While a cost-benefit approach may be highly relevant in explaining risk-laden behavior, its relevance for other actions is limited. The relationship between historical schema, rationality, and emotion is complex and controversial.

to warrant the emotion, but also in its role of perpetuating attitudes which themselves serve to justify the practices of the communities in question. 'Hatred' involves critical attitudes, such as the appraisal of the object as in salient respects 'unpleasant' or 'bad,' and appetitive attitudes, in so far as they are used to dehumanize the object of 'hatred,' can be regarded as sociofunctional in that dehumanization is necessary to the agent's justification of his otherwise immoral treatment of the object.[7]

Hatred, with its history of negative appraisals, provides a ready means of essentialization and dehumanization necessary for justifying ethnic conflict.

Fourth, hating in the sense of Hatred may not be particularly unpleasant, in fact there may be some sense of fulfillment in acting as the avenger of one's ethnic group. Ivo Andric, the Nobel-winning author from Bosnia, wrote a classic description of "ancient hatred" in his short story "A Letter From 1920."[8] One of Andric's characters describes the emotional character of Bosnia with a particular and sophisticated view that summarizes Hatred:

Yes, Bosnia is a country of hatred. That is Bosnia. And by a strange contrast, which in fact isn't so strange, and could perhaps be easily explained by careful analysis, it can also be said that there are few countries with such firm belief, elevated strength of character, so much tenderness and loving passion, such depth of feeling, of loyalty and unshakeable devotion, or with such a thirst for justice. But in secret depths underneath all this hide burning hatreds, entire hurricanes of tethered and compressed hatreds maturing and awaiting their hour. The relationship between your loves and your hatred is the same as between your high mountains and the invisible geological strata underlying them, a thousand times larger and heavier. And thus you are condemned to live on deep layers of explosive which are lit from time to time by the very sparks of your loves and your fiery and violent emotion. Perhaps your greatest misfortune is precisely that you do not suspect just how much hatred there is in your loves and passions, traditions and pieties. And just as, under the influence of atmospheric moisture and warmth, the earth on which we live passes into our bodies and gives them colour and form, determining the character and direction of our way of life and our actions – so does the strong, underground and invisible hatred on which Bosnian man lives imperceptibly and indirectly enter into all of his actions, even the best of them.

There are several revealing qualities of this passage. First of all, there is a sense of the *enjoyment* of this form of hatred. Being able to passionately

---

[7] Claire Armon-Jones, "The Social Functions of Emotion" in Rom Harre, *The Social Construction of Emotions* (New York: Basil Blackwell, 1986), p. 73.

[8] From *The Damned Yard and Other Stories* (London: Forest Books, 1992), pp. 107–19. The quote is from p. 115. This passage is commonly cited; Robert Kaplan and Russell Hardin also discuss this passage.

hate heightens and develops other passions, even tenderness and love. The bedrock of hate supports and produces the woundrous peaks of other emotions and desirable qualities. One wonders what geographical analogy Andric would use for some Western European countries – perhaps Sweden would be a flat plane. Would Andric trade his hate-based terrain? Probably not. Radovan Karadzic is known to recommend this story to foreigners to explain the nature of Bosnia;[9] certainly, he does not recommend it because he believes it casts a negative light on Bosnian Serbs. It is likely that other Bosnians, especially rural Serbs and Croats whose actions were so critical in the mobilization of ethnic violence, also see their hatred in this light.

Fear

Fear: Structural changes such as the collapse or weakening of the political center eliminate institutional constraints and guarantees to produce a situation characterized as anarchy or emerging anarchy. Under these conditions, Fear heightens the desire for security. *The target of ethnic violence will be the group that is the biggest threat.* The theory is not supported if the target of attack is not a threat.

Following Figure 2.1, ethnic violence results from changes in both desires (heightened by emotions) and beliefs. Individuals come to want to commit ethnic violence and they need to believe it is a feasible strategy. There are multiple versions of the Fear narrative with differing emphases on belief versus emotion. Perhaps the most common Fear accounts are security dilemma accounts derived from International Relations theory. These accounts never directly refer to any microlevel mechanisms at all, let alone emotion. In these versions, reference to emotion would provide no added value; beliefs about structural change are sufficient in themselves to explain why individuals commit ethnic violence. The series of Fear arguments presented below begin with purely structural and belief-centered theories and then move toward those that include reference to the individual and explicit discussion of emotion.[10] All of these theories, however, rotate on a common assumption: that dangerous threats actually exist.

---

[9] Personal communication with Gordon Bardos, former translator for the U.S. military in Bosnia.

[10] Many of these theories are also covered in David A. Lake and Donald Rothchild, "Containing Fear: The Origins and Management of Ethnic Conflict" *International Security* 21 (2) (1996): pp. 41–75.

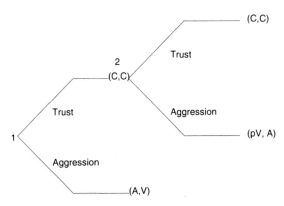

Figure 4.1   Reciprocal Vulnerability Game

Barry Weingast's Reciprocal Vulnerability Game

When two sides have the ability to attack one another without having a means to convincingly signal peaceful intentions or credibly commit to nonaggression, a security dilemma exists.[11] One game theory application of a form of the security dilemma illustrates the fundamental properties of that dilemma. Barry Weingast has laid out a "Reciprocal Vulnerability Game." There are four relevant aspects to the game: a one-time pay-off for aggression (A), a pay-off for cooperation (C), a pay-off for victimhood (V), and a probability for being attacked (p). The game assumes two players of roughly equal strength, that is, both possessing enough force to inflict heavy damage on their opponent in a first strike. The strategies are cooperation and aggression with the players acting sequentially. The pay-off for Player 1 is listed first. The game is represented in a slightly modified version in Figure 4.1.[12]

The basic insight of Weingast's game, and the security dilemma on the whole, is that even if both groups are "peaceful" or "trusting" by nature,

---

[11] See in particular, Robert Jervis, "Cooperation under the Security Dilemma" *World Politics* 2 (1978): pp. 167–213, and Robert Jervis, *Perception and Misperception in International Politics* (Princeton, NJ: Princeton University Press, 1976).

[12] Barry Weingast, "Constructing Trust: The Political and Economic Roots of Ethnic and Regional Conflict" (unpublished manuscript, 1994). The diagram is a slightly revised version of the game on p. 6. I have added the p term to the figure. I believe this addition captures Weingast's discussion of group one's subjective estimate of the aggressive or trusting nature of group two, a distinction that plays a crucial role in the analysis of the game.

and even if long-term cooperation (C) will produce the most benefits, the group playing first is likely to choose aggression.[13] Three factors work to produce this outcome. First, the cost of victimhood is assumed to be so enormous that even a small probability of being attacked in the second round yields a heavy negative expected value. Second, in the presence of anarchy, or at least in the absence of effective institutions, the group playing second has no way to commit itself to playing cooperation. Third, the cost of aggression is lower in earlier stages of conflict before the other side can build its defensive capabilities. In sum, because groups cannot commit themselves to cooperation, p is judged to be significantly greater than zero. Aggression by Player 1 becomes the rational choice because it precludes any possibility of receiving the high costs of victimhood. As an illustration, Weingast discusses the ethnic violence in the Krajina region of Croatia. Krajina Serbs launched a strike to separate themselves from Croats for basic security dilemma reasons: The Croats could not guarantee fair treatment in the future and the Serbs had a short-term advantage in the balance of military power.

There need be no reference to individual human beings or emotions in this game. Two unitary actors representing corporate ethnic groups engage in ethnic war for purely rational reasons.[14] The actor is driven entirely by perception of threat and the heightened concern for security at all costs, even bloody ethnic war.

Barry Posen's "Emerging Anarchy"

While Weingast's interpretation rotates around the high cost of victimhood, other security dilemma explanations of ethnic conflict have a somewhat different emphasis. Barry Posen specifies additional reasons why the perception of threat, the essence of the Fear argument, is the main cause of ethnic conflict.[15] First, when offensive strategies cannot be readily stopped by existing defensive countermeasures, concern with threat naturally heightens. Second, threat becomes more salient when the offense cannot be distinguished from the defense. Third, threat becomes the chief motivator of action if the opposing groups have a history of ethnic bloodshed.

---

[13] This game is similar to the prisoner's dilemma, only in sequential form and with a more extended view of the probability term.

[14] For further discussion of rationality and war, see James Fearon, "Rationalist Explanations for War" *International Organization* 49(3) (1995): 379–414.

[15] Barry R. Posen, "The Security Dilemma and Ethnic Conflict" *Survival* 35 (1993): 27–47.

Posen shows why periods of state collapse, what he terms "emerging anarchy," are especially likely to engender these conditions. First of all, when an ethnic group organizes and arms itself, other groups will not be able to determine whether that mobilization is for defensive or offensive purposes. The form of organization, that of loosely and rapidly formed infantry, is suited for offensive operations. In ethnic war, there is no readily available deterrent (as with nuclear weapons) and few technologies that allow for easy defensive superiority (as in World War I, as Posen argues). Furthermore, in order to induce men to join these units, leaders often appeal to group solidarity and refer to bloody interethnic histories. These words will undoubtedly create an aggressive aura to mobilization. Second, the offense is likely to dominate the defense when "ethnic islands" exist within regions demographically dominated by another ethnic group. The regional majority will have strategic incentives to attack these vulnerable ethnic pockets, while ethnic brethren have an incentive to quickly rescue them. This situation is completely unfavorable for cool-headed diplomacy. If a violent interethnic history exists alongside these factors, then the intentions of the other group, and the probability of attack, must be interpreted in the worst light and may well lead to preemptive strikes along the lines of the logic outlined by Weingast. In either case, it is fear of physical attack, and balance-of-power advantages in the present, that drive ethnic conflict.[16]

Posen's treatment of ethnic violence is structural and rational. The perception of threat is not created by human beings, but by the nature of the situation. As Posen writes in defense of his structure-based argument,

Analysts inclined to the view that most of the trouble lies elsewhere, either in the specific nature of group identities or in the short-term incentives for new leaders to 'play the nationalist card' to secure their power, need to understand the security dilemma and its consequences. Across the board, these strategic problems show that very little nationalist rabble-rousing or nationalistic combativeness is required to generate very dangerous situations.

Within Posen's discussion and case examples, though, it is possible to glean a good deal of material relating to individual-level motivations. Clearly,

---

[16] Jim Fearon's paper, "Ethnic War as a Commitment Problem" (unpublished manuscript, 1993), might be considered here as a security dilemma approach if a broad view of the security dilemma is taken. My own interpretation of Fearon is that he is specifying the low value of cooperation in the first round and that "fear" is not the driving motivation behind his model.

perception of threat and heightened concern for security motivate the mass of individuals operating within security dilemma conditions. Posen boldly states, "the drive for security in one group can be so great that it produces near-genocidal behavior toward neighboring groups."[17] Groups that engage in conflict, like the Serbs and Croats, have a "terrifying oral history" of violence that affects their understanding of probabilities in times of emerging anarchy.

Other scholars emphasize individual-level, emotional factors to a much greater and more explicit extent. David A. Lake and Donald Rothchild cite the security dilemma as a cause for ethnic violence but see emotions as important magnifiers and accelerators of conflict. They mention the unifying effects of fear: "People who have little in common with others may unite when they feel threatened by external enemies."[18] Charles Taylor, in an argument that will come up again, sees Resentment inspiring elite behavior and Fear driving the mass of individuals acting in the wake of elite action. While elites are motivated by a desire for recognition and dignity, "for the masses the motivation may have little to do with a call to difference, and a sense of threatened identity. It is a nationalism born of a sense of physical threat, of the fear of displacement, even extermination, by a hostile other. Each community has the sense that the other united first against its unsuspecting members, and that its own mobilization is secondary and defensive in nature."[19] Taylor gives the power of the security dilemma life at the individual level. More biologically oriented social scientists could further specify the individual level story. Rapid structural collapse of the state, caused by war or disintegration, produce a situation in which guarantees of protection no longer hold. The cognitive-emotive cycle then comes into play. Information regarding the collapse of previous protections and the build-up of the "other side" produces a belief that one's life, family, and property are in danger. This belief produces an emotion, an action tendency, that affects not only the nervous system of individuals, but further sensitizes their cognitive capacities. The fearful individual is "activated" to become exceptionally alert to any signals

---

[17] Posen, "The Security Dilemma and Ethnic Conflict" p. 106.
[18] Lake and Rothchild, "Containing Fear" p. 56.
[19] Charles Taylor, "Nationalism and Modernity" in John A. Hall, ed., *The State of the Nation: Ernest Gellner and the Theory of Nationalism* (Cambridge: Cambridge University Press, 1998), p. 19.

regarding the safety of the environment. The emotion then works to filter information, selecting out the evidence of danger. The result is a confirmation of previous beliefs and a further heightening of fear. By this time, the state of "action readiness" has changed and the individual is ready for fight or flight. While this story fits many descriptions of ethnically violent events, the theoretical social science treatment of Fear usually fails to specify all of these links, especially any systematic link to emotion.

Russell Hardin's One for All: The Logic of Group Conflict

Posen concludes that "if outsiders wish to understand and perhaps reduce the odds of conflict, they must assess the local groups' strategic view of their situation. Which groups fear for their physical security and why?"[20] For Posen, the perception of threat arises from the situation. In other versions, the perception of threat is largely created by elites and then magnified by group norms and ignorance.

Hardin summarizes his approach by stating, "In this study, I wish to go as far as possible with a rational choice account of reputedly primordial, moral, and irrational phenomena of ethnic identification and action."[21] Although not listed in this statement, Hardin clearly wishes to make no explicit reference to emotion. Yet, like Posen and Weingast, Hardin's argument is a Fear argument in that the perception of threat motivates individual action. Furthermore, at a certain point in Hardin's story, the security dilemma structure arises. One of Hardin's main contributions is specification of the coordination mechanisms that unite individuals into the unitary actors assumed in the game tree above.

Conflict is described in terms of a progression. First, political elites ("jingoists") begin the process of ethnic group coordination for self-interested reasons. Their calls for ethnic group solidarity trigger norms of exclusion in the mass population. These norms overcome the collective action problem largely through their appeal to self-interest. For instance, once the other group is identified as a threat, appeals to rally around the group for safety carry normative strength, but their power also derives from the interest of safety. Participating in the group may provide

---

[20] Posen, "The Security Dilemma and Ethnic Conflict" p. 119.
[21] Russell Hardin, *One for All: The Logic of Group Conflict* (Princeton, NJ: Princeton University Press, 1995) p. 16.

protection from outside attacks and help secure refuge if needed. Individuals in the mass population follow the "jingoists" for several reasons. These individuals are rational but rather ignorant as well. This ignorance stems from several sources: the jingoist elite's control of the media, the predisposition not to seek better knowledge but instead rely on the "epistemological comforts of home" – stereotypes, slogans, and so on.

This combination of elite self-interest, exclusionary norms, and epistemological flaws and limitations of the masses produces even higher coordination power. As the ethnic group achieves yet higher levels of solidarity and organization, the political and physical capabilities of the group and its leaders grows. A point is reached when even those previously on the sidelines cannot resist the pressures to participate. Even those adamantly opposed to the aggressive regime may not be able to avoid the sanctions involved with dissent. Given ethnic group mobilization and the lack of credible commitment to act differently, the logic of the Fear hypothesis comes into play. With both sides mobilizing, a preemptive strike becomes necessary. Ethnic conflagration becomes almost inevitable.

In contrast to Posen, Hardin sees "rabble-rousers" as a far more crucial element of ethnic violence. In the beginning stages, they create fear. First, their ability to mobilize ethnic groups breaks down the fabric of the state and creates the structural breakdown that characterizes the Fear scenario. As the constraints of the state break down, these elites build on the emerging anarchy they themselves have created by appealing to exclusionary norms and using their control of the media to manipulate the general population. In the end, the fearful structural logic of the security dilemma may unfold. The perception of threat, a real threat in the final stages of the processes, becomes the motivating force behind much individual participation in ethnic violence. Hardin, however, concentrates on the agency of elites in making this result come about.

Summary of Fear

There are three popular versions of the Fear story that can be discussed along lines of the relative weights of structure versus emotion. In one, the fears of the mass and the political elites are similar and both respond to an existing anarchic structure that has unfolded through processes outside the agency of actors. In a second, the fears of the population are manipulated and artificially heightened by a political elite for their own ends. A third version, a modification of the second, primarily focuses on a political struggle between elite factions. One faction creates fear, and possibly a security dilemma, as an effective mobilization strategy against the other.[22]

As presented here, the Fear narrative holds that an actual threat does exist. It rests on an observable reality regarding power structures: Identifiable groups have the mutual ability to inflict physical attacks against each other. This reality makes the hypothesis falsifiable. Fear assumes that when the perception of threat becomes the primary concern, then the most threatening ethnic group becomes the most likely target of attack. Thus, Fear creates a specific prediction.

The Fear narrative subsumes situations when the security dilemma structure exists. It can incorporate both situations in which this structure developed outside the agency of elites and situations when elites created it. However, the hypothesis does rest on an observable structural property. It does not incorporate a situation when elites have totally manufactured fear in the absence of any realistic threat. While it may be true that there is an "art" to the creation of fear, that certain charismatic leaders can manipulate fear to their own ends, it is also true that this "art" and "charisma" is basically impossible to systematically compare and test across diverse cases. It may be true that leadership can be a decisive force in ethnic conflict, but that factor, like many others, is not directly tested here.

Rage: Noninstrumental Emotion

The primary purpose of this work is to explain variation in the timing and targets of ethnic violence. Resentment, Fear, and Hatred all explain this variation by telling a narrative in which cognition precedes emotion. For these instrumental emotional paths to ethnic violence, the source of the process is an observable change in status, power, and overall conditions. A relatively straightforward course linking belief, emotion, and change in desire then leads to a choice of a specific ethnic target. The instrumental emotions are defined as instrumental because they work to change the relationships among groups in a particular way through specification of an ethnic target. There are several alternative theories that see a period of multiple or long-term frustrations leading to an ill-defined desire to "lash out." The individual then creates "enemies" to be attacked; these targets are only sometimes, or partially, directly connected to realistic conflicts.

[22] See V. P. Gagnon for a discussion on the collapse of Yugoslavia. Among other articles, see "Serbia's Road to War" *Journal of Democracy* 5 (1994): 117–31.

With this thinking, the emphasis is on committing the violent action itself and less on the relational properties of groups that might motivate that action. While many approaches strike a balance among these elements, several important schools of research do follow a certain general form that rotates around a heightened desire to lash out. The broad outlines of form, here entitled Rage, can be briefly summarized:

1. Rage narratives often see the process beginning from a diffuse or unconscious source – multiple sources, long-term sources, and culturally formed personalities. The instrumental paths, on the other hand, begin with observable structural changes that provide blunt information about power and status relationships.
2. In Rage explanations, this diffuse source creates an emotion early on in the process. With Rage, emotion precedes cognition. In the instrumental paths, information converts into beliefs which only then create the emotion.
3. In Rage, the search for a target happens after the emotion is operative. The emotion elevates a desire to lash out. But at whom? Irrational psychological mechanisms may work to identify and justify a particular target.

Rage would seem a plausible explanation for ethnic violence in twentieth century Eastern Europe. The region has suffered immensely. Wars, occupations, hunger, political upheavals, economic depression, and a host of other privations have hit Eastern Europe like biblical plagues. It would not be surprising if masses of frustrated and alienated individuals occasionally lashed out against their lot. Undoubtedly, there is an element of rage (lower case) in most events of ethnic violence. The key question here is how often Rage, a path centered on the overwhelming desire to simply lash out, has commanded the process. The obvious next question is how to identify when Rage is dominant.

Rage differs from the instrumental emotions in terms of source of the emotion, nature of target selection, and justification for violence. These issues are addressed in turn.

The Sources of Rage

Where does the emotion directing one to lash out come from? As opposed to the instrumental emotions, the source may be general and perhaps amorphous. This makes sense. If the source of the emotion produces blunt information about status and power, then one of the instrumental paths defined by that source is likely to obtain. If the source itself is general, or perhaps hidden in some way, Rage would be more likely.

One such source is found in culture and personality. In the wake of the Second World War, numerous studies attempted to uncover the forces behind the rise of Nazism. The roots of this virulently nationalist, racist, and antisemitic force were often sought in prejudiced and highly ethnocentric personalities. The work of Theodore Adorno and his colleagues is a well-known example of this approach.[23] In *The Authoritarian Personality*, the Adorno group identified characteristics of a personality type prone to the appeals of ethnocentrism and fascism. These traits included submissive attitudes toward authority figures of the in-group, opposition to the imaginative and tenderminded, the belief in mystical determinants of fate, preoccupation with power and toughness, generalized hostility, the disposition to believe wild and dangerous things, and, perhaps most importantly, generalized hostility. The authoritarian personality lives in a harsh psychic environment, a rigid world without imagination, pity, or love. In response to this conflicted and painful existence, the individual seeks to find a villian to lash out against. For this to happen, cognitive distortions concerning out-groups are likely. The authoritarian personality comes to see out-groups as threatening and hostile. In effect, Adorno et al. believed that the modern world had created a new type of "anthropological species," an individual with a generalized destructive urge that could be targeted against almost any group. Here are the key elements of Rage.

Hans Magnus Enzensberger claims that modern civil wars are "about nothing at all."[24] Perpetrators of violence act from a position of complete alienation. There is no specific source of emotion and no specific target: "Their aggression is not directed only at others but at themselves. It is as if it were all the same to them not only whether they live or die, but whether they had ever been born, or had never seen the light of day."[25] Here again is a new type of "anthropological species" ready to commit

[23] Theodor W. Adorno et al., *The Authoritarian Personality* (New York: Harper, 1950).

[24] Han Magnus Enzensberger, *Civil Wars: From L.A. to Bosnia* (New York: The New Press, 1993), p. 30.

[25] Ibid., pp. 27–28.

violence against a variety of targets in response to some vague, unconscious angst.[26]

Another source of the Rage process, perhaps one more relevant for the case material here, might be seen in "frustration." In 1939, John Dollard and a group at Yale wrote that "aggression is always a consequence of frustration."[27] In the ensuing six decades since this work, frustration-aggression theory has been worked and reworked in a variety of directions. The core definitions and propositions of Dollard et al., however, have been maintained in most forms of the theory. Dollard et al. defined frustration as a thwarting of expected goal attainment. It is important to note that the Dollard group was concerned with the external thwarting of an expected goal. In clear opposition to the personality forms of Rage just discussed, Dollard et al. focused on external occurrences rather than internal psychological developments. Relatedly, frustration arises not from unconscious forces, not from a battle between the superego and the id for example, but from the failure to receive an expected gratification. Individuals learn to expect a reward to result from a given action; frustration stems not from general deprivation, but rather deprivation of an expected reward.

Only certain forms of a frustration-agression argument would fit Rage. Rage would *not* fit the following sequence: An accurate belief forms that an agent is responsible for the thwarting of a goal; emotion follows that heightens the saliency of the blocked concern; emotion then directs the individual to take aggressive action against this agent. Here, beliefs precede emotions, no cognitive distortions can be identified. This version of frustration-aggression fits an instrumental view of emotion. Two versions of frustration-aggression do fit Rage, though.

---

[26] As Enzensberger notes, this general orientation toward violence has some resemblance to perpetrator mentalities of the interwar years. A general rage can be seen as the essence of 1920s and 1930s fascism. It is captured in the phrase, "Born a man, died a grocer." The entire materialistic and rationalistic bourgeois world was held in contempt by significant numbers, especially those alienated through experiences in the First World War. In the vein of Rage, they were searching for an outlet for their destructive impulses. Violence was glorified even when a specific target (the bourgeosie cannot be labeled specific) could not be readily identified. Enzensberger rejects parallels between the two periods by stating that ". . . in contrast to the thirties, today's protagonists have no need for rituals, marches and uniforms, nor for agendas and oaths of loyalty. They can survive without a Fuhrer. Hatred on its own is enough" (Ibid., p. 27).

[27] John Dollard, L. Doob, N. Miller, O. Mowrer, R. Sears, *Frustration and Aggression* (New Haven, CT: Yale University Press, 1939), p. 1. For an examination of Dollard's hypothesis, see Leonard Berkowitz, "Frustration-Aggression Hypothesis: Examination and Reformulation" *Psychological Bulletin* 106 (1989): 59–73.

Any frustration-aggression approach where the frustration comes from many sources over a relatively long time period may fit Rage. In this case, frustration may form a general mindset disconnected from any single source. This phenomenon is sometimes referred to as cumulative ethnic aggression. Donald Horowitz provides a definition – "aggression produced by the conjunction of different sets of frustrations or grievances but directed at fewer than all of the frustrating groups."[28] Under this conception, multiple thwartings arise from multiple agents. Frustration "builds up" from a variety of sources and then explodes against one or a few targets. Clearly, any frustration-aggression theory incorporating cumulative aggression does not accept a one-to-one correspondence between the source of frustration and the target of attack. Frustration is at least a somewhat generalized state, a pent-up force. Release is required, but the direction, the target, of the release of cumulative frustration cannot possess any determinative logic.

Consider, for example, the following hypothetical sequence: Group A prevents Group X from reaching a highly important goal in Time Period One; Group B prevents Group X from achieving an equally important goal at Time Period Two; Group C thwarts Group X regarding a much lesser goal during Time Period Three. Frustration is accumulating over time. If and when violence occurs, who will be the target? Several possibilities exist. Despite thwarting a lesser goal, Group X might attack Group C, the most recent frustrating agent. The action of Group C might be the "straw that broke the camel's back" or they may have pushed the group "over the brink," or "raised the temperature past the boiling point." The English language is filled with metaphors describing processes of cumulative frustration that result in a rapid collapse or explosion. It makes sense that this explosion might be directed against the most recent, and thus most visible, frustrating agent.

Alternatively, aggression might be directed against Group A or Group B, agents that blocked similarly valued goals. But which of these two groups would be the target? Here is the crux of the matter. With cumulative frustrations, the nature and level of frustration at a latter time period relates to actions connected to many groups and events, but not to any single group or event. With an increasing number of time periods and frustrating events, the connection between this increasingly generalized

---

[28] Donald Horowitz, "Direct, Displaced, and Cumulative Ethnic Aggression" *Comparative Politics* 6(1) (1973): 1–16. Also see Horowitz, *The Deadly Ethnic Riot* pp. 136–47.

type of frustration and the specific form of aggressive action that might be taken becomes weaker and weaker. The attack on any given single group cannot be a direct response toward a frustrating agent because the existing frustration is the result of the actions of several groups and several different types of frustrations. At a certain point, this generalized frustration must be seen as having a life of its own. It drives the individual to seek relief, to strike out.[29]

A second form of frustration that can be seen as the source of Rage can be labelled residual frustration. Imagine that Group A prevents Group X from reaching a certain goal, thus creating a frustration. It is possible that Group A flees or disappears. Although the frustrating agent is no longer available for redress, the frustration remains. The emotion still compels the person to lash out. The emotion can now be seen as the prior element in the sequence of emotion and cognition. The individual needs a target to lash out against. The existing emotion will affect, and possibly distort, subsequent information collection and belief formation.

Nature of the Target

As a key feature of Rage, the emotion exists before targets are selected. Building on the previous paragraph, residual frustration might operate to find a target through substitution. The group that is the cause of the frustration is unavailable, but the emotion remains and drives the individual to find a new object, a substitute target.[30] For the instrumental emotions,

---

[29] Perhaps the most well-known work employing the assumptions of cumulative aggression is Ted Gurr's *Why Men Rebel*, the classic statement of relative deprivation theory. There are many versions of this theory, but most involve some conception of cumulative discontent. For Gurr, a necessary factor for political violence is a discrepancy between average value expectations, what members of a collectivity believe they deserve, and value capabilities, what members believe themselves capable of receiving or maintaining. In Gurr's theory, and many other similar theories, this gap develops over time and may involve numerous events and many thwartings of diffuse goals. See Ted Robert Gurr, *Why Men Rebel* (Princeton, NJ: Princeton University Press, 1970). For a summary and critique of the relative deprivation literature see Barbara Salert, *Revolutions and Revolutionaries* (New York: Elsevier, 1976), especially Chapter 3, "The Psychological Basis of Revolutionary Action."

[30] Horowitz uses the term *displaced* instead of *substitute*. The term *substitute* is used here to avoid confusion with Freudian displacement, a mechanism associated with the authoritarian personality school.

the targets are direct targets, that is, groups that are connected to the source of the problem whether it be in terms of status, threat, or historical rivalry. An attack on a clear substitute target suggests that the individual is being driven largely by the need to lash out rather than being directed by an instrumental emotion.

It is often very difficult to identify a clear substitute target, however. Horowitz points this out in his discussion about targets under the effects of cumulative frustration.[31] He points out that targets may be both direct and substitute. The target may not be the primary source of frustration, but may be a source of frustration nonetheless. Second, it might be hard to draw any conclusions from the intensity of the violence against a single target. Horowitz writes:

> If a target group simultaneously receives direct and displaced aggression, then it is easier to understand the intensity of certain violent outbursts, which otherwise seems inexplicable. Some initiators of violence may well be fighting what amounts to two wars on two fronts, but all their fire may be trained on one target.[32]

Irrational Mechanisms of Target Selection

Within the course of Rage, emotion-laden searches for targets may trigger irrational psychological mechanisms. The individual may feel the need to find a target and justify aggression in any possible manner. There are many such relevant mechanisms, but the two most relevant for the cases here are projection and attribution. As defined by Gordon Allport in his classic text, "Projection may be defined as the tendency to attribute falsely to other people motives or traits that are our own, or that in some way explain or justify our own."[33] With attribution, the individual believes that an outgroup's behavior derives from inherent characteristics.

---

[31] Horowitz, *The Deadly Ethnic Riot* pp. 146–47.

[32] Ibid., p. 138.

[33] Gordon Allport, *The Nature of Prejudice* (Reading, MA: Addison-Wesley, 1979), p. 382. Allport discusses three types of projection: direct, mote-beam, and complementary. For something of a recent revisiting of Allport's work, see Elisabeth Young-Bruehl, *The Anatomy of Prejudice* (Cambridge, MA: Harvard University Press, 1996). For a broad discussion of psychological defense mechanisms and their relation to ethnic conflict, see Vamik D. Volkan, "Psychoanalytic Aspects of Ethnic Conflicts" in Joseph V. Montville, ed., *Conflict and Peacemaking in Multiethnic Societies* (Lexington, MA: Lexington Books, 1987), pp. 81–92.

Distinguishing Rage from Hatred: Comparing Justifications for Violence

A final task at this point is to distinguish Rage from Hatred. Rage is closely related to hatred in a general form. Emotion theorists often categorize and define emotion by whether the emotion is event based or object based. Fear and Resentment are event based. With these two emotions, there is nothing intrinsic about other ethnic groups that produces the emotion. Rather, events have produced conditions that create antipathy toward the other ethnic group. For Fear, it is the condition of vulnerability that produces the antagonistic emotion; if new events remove the threat of attack, the emotion will fade. For Resentment, events that change the status hierarchy produce negative emotions; the emotion arises even in the absence of any preexisting negative feeling toward the other ethnic group and the emotion can fade with changes in the status hierarchy. Hatred is another matter. Hatred is about the object itself, in this case the object being another ethnic group. For the Hatred path identified above, the other ethnic group possesses an intrinsic property as the traditional enemy. There is a constant, underlying, historically developed and ingrained antagonistic property of the "anciently" hated ethnic group. The violent and conflictual role between such groups is always present. Events are important in taking off constraints, in cueing individuals when to actively take on the violent role, but the role itself, based on properties of the groups, is a constant.

Rage is also object-oriented, not event-based. In both Hatred and Rage, the target group, as an object, is the focus of aggressive action. However, the two predict very different qualitative forms of aggression. The Hatred path involves a role, a tradition of a form of qualitative violence or humiliation. The reasons for aggression, embedded in historical grievances, remain constant and recognizable. Both Hatred and Rage involve negative images of the opponent, but with Hatred that image remains fairly constant, framed by historical schemas. With Rage, the negative images change to fit any current situation that requires release of internalized tensions. With Rage, the forms of violence and discrimination can also widely vary.

In effect, the target of Rage can be somewhat of a "living inkblot," a Rohrschach inkblot upon which the aggressor can inject various meanings at different times and under varied conditions. The Rage emotion can usually generate a reason for attacking or discriminating against the target: At one time, the group will be too rich, at another too poor; at one time the group is an economic threat, at another it will be a security threat; at one time, members of the group will remain too separate from society, at another their efforts at assimilation will prove disturbing.

The following example can serve as an illustration. Some have claimed that Serbs possess a historical antipathy against Bosnian Muslims, an antipathy that came to the fore with the collapse of the former Yugoslavia. In other words, they posit that Serbian violence against Bosnian Muslims was motivated by Hatred. Hatred, based on culturally embedded schemas and roles, should generate familiar historic justifications for violence. With this in mind, consider the following passage:

In justifying the atrocities in Bosnia, Serb nationalists would point to atrocities by Croatian army forces in World War II or in the 1991 Serb-Croat war. When it was pointed out that the largely Muslim population selected for extermination had nothing to do with the Croat army and indeed had been attacked by the Croat army in 1993, Serb nationalists would shift to blaming all Muslims for the acts of those who fought with the Ustashe in World War II. When it was pointed out that many of the families who suffered worst in the Serb army onslaught in Bosnia were families of World War II partisans who fought against the Ustashe, Serb nationalists would shift to claims of Ottoman depravity and treat the Muslims as Turks. When it was pointed out that the Slavic Muslims were just as indigenous to the region as Orthodox Christians or Catholics, the discussion would then shift to allegations that the Bosnian Muslims were funda-mentalists and that Serbia was defending the West against the fundamentalist threat of radical Islam. When it was pointed out that most Bosnian Muslims were antifundamentalist by tradition and character, the Serb nationalist would move to a final fallback position: that this was a civil war in which all sides were guilty, there were no angels, and the world should allow the people involved to solve their own problems.

In comparing Hatred and Rage, this passage provides clear evidence against Hatred. If emotion connected to a historical schema is guiding action, the perpetrators of violence would be readily able to employ that schema in their justifications. Here, the quality of the target, the object of hatred, continually shifts. In comparing Hatred and Rage, the passage clearly supports Rage – the perpetrators simply wish to commit violence, have found a target, and will commit it for any of several reasons.[34]

---

[34] This passage is from Michael Sells, *The Bridge Betrayed: Religion and Genocide in Bosnia* (Berkeley: University of California Press, 1998), pp. 66–67. In Chapter 10 I will argue that, while elements of Rage were present, the larger pattern supports Resentment as the driving force of Serbian action against Bosnian Muslims.

Application of Rage to the Case Material

Rage is a general form of a noninstrumental path, a path that resonates with strands of the psychological literature. The goal is to assess the prevalence of this phenomenon in comparison to Fear, Hatred, and Resentment. The question becomes how best to define and distinguish these different paths to ethnic violence.

Rage tells a plausible story in which a frustrated, alienated, or beaten down ethnic group develops a general emotion that heightens a desire to lash out, a general desire that can be satisfied without a specific target. The path of Rage delineated here allows an outside observer to judge whether such a path is operating by examining the possible sources of the emotion (although this is very difficult), the nature of the target, the nature of targeting, and the justifications for violence. The presence of a type of Rage must be evaluated on a case-by-case basis. If the process contains significant cognitive distortions in target selection, Rage gains support. If the target is clearly a substitute target, Rage gains support. If the target is an "inkblot," Rage gains support. In many of the cases, elements of Rage will be observable. There will be evidence of projection and attribution. It is a judgment call whether these are only minor phenomena within the contours of Fear, Hatred, or Resentment or whether their sum and coherence constitutes a process on their own.

Summary

The second chapter laid out four paths to ethnic violence in theoretical terms. The third chapter outlined Resentment and identified its specific and general implications. The present chapter has summarized the intellectual heritage of three alternative paths to ethnic violence and persecution. It is now time to apply this knowledge to the case material, beginning with an overview of the Baltics.

PART II

Comparisons: The Baltic States in the Twentieth Century

The histories of Lithuania, Latvia, and Estonia contain all of the elements necessary for a study of Fear, Hatred, Resentment, and Rage. In the course of the twentieth century this region witnessed the slow structural change of modernization, rapid changes created by numerous wars and occupations, reorderings and reversals of ethnic hierarchies, and changing power balances among ethnic groups. This section contains three historical chapters: (1) Chapter 5: "1905"; (2) Chapter 6: "In the Wake of Barbarossa"; and (3) Chapter 7: "The Reconstruction of Independent States." Proceeding chronologically across the entire twentieth century, these chapters cover, to varying extents, the entire periodization outlined in the Introduction. The section as a whole aims to assess and compare the explanatory and descriptive abilities of the four emotions. The fifth chapter provides historical background while addressing the 1905 failed Russian Revolution. The sixth and seventh chapters address specific puzzles regarding variation in ethnic targets and nature of violent action. These three chapters are used to assess the "fit" of the Fear, Hatred, Resentment, and Rage narratives, that is, how well each can explain important enigmas in target patterns and general processes within a given period. A summary chapter, Chapter 8, assesses the "fit" of each emotion across time and draws some general conclusions.

5

Baltic 1905

The Slow Changes of a Modernizing Empire

In the period immediately preceding the 1905 Russian Revolution, the demographic situation in Latvia and Estonia typified Eastern Europe and its modernization. The majority ethnic group was overwhelmingly rural, but beginning to filter into the cities, while the urban population was dominated by Russians, Jews, and others.

Records show that 94.9% of Latvians and 96.9% of Estonians were categorized as peasants (*bauerliches Standes*) in 1905.[1] In contrast, 97.7% of Jews lived in cities or towns (*kleinburgerstand*). While 49% of Russians were characterized as *bauern*, or farmer/peasant, most of these rural dwellers were really soldiers stationed in rural areas. The position of the Germans, however, is of greatest interest here. Like Jews, the overwhelming majority of Baltic Germans were concentrated in the cities. Although 12.5% of the German population was categorized with an official peasant status in 1905, even the majority of these individuals were living in the cities at the time.[2] More importantly, Germans, comprising just a tiny percentage of the population, owned 73.9% of the rural land in Estonia and 54.7% in Livland (the Russian Empire's district containing most of present day

---

[1] Some individuals who had moved to towns were probably still categorized as peasant. The figures for the city of Riga that will be mentioned shortly would seem to confirm this.

[2] Tonu Parming, "Population and Ethnicity as Intervening Variables in the 1905/1917 Revolutions in the Russian Baltic Provinces" in Gert von Pistohlkors et al., eds., *Quellen und Studien zur Baltischen Geschichte: Die Baltischen Provinzen Russlands Zwischen den Revolutionen von 1905 und 1917* (Koln: Bohlau Verlag, 1982), p. 3.

Latvia);[3] Germans comprised 83% of pastors, a socially and politically influential group; Germans also possessed a disproportionate number of positions in the bureaucracy.[4]

Underlying these striking numbers was the reality of day-to-day living. The language of state and business was not Latvian, but German or Russian. The institution of Ritterschaft, which involved designation of knighthood, virtually guaranteed German dominance in several areas. Positions in law, the police forces, and the church were determined by Ritterschaft, where the German-dominated church had a huge influence. In effect, Latvians and Estonians who wished to rise through the ranks had to become German.[5] Meanwhile, several commentators described the relations between Baltic communities as being separated by a glass wall where they "could see each other but not meet or touch."[6]

The onset of modernization, with its rapid urbanization and increasing numbers of literate workers and peasants, changed the relationship among groups. The extent of the modernization process can be illustrated by a few basic indicators. For instance, the population of Riga expanded from 102,000 in 1867 to 482,000 in 1913. The Latvian population of the city increased from 23.6% to 38.8%; in terms of absolute numbers, the Latvian population of Riga increased from 24,200 to 187,000. These figures meant that roughly 163,000 more Latvians were exposed to the possibility of greater contact with minority groups. The population of Tallinn, only 31,300 in 1867, also increased over 300% during the same period with the percentage of Estonians rising from 51.8% to 71.6%. As Anatol Lieven has summarized, the leaders of Latvian and Estonian national movements would emerge from this urban and newly educated strata:

The spread of education allowed these men to educate their sons, and the general growth in the economy provided jobs in the town for this new intelligentsia. The great majority of the first and indeed the second generation of Baltic intelligentsias

---

[3] Two-thirds of the peasantry, in contrast, owned no land at all. Toivo Raun, "Estonian Social and Political Thought" in Gert von Pistohlkors et al., eds., *Quellen und Studien zur Baltischen Geschichte: Die Baltischen Provinzen Russlands Zwischen den Revolutionen von 1905 und 1917* p. 61.

[4] Andreas Kappeler et al., *Die Deutschen im Russischen Reich und im Sowjetstaat* (Koln: Markus Verlag, 1987), p. 15.

[5] Reinhard Wittram, *Baltische Geschichte* (Darmstadt: Wissenschaftliche Buchgesellschaft, 1973), pp. 138–42.

[6] See Anatol Lieven, *The Baltic Revolution: Estonia, Latvia, Lithuania and the Path to Independence* (New Haven CT: Yale University Press, 1993).

came from this background. So did virtually all the political leaders of the Baltic states in their first period of independence. The absence of famine, war, and plague facilitated the growth of the rural population, and in the latter part of the nineteenth century the growth of industry pulled this population to the towns. Cities which, since their foundations six hundred years before had been overwhelmingly German found themselves within a few decades with Latvian or Estonian majorities or at least pluralities.[7]

The expansion of education and literacy proceeded rapidly in both countries during this period, and not only in the cities. The membership figures of social-patriotic organizations illustrate the manner in which these processes spread national identity even into the countryside. The Estonian Literary Society's founding membership was nearly 50% rural teachers and intelligentsia, a group that had not previously existed (until the 1860s and 1870s, education had been in the hands of German pastors).[8] This new literate rural segment carried nationalist ideas to newly literate peasants and smallholders as well as the urban strata of artisans, officials, and shopkeepers. While peasants and smallholders made up 9.3% of the Estonian Literary Society in 1878, their percentage more than doubled in four years. In terms of total numbers, the Society increased from 280 members in 1878 to 1,118 members in 1882. The ideas of these newly born patriotic societies would find even more fertile ground as the century turned.

In summary, on the eve of the 1905 Revolution the most salient societal cleavage in the Baltics separated peasant and landlord. Yet on top of the economic conflict, the forces of modernization were breeding experiences and social organization that fostered an increasingly stronger perception of ethnic hierarchy. Clearly, in the northern Baltic region, the Russians were at the top of this hierarchy with Russian administrators and Russian soldiers being the ultimate arbiters of policy. Second in line, however, were the Baltic Germans, dominant in land holding and the church, but owing their authority to Russian support. The Latvians and Estonians followed, in a position similar to that of other minorities such as the Poles, Jews, Swedes, and West Ruthenians.

---

[7] Ibid., p. 50.
[8] All figures concerning the Estonian Literary Society are from Miroslav Hroch, *Social Preconditions of National Revival in Europe: A Comparative Analysis of the Social Composition of Patriotic Groups among the Smaller European Nations* (Cambridge: Cambridge University Press, 1985), pp. 78–79.

The 1905 Revolution: A Rapid Collapse of Constraints

In the Baltics, the beginning stages of the Revolution were characterized by peaceful demonstrations and moderate demands by workers and students. By late January, violence appeared. Armed mobs presented demands to the overseer or directly to the estate owner, an action often accompanied by violence.[9] Despite the arrival of troops, the violence and arson escalated, especially in Latvia. Police officials around Riga and Mittau, positions held by Russians and Germans, were specifically targeted. During the 1905 Revolution, insurrectionists burned down 184 manor houses and killed 82 German nobles as well as hundreds of other German and Russian landowners.[10] It is estimated that over half of the peasants in Estonia, Livonia, and Kurland violently rose against their landlords.[11]

Although the violence struck landowners in general, there were some ethnic differences in its targeting. Russian-Latvian alliances against the Baltic Germans were not uncommon.[12] During the Revolution, the most obvious form of anti-German violence was against German pastors.[13] Often, pastors were allowed to speak until they began blessing the Kaiser and the German nobility, at which point shouts and yells broke out.[14]

Although most violence may have been class based, the actual nature of violence could potentially transform into ethnic conflict. Consider the attack on Pastor Ehrmann in Lasdohnschen:

An unknown attempted to knock down the pastor while he spoke. At this point, three other unknown persons carried him out of the church after having grabbed him by his shoulders. Outside, he was to be forced to carry a red flag. After refusing to do so, he was thrown into a puddle and beaten with fists, sticks, and kicked with their feet and afterwards dragged along with the red flag-carrying procession.[15]

---

[9] Ernst Benz, *Die Revolution von 1905 in den Ostseeprovinzen Russlands* (Mainz: Johanes-Gutenberg Universitat, 1990), p. 155ff.

[10] Lieven, *The Baltic Revolution* p. 51. Georg von Rauch, *The Baltic States: The Years of Independence 1917–1940* (New York: St. Martin's Press, 1974), p. 15. Benz, *Die Revolution* pp. 260, 276 lists 412 damaged estates in South Livland and Kurland, and 161 damaged estates in Estonia and North Livland.

[11] Martin Gilbert, *Atlas of Russian History* (Great Britain: Dorset Press, 1972), p. 75. In the other two Baltic provinces, Kovno and Vilna, there was far less violence, an issue addressed shortly.

[12] Lieven, *The Baltic Revolution* p. 50; Jurgen von Hehn p. 4.

[13] von Rauch, *The Baltic States* p. 14; Lieven, *The Baltic Revolution* p. 51; Benz, *Die Revolution* pp. 177–78, 186, 188.

[14] Benz, *Die Revolution* p. 186.   [15] Ibid., p. 183.

In some cases, the congregation's response to this type of violence was to start attending church with weapons. In addition to possibly escalating the violence, this response created ethnic overtones when the congregation was German and the assailants were Latvian or Estonian. The conflict was no longer about the red flag, but about German dominance. As Lieven has summarized, the atrocities of the 1905 Revolution had an effect on the Baltic Germans that could be fruitfully compared to the effect of the Indian mutiny on British colonials: "A hitherto image of loyal and simple peasants was replaced by a hostile one, and the way opened to mutual atrocities."[16]

The targeting of Germans is less clear than the absence of targeting of other groups. Relevant to the chapters that follow, Jews were not a primary target. Records indicate no major pogrom type violence against Jews in the Russian Empire's provinces of Vilna, Kurland, Livonia, and Estonia, and only one incident in Kovno (Dusiata).[17] In fact, the political fallout from the Revolution witnessed collaboration between Lithuanians and Jews as the two groups formed an alliance in order to win seats in the early Dumas of the proceeding years.[18]

Due in part to the absence of a significant urban working class, the Revolution passed more quietly in Lithuania. The aggression that did occur, however, targeted a rather surprising group, not the Poles nor the Jews, but rural Russians. As von Rauch summarizes: "(T)he unrest was restricted mainly to the rural areas, and consisted of spontaneous attempts to depose Russian parish clergy and country schoolteachers. The basic trend was neither anti-Polish nor anti-clerical but anti-Russian."[19]

Summary

The Russian Empire's modernization necessitated broad structural change. As throughout most of the Russian Empire, and the other multinational empires of Eastern Europe, this change brought urbanization, literacy, and education to the offspring of isolated and illiterate peasants. New types of contact wrought new types of conflict; more importantly, new types of contact created and intensified new identities. National identity competed, or conjoined, with religious and class identity. Still, at the time of the 1905 Revolution, class orientation seems to have predominated in drawing the

---

[16] Lieven, *The Baltic Revolution* p. 136.   [17] Gilbert, *Atlas of Russian History* p. 75.
[18] von Rauch, *The Baltic States* p. 23. This alliance failed to be very effective, winning only eight seats in the first and second Dumas.
[19] Ibid., p. 22.

lines of violent conflict. On the whole, peasants attacked landlords, although ethnic identity was becoming a salient element in the conflict.

This brief chapter, addressing aspects of the first of the six periods, illustrates several features which repeat throughout the remaining five periods. First, slow macrostructural changes are punctuated by a collapse of state control and the breakdown of constraints on violence. This sequence repeats when the political progression of nationalizing states (Period Three) is punctured by war and occupation (Period Four). The sequence repeats once more when the broad changes and evolution of the Communist period (Period Five) are followed by the rapid breakdown of Communist regimes. In each case, the slow changes in power and identity created the nature of the "playing field" for the emotions that were unleashed in the time of structural collapse.

In the Baltics, variation in targets can be summarized as follows: Antipathy toward landlords, German landlords in particular, drove the burning of manor houses and killing of nobles. The nature of the violence, although primarily class based, possessed an ethnic and anti-German flavor. Jews were not major targets; Russians, as an ethnic entity, were not targets; other minorities were not targets.

Which emotions motivated this pattern of violence in 1905? The Hatred narrative would not seem to fit. Hatred sees individuals accepting established and antagonistic schemas and roles; once accepted, the negative characteristics of the target group motivate the direction of the violence. The problem is that prior to the 1905 Revolution the existence of an anti-German role or schema cannot be firmly established. Indeed, at the beginning of the hostilities, for example, many Germans did not seem to even be aware of the level of antipathy felt by large sections of the eponymous peoples. This ignorance is recorded in a British journalist's account of a German pastor, sympathetic to the Latvian language and culture, who became an unwitting victim during the upheaval:

His chief delight had been the collection of Lettish songs, riddles, proverbs, and legends. Over this labour he had gone blind, but, with wife and grandchildren around him, he had resolved to write one more book, to be called 'The Happy Life,' when suddenly the peasants attacked his parsonage, shot his sexton, threatened his daughter, burnt his library, smashed his china, trampled on his harpsichord, and made a bonfire of his furniture in the garden, kindling it with his manuscripts.[20]

---

[20] Recounted in John Hiden and Patrick Salmon, *The Baltic States and Europe: Estonia, Latvia, and Lithuania in the Twentieth Century* (London: Longman, revised edition, 1994), p. 21.

As quoted above, "A hitherto image of loyal and simple peasants was replaced by a hostile one, and the way opened to mutual atrocities." The key here is that images were "replaced," new images pushed aside old ones. Hatred, in contrast, rests upon old images being accepted over and over.

Rage also fails to present a convincing case. Rage gains support if the target is a substitute rather than a direct target. Rage gains plausibility when the process leading toward violence contains clear cognitive distortions. Neither of these is evident in the 1905 Baltic case. Although Russians held decisive political power, German landlords, owning close to three-fourths of the land in Latvia and over half in Estonia, were a logical target for both economic and political reasons. For most Latvians and Estonians, the conflict with Russians was less local, less a part of daily life. Friction with Germans, on the other hand, provided day-to-day experiences of subordination. Note that in Lithuania, where Germans did not play the same economic and political role, Germans were not a target of attack. When the constraints came off in 1905, rural Lithuanians, if they acted at all, confronted Russians and symbols of Russian dominance. On the whole, there is little evidence that the attacking mobs were driven by irrational psychological mechanisms. Furthermore, a vulnerable substitute target, Jews, was readily available but not chosen.

Fear does not fit well either. It is difficult to make the case that the peasants and workers feared, in terms of physical safety, the ethnically distinct landowners, and particularly the clergy, when they attacked. Indeed, the actions of peasants and workers created a high chance of reprisal, a probability that became a harsh reality.

If any of the four emotions yields explanatory insight, it is Resentment. This emotional narrative predicts that the target of conflict will be the group farthest up the hierarchy that can be brought down through aggression. Consider the ethnic hierarchy in Latvia and Estonia as it stood in 1905:

Russians
Baltic Germans
Latvians – Jews – Others

While it was clear that in Latvia and Estonia the Russians could not be brought down as masters of their empire at this time, the Baltic Germans were vulnerable. In fact, the violence was very effective in changing the relations between Balts and Germans forever. One German aristocrat described the experience of returning to his burned estate as returning "as a mere stranger, walking amidst the servants, still living untroubled on my estate, who watched me with mocking expressions."[21] Violence had indeed provided a measure of reversal between the formerly dominant and subordinate groups; while the change may have been as much class based as ethnic, the latter factor cannot be denied.

In Lithuania, intensity and targeting differed. Lithuania was unarguably the least developed region in the Baltic and arguably the least nationally conscious. Correspondingly, the intensity of conflict was lower in Lithuania. Furthermore, a German group, for all practical purposes, did not register on the ethnic hierarchy. The group clearly above Lithuanians were Russians, who, again in line with the instrumental logic of Resentment, were targets where they were the most vulnerable, in the countryside.

Finally, the qualitative nature of some of the violence again conformed to the pattern of Resentment. In both the Latvian-Estonian case as well as the Lithuanian case, insurrectionists consciously targeted clergy, the most visible symbols of their community.

In 1905, the Russian Empire exhibited signs of exhaustion. Modernization forced changes in methods of administration and challenged the stability of existing political and economic relationships. The position of Baltic Germans, a long-time powerful player in most of the region, was most vulnerable. Conflict in 1905 challenged the Germans mainly as landlords. Modernization and the establishment of independent Baltic states would produce different types of strife, deeply emotional strife, among different players in the not-too-distant future.

[21] Ibid., p. 21.

6

In the Wake of Barbarossa

On the 22nd of June, 1941, the Germans launched a blitzkrieg war into Soviet territory. Avoiding urban areas, reconnaissance detachments rushed ahead moving at speeds of up to twenty-five miles per hour. A column of mechanized infantry and artillery followed.[1] Thus began the war on the Eastern Front – the largest and most brutal battle of modern history ending only after the deaths of tens of millions of human beings.

While the main event was the mechanized war fought mainly by Germans and Russians, many highly significant sideshows occurred among other peoples and nationalities. This chapter covers one of them: violence in the Baltic states and eastern Poland in the anarchic days of the last week of June 1941. The Molotov-Ribbentrop Pact divided northern Eastern Europe between the Soviets and the Germans. Stalin's regime incorporated the eastern half of Poland (henceforth called Poland B) in 1939 and then annexed the Baltic states in 1940. This ethnically diverse region thus encountered a rapidly changing political environment moving in a short period of time from independent states to Soviet occupation and then German occupation.

This project aims to isolate the effects of mass-based emotion on ethnic violence. There is perhaps no better period in twentieth century Europe to isolate this force than in the days immediately following the launch of Barbarossa. These few days approximated a Hobbesian state of anarchy with a thorough disintegration of social and political control. The Soviet occupation had done much to wipe out the longstanding elites and organization of independent Lithuania. In two sizable and merciless waves, the

---

[1] Perhaps the best book on Operation Barbarossa is Alan Clark's *Barbarossa: The Russian-German Conflict, 1941–45* (New York: Quill, 1965).

Soviets killed or deported most identifiable political leaders of the independence period. The newly installed Soviet leadership fled, if it was fortunate enough to escape being killed by the locals. Given the speed of blitzkrieg warfare, political control lagged behind military victory; the Germans would not establish any semblance of control for several days, and full control would take even longer. In short, a rapid lifting of constraints produced masses of leaderless individuals milling around in the streets, celebrating the end of the hated Soviet occupation, looking to even scores with collaborators – and most relevant to this project, sometimes looking to commit violence against other ethnicities. Most critically, the variation in this ethnic violence was sometimes striking.

Lithuanians, Jews, and June 1941

During the World War II German occupation, roughly 200,000 of Lithuania's 240,000 Jews would perish. As is well known, elements of the Lithuanian population took advantage of the chaos in the opening days of the German-Soviet war to engage in pogroms against Jews after the Soviets had been routed but before the Germans took control. Commonly cited figures put the number of Jewish dead, in Kaunas alone, during this brief period at about 3,800.[2]

---

[2] This figure is mentioned by Daniel Jonah Goldhagen, among others. Goldhagen's account, however, like many others, attributes too much control and initiative to the Germans and is misleading. See Goldhagen, *Hitler's Willing Executioners: Ordinary Germans and the Holocaust* (New York: Alfred A. Knopf, 1996), pp. 151, 191–92. Zvi Gitelman provides a figure of seven to eight thousand Jewish deaths in all of Lithuania during the initial days of German occupation. See Zvi Gitelman, "The Soviet Union" in David S. Wyman, ed., *The World Reacts to the Holocaust* (Baltimore, MD: Johns Hopkins University Press, 1996), p. 305.

This event has been a relatively recent subject of controversy. See particularly, Benjamin Frankel and Brian D. Kux, "Recalling the Dark Past of Lithuanian Nationalism" *Los Angeles Times*, April 29, 1990, p. M2. This article brought numerous letters of reply published in the May 5 *Los Angeles Times*. Some responses went unpublished. One unpublished letter, "An Open Response to the Editorial Board of the *Los Angeles Times*, written by the Lithuanian Research and Studies Center of Chicago, questions Frankel and Kux's selective use of SS documents. Additionally, in the immediate aftermath of Lithuanian independence, *The New York Times* published several articles concerning possible amnesties to former Nazi collaborators which included references to the June 1941 events. On September 5, 1991, the *Times* ran a front page story entitled "Lithuania Starts to Wipe Out Convictions for War Crimes" and followed up on the story in proceeding editions. In the same paper on September 10, A. M. Rosenthal commented on Lithuania in an editorial entitled "Absolutions for Killers" (p. A19) and the *Times* editorial board itself followed with its own view on September 14. Alan Dershowitz also weighed in on the issue in his *Contrary to Popular Opinion* (New York: Pharos Books, 1992), p. 338–40.

The pogrom involved more than just killing Jews – at times the persecution took on the aura of public humiliation.[3] One of the most infamous
such events was the slaughter at Lietukis garage on Vytautas Prospect in
Kaunas. There, apparently in the presence of onlookers, Jews were forced
to clean manure from the floor with their bare hands and then were beaten
with shovels, crowbars, and pipes. Water hoses were shoved in mouths and
turned on as a form of torture. When one group of Jews had died, another

On the scholarly side, Tomas Venclova's "Jews and Lithuanians" *Cross Currents* 8
(1989): 55–73, is a key piece. For an excellent article on Polish-Jewish relations of the
same time, see Jan T. Gross, "Polish-Jewish Relations During the War: An Interpretation"
European Journal of Sociology 27 (1986): 199–214.

The most recent work centering on these events are two articles found in Zvi
Gitelman, ed., *Bitter Legacy: Confronting the Holocaust in the USSR* (Bloomington, IN:
Indiana University Press, 1997). See Sara Shner-Neshamit, "Jewish-Lithuanian Relations
during World War II: History and Rhetoric" pp. 167–85 and Sima Ycikas, "Lithuanian-
Jewish Relations in the Shadow of the Holocaust" pp. 185–213.

The first discussions of the days immediately after Barbarossa were held in Munich in
1947. Much of the debate, especially Jewish charges of Lithuanian collaboration with Nazis
and Lithuanian countercharges of Jewish collaboration with the Soviets, has remained the
same for fifty years.

[3] Three separate memoirists describe nearly identical events: Avraham Tory, *Surviving the
Holocaust: The Kovno Ghetto Diary* (Cambridge, MA: Harvard University Press, 1990), p. 9;
Frieda Frome, *Some Dare to Dream: Frieda Frome's Escape from Lithuania* (Ames: Iowa State
University Press, 1988), pp. 24–25; Walter Mishell, *Kaddish for Kovno: Life and Death in a
Lithuanian Village, 1941–1945* (Chicago: Chicago Review Press, 1988), pp. 18–19. A few
comments about the reports of SS commanders, an alternative source of information on
these events, should be made. I am familiar with the reports of SS commander Stahlecker
who led Einsatzgruppe A, and those of Karl Jager, chief of Einsatzkommando 3. The
problem with these reports are twofold. First, they are contradictory; second, they may
have been written with certain political motivations in mind. For instance, in the aforementioned article by Frankel and Kux (see the first footnote), the authors state "Internal
SS memos marveled at what they called the Lithuanian 'self-cleaning action.'" Yet, at
another point in these documents, Stahlecker writes "It was astonishingly difficult at first
to set into motion an extensive pogrom against the Jews." Arno Mayer, in *Why Did the
Heavens Not Darken?: The Final Solution in History* (New York: Pantheon Books, 1988), also
recognizes that Stahlecker and Jager may have had motivations to "spin" their accounts of
the June 1941 in a certain way. Mayer, recognizing the fact that Stahlecker and Jager
claimed a great deal of credit for the Lithuanian actions (contrary to Lithuanian "self-
cleansing") but not believing them, speculates on reasons they had for inaccurate reporting: "Since by the time they drafted their reports the brutalization of war, including
the mass killings of Jews, was official policy, probably both Stahlecker and Jager claimed
excessive credit for what the Lithuanians were inclined and able to do on their own,
especially as there was neither army nor police to restrain them (p. 259)." I would prefer
not to speculate on the motivations and possible inaccurate reporting of these SS
commanders, and don't feel it necessary given the consistency of the memoirs of Jewish
survivors.

group of Jews was forced to clean up the mess before being executed themselves. Several times during the pogrom, religious Jews had their beards publically shaved, jerked, or set on fire.

There is some debate about the organization of these pogroms. The Lithuanian Activist Front, with contacts in Berlin, did plan and organize the assault on the Soviet government that coincided with the beginning of Barbarossa. Some have assumed that this organization also directed the pogroms that followed in the wake of this assault. In previous work, I have thoroughly researched the formation of local units of the LAF.[4] It is my strong impression that the LAF rapidly lost any control over the events of late June 1941.[5] It is also my strong impression that the Germans did not control events in Lithuania until several days after Barbarossa began. In all my reading of cases of ethnic violence in Eastern Europe, this case (comprising only the few days in June before the establishment of German rule) comes as close to anarchy as one can expect to see. Yet despite the general chaos, in many locations significant segments of the Lithuanian population focused their aggression against one particular target. How did this happen? As put forth in the introduction, widespread emotional antipathies can substitute for leadership in these situations.

---

[4] See Roger Petersen, *Resistance and Rebellion: Lessons from Eastern Europe* (Cambridge: Cambridge University Press, 2001). The third and fourth chapters of this book deal extensively with the formation of the LAF. My theoretical and substantive focus in these chapters was almost entirely on the formation of local cells, not elite politics.

[5] This impression is gleaned from approximately two dozen interviews and conversations, both with former LAF members and non-LAF members. My finding was that the LAF never had firm control over local cells. These cells formed in various communities without much outside direction and were incorporated, often very loosely incorporated, into the LAF. Given the nature of Soviet control, with its early decapitation of leadership, it would have been difficult to form such a widespread organization in any other way. It should also be kept in mind that the organization existed for only a matter of months; it had little time, especially in the face of Soviet police control, to become a tight, centrally directed organization. In terms of personal political ideologies, the members of the LAF covered the spectrum, although my research indicates that local resistance cells often had foundations in prewar Catholic organizations – more so than prewar right-wing nationalist organizations.

The assumption of LAF direction and control is often based on documents written in Berlin. I find these documents to be a dubious source for understanding what went on in the streets of Kaunas and other towns. First, these documents were likely more for the Germans than anyone else. Lithuanians knew that regaining independence depended on German goodwill so they were inclined to tell the Germans what they wanted to hear. Second, the Lithuanians in Berlin were not necessarily representative of the LAF in Lithuania. The former were comprised of many Voldemarists, a Lithuanian fascist group; the latter were based to a greater extent on Catholic networks that had been at odds with the

As the Germans began their relentless advance under Operation Barbarrossa, there was great regional variation in attacks on Jews. The events in Kaunas were by no means the rule. Five specific "puzzles" based on variation in timing, ethnic target, and the nature of ethnic violence are outlined below.

Five Puzzles

Lithuanian-Jewish Violence over Time   Contrary to common opinion today, one of the most significant aspects of Lithuanian-Jewish relations prior to June 1941 was the relative lack of major mass violent action against Jews.[6] Anarchic conditions held in the post-World War I era, but mass violence by Lithuanians against Jews is seldom recorded.[7] Even after the democratic government was suspended in 1926 the mild authoritarian government of Smetona did not carry out or encourage violent actions against Jews.[8] Ezra Mendelsohn, the author of a major comparative study on Central European Jewry, sums up the situation in the following words:

But the "Jewish question" in Lithuania never was the subject of obsessive attention, as it was in Poland, Romania, and Hungary, and no Lithuanian government

Voldemarists. Documents written by Voldemarists in Berlin were not likely to be taken as a hard and fast matter of policy direction in Kaunas or Vilnius. Third, and most importantly, I argue that no group had control over events in the immediate wake of Barbarossa. Soviet deportations had begun one week prior to the invasion sending thousands into hiding and the entire society into disruption. When the invasion began, prisoners were freed from jail who had their own agendas, there was a great deal of alcohol consumption, tens of thousands of previously unorganized individuals flooded the streets. As I mentioned above, the LAF was not a tightly centralized organization. This type of organization was not in a position to control events, or even the bulk of its own membership, in the situation that unfolded after Barbarossa. This certainly does not mean that members of the LAF did not commit atrocities against Jews. It does mean that these actions were likely done primarily on the perpetrators' own volition rather than as a matter of following orders from the LAF. Finally, I would note that this commentary is certainly no apology for Lithuanians. Its implication is that a significant segment of Lithuanian society was oriented to attack Jews. I will make a similar argument about Serbs in Chapter 10.

[6] Martin Gilbert, in his *Atlas of Russian History* (Great Britain: Dorset Press, 1972), pp. 69–70, 75, lists one pogrom occurring in the region from 1871–1906: Dusiata, in northern Kovno in 1905–06.

[7] There were actions against Jews in Vilnius, but that city was Polish controlled and populated at the time. It is possible to find scattered reports of isolated actions. For example, there is mention of a pogrom in Panevyzys in 1919. However, the conclusion that Lithuanian-Jewish relations were nonviolent, especially in comparison with neighboring regions, is generally noncontroversial.

[8] Smetona often visited a synagogue on high Jewish holidays.

attempted to revoke Jewish emancipation. Moreover, Lithuania suffered little of the anti-Semitic violence endemic to Poland.[9]

Joseph Rothschild has stated that Jews "were relatively the best-treated of the country's interwar minorities."[10]

Vilnius versus Kaunas Compared to Kaunas and many other cities in Lithuania, Vilnius witnessed little action against Jews in the wake of Bar-barrosa. As Yitzhak Arad sums up:

During the brief period of joint German-Lithuanian administration, no mass executions of Jews in Vilna nor any anti-Jewish pogroms were carried out. There were persecutions and molestations and Jews were murdered, but these were not the type of pogroms and massacres that occurred in those days in the other cities of Lithuania, especially in Kovno (Kaunas) and Shavli (Sauliai).[11]

This difference is even more interesting when seen in historical context. During the immediate post-World War I period, Vilnius, under Polish control and with a largely Polish population, witnessed several pogroms while Kaunas remained relatively quiet. The evaluation of the Jewish leader Vygodski on the general experiences of Jews in Kaunas and Vilnius sets up a basic puzzle:

Taking into account the experience we had with Kovno Lithuania (that is, with the independent Lithuanian state) and with Vilna Lithuania (that is, with the Poles), it was entirely clear to us that Kovno Lithuania was a paradise in comparison with Vilna Lithuania.[12]

Shortly more than twenty years later, Lithuanians beat Jews with iron bars in the "paradise" while neither Lithuanians nor Poles committed massive riotous acts against Jews in Vilnius.

In Vilnius, Lithuanians were much more concerned with solving the "Polish problem" than with the Jews. In the period before the Germans

---

[9] Ezra Mendelsohn, *The Jews of East Central Europe Between the World Wars* (Bloomington: Indiana University Press, 1983), p. 236.

[10] Joseph Rothchild, *East Central Europe between the Two World Wars* (Seattle: University of Washington Press, 1974), p. 378.

[11] Yitzak Arad, *Ghetto in Flames: The Struggle and Destruction of the Jews in Vilna in the Holocaust* (Jerusalem: Ahva Cooperative Printing Press, 1980), p. 46. In a footnote contained within this passage, Arad refers to the murders of Jews along with Soviet soldiers on June 24 in the garden of the Franciscan Church.

[12] Quoted in Mendelsohn, *The Jews of East Central Europe* pp. 221–22.

established control, Lithuanians targeted Poles by closing down Polish cultural institutions and trying to implicate Poles in anti-German activities. As an Einsatzgruppe report stated: "In the view of the Lithuanian population in the Vilna district, the Jewish question takes second place after the Polish problem."[13]

Belorussia, Estonia, and Latvia   In each of these cases, Operation Barbarossa and the subsequent Soviet withdrawal introduced a period of anarchy. In Latvia, events resembled those in Lithuania.[14] Again, Latvians and Jews had lived without violence during the interwar period; the Latvian government, like the Lithuanian, supported Jewish education; again, Latvians committed pogromlike violence against an unwitting and defenseless Jewish population. Scholarly summaries of Lithuania and Latvia sound very similar. As one scholar describes, the Latvians "wasted no time in 'getting even' with the helpless Jews, who had lived on Latvian soil for centuries. In cities, towns, and villages all over Latvia, whole groups of Jews were murdered even before the arrival of the Germans. It came as a shock to Latvian Jews, who had never thought that their erstwhile neighbors hated them with such passion."[15]

In Estonia, mass public anti-Jewish action on the scale seen in Latvia and Lithuania did not occur. In neighboring Belorussia, there was again an absence of aggression. In fact, as the leader of the Minsk ghetto, Yefim Stolerovitch, was to state, "Though the Germans found their individual collaborators among the Byelorussians, these were the exception and not the rule. The dominant characteristic of the Byelorussian population was one of friendship and sympathy toward the Jews."[16]

---

[13] Einsatzgruppe A, Report of October 15, 1941, YVA, 0-51/57-1, p. 112. This passage is cited by Arad on p. 49.

[14] Events in Latvia are discussed and interpreted in Hans-Heinrich Wilhelm, "'Inventing' the Holocaust for Latvia: New Research" in Zvi Gitelman, ed., *Bitter Legacy: Confronting the Holocaust in the USSR* pp. 104–22. In the first pages of this article, Wilhelm summarizes Berhard Press, *Judenmord in Lettland, 1941–1945* (Berlin, 1988). Press, a Latvian Holocaust survivor wrote, "a bloody, drunken orgy seized the land and whoever did not raise his hand to kill, at least tried to browbeat us. No one comforted us, no one stood up for us. Suddenly we became strangers in our own homeland . . ." (p. 17).

[15] Gertrude Schneider, "The Two Ghettos in Riga, Latvia, 1941–1943" in Lucjan Dobroszycki and Jeffrey Gurock, eds., *The Holocaust in the Soviet Union* (New York: M. E. Sharpe, 1993), pp. 182–83.

[16] Yuri Suhl, ed., *They Fought Back: The Story of the Jewish Resistance in Nazi Europe* (New York: Crown Publishers, 1967), p. 153. Cited in Jan Zaprudnik, *Belarus: At a Crossroads in History* (Boulder, CO: Westview Press, 1993), p. 97.

Other Minorities within Lithuania   Although the June 1941 outburst followed the withdrawal of the hated Soviet regime, Lithuanians apparently committed little violent action against the Russian minority. Commonsense might hold that Russians would have been likely targets of Lithuanian wrath in this period, yet they and other minorities, such as Belorussians, were largely left alone.

Rabbis and Religious Jews   There is evidence that Rabbis and religious Jews were especially targeted.[17] As this outburst had anti-Soviet and anti-Communist overtones, why were these religious figures targeted? Dov Levin states that thirty six rabbis were "brutally tortured."[18]

The Background of June 1941

These puzzles exemplify the variation in targets and actions that occurred in the beginning of the fourth period profiled in the introduction – the time of occupation and war. In order to address these puzzles and assess the explanatory power of the four emotional paths, it is necessary to outline the evolution of power and status relationships throughout Periods Two (the collapse of empire) and Three (interwar nationalizing states). In effect, the following historical narrative continues where the previous chapter left off.

Before the First World War, both Lithuanians and Jews were simply two groups within the Russian Empire, neither having the capacity to challenge Russian political dominance. With the onset of war and the collapse of the tsarist regime, all this changed. Encouraged by their German occupiers, a significant number of Lithuanians and Jews saw the creation of an independent Lithuanian state as a chance to free themselves from Russian, and possible Polish, hegemony. Jewish leaders believed that in this new state terms of Jewish autonomy could be arranged that would free Jews from outside political dominance. In effect, Jews believed that a consociational system could be established with elite-bargained cultural autonomy and a great deal of political autonomy as well. Mendelsohn sums up the logic of the Lithuanian-Jewish political alliance:

[17] See Zvi Kolitz, "The Physical and Metaphysical Dimensions of the Extermination of the Jews in Lithuania" in Lucjan Dobroszycki and Jeffrey Gurock, eds., *The Holocaust in the Soviet Union* p. 199; Mishell, *Kaddish for Kovno* pp. 20–21. Rabbi Osowski is specifically mentioned.

[18] Dov Levin, "Lithuania" in David S. Wyman, ed., *The World Reacts to the Holocaust* (Baltimore, MD: Johns Hopkins University Press, 1996).

What seemed a good bargain from the Lithuanian side appeared no less attractive to many Jews. If the Ukrainians were not the most desirable of partners because of the fierce anti-Semitic tradition in the Ukraine (and the Jews needed no reminder of this tradition during 1918–20), the Lithuanians, as we know, were a different case. If the Poles refused to consider Jewish national demands in eastern Galicia and Congress Poland, the Lithuanians promised them everything they desired. Moreover, Jewish nationalists welcomed the idea of an independent Lithuanian state because the Jews living in such a state would not be tempted to assimilate into the dominant culture, but would (so it was assumed) concentrate on developing their own national life. . . . It made sense, therefore, for the Jews to support a Lithuanian state which would be by definition a multinational, federal state in which all the nationalities – Jews, Poles, Belorussians, and the majority Lithuanian people – would band together against the imperialist powers to create a kind of East Europe and Switzerland.[19]

In avoiding political control by outside great powers, Jews and Lithuanians became allies and the ethnic boundary between them had few overtones of subordination or domination despite Jewish economic concentration (which was probably more pronounced in 1920 than in the late 1930s) and despite any religion-based animosity stemming from Lithuania's intensely Catholic population. The ethnic boundary, it seems, was shaped by the goal of reducing common political subordination.

For the first several years, extraterritorial national automony appeared to have a chance of implementation. On August 5, 1919, a nonbinding declaration on the status of the Jewish minority promised proportional Jewish representation in the legislature, a special minister for Jewish affairs, autonomy in "religion, welfare, social help, education, and culture in general," state-paid education in Jewish schools, free use of Jewish languages in the government and courts, and recognition of the authority of Jewish national institutions to levy taxes and administer other governmental functions binding on all Jews. Similar promises were made to Poles and Belorussians. In the beginning, the chances for actual legal enactment of these proclamations seemed promising. Some Jewish deputies addressed the parliament in Yiddish, and Hebrew street signs appeared in Kaunas. As Dov Levin sums up, "Lithuanian Jewry could feel the hope for a new era of cooperation between their two newly liberated peoples."[20]

---

[19] Mendelsohn, *The Jews of East Central Europe* p. 218. Also see John Hiden and Patrick Salmon, *The Baltic States and Europe: Estonia, Latvia, and Lithuania in the Twentieth Century* (London: Longman,1994), p. 146 ff. for an overview of the minority rights and roles established in the constitution, as well as the minority role in the parliamentary politics.
[20] Levin, "Lithuania" pp. 326–27.

However, when the minority-filled Vilnius region fell into the hands of the Poles, demographically Lithuania became a predominantly Lithuanian state. The incentives to maintain the political balance and to continue to build institutional checks on the power of the majority became weak or nonexistent. Demographic and political checks disappeared. Nothing could deter Lithuanians from creating "Lithuania for Lithuanians," the pattern of majority dominance sweeping through all of Eastern Europe. In effect, the actual establishment of a sovereign state of Lithuania profoundly changed the previous cooperative ethnic boundary between Lithuanians and Jews within a relatively short period. The 1922 constitution failed to grant legal status to either the Jewish ministry or Jewish languages. By 1925, the Ministry for Jewish Affairs and the Jewish National Council had been abolished; of the long list of guarantees proclaimed in 1919, only the autonomous and state-funded Jewish educational system was actually implemented. After the 1926 coup, the state became more and more synonymous with the Lithuanian nation with almost no Jews in any branch of government or at the universities. For the many Jews living entirely within their separated religious community, Lithuanian political dominance in the bureaucracy and state was perhaps of little consequence. However, for secular or assimilated Jews, state policy meant a loss of opportunity. By the 1930s, Jews were clearly a subordinate people within the Lithuanian polity.

Several remarks can be made about the links between structural change, ethnic hierarchies, and ethnic violence. First, in the period of relative anarchy at the end of the First World War, Lithuanians did not use the opportunity to wreak massive violence against Jews. In the immediate aftermath of independence, Lithuanians and Jews clearly cooperated. In essence, two groups, both having been subordinate in the Russian Empire, became temporary allies.

Structural changes helped end this cooperation. Less importantly, the loss of Vilnius and its large Jewish population to Polish control changed the balance of power between the groups.[21] More importantly, the fact of Lithuanian sovereignty and the building of a Lithuanian nation-state profoundly changed the ethnic hierarchy. With the creation of a state came the need for a bureaucracy which needed to be staffed, a military with an

---

[21] Jews were assumed to be about 13% of the population if the Vilnius region was included. The 1923 census revealed that Jews were only about 7% of the total of truncated Lithuania. Figures for other minorities would also reveal declining proportions.

officer corps, a police force, and an official language. All of these would
reflect Lithuanian dominance partly due to the large Lithuanian majority
and partly due to policy.[22] This sense of being the dominant group would
soon be shaken with another structural change – the Soviet occupation of
1940. An abrupt structural change would result in a reordering of an ethnic
hierarchy.

The First Soviet Occupation

The Soviet takeover in 1940 radically altered the Lithuanian social landscape, in some ways allowing a turning of the tables. Clearly, for Jews the
Soviets were to be preferred to the Germans. Furthermore, the Soviet
occupation created new opportunities in the government that had been
previously closed off to Jews. In short, the Soviet occupation allowed at
least a certain minority of Jews to free themselves from the fetters of the
Lithuanian state's discriminatory policies. Levin sums up Jewish thinking
upon the entry of the Soviets: "Between these two alternatives Lithuanian
Jews had no real choice, and some Jews played a significant though by no
means exclusive role in the Sovietization of Lithuania, taking managerial
and official jobs shunned by Lithuanians. The genuine interests of both
groups were clearly in conflict. Consequently, the Jews would later bear
the brunt of the anger of patriotic Lithuanians."[23] Other sources describe
the change that took place in more emotional terms. Describing the Soviet
arrival, the words of one Jewish memoirist capture the switch of relationships and emotions that colored the Lithuanian-Jewish ethnic boundary
and provide a preview of the Lithuanian response and the events of
June 1941:

Every Jew held his head high. If he met a Lithuanian on the sidewalk, the Lithuanian would step off the curb to let him by. Before the Russians came, it had been
just the reverse. The anti-Semites' eyes were popping out of their heads from the
pressure of having to keep their mouths shut! But there were some who just
couldn't hold their tongues. Even with the threat of never seeing the light of day

---

[22] A similar progression occurred in the other two Baltic states. During the early years of
the new states, cooperation among ethnic groups held. The Estonian Law on Cultural
Autonomy, passed in 1925, was considered exemplary for the time. By the 1930s, however,
the guiding theme of the Ulmanis regime in Latvia, for example, had become "Latvia for
Latvians." Although it should be said that the Latvian Constitution could be characterized as exceptionally tolerant.
[23] Levin, "Lithuania" p. 330.

again they still would take the risk and speak: Hey, you! Jew! You think that Stalin is your Daddy? You think you are in heaven? It isn't going to last! . . . There is a Jewish saying: 'If we are on the horse today, then the Lithuanians are ten feet under.' We would enjoy it while it lasted. What would happen later we didn't want to know. We lived for the day. But the anti-Semites knew what they were talking about; what they would show us we would remember for generations to come.[24]

Understandably, given the German alternative, many elements of the Jewish population greeted the Soviet arrival, and the end of Lithuanian sovereignty, with relief if not joy. Even in smaller cities, the reaction to the end of independent Lithuania differed between the two populations. The following is a passage from an interviewee who was a Lithuanian high school student in 1940:

I was young and sided with the Left. I thought a Communist regime would come to Lithuania. I heard beautiful stories about traveling over the plain in Russia, and so on. And then they came in 1940. I was secretary of my class at school and I was tempted to go out and greet them. When I saw who greets them, I saw that all my friends and all the general population, mostly farmers and workers, were standing in the distance, not waiting, but just standing. Their attitude impressed me to such a degree that I chose right away. Those that greeted them were different you see. It's very easy to become anti-Semitic, apparently anti-Semitic, when you try to portray the picture of what was happening there. Now the invaders are coming and they are greeting them and we are standing on the other side, and somehow this was not very acceptable, especially for young Lithuanians. We got some sort of a fear, that this minority was siding with them.[25]

Although the vast majority of the Jewish population would suffer along with Lithuanians, the visibility of Jews in the Soviet governmental apparatus worked to totally change perceptions of the ethnic hierarchy. Clearly, many Lithuanians believed that they had become subordinate to Jews. At the very least, Lithuanians were no longer dominant in the ethnic hierarchy simply on the basis of being Lithuanian.

Jews had not held a seat as minister or deputy minister for eighteen years, but during the first Soviet occupation they filled certain sections of the government and Party. The Minister of Industry as well as many of the highest officials of the Ministry of Industry were reported to be Jews.[26] Of commissars appointed to nationalize industry, Jews made up a propor-

[24] Harry Gordon, *The Shadow of Death: The Holocaust in Lithuania* (Lexington: University of Kentucky Press, 1992), p. 16.
[25] Interview Cl-2 from my own fieldwork.
[26] Juozas Prunskis, *Lithuania's Jews and the Holocaust* (Chicago: Lithuanian American Council, 1979), p. 13.

tion five times that of their numbers in the general population.[27] While holding only five of the twenty-one seats on the Central Committee, key city and regional Party positions were often held by Jews, and not only in Kaunas and Vilnius but also in the smaller cities of Panevezys, Sauliai, Birziai, Utena, and Taurage.[28] Additionally, as was known to the population, some of the top Lithuanian leaders of the Communist Party (Snieckus, Didziulis, Gailiavicius) were married to Jews, a fact that made them not "fully Lithuanian" in the eyes of many in the population.

The Jewish presence in the Komsomol was even higher than in other government organs. Moreover, the actions of these young Communists were very visible in the day-to-day life of the general Lithuanian population. Komsomol members worked as propagandists for the elections and Jews probably composed significant percentages of the Komsomol representatives on the electoral commissions (forty-six of sixty-five in Vilnius).[29] Komsomol youth were also sent into the countryside to organize "socialist competitions." Lithuanian peasants were forced to sit and listen to young Jews, who often spoke poor Lithuanian, on the merits of the Soviet state and how it would transform the countryside. Needless to say, these lectures were less than appreciated.[30]

More than any other aspect of Soviet rule, Lithuanians were outraged by their perception of the Jewish role in the People's Commissariat of Internal Affairs (NKVD). These important positions were only doled out to the most trusted elements in the prewar Lithuanian Communist Party, and since the tiny prewar Party had been disproportionately Jewish it was natural that some Jews would fill the ranks of the security organs. Gladkov, the supreme commander of the NKVD in Lithuania, was a Jew

[27] Dov Levin, "The Jews and the Socio-economic Sovietization of Lithuania, 1940–41" *Soviet Jewish Affairs* 17 (1987): 17–30.

[28] Dov Levin, "Jews in the Soviet Lithuanian Establishment, 1940–41" *Soviet Jewish Affairs* 10 (1980): 21–37.

[29] Ibid., pp. 31–32. For a more extensive treatment of these election campaigns, see Dov Levin, "The Jews and the Election Campaigns in Lithuania, 1940–41."

[30] Even within the Komsomol, relations between Jews and Lithuanians were not good. Levin reports the following memo from a Central Committee member visiting Panevezys: "Sitting by a table in the Komsomol club is a Jewish committee member and round him are Jewish comrades speaking Yiddish loudly, while on the other side of the club sits a Lithuanian committee member and round him are Lithuanian members speaking Lithuanian. The Jewish Komsomol members explained the phenomenon by saying that it is impossible to become friends with them (the Lithuanians) there." Levin, "Jews in the Soviet Lithuanian Establishment, 1940–41" p. 33. Other similar examples are cited.

and the names of his Jewish lieutenants were well known to many in the Lithuanian population: Finkelstein, Dembo, Rozauskas, Singeris, Sermanas, Todes, Komodos, Bloch, Margolinas, Slavin, and so on.[31] Additionally, Jews were perceived as taking significant numbers of the political positions within the Soviet Army in Lithuania.[32] As extensively discussed as follows, it was not the *number* of Jews who occupied these positions that is critical. Rather, the fact that Jews occupied any of these positions of authority at all is most crucial.

The Soviet regime was well aware of the impression being made upon the general Lithuanian population and took corrective measures.[33] Lithuanians were actively recruited into the Party to help promote some semblance of proportionality ("the policy of national cadres").[34] Furthermore, the more symbolic posts, such as "elected" representatives to the national legislative bodies of the USSR were held almost exclusively for non-Jews. Only one of thirty-five designates to the Soviet and the Soviet of Nationalities was Jewish.[35] But the damage had already been done. The relations between Jews and Lithuanians had been poisoned and the deportations of mid-June 1941, associated by Lithuanians with Jews, were yet another blow. The following passage might be considered typical of the Lithuanian perception and interpretation of the relationship between Jews and the Soviet regime and is worth quoting at length:

---

[31] Ibid., p. 22; Prunskis, *Lithuania's Jews* pp. 12–13; Algirdas Martin Budreckis, *The Lithuanian National Revolt of 1941* (Boston: Lithuania Encyclopedia in Press, 1968), pp. 17–18. Zvi Gitelman sees in this process a repetition of the early days of the Soviet Union: "Again, as in 1918–21 in the Soviet Union proper, the new regime relied on Jewish Communists to identify and arrest 'class enemies' and 'reactionary elements.' Naturally, this did not endear the Jews to the local populations, who had just lost their political independence, acquired only two decades earlier, to the Communists," from "The Soviet Union" p. 303. One might speculate that the Soviets preferred Jews in the most sensitive areas of the Party on grounds of controllability. Milovan Djilas made such a speculation after a meeting with Stalin: "He boasted of how 'Comrade Zhdanov purged all the Jews from the apparatus of the Central Committee!' – and yet he simultaneously lauded the Hungarian Politburo which at that time consisted almost entirely of Jewish emigres, which must have suggested to me the idea that, despite its covert anti-Semitism, the Soviet Government found it convenient to have Jews at the top in Hungary because they were rootless and thus all the more dependent upon its will." *Conversations with Stalin* (New York: Harcourt, Brace & World, 1962), p. 171.

[32] Prunskis, *Lithuania's Jews* p. 14.

[33] Gitelman sees the replacement of Jews from visible positions as common across the newly occupied regions. See Gitelman, "The Soviet Union" p. 303.

[34] Levin, "Jews in the Soviet Lithuanian Establishment, 1940–41" p. 28.

[35] Levin, "Jews and Election Campaigns" p. 46.

If you had only seen what happened when the Soviet tanks entered Lithuania. The Lithuanians wiped away their tears, while the Jews took great efforts to come out to throw flowers to the tank divisions at the risk of falling under the caterpillars. Their joy knew no end!

With the establishment of Soviet power in Lithuania the Jews' influence and position grew extraordinarily. In many government departments there were only Jews. They interfered in everything and told everyone how to live. Jewish agitators flooded the villages. They called upon the peasants to begin the sowing or the reaping. The people were silent and bit their tongues. But as soon as the agitators left, the people began to spit in rage: Of what value is the advice of a person who had never in his life held a scythe in his own hands, who had never pushed a plow in his life. . . .

All this led to the fact that Lithuanians, who had lived peacefully for centuries together with the Jews, in the course of a single year literally came to hate them. Almost no one among the people spoke of "Soviet power"; people spoke of "Jewish power." Those who collaborated with the authorities were called Jewish grovellers.

The Jews went too far. Only this can explain their behavior. Many people have told me how the Jews at that time cried out to the Lithuanians: 'Yesterday it was you who governed, today – it is our turn!'[36]

When the Soviets fled the advancing German forces, constraints on violent action against Jews were lifted. Unlike earlier periods of Lithuanian history, this time a lack of constraints coincided with a desire to do violence.

Returning to the Five Puzzles: Assessment of the Four Emotions

How should this desire to commit violence be explained? Which of the four emotion-based stories plausibly addresses the puzzles created by the variation of these Baltic events? Of the four emotions, Resentment possesses the most convincing overall fit with elements of Rage also plausible. This brief summary section first applies Resentment to the post-Barbarossa Baltic violence and then discusses Fear, Hatred, and Rage.

Following the links in Figure 2.1, the Soviet occupation of 1940 brought rapid structural change. Most critically, the Soviet occupation of the Baltic states ended Lithuanian sovereignty and ethnic dominance. The everyday experiences of meeting minority individuals on the street, of dealing with the bureaucracy, of encountering police, produced information that confirmed the new status relations. In turn, the change in ethnic hierarchy produced beliefs of injustice and emotions of Resentment. The

---

[36] A. Zuvintas, "An Open Letter to Tomas Venclova" *Cross Currents* 8 (1989): 62–67.

desire to put others "back in their place" was strong. With the collapse of Soviet rule in June 1941, these desires led to acts of violence that quickly resubordinated minority groups, especially Jews. The violence against Jews was highly emotional, immoral, and pathological. Yet, in terms of Resentment, it was instrumental and highly effective in accomplishing basic goals of much of the Lithuanian population.

Why June 1941?

Why was there brutal violence against Jews in June 1941 but not earlier? Before the political structure of the Lithuanian state had been firmly formed, Jews and Lithuanians were allies in a quest to end mutual subordination. Ethnic violence among those groups was not prevalent. During the 1920s and 1930s, the requirements of modernization strengthened perceptions of status hierarchy which were, in turn, affirmed through political policies and position-holding controlled by the majority group. The Soviet takeover of 1940 not only stripped Lithuania of its sovereignty, but, as indicated by the statements above, created a powerful perception of a status reversal. The sense of injustice produced by this status reversal was heightened by the fact that Jews were a relatively small minority with no tradition of occupying positions of authority, especially positions in the police. Aggression could and did serve to reduce Jews to a clearly subordinate position. The desire to reestablish dominance was intense.

Vilnius versus Kaunas Why was there little aggression in Vilnius? The ethnic target in Vilnius, as far as one existed, was the Poles. Until the first Soviet occupation, Poles had unquestionably been on top of the ethnic hierarchy in Vilnius. In the period immediately following the First World War, Polish administrators instituted Polish as the only language of administration in the Vilnius region; moreover, a commission composed entirely of Poles governed the district.[37] Of possible targets in Vilnius, the Poles were the greatest impediment to present and future Lithuanian status dominance. Far from being a blind, knee-jerk reaction against "ancient enemies" in a period of few constraints, the differentiation of targets indicates the instrumental nature of this ethnic conflict.

[37] See von Rauch, *The Baltic States: The Years of Independence 1917–1940* (New York: St. Martin's Press, 1974), pp. 101–02.

Latvia, Estonia, and Belorussia   Why the variation among Belorussia, Latvia, and Estonia? Belorussians committed no similar outburst against its Jewish population. Of course, Belorussia had not been a sovereign state but only a federal unit within the Soviet Union; the strength of its ethnic hierarchy reflected that fact. There had been no "Belorussia for Belorussians" policy similar to that in the independent Eastern European states. It was not occupied in 1940 and experienced no status reversals. In short, aggression had no value in reordering a status hierarchy. This could not be said for the Baltic states. The situation in Latvia most resembled that of Lithuania in terms of change and perception of status reversal as well as the nature of the aggression against the Jewish minority. In Estonia, there is no evidence of a public mass action against the Jewish minority, but that minority had been so small (5,000 total) that it simply did not register on the ethnic hierarchy.

Russians   Why was there little aggression against Russians as a group?[38] There are two reasons violence would not have the same utility in status reduction against Russians as against Jews. First, the Russian minority gains status from being connected to the tens of millions of Russians living next door. Aggression at the local level cannot affect this status. The same could not be said for Lithuanian Jews. Secondly, the sense of injustice incurred through subordination to the traditionally "weak" Jews is far greater than the sense of injustice produced by subordination to the traditionally "strong" Russians. Chapter 8 discusses the lack of violence against Russians at greater length, as does the section on Poland B as follows.

Rabbis   Finally, why target Rabbis rather than the secular Jews who might actually have collaborated with the Soviet occupier? If, as Resentment posits, the value of aggression is in reducing the status of *groups*, then aggression should logically be targeted against the clearest symbols of those groups. Secular Jews could not be easily distinguished from Lithuanians, but Rabbis and other religious Jews were clear symbols of Jews as a group.

  Resentment heightens the saliency of status concerns; it impels individuals to rectify correctable status imbalances. Resentment provides an answer for the overall pattern seen across the Baltic in the wake of Barbarossa – mass violence against Jews in Kaunas and the rest of interwar Lithuania and Latvia, no mass violence against Jews in Vilnius (with

[38] There was, of course, a great deal of violence against Soviet officials, a group with many Russians; however, there is little evidence of action against Russians simply because they were Russians.

some action against Poles), or in Estonia and Belorussia. Resentment also explains the reversal of the World War One pattern. Recall that Jews had been attacked in Vilnius but not in Kaunas in that earlier period.

Fear and Hatred

Fear definitely has little applicability. In the wake of Barbarossa, Lithuanians did not feel threatened by Jews. Any Jew who had possessed any political power or had access to weapons had probably fled with the Soviet regime. The conflict between Lithuanians and Poles in Vilnius might fit the Fear story. Both were in a position to contest the coveted Vilnius region. Lithuanian actions, however, were not a preemptive strike against Polish force potential, but rather intended to convince the Germans to maintain Lithuanian sovereignty of the region.

As defined previously, Hatred involves historical roles of enmity. As discussed previously, Lithuanian-Jewish relations were decent by regional standards. At the very least, no pervasive historical record of violent pogroms against Jews pervaded Lithuanian minds. During the reign of the Russian Empire, Lithuanians and Jews were two subordinate groups. Jews and Lithuanians were political allies twenty years earlier. The brutal and humiliating actions of Lithuanians were not the resumption of a historical pattern; indeed, they came as a shock to most of the Jewish victims. In the aforementioned quoted passages, the actors make reference only to recent events. They do not seem to be taking on historical roles embedded within a shared cultural schema. Furthermore, Hatred, as a general national cultural phenomenon, does not help explain the difference in Lithuanian behavior in Vilnius and Kaunas.

Rage

As opposed to Fear and Hatred, Rage provides a plausible alternative narrative and is Resentment's major competitor. In assessing the explanatory merits of Rage, it is worthwhile to recall the defining features of the Rage narrative:

1. Often, a general or diffuse and largely unconscious source provides the basis for the emotion.
2. The emotion heightens a desire to lash out.
3. The emotion occurs prior to cognitive processes involved with finding a target. Identifiable distortions such as projection, attribution and others are likely to result.

4. The target may be a substitute target.

5. In opposition to Hatred, the justification for violence may lack a precedent.

Following Figure 2.3, Rage provides a general story that fits the events of June 1941. Here is a rendition. The Soviets eliminated the independent Lithuanian state. They deported the country's leadership in the summer of 1940. They nationalized property and planned to collectivize agriculture. Living standards fell. The Soviet secret police created an aura of fear and suspicion. The new regime elevated minorities into positions of power. The Soviets carried out a second deportation on June 13, 1941 only nine days before Barbarossa. Immediately before the German invasion, Moscow's regime deported over thirty thousand individuals (1% of the population) in an inhumane manner, characterized by the separation of families. Many went into hiding, and bitterness toward the Soviet regime greatly increased. Looking across an entire year of Soviet occupation, frustrations were numerous and diverse. In effect, cumulative frustration developed. From this general source, an emotion developed that motivated individuals to lash out. But against whom?

Continuing the Rage narrative, Lithuanians could not blame themselves or their own leaders for their misfortunes, so they looked for someone else to blame. Based on existing antisemitism, Jews were a natural target. Some Jews were active in supporting the Soviet Communist Party, some were even active in the secret police and government. At that point, cognitive distortions occurred in the form of attribution errors: The numbers of Jews active with the Communists were wildly distorted. Selective and distorted information collection then led to twisted beliefs. Everywhere Lithuanians looked they tended to see the myth of Judeo-Bolshevism coming to life.[39] A faulty conclusion was drawn – Jews are to blame. Certainly, no more than a small percentage of Jews were ever actively working with the Communists. The previous quotes indicate attribution errors. Further, even if prewar Lithuanian culture and history were "relatively" free of obsessive anti-Semitism, Lithuania was subject and home to Eastern European stereotypes of Jews; Lithuania's deeply Catholic culture was prone to Jew hatred that would help select Jews as a blameworthy target; Jews could be seen as inherently capable of evil and willing collaborators with an anti-Christian occupier.

[39] See Arno Mayer, *Why Did the Heavens Not Darken?*

With the coming of Barbarossa constraints disappeared. A high level of frustration and the ability to act converged. Rage was unleashed. Attacking Jews brought some relief to the frustrated Lithuanians.

Jews fit the profile of a substitute target, or at least a target that is both substitute and direct. Lithuanians immediately attacked as many Soviet functionaries as they could, but most of the Soviet administration had fled the country. This meant that the group most responsible for Lithuanian suffering, or the direct target, was largely unavailable. The frustration, cumulative and residual, remained and demanded outlet. Jews were an available, and vulnerable, substitute target; they were also partially a direct target in the sense that some Jews had taken positions in the Soviet apparatus. Clearly, Rabbis were not a direct target in any sense.

Evaluating Rage and its Relationship to Resentment

The Rage narrative provides answers to some of the five puzzles. Rage has a ready answer for the fourth and fifth puzzles. Rabbis, and Jews in general, are a substitute target, an available and easy target in comparison to the fleeing Soviet functionaries or Russians. Regarding the first three puzzles, on the other hand, Rage does not provide such a ready solution. While the entire region suffered deprivation or frustration, Jews were not always a target of violence. They did not serve as scapegoat targets in Vilnius, in Belorussia, or in Estonia. Nor were Jews a consistent target of wrath across time; never before had such a mass of Lithuanians acted against them in such a violent manner.

In order to explain the wider pattern of variation, Rage would need to be supplemented with reference to other specific factors. For instance, Lithuanians may have felt the same levels of frustration in both Kaunas and Vilnius, but the lower percentage of Lithuanians in the latter served as a check on the release of that frustration. However, this explanation does not tell us why Poles and Lithuanians, together forming a majority of the Vilnius population, would not attack Jews (especially since attacks did occur in Vilnius in an earlier period of Polish control).

While the Rage narrative as a whole does not do as well as Resentment in explaining overall variation, it cannot be denied that elements of Rage were at work in Lithuanian violence against Jews. Antisemitism helped select the target and surely intensified the violence. Cognitive distortions occurred in processing information. The conclusion here is that antisemitism and attribution errors are important and, perhaps in some locations, critical elements within the Resentment path.

Despite possibilities for reconcilation and combination of these two paths, the essential conceptual differences between Rage and Resentment should be emphasized and clarified in light of this case. Perpetrators acting under the influence of Rage selectively use evidence and develop faulty or irrational beliefs. Resentment, in contrast, makes no reference to these phenomena. In the June 1941 case, the Rage story envisions the following belief: "Jews are responsible for the troubles of Lithuania and they should be punished." Resentment envisions a very different belief: "Jews occupy a position above Lithuanians and they should be brought down." The differences directly relate to essential conceptual issues regarding information processing and instrumentality.

Assume that 3% of the Jewish population and 1% of the Lithuanian population were visibly active in the Soviet administration.[40] Further assume that most of these individuals fled eastward at the beginning of Barbarossa. The question becomes why attack members of the 97% who were not active and who may have suffered under Soviet rule themselves? Rage provides two answers. First, these numbers do not matter because internalized frustration and the act of lashing out matter above all else. Perpetrators naturally develop a justification for their actions, but the story they tell themselves need not be firmly connected to actual events. The second answer is that cognitive distortions, especially attribution errors, greatly inflate these numbers – perpetrators perceive not 3% but rather 30% of the Jewish population as active. Both factors can operate together.

For Resentment, the question does not concern the overall percentage of the group that is engaged in action, but whether that action is able to change status relations. The relevant issue is whether the actions of the 3% changed the status of the group as a whole. Consider the quote: "Every Jew held his head high. If he met a Lithuanian on the sidewalk, the Lithuanian would step off the curb to let him by. Before the Russians came, it had been just the reverse." Although unconnected to the Soviet regime, group status changed for this Jewish memoirist – and apparently for many of the Lithuanians he encountered during the first Soviet occupation.

In this light, violence against the inactive 97% serves an obvious purpose. Even if the active 3% flee, the group status effects they created

---

[40] Or one could assume that equal percentages of the literate and urban populations joined the Communists. Those numbers would produce a far more skewed ratio of participation.

remain for the inactive 97%. In undoing those effects, and undoing them quickly, nothing is more effective than humiliation-tinged violence against symbolically significant group members. Thus, unsurprisingly, we witness public Lithuanian violence against rabbis.

Such violence is unjust; the victims bore no guilt. Justice, however, may have little to do with the emotions that drive group-based ethnic violence. For the individuals likely to commit violence, Resentment sees questions of individual guilt or innocence as far less motivating than the day-to-day experiences of domination/subordination. The emotion-based approach, especially in its Resentment form, emphasizes the compulsions that may be hardwired into human biology. In contrast, individual justice is largely a matter of human intellect and human agency. Intellect can overcome group-centered emotion, but it may not.

Which process occurred in the Baltic during the first Soviet occupation? The cognition-led, instrumental path of Resentment or the emotion-led, distortion-filled path of Rage? Undoubtedly, Rage and straightforward antisemitism drove many individuals toward violence. However, the Resentment story is also plausible and, critically, does a better job of explaining overall variation in targets. The following section provides more substantive material to compare the two paths.

Poland B: Similarities

In the wake of Barbarossa, the situation in the Soviet-occupied territory of former Poland (Poland B) witnessed events similar to those just described in Lithuania: Jews were viciously attacked; the perpetrators justified their aggression with charges of Jewish collaboration with the Soviets. In one locality, Jews were forced to tear down a statue of Stalin, while in another a Jew was made to stand on a monument to Stalin while other Jews were forced to jeer him and shout "You are a stupid Stalin!"[41]

As in the Lithuanian case, some interesting patterns emerged within the overall event.[42] I am going to rely on Table 6.1 created by Andrzej

[41] Andrzej Zbikowski, "Local Anti-Jewish Pogroms in the Occupied Territories of Eastern Poland, June–July 1941" in Lucjan Dobroszycki and Jeffrey Gurock, eds., *The Holocaust in the Soviet Union* pp. 173–79.

[42] For a collection of essays on the Soviet occupation of Eastern Poland covering a range of topics, see Keith Sword, ed., *The Soviet Takeover of the Polish Eastern Provinces, 1939–41* (New York: St. Martin's Press, 1991).

Table 6.1. *Anti-Jewish Pogroms that Resulted in Fatalities,*
Eastern Territories of Poland

Region	Population	Number of Reports
1. Bolechow	Ukrainian	3
2. Boryslaw	Ukrainian	8
3. Borczow	Ukrainian	—
4. Brzezany	Ukrainian	2
5. Buczacz	Ukrainian and German	2
6. Czortkow	Ukrainian and German	3
7. Drohobycz	Ukrainian	5
8. Dubno	Ukrainian and German	1
9. Grodek Jag.	Ukrainian	1
10. Jaworow	Ukrainian	1
11. Kolomyja	Ukrainian	4
12. Korzec	Ukrainian	1
13. Korycin	Belorussian	1
14. Kowno	Lithuanian	2
15. Krzemieniec	Ukrainian	1
16. Lwow	Ukrainian	23
17. Radzilow	Polish	2
18. Sambor	Ukrainian	2
19. Sasow	Ukrainian	2
20. Schodnica	Ukrainian	1
21. Sokal	Ukrainian	1
22. Stryj	Ukrainian	3
23. Szumsk	Ukrainian	2
24. Tarnopol	Ukrainian	6
25. Tluste	Ukrainian	3
26. Trembowla	Ukrainian	2
27. Tuczyn	Ukrainian	1
28. Wizna	Polish	1
29. Woronowo	Lithuanian	1
30. Zaborow	Ukrainian	1
31. Zloczow	Ukrainian and German	4

Source: Accounts and memoirs in the archives of the Jewish Institute in Warsaw. Reprinted from Andrez Zbikowski, "Local Anti-Jewish Pogroms in the Occupied Territories of Eastern Poland, June–July 1941" in Lucjan Dobroszycki and Jeffrey Gurock, eds., *The Holocaust in the Soviet Union* (Armonk, NY: M. E. Sharpe, 1991). Reprinted with permission of M. E. Sharpe.

Zbikowski from information from the archives of the Jewish Institute in Warsaw in order to produce a field of variation. Demographically, this region consisted of Poles, Ukrainians and Jews with smaller concentrations of Germans and Belorussians. Yet, of the thirty-one locations reporting anti-Jewish pogroms involving a fatality, twenty-two occurred in primarily Ukrainian regions, four more in mixed Ukrainian-German areas. Anti-Jewish pogroms are reported in only two Polish areas.

The Ukrainian violence in the very first days of the German occupation becomes more puzzling when it is compared to the first days of the Soviet occupation in late September 1939. Then, the Soviets stood by while Ukrainians assaulted Poles as the primary target, not Jews. Several thousand people died in locally based actions in the first two weeks of Soviet occupation – mostly Poles killed by their Ukrainian neighbors.[43] As Jan Gross points out, this violence created lasting effects due to its spontaneous and localized nature. Again, neighbors attacked one another. Because these brutal acts were not directed from without, blame could not be diverted to short-term interlopers:

> It was the intimacy of violence which, I think, had the most lasting consequences. For it showed that *within* the affected communities a destructive force lay dormant which could be unleashed with devastating effect. To be sure the outside invader served as a catalyst, but, as the historical record shows without a doubt, local communities were primarily unhinged and subdued from within, as it were, by their own efforts.[44]

Three Puzzles

Ukrainian Violence in 1939 versus Ukrainian Violence in 1941   Why attack Poles at one instance of structural upheaval and assault Jews, but not Poles, two years later under another period of transition?

There is an obvious answer to this question. In the first case, the Soviets used class-based incitements to encourage Ukrainians to commit violence against Polish landowners and capitalists; in the second case, virulently antisemitic Germans encouraged Ukrainians to attack Jews. Following

---

[43] This description is taken from Jan T. Gross, "The Sovietization of Western Ukraine and Western Byelorussia" in Norman Davies and Antony Polonsky, eds., *Jews in Eastern Poland and the USSR, 1939–1946* (New York: St. Martin's Press, 1991), p. 65.

[44] Ibid., p. 65.

these lines, Ukrainian perpetrators could be seen as simply anticipating the targets of incoming occupiers and acting accordingly. No doubt there is some truth to this logic. However, it is not clear that the level of Soviet control during this violent transition was so high that the Soviets could have prevented actions against Jews if the Polish and Ukrainian populations were intent on committing them.[45] The key point is that there appears to have been a clear target of the violence when alternative targets were at least possible. In the 1941 case, perpetrators came from a wide strata of Ukrainian society. It is unclear that rural peasants, for instance, were acting strategically in order to receive benefits from the incoming German regime. Zbikowski writes, "Exceptionally tragic was the lot of the Jewish population living in small concentrations in purely Ukrainian villages. Several reports from the quoted collection certify that these groups of Jews were put to death by their Ukrainian neighbors without any assistance from the German occupiers."[46]

Limited Polish Action in 1941   While Poles did commit violence against Jews, the table suggests that their action was far less frequent in comparative terms than that of Ukrainians.

The Role of Belorussians   As a significant proportion of Poland B's population, Belorussians might be expected to be involved in the multiethnic fray in some fashion. Yet, Belorussians seem to be perpetrators and victims less than other groups. It is a possibility that scholars simply do less research on Belorussians than other groups and thus we do not know the violence in Belorussian history very well. However, as argued as follows, there are good reasons to believe that Belorussians were not as active as other groups.

In addition to these three puzzles, I will conclude the section with a short discussion of Jan T. Gross's work *Neighbors: The Destruction of the*

---

[45] Jan Gross argues that there was no special relationship between Soviets and Jews, suggesting that the Soviets would have been unlikely to go out of their way to provide special protections for Jews. See Jan T. Gross, "A Tangled Web: Confronting Stereotypes Concerning Relations between Poles, Germans, Jews, and Communists" in Istvan Deak, Jan T. Gross, and Tony Judt, eds., *The Politics of Retribution in Europe* (Princeton, NJ: Princeton University Press, 2000), pp. 74–130.

[46] Zbikowski, "Local Anti-Jewish Pogroms in the Occupied Territories of Eastern Poland, June–July 1941" pp. 178–79.

Jewish Community in Jedwabne, Poland.[47] To repeat a point from the introduction, this work is most interested in periods most resembling anarchy. When a regime or occupier is in control, new constraints and opportunities come to the fore to cloud and complicate individual motivation, the primary focus of the study. Gross discusses two massacres in *Neighbors* – Radzilow and Jedwabne. The former occurred on July 6, 1941 apparently with the total absence of Germans. The latter took place on July 10, with Germans present. While Radzilow better fits the purpose here, Gross claims the perpetrators of Jedwabne also acted on their own volition. Both cases will be briefly considered. Gross's study essentially asks the same question as this study – how do members of one group come to want to attack members of another group.

As in the previous Lithuanian case, these puzzles concern variation occurring during Period Four. Again, a review of the evolution of power, status, and culture during Periods Two and Three is necessary before attempting to assess the ability of the four emotion-based explanations to answer these puzzles.

The Interwar Polish State

Poland was born from the death of the Russian and Austro-Hungarian Empires. It was a painful birth. In Eastern Galicia and Western Volhynia, Ukrainian nationalists challenged the emerging Polish state resulting in a war with 15,000 Ukrainian and 10,000 Polish casualties.[48] In the chaotic period following the First World War, the Ukrainian National Council governed a territory of four million people for eight months. As in Lithuania, Ukrainians, the regional majority, made deals with minorities in order to create an alliance powerful enough to withstand the hegemonic aspirations of a threatening nation, in this instance, the Poles. The National Council promised that 30% of seats in the future parliament would be reserved for minorities. With pledges like these, combined with Polish pogroms,[49] Jews were not entirely averse to siding with Ukrainians; in fact, an all-Jewish unit composed of 1,000 soldiers served as part of the

---

[47] Jan T. Gross, *Neighbors: The Destruction of the Jewish Community in Jedwabne, Poland* (Princeton, NJ: Princeton University Press, 2001).
[48] Orest Subtelny provides a succint summary of events in *Ukraine: A History* (Toronto: University of Toronto Press, 1988), pp. 367–72.
[49] A three-day pogrom occurred in Lviv after Poles retook that city.

West Ukrainian Army.[50] Despite such forms of cooperation, Polish numbers overwhelmed the Ukrainian forces and established control, brutal control, over Eastern Galicia and Western Volhynia, the territories known after Soviet occupation as Poland B.

When the Soviets occupied Eastern Poland on September 17, 1939, they gained control over a territory that had held 51.6% of Poland's land and 37.1% of Poland's population at the end of the independent period.[51] This region was the backward and impoverished half of Poland, home to only 15% of Poland's industrial labor and consumer of less than 9% of Poland's electricity.[52] Demographically, Poles and Ukrainians made up equal thirds of the population while the remaining third was divided among Jews, Belorussians, and a mixed Orthodox peasantry.[53] In geographic terms, Ukrainians predominated in the south of the area, Poles and Belorussians in the north. As elsewhere in this region of Eastern Europe, the populations of the towns and cities greatly differed from the surrounding countryside. In 1931, over 80% of the population was rural and overwhelmingly Slavic. In contrast, Jews, 10.2% of the total population of Eastern Poland, made up 38% of the urban population, 79% of those involved in commerce, and probably over half the numbers of doctors and lawyers.[54] Despite skewed occupational figures, the

---

[50] Subtelny, *Ukraine* p. 369.

[51] Wladyslaw Bartoszewski, "Polish-Jewish Relations in Occupied Poland, 1939–1945" in Chimen Abramsky, Maciej Jachimczyk, and Antony Polonsky, eds., *The Jews in Poland* (Oxford: Basil Blackwell, 1986), p. 149.

[52] Norman Davies and Antony Polonsky, "Introduction" in Norman Davies and Antony Polonsky, eds., *Jews in Eastern Poland and the USSR, 1939–1946* (New York: St. Martin's Press, 1991), p. 2.

[53] Jan Gross, "The Sovietization of Western Ukraine and Western Byelorussia" p. 64. Davies and Polonsky, "Introduction" p. 3, present precise figures from the wartime Polish government-in-exile: (in millions) Poles, 5.274; Ukrainians, 4.125; Belorussians, 1.123; Jews, 1.109; Russians, 0.134; Lithuanians, 0.084.

[54] The first two figures are from Maciej Siekierski, "The Jews in Soviet-Occupied Eastern Poland at the End of 1939: Numbers and Distribution" in Davies and Polonsky, eds., *Jews in Eastern Poland and the USSR, 1939–1946* p. 111–12. Urban centers are defined by a minimum twenty thousand population. In the largest cities, Siekierski provides the following figures: 31.9% Jewish in Lviv; 28.2% in Vilnius; and 43.0% in Bialystok.

Regarding figures on doctors and lawyers, Aharon Weiss states that at the end of the 1930s, 72% of all lawyers and 51% of all doctors in Eastern Galicia were Jewish. See Aharon Weiss, "Some Economic and Social Problems of the Jews of Eastern Galicia in the Period of Soviet Rule (1939–41)" in *Jews in Eastern Poland and the USSR, 1939–1946* p. 80. The numbers in Volhynia may have differed. Davies and Polonsky, "Introduction" p. 4 estimate "slightly more than half."

dominant characteristic of Poland B was general poverty among all ethnic groups.

The Soviets also inherited provinces that had experienced the nationalizing policies of the Polish regime. The Polish interwar government, refusing to recognize Ukrainian and Belarussian cultures as capable of nationhood, embarked on a campaign of assimilation. The government banned the use of Ukrainian language in state agencies in 1924. While Ukrainian language schools became nominally bilingual, the Polish language predominated. The promised Ukrainian university never materialized.[55] Land policy also established Polish dominance in Eastern Poland. In the face of the land hungry, overpopulated, and overwhelming rural Ukrainian and Belorussian populations, the Polish regime settled Poles, many of them veterans, on the region's estates.[56] Attempting to build cohesion among the Poles in the East, the Polish government, with the use of genealogies, attempted to persuade the *szlachta zagrodowa* (peasant-nobles) of their historic rights to privilege in the region.[57]

Polish state policy also discriminated against Jews. The regime systematically excluded Jews, as well as Ukrainians and other groups, from government service. The state made efforts to eliminate the Jewish presence in business throughout the country.[58] Further, Poles discussed stripping Jews, at least those living in the East, of citizenship. Many Poles saw emigration as the best possible solution to the Jewish problem: "If Zionism meant Jewish emigration to (Palestine), no one was more Zionist than Poland's leaders in the late 1930's."[59]

In short, as in Lithuania, the ruling regime instituted a set of policies strengthening and reinforcing perception of an ethnic hierarchy and establishing the indisputable dominance of the titular ethnic group. By every

---

[55] Subtelny, *Ukraine* p. 429. Rogers Brubaker, *Nationalism Reframed: Nationhood and the National Question in the New Europe* (Cambridge: Cambridge University Press, 1996), pp. 97–103, specifically discusses Poland's nationalizing policies in the eastern border-lands.

[56] The exact figures for Polish settlers are a matter of considerable dispute. Ukrainian sources put the figure at 200,000 rural and 100,000 urban Polish newcomers while Polish writers claim a number of less than 100,000 total. See Subtelny, *Ukraine* p. 429.

[57] Pawel Korzec and Jean-Charles Szurek, "Jews and Poles Under Soviet Occupation (1939–1941): Conflicting Interests" pp. 393–94.

[58] Brubaker discusses interwar policy toward Jews in a section entitle "Nationalizing the Urban Economy" pp. 93–97 in *Nationalism Reframed*. Also see Korzec and Szurek, "Jews and Poles Under Soviet Occupation" pp. 391–92.

[59] The quote is from Brubaker, *Nationalism Reframed* p. 97.

status indicator – language, educational policy, government and military service, land redistribution – Poles were on top.

Violence also exacerbated the awareness and volatility of ethnic dominance. In 1930, Ukrainians began a series of attacks on Polish estates in Galicia.[60] Rebels committed over 2,000 acts of sabotage. Polish police and cavalry units responded in ruthless fashion. Over 2,000 arrests and hundreds of lengthy prison terms resulted. Polish nationalists responded with political assasssinations. In turn, the Polish regime extinguished self-government in many Ukrainian villages and set up a concentration camp in Bereza Kartuzka. This spiral of rebellion and repression cemented the boundaries between Ukrainians and Poles. In several ways, interwar eastern Poland resembled an occupied land.

The Events of September 1939

Given the nature of the interwar Polish regime, it is hardly surprising that members of non-Polish groups in eastern Poland greeted the incoming Soviets with joy. Mistakenly, most believed that nothing could be worse than Polish rule. Apparently, members of almost every minority set about attacking the participants and symbols of Polish rule. As Jan Gross has written:

(T)he principal victims were Poles: the military colonists, the minor nobility of the borders, the landowners, the police, the forest guards, as well as small groups of soldiers and officers from units of the Polish army broken up by the German offensive. In the course of a few days in September, the Ukrainians, the White Russians, and the 'locals' had made those who had been instruments of Polonization of the provinces of the south-east of the past twenty years pay for it.[61]

The Soviets encouraged this action to take place as "rightful anger of the masses."[62] Much of this vengeful action may have been directed at agents of Polish control rather than against Poles as Poles, but, in this case, it is difficult to separate out these motivations with the available information.[63] Multiple factors were at play. For example, Soviet occupation encouraged

---

[60] This paragraph relies on Subtelny, *Ukraine* p. 430.

[61] This quote is from Jan Gross and Irena Grudzinska-Gross, "W czterdziestym nas matko na Sybir zeslali" in *Polska a Rosja 1939–42* (London, 1983). The translated passage here is from Korzec and Szurek, "Jews and Poles Under Soviet Occupation" pp. 396–97.

[62] Korzec and Szurek, "Jews and Poles Under Soviet Occupation" p. 397.

[63] This problem is similar to the Latvian and Estonian attacks on German landowners discussed in the previous chapter.

general Ukrainian hopes for an independent state. The Soviet arrival, rather than the German alternative, also produced relief for the Jews who were familiar with the the German regime now stalled in the center of Poland.[64]

Yet, given this complexity, it is clear that after the breakdown of government constraints Poles were the primary target in September 1939.

The Nature of the Soviet Occupation

Eager to win converts to the new Communist regime, the Soviets instituted many changes that effectively reversed the interwar positions of Poles and Ukrainians.[65] The highly popular expropriation of Polish landlords followed basic Communist principles. The Soviets went far beyond these economic measures, though. The University at Lviv, a symbol of regional Polish cultural dominance, switched its language of instruction from Polish to Ukrainian; further, in a blatant affront to Poles, the Soviets renamed Lviv University for Ivan Franko, a Ukrainian hero. Elementary schools made the switch as well and by 1940 6,000 of the region's 6,900 schools were operating in Ukrainian. In an important symbolic gesture, General Semen Tymoshenko, possessing a clearly Ukrainian name, led the Soviet forces into Galicia. No longer would only Poles control the means of force in the region. Poles could not display their national colors or national symbol, the white eagle. In time, the Soviets would deport 1.2 million from Poland B during the brief occupation from 1939–41. Most of these deportees were Poles. As Orest Subtelny has summarized, "The catastrophe reflected the dramatic plunge in the political fortunes of the once dominant Poles, who, deprived

---

[64] As in Lithuania, the nature of local knowledge of the ultimate nature of German intentions is not clear. On the one hand, 300,000 to 350,000 Jews fled Western Poland and the German invasion. On the other hand, significant numbers of these refugees decided later to return to the German-occupied zone. Ben-Cion Pinchuk has written, "In spite of a constant stream of updated information on Nazi atrocities, mass executions, wearing of yellow stars, ghettos and so on, that came with the refugees from German regions, nothing of it was disseminated. On the very eve of the German attack, Jews and non-Jews were left in the dark as to the real dangers of Nazism." "Sovietization and the Jewish Response to Nazi Policies of Mass Murder" in Davies and Polonsky, *Jews in Eastern Poland and the USSR* p. 132. Pinchuk also cites the long-held view of Germans as the more civilized of the two powers. The Soviet occupation of 1939–41, especially in 1940–41, did little to persuade inhabitants otherwise.

[65] This paragraph summarizes Subtelny, *Ukraine* pp. 454–57.

of government backing, suddenly found themselves transformed from oppressors into the oppressed."[66]

While the Poles descended the ethnic hierarchy, the Ukrainians ascended. The Ukrainian language could be heard in the schools and the university. The public witnessed Ukrainians, as members of newly founded militias, openly bearing arms. By 1940, the Soviets instituted a much harsher form of rule with the threat of deportation hanging over members of every ethnic group. Land reform, expected to put land into the hands of many smallholders, never came to pass. Most state business was transacted in Russian. Yet, in terms of relative positions, the Ukrainian hierarchical position in the region was clearly above that of the decimated and humbled Poles.

While the Polish-Ukrainian reversal was dramatic, the position of Jews also changed. As in Lithuania, the Communists had little alternative to reliance on Jews.[67] In the prewar period, Jews comprised over half of local party leaderships, a majority of the Central Committee, and roughly a quarter of the overall membership in the Communist Party.[68] Being 95% rural, not many Ukrainians or Belorussians in Poland B fit the desired social categories for Party leadership. Perhaps most crucially, Jews did not have the nationalist ambitions that made Ukrainians so suspect.

In the beginning stages of the occupation, there is little doubt that Jews occupied a number of positions in the Soviet administration that was disproportionate to their numbers in the general population. As Aharon Weiss sums up:

From the first days of Soviet rule, the Jews were absorbed into the state administration, together with all its offshoots, without any restriction, and they were represented in it to an extant exceeding their proportion of the population as a whole. . . . The Soviets saw in the Jews an element loyal to the new regime, and sometimes even sympathetic to it. . . . And so the Jews, perhaps more than the other two nations in Eastern Galicia, met the requirements of the authorities. The Jews at

---

[66] Ibid., p. 456. Neal Ascherson writes, "Yet in its brutality and the sheer scale of its cold-blooded attempt to obliterate the Polish nation physically and culturally, this 21-month Soviet occupation far outdid all the crimes committed against Poland during this century and a quarter of Russian occupation under the Tsars," in *Struggles for Poland* (London: Pan Books, 1988), pp. 94–95.

[67] Davies and Polonsky, *Jews in Eastern Poland and the USSR* pp. 19–21.

[68] Michael C. Steinlauf, "Poland" in David S. Wyman, ed., *The World Reacts to the Holocaust* (Baltimore, MD: Johns Hopkins University Press, 1996), pp. 81–155.

this time had no political ambitions such as would have excited the suspicions of the Soviets or given them cause to exercise reserve."[69]

The actual numbers and proportions were not as important as the fact that Jews could be found in positions that they had never held. The effect of meeting a Jew in a position of authority or a Jew holding a gun, possessing means of force, was stunning for both Jews and non-Jews. In some memoirs, Jews recall feeling "ten feet tall" after meeting Jews in the Red Army.[70] As one Jew remarked, "(F)or the first time, the Jew was not a second-class citizen."[71] Michael C. Steinlauf sums up: "Some of the working class youth, suddenly offered unprecedented educational and vocational opportunities, enthusiastically embraced a system in which being born Jewish was declared irrelevant; some, indeed, even joined the Soviet security apparatus."[72] Things would change during the course of the Soviet occupation, but, as Gross states, "At the beginning what mattered above all was the newly introduced equality, and with it a restored sense of dignity."[73]

The Soviet occupation allowed Jews to turn around a common inter-war Polish phrase and taunt Poles by saying "You wanted Poland without Jews, now you have Jews without Poland."[74] The response of non-Jews was similar to that seen in the Lithuanian case. The gentile population saw and categorized Jews as collaborators, traitors; they recall Jews welcoming the Soviets and becoming their willing servants.[75] Most scholars agree that participants justified violent pogroms against Jews in the first days of the German occupation with this charge of collaboration.[76]

---

[69] Weiss, "Some Economic and Social Problems of the Jews" p. 97. Weiss also discusses the new opportunities for state positions for Jewish doctors, lawyers, and engineers. For all of these occupational categories, Jews had been previously barred from state employment but were able to obtain positions under Soviet rule.

[70] Davies and Polonsky, *Jews in Eastern Poland and the USSR* pp. 17–18, citing historical work conducted by Dov Levin.

[71] Korzec and Szurek, "Jews and Poles Under Soviet Occupation" p. 398.

[72] Steinlauf, "Poland" p. 104.

[73] Jan T. Gross, "The Jewish Community in the Soviet-Annexed Territories on the Eve of the Holocaust: A Social Scientist's View" in Lucjan Dobroszycki and Jeffrey Gurock, eds., *The Holocaust in the Soviet Union* (New York: M. E. Sharpe, 1993), p. 159.

[74] Gross, "The Jewish Community in the Soviet-Annexed Territories on the Eve of the Holocaust" p. 159.

[75] As in the Lithuanian case, stories about Jews physically kissing and embracing Soviet tanks seem to be common.

[76] Zbikowski, Korzec and Szurek, Subtelny, Davies and other authors cited in the footnotes of this section all concur that the charge of collaboration was pervasive throughout Poland B.

The nature of the response in Poland B is exemplified in the Karski report. Jan Karski was a Polish courier who made reports to the Polish government in exile on the nature of the Soviet and German occupations. His February 1940 report related the position of Jews under Soviet occupation.[77] Although Karski describes Polish thinking and emotion, there is little reason to doubt that many Ukrainians held the same views. Karski stated, among other observations:

They (Jews) are entering the political cells; in many of them they have taken over the most critical political-administrative positions. They play quite a large role in the factory unions, in higher education, and most of all in commerce; but, above and beyond all of this, they are involved in loansharking and profiteering, in illegal trade, contraband, foreign currency exchange, liquor, immoral interests, pimping, and procurement. In these territories, in the vast majority of cases, their situation is better both economically and politically than before the war.

Karski further stated:

The attitude of Jews towards the Bolsheviks is regarded among the Polish population as quite positive. It is generally believed that the Jews betrayed Poland and the Poles, that they are basically communists, that they crossed over to the Bolsheviks with banners waving.

Karski went on to qualify these statements by noting that Jews had been previously oppressed. Nevertheless, he notes how Jewish police officers commonly treated the Polish population with disdain and disrespect. This comment brings up a point also made by Jan Gross – the number of Jews who occupied these positions is not critical. Rather, it was the fact that a Jew *could* obtain such a position of authority that was so disturbing. Jan Gross writes of the Polish experience of seeing Jews in these positions:

What about the shared memory of Jews lending a helping hand to the Soviet invader? Well, there were Jews in the Soviet administrative apparatus, in the local militia, and in the secret police. And there is no reason to think that they would have been less rude or abusive than any other such Soviet functionary. But that they were remembered so vividly and with such scorn does not tell us necessarily that Jews were massively involved in collaboration. Rather, I think, it is a reflection of how unseemly, how jarring, how offensive it was to see a Jew in a position of authority.[78]

---

[77] Karski's February 1940 report is summarized by Korzec and Szurek, "Jews and Poles Under Soviet Occupation" pp. 386–90 and in Davies and Polonsky, *Jews in Eastern Poland and the USSR* pp. 13–14.

[78] Jan T. Gross, "The Jewish Community in the Soviet-Annexed Territories on the Eve of the Holocaust" p. 161.

As in Lithuania, the Soviet authorities realized the effect that Jewish participation had upon the general population and they took action to reduce Jewish numbers. No Jew was elected to the Supreme Soviet in the elections of March 1940; Jews were underrepresented in the national assemblies of Western Ukraine and Western Belorussia; Jews were removed from senior, and highly visible, positions.[79] But the damage was done. The popular perceptions of Jewish status and collaboration continued (and continue to the present day).

In the days preceding Barbarossa, Polish power in the region had been broken through Soviet brutality and deportations. The settlers and soldiers that had maintained Polish rule were gone. In terms of political status, the Polish position had also been reduced. As Subtelny stated, the oppressors had become the oppressed. By all indicators of ethnic status a new hierarchy had been created with Ukrainians and Jews in positions below Soviet functionaries but above Poles.

Returning to the Three Puzzles

Resentment produces a coherent answer to the three puzzles of Poland B. Interwar Polish administration had created a clear ethnic status hierarchy with Poles at the peak and all other ethnic groups below. The Soviet takeover of September 1939 allowed Ukrainians to use violence to reduce the position of Poles. After the humiliations of the first few weeks of Soviet rule, Poles knew that they were no longer masters in this region. Soviet language, education, and land policies cemented the inferior position of Poles. As Jan Malanowski sums up, "All paths of promotion were soon closed to Poles who inevitably began to think of themselves as second-rate citizens."[80] Although possessing an antisemitic tradition, Ukrainians were apparently not compelled to commit violence against Jews, another group as far or farther beneath the Poles as the Ukrainians.

When the Germans entered in June of 1941, the Poles were no longer the focus of Ukrainian violence. During the brief period of Soviet rule, Poles and Ukrainians perceived that Jews had risen to a status position

---

[79] Davies and Polonsky, *Jews in Eastern Poland and the USSR* p. 21–22. They are citing Weiss on the subject of senior positions in Eastern Galicia.

[80] Jan Malanowski, "Sociological Aspects of the Annexation of Poland's Eastern Provinces to the USSR in 1939–41" in Keith Sword, ed., *The Soviet Takeover of the Polish Eastern Provinces, 1939–41* (New York: St. Martin's Press, 1991), p. 77.

equal or higher than that of Ukrainians. When constraints were released by the German invasion, Ukrainians were not impelled to attack Poles, the target just two years earlier. Soviet policies, and especially Soviet deportations, had reduced the position of Poles to a hopelessly inferior level. This time, Jews were the status rival. Humiliations and violence "put them back in their place."

The second puzzle asks why Poles participated to a lesser extent than Ukrainians in attacking Jews in the wake of Barbarossa. After all, Poles were well known for anti-Jewish pogroms in the region in earlier periods of semianarchy. They would commit violence against Jews in the postwar period as well. Here, without a doubt, was another opportunity. Rage would predict violence. Here, a badly downtrodden group is presented with opportunity to lash out. Furthermore, a traditional scapegoat, the Jewish population, is available as a vulnerable target. Resentment, on the other hand, predicts inaction for ethnic groups if violence would clearly not produce a change in status position. Unlike the Ukrainians, the Polish position had become so weak that violence would not have obtained any significant result in changing status position.[81] Additionally, the Poles, again unlike the Ukrainians, held little hope that the Germans would propel them into a position of regional dominance.

The third puzzle concerns the irrelevance of Belorussians. Although as numerous as Jews, their rural and poorly educated situation kept them from making advances during the Soviet occupation.[82] They were in a lower position during the interwar Polish administration and they remained in that lower position under the Soviets. They experienced no status reversal that would have created the emotion of Resentment nor did they create this emotion in any other group by rising above them on the status hierarchy. Notice, though, that they did not take out their frustrations, which were numerous under Soviet rule, with antiminority violence.

Fear and Hatred poorly explain the overall pattern of ethnic violence witnessed in Poland B. The targets are not rivals in terms of force or threat. As noted above, Hatred does an inadequate job in explaining frequent changes in targets or regional variation within a particular ethnonational culture.

---

[81] Ibid., especially pp. 80–84. Malanowski comments on the poor psychological state of Poles at the end of the Soviet occupation.

[82] Due to this position, it is not clear that Belorussian perception of status hierarchy was as powerful as that of Poles, Ukrainians, or Jews.

As in the Lithuanian case, Rage is the most powerful challenger to Resentment. The same story concerning the conjuction of societal frustration, traditional antisemitism combined with cognitive distortions, and release of constraints can be told for both the Baltic and Poland B. Again, Rage fails to explain the overall targeting pattern as well as Resentment. Not all frustrated groups lashed out in anger and violence. Ukrainians varied their targets in line with changing status hierarchies. Again, a Rage-based explanation would require the addition of other specific local factors to fit the observed differences in target and timing. Of course, elements of Rage and Hatred present themselves within the Resentment narrative. Also, Rage and Hatred may be the dominant path in certain locations, a point that is addressed in the following section.

Neighbors

Jan T. Gross's book, *Neighbors: The Destruction of the Jewish Community in Jedwabne, Poland*, provides details for the Polish cases listed in Zbikowski's table (Table 6.1).[83] Zbikowski lists only three reports of anti-Jewish pogroms in predominately Polish localities. The Radzilow region is credited with two reports. As Zbikowski mentions Jedwabne in the text of his article, these two reports would seem to be Radzilow and Jedwabne, the two neighboring villages that Gross discusses in detail. Gross briefly mentions the other listed case, Wizna.[84]

The Radzilow case is perhaps of most interest here. The primary goal of the present project is to isolate emotional mechanisms operating among peoples with a long history of living together. The possibility of isolating these mechanisms is best in the absence of the effects of firm control of occupying regimes. Thus, the first focus should be on the first few days of near anarchy before German establishment of rule, basically June 22 and a few following days. In both Radzilow and Jedwabne, events resembled those described above in the Lithuanian case. Violence occurred in these days but with a focus on humiliation, and perhaps plunder of Jews, not extermination. As Gross sums up, "Some people were killed, but the principal threats Jews faced at the time were beatings, confiscation of material property, and humiliations – men caught in the street could be

---

[83] Gross cites Zbikowski's article containing this table as "a concise article with summary data" in "A Tangled Web" footnote 71, p. 125.
[84] Gross, *Neighbors* pp. 70–71.

ordered to clean outhouses with their bare hands, for example."[85] Gross's work and this book are in basic agreement with a central issue: When given an opportunity, significant segments of one group are able to target another group even without much direction or any significant prior organization.

Even with more consolidated German control, Gross stresses the volition of Poles in participating in the Germans' extermination project. Radzilow is the best example here. Based on the testimony of survivors, "not even a single German was present" during the massacre in Radzilow.[86] In Jedwabne on July 10, as Gross notes, "No sustained organized activity could take place there without their (German) consent."[87] Still, Gross makes a convincing case that Poles were given reign to act on their own, and they chose to use the opportunity to mass murder the Jewish population of the town.

The quality of the mass murders is perhaps most interesting for the comparative approach employed here. Although motives of plunder and political ingratiation with the new occupiers are no doubt at work, the specific nature of the humiliations show something more at work. In Jedwabne, Poles made Jews carry a statue of Lenin around the town while singing. A rabbi was forced to lead the procession to the barn where the mass burning would take place. Testimony also holds that a rabbi and a kosher butcher were given a red banner before being chased into the barn. As one survivor of the Radzilow events sums up, "The Jewish population became a toy in the hands of the Poles."[88] As in Lithuania, the quality of the violence indicates that local Poles firmly connected Jews to the Soviet occupying regime. As in Lithuania, Poles felt compelled to humiliate Jews, to turn them into toys, in ways that specifically linked them to the outgoing Soviet regime.

Neighbors in Comparison

Gross's interpretations are not much help in explaining the three puzzles that guide this section. Gross's work is not comparative. He does not compare Jedwabne and Radzilow to any cases in which violence was absent. He does not compare Polish regions to Lithuanian or Ukrainian regions. If one looks only at the single case of Jedwabne, one might form

---

[85] Ibid., p. 54. [86] Ibid., p. 65 and p. 69. [87] Ibid., p. 77. [88] Ibid., p. 64.

the inference that Poles were exceptionally cruel to Jews. When seen in light of the violence that occurred at the same time in surrounding Lithuanian, Latvian, and Ukrainian regions, the puzzle becomes the one formulated above. That is, what accounts for the comparative *infrequency* of Polish violence in the regions of Poland B?

Comparative political science seeks to identify general processes and mechanisms that are able to help explain variation in social phenomena. Fear, Hatred, Resentment, and Rage are narratives of processes centered around different motivations. They are decidedly simplified versions of reality designed to compare competing theories linking individual motivation to ethnic violence. *Neighbors* is a historical work that does not seek simplification or comparison of alternative ideas of motivation. In fact, Gross provides little insight into the motives of the killers. He makes two unsurprising points on this issue. First, he states that the Jedwabne murders should be seen as a series of episodes in which various motivations came together to create the outcome. He writes, ". . . we must also be able to see it as a mosaic composed of discrete episodes, impro- vised by local decision-makers, and hinging on unforced behavior, rooted in God-knows-what motivations, of all those who were near the murder scene at the time."[89] It is undoubtedly true that various individuals with a myriad of motivations participate in these events. Given a comparative lens, however, it would seem that some more general force is behind the patterns seen within the field of variation, some variable or turn in the process that explains differences among regions. It is the goal of compar- ative political scientists to seek this force and see if it has generalizable properties.

Gross identifies a general force behind the murders – antisemitism. At different junctures in his works, he mentions antisemitism's deep roots in the region; he specifically mentions medieval prejudices about ritual murder, for instance. Again, there is an obvious problem for the compar- ativist. Undoubtedly, antisemitism is a primary factor, and probably a nec- essary one, in explaining the ferocity and prevalence of the violence against Jews in June 1941. However, antisemitism, especially when linked to medieval origins, is a constant. Constants cannot explain variation. Poles did not like Jews, Ukrainians did not like Jews, Russians did not like Jews, Lithuanians did not like Jews, Latvians did not like Jews, Germans did not

---

[89] Ibid., p. 125.

like Jews. Yet the type, timing, and prevalence of violence varied among and within these nations.

What does Gross's case study indicate about Fear, Hatred, Resentment, and Rage? It would seem that Gross tells a tale of Hatred. An antisemitic schema arises during a series of structural changes and collapses. Resulting from this schema, the emotion of hatred heightens a desire for historically framed revenge. In the grip of this emotion, individuals essentialize the opposing group. Dehumanizing violence results. This narrative is certainly plausible. However, an examination of the details in Gross's history suggests that Resentment may be at work in this particular Polish region. Resentment's foundation is group comparison and the narrative directs the analyst to try to understand the nature of the group comparisons made by the perpetrators at the time of ethnic violence. With this point in mind, it is fruitful to reconsider some of the events that occurred in these Polish localities.

First, consider Gross's treatment of the Soviet destruction of the local Polish underground in June 1940.[90] After a Soviet attack on the Polish underground headquarters, the Soviet regime imprisoned 250 people from the area of Jedwabne, Radzilow, and Wizna – the towns where the mass murders of Jews occurred one year later. Gross rightly states, "Naturally, a historian investigating the trail of violence in the area would like to know whether any connection can be established between these two extraordinary events: the destruction of the Polish underground organization in June 1940 by the Soviets and the mass murder of Jews in July 1941 by the Poles."[91] Gross cites documents that show that Jews were not among the informers who betrayed the Polish underground to the Soviets. Therefore, Jews cannot be logical targets of revenge a year later. He concludes the section by stating, "In any case, the Jews from Jedwabne were not implicated in this whole affair."[92] However, if one views the perpetrators as driven by group comparisons, as Resentment holds, it would seem impossible to so easily disconnect this event from the one that happens only a year later. Local Poles suffered imprisonment and death under Soviet occupation. Even if Jews were not the direct cause of this suffering, they did not suffer in the same way as Poles.[93] In the region, Jews were

---

[90] Ibid., pp. 47–53.   [91] Ibid., p. 48.   [92] Ibid., p. 53.

[93] Gross argues that Jews probably suffered more than Poles during the Soviet occupation, but it is highly doubtful that Poles saw it that way at the time. See Gross, *The Tangled Web* p. 103.

not organizing a local underground, NKVD troops were not "ferociously attacking" Jewish positions, the Soviets apparently did not arrest and interrogate Jews for participation in anti-Soviet activities. Resentment holds that Poles in this area would have compared their lot to that of other groups. Through comparison, they would likely come to a belief that Poles are anti-Soviet resisters and Jews are not. Gross points out that Jews were not active collaborators and thus makes the case that the killing of Jews could not be revenge. Resentment is not revenge, however. Revenge drives action against active treachery, but Resentment predicts action against an ethnic group even in the absence of specific betrayal. The most relevant factor is perception of change of group position. Consider again the specific nature of the violence. On July 10, 1941, the Poles of Jedwabne made the rabbi carry a red flag before they killed him. These perpetrators knew that the rabbi was not a Soviet collaborator; they were not seeking revenge for a specific betrayal. Resentment suggests that the Polish population wanted a symbol of the population that had risen above them, a symbol that they could turn into a "toy," thus showing that the positions between the two groups had once again turned.

Of course, these local events occurred within the broader contours of the Communist takeover in Poland B. Building on a point made earlier in the Lithuanian case, an emotion-based approach generates a viewpoint concerning how Poles were likely to perceive Jewish participation in the new Soviet regime. As Gross recognizes, Jews took positions in the Soviet administration. He even suggests that young Jews took these positions in order to escape the suffocating atmosphere of Jewish social life of that time.[94] Gross makes the case that this collaboration was not extensive, it was normal given the circumstances, that "it is impossible to identify some innate, unique characteristics of Jewish collaboration with the Soviets during the period 1939–1941."[95] From the point of view of the emotion–driven Polish population, what does it matter if Jewish collaboration was nonextensive and normal rather than "innate and unique"? In the comparative thinking of the Poles, Jews were a subordinate group in interwar Poland but under Soviet occupation indicators showed that they gained a measure of equality. That fact alone, without regard to why it happened, created an emotional reaction in the Polish population. Under the sway of this emotion, Poles were more likely to think in terms of group status and talk about "the Jews" as an enemy group. While antisemitism

[94] Gross, *A Tangled Web* pp. 102–03.   [95] Gross, *Neighbors* p. 155.

helps explain the ease and intensity of group essentialization, the phenomenon itself is a general one.

Finally, it is important to keep in mind the obsessiveness of group consciousness that pervaded northeastern Europe at this time. From the ruins of the First World War, the Baltic states and Poland emerged. An independent Ukrainian entity also briefly existed. This was an era of emerging national consciousness, a consciousness only heightened by the loss of statehood in the early stages of World War II. It was also an era when remnants of an older social system lingered. Although engaged in increasing interactions, ethnic groups mostly kept to themselves. For instance, after giving a largely positive review of Jewish-Latvian relations, Andrew Ezergailis writes, "But there is no reason to portray the relationship too idyllically; there was little contact between the two peoples. They lived like oil and water, separated by tradition, religion, and language."[96] The same could be said for the rest of the region, including Poland B. The birth of national consciousness and the nation-state in a time when groups still lived as oil and water could not bode well for minorities. Acute awareness of group and group status heightened the comparative processes underlying Resentment. Resentment suggests how local factors, in conjunction with national events and the east European milieu, created group comparisons that motivated the violence seen in *Neighbors*. In addition to providing an explanation for the variation witnessed in the broader region, Resentment offers an alternative view for the action in these Polish localities.

Summary

By the end of the 1930s, the perception of ethnic hierarchy pervaded daily life in the Baltic countries and Poland B. In the Baltic countries, and especially in Poland, the state worked to cement the perception of the titular group's dominant position. The Soviets and Germans reversed status orderings and destroyed stable hierarchies. As the quoted passages above illustrate, powerful emotions followed, strong desires developed, violent actions resulted. When constraints were lifted, perpetrators selected targets with a logic often fitting Resentment.

[96] Andrew Ezergailis, "Latvia" in David S. Wyman, ed., *The World Reacts to the Holocaust* (Baltimore, MD: Johns Hopkins University Press, 1996), p. 360.

The war would end. A Partisan war against Soviet control of the Baltic would follow. But eventually another period of stability emerged to create a stable set of power and status relations in the Baltic. This period of Communist stability (Period Five) would break down in the late 1980s and early 1990s. Ethnic conflict would again result. But it would play out in a different way.

7

The Reconstruction of Independent States

John Ginkel

As Germans and Jews had been eliminated through murder, deportation, or flight during the 1940s, ethnic relations in the Baltic in the post-Communist period (post-1991) have primarily involved interactions among the eponymous peoples, the Russian diaspora, and in Lithuania, the Polish population in the Vilnius region.[1] No significant ethnic violence occurred during the reestablishment of independence. Given this fact, this chapter, in effect, changes the dependent variable. Here, the puzzles involve state policies of the early and mid-1990s. Fear, Hatred, and Resentment still provide the framework for analyzing variation, but here that variation is measured by differences in the formation of institutions. For these cases, emotion may not be as dramatic or intense, but it still motivates action and influences outcomes. The linkage between emotion and individual actions may not be as tight or direct in this chapter as in the sections focusing on violence. However, by expanding the approach, this chapter tests the ability of an emotion-centered explanation to address a wider spectrum of ethnic politics.

The Baltic states' ethnic policies have exhibited considerable variation. To take one fundamental example, the three Baltic states showed signifi-

---

[1] By the time Estonia and Latvia were annexed by the USSR in 1940, over 90% of all Baltic Germans had already left. See Hans Hecker, *Die Deutschen im Russischen Reich, in der Sowjetunion und ihren Nachfolgerstaaten* (Koln: Verlag Wissenschaft und Politik Claus-Peter von Nottbeck, 1994) p. 80. Of course, most Jews had been killed in the Holocaust. On Polish-Lithuanian relations, see Stephen R. Burant and Voytek Zubek, "Eastern Europe's Old Memories and New Realities: Resurrecting the Polish-Lithuanian Union" *East European Politics and Societies* 7 (1993): 370–93. Also see Anatol Lieven, *The Baltic Revolution: Estonia, Latvia, Lithuania, and the Path to Independence* (New Haven, CT: Yale University Press, 1993), pp. 158–73.

cant differences on the question of citizenship. In Lithuania, all residents were granted automatic citizenship regardless of ethnic history.[2] In Estonia, the Supreme Council reinstated Estonia's citizenship of 1938. All those who could not trace their roots back to the interwar republic were required to go through an application process and, most importantly, were required to know the Estonian language. The law effectively disenfranchised the Russian-speaking minorities. In Latvia, the situation was murkier but probably even more restrictive; the Latvian Saeima legislated language proficiency and residency requirements even stiffer than those of its northern neighbor. This variation cannot be attributed to broad national/cultural heritages. As previous chapters have shown, all three Baltic states possess checkered histories with both intolerant and tolerant policies. Further clouding the picture, Lithuanian treatment of Poles in the post-1991 era, despite its tolerant posture toward Russians, has involved some types of institutional discrimination. Baltic history defies simplistic statements based on assessment of national character.

Here then are the puzzles that drive this chapter:

1. Why did Estonia and Latvia choose highly restrictive citizenship policies that denied the majority of the Russian-speaking population access to the political process while Lithuania adopted an inclusive citizenship policy that enabled ethnic Russian migrants from the Soviet time period to become naturalized citizens?
2. In Lithuania, why is there evidence of institutional discrimination against Poles in Lithuania but not Russians?

Answering these questions requires an understanding of the administrative policies of the postwar Soviet regime. This chapter begins by reviewing Period Five, the consolidation and implementation of Soviet control, before returning to the above puzzles that appear in Period Six, the post-Soviet era.

Period Five: Soviet Administration and its Consequences

As a part of the Soviet Union, the Baltics were constituent Soviet Socialist Republics. Ultimate political power resided in Moscow, but each republic possessed its own legislative body, the local Supreme Soviet. These republic-level legislative bodies administered local issues and were elected

---

[2] There were a few exceptions regarding members of the Soviet security forces.

bodies. Voters were citizens of each republic regardless of ethnicity. However, real power within each republic resided in the hands of the local branch of the Communist Party (CP) which was constitutionally charged with the leading role in society.

In order to insure that the local CP branches would remain loyal to the Soviet Union, Moscow imported communist officials from elsewhere in Russia to staff the most important positions. When possible the Soviets imported ethnic Balts who had grown up in the Soviet Union and had been completely "Russified." In Latvia these Russifed Latvians were known as *latovichi*. In Estonia, due to their heavy Russian accents, the Russian-Estonians were called *Yestonians*. Throughout the Baltics, the indigenous population regarded the Russified imports as outsiders despite their ethnic heritage.

Although the communist officials were not fully accepted by the local population, they assumed enormous political power. In Estonia, Russian-Estonians monopolized the top spots in the Estonian communist party from the 1950s until the late 1980s and the growth of the independence movement.[3] And in Latvia, only two members of the republic's thirteen-person politburo were born in Latvia.[4]

In Estonia, Yestonians were thrust into power following a 1950 purge of the indigenous Estonian communist membership. Johannes Kabin, a Russian of Estonian extraction who reputedly could not even understand a word of Estonian, became the First Secretary. A similar purge of the communist leadership occurred in Latvia in 1959. Arvids Pelse, a *latovichi* who had been born in Russia, became the First Secretary of the Latvian Communist Party. In the first years of his leadership he endeavored to remove every indigenous Latvian from a position of responsibility in the party membership. In Lithuania, events were somewhat different, for the Soviets found a Lithuanian communist, Antanas Snieckus, who was loyal to the cause of communism. Though he was noted as a ruthless leader, who deported even his closest relatives, he is credited with saving Lithuania from the most brutal aspects of Stalinization, and some Lithuanian intellectuals today believe that he did, indeed, serve his country.[5]

[3] Rein Taagepera, *Estonia's Return to Independence* (Boulder, CO: Westview Press, 1993).
[4] Juris Dreifelds, "Latvian National Demands and Group Consciousness since 1959" in George W. Simmonds, ed., *Nationalism in the USSR and Easteren Europe in the Era of Brezhnev and Kosygin* (Detroit, MI: University of Detroit Press, 1977).
[5] Lieven, *The Baltic Revolution* p. 96.

Thus, despite the fact that ethnic Russians constituted a minority of the population as a whole, they were a disproportionately powerful ethnic group in Estonia and Latvia. In Lithuania, ethnic Lithuanians were better represented in the upper echelons of the CP, but Russian party officials still exerted influence in excess of their demographic status. Given that the Communist Party in the Baltic republics was disproportionately Russian in composition, it is not surprising that the party staffed the most important and sensitive civil service positions with coethnics. The composition of police and security forces provide a prime example. At the time of independence in Latvia, most of the republic's 10,000 police officers were non-Latvian and had poor Latvian language skills.[6]

During Soviet times, the primary characteristic used to select police personnel was political reliability.[7] All applicants were scrutinized by the Communist Party and the KGB, and family histories counted as much as personal qualifications. An applicant with a relative who had violated the law forty years earlier might be rejected. Thus, Balts regarded the police as functionaries of the Soviet regime. The OMON (Special Purpose Militia Detachments), a division of the central police, targeted nationalist demonstrations during the Baltic independence movement and orchestrated a raid on a Lithuanian television station in January 1991, in the bloodiest moment of the Baltic independence struggle.

Beyond the obvious political and economic legacies left by fifty years of communism, Soviet annexation also greatly affected the underlying demographic structure of the Baltic states; an influx of Russian speakers into the Baltic regions of the Soviet empire significantly changed the ratio of ethnic Balts to ethnic Russians.

The population figures in Table 7.1 clearly show that Estonia and Latvia have endured the most dramatic demographic changes between the interwar period and today. Ethnic Estonians and ethnic Latvians constitute a bare majority of the population in their respective states. Most of this difference is due to differing patterns of Soviet migration in the Baltics.

Estonia and Latvia were favored sites for Russian relocation during the Soviet period. Ethnic Russian workers were brought in to aid in postwar industrialization and construction and many remained. Furthermore, Estonia and Latvia were traditionally favored retirement locations for the

---

[6] Juris Dreifelds, *Latvia in Transition* (Cambridge: Cambridge University Press, 1996), p. 106.
[7] Loiuse I. Shelley, *Policing Soviet Society: The Evolution of State Control* (New York: Routledge, 1996), p. 87.

Table 7.1. *Population Trends in the Baltic Republics*

Republic Nationality	Number 1989 (thousands)	Percentage of Republic Population					Change 1959–1989
		1926	1959	1970	1979	1989	
Estonia	**1,556**						
Estonians	963	88.2	74.6	68.2	64.7	61.5	−13.1
Russians	475	8.2	20.1	24.7	27.9	30.3	+10.2
Ukrainians	48	—	1.3	2.0	2.5	3.1	+1.8
Belorussians	28	—	0.9	1.4	1.6	1.8	+0.9
Latvia	**2,667**						
Latvians	1,388	76.0	62.0	56.8	53.7	52.0	−10.0
Russians	906	10.6	26.6	29.8	32.8	34.0	+7.4
Belorussians	120	1.4	3.0	4.0	4.5	4.5	+1.5
Ukrainians	92	0.1	1.4	2.3	2.7	3.4	+2.0
Lithuania	**3,675**						
Lithuanians	2,924	81	79.3	80.1	80.0	79.6	+0.3
Russians	344	2	8.5	8.6	8.9	9.4	+0.9
Poles	258	3	8.5	7.7	7.3	7.0	−1.5

Source: Harris and Chauncy, 1993. "The New Russian Minorities: A Statistical Overview," *Post-Soviet Geography* 34(1): 1–27. Reprinted with permission from V. H. Winston & Son, Inc., Palm Beach, FL. All rights reserved.

Soviet military, and large numbers still reside there today. Lithuania, though, remained relatively untouched by Russian influences. Lithuania did not enjoy the same level of industrialization as Latvia and Estonia, and Lithuanians were traditionally less hospitable toward Russian settlers, making the country less inviting to retirees.

Period Six: From Secession to Independence

As the Soviet system collapsed, the Baltic states began a political process not of establishing independence, but rather of *r*eestablishing independence. In this particular process, the fundamental question of ethnic relations concerned citizenship. The ethnic conflict concerned who belonged and what were the rights of those who did not belong. Other essential issues – language, education, jobs – would follow from the resolution of the citizenship question. This section concentrates on the path that each country took in determining its citizenship policies following independence from the Soviet Union. The focus is on how the initial political parties in these three states positioned themselves on the issue of citizenship. Who were their constituents? What was the nature of their support? Their opposition?

In contrast to other cases in the book, this chapter considers a different type of structural collapse. In this case, the chaos was institutional; old patterns of social organization were replaced by new, emerging, and untested institutions. The chaos was also tempered by the fact that Russians in the Baltic states resided under an implicit veil of protection from Moscow. Furthermore, Baltic leaders exploited Boris Yeltsin's assistance as a counterbalance to Moscow's hardliners to crystallize independence. Thus, there was a concerted effort to avoid violent confrontation between Balts and Russians.

However, Baltic independence has nonetheless motivated a reordering of the ethnic hierarchy in Estonia, Latvia, and Lithuania. While we may not be able to point to acts of violence perpetrated on ethnic Russians trapped in the newly independent Baltic republics, it is important to look at how ethnic differences have been exacerbated by symbolic actions. What rhetorical devices have politicians used to describe the nature of ethnic relations in the Baltic states? What actions have occurred within the public, nonpolitical, sphere of life?

Estonia

Immediately following independence, Estonia was represented by a legislature that had been elected under Soviet election rules with Estonian residents of all ethnicities participating in the election process. The Estonian Popular Front, which had a more moderate position concerning independence and Estonian nationalism than some of the other Estonian parties, captured the most votes during the last Soviet elections of March 1990, winning 49 seats in the 105-seat Estonian Supreme Soviet. The more radically nationalist Free Estonia Association won 29 seats, and the remaining 27 seats were won by hard-line Soviet candidates under the umbrella of a worker's collective called Intermovement.

The first major challenge that this legislature faced was deciding who would be a citizen of the new state. A special commission on citizenship submitted Estonia's first draft law on citizenship to the legislature less than a month after the failed Soviet coup.[8] The initial draft was fairly inclusive in nature and included the following provisions:

---

[8] Lowell Barrington, "The Domestic and International Consequences of Citizenship in the Soviet Successor States," *Europe-Asia Studies* 47 (1995): 735.

- Citizens from the interwar state and their descendants would be granted automatic citizenship.
- Permanent residents during the transition period to independence could apply for citizenship and waive the two-year naturalization period, language exam, and ten-year residency requirement.
- For others, the requirements listed above and an oath of loyalty would be required.
- Elimination of automatic citizenship for spouses of citizens, but allowed parents to pass on citizenship to their children.

The law's inclusiveness sparked controversy, and the legislature amended it on the floor.

Following extensive floor debate, the legislature, on February 26, 1992, decided to reenact the Estonian citizenship law of 1938 with a few amendments.[9] This new law provided automatic citizenship only for pre-1940 citizens and their descendants. The special waivers for permanent residents during the transition period were eliminated. This more restrictive citizenship law made it impossible for approximately 75% of the non-Estonian (i.e., those who were not ethnic Estonian) population to receive citizenship.

This law affected the composition of the voting pool for the referendum on the new Estonian constitution and the next election, for the Estonian legislature declared that naturalized citizens would not have a chance to participate in these votes, only those with restored citizenship.[10] Russian speakers in Estonia responded to the new law and the declaration on elections with a demonstration in Tallinn on March 21, 1992 where 4,000 protesters demanded minority ethnic, linguistic, and cultural and religious protections and rights.[11]

The new Estonian constitution allows noncitizens an array of social protections, such as unemployment benefits, pensions, and the right to conduct business, but they are conditional rights. The constitution allows for these rights to be restricted by later legislative acts.[12] More immediate restrictions apply to electoral participation. Noncitizens may vote in local elections, but they cannot hold office, cannot belong to a political party, and cannot cast ballots in national elections.

---

[9] Paul Kolstoe, *Russians in the Former Soviet Republics* (London: Hurst and Company, 1995), pp. 120–21.
[10] FBIS-SOV-92-059, p. 80.   [11] FBIS-SOV-92-059, p. 81.
[12] Kolstoe, *Russians in the Former Soviet Republics* p. 122.

In September 1992, Estonia held its first postindependence elections, and the political saliency and effect of the new citizenship legislation and constitutional changes were immediate. The Popular Front had collapsed as a political force due to the inclusive stance that it had held on the citizenship debate, yielding dominance to the new, more nationalistic, Fatherland Party. And, no Russians or Russian-speakers were elected to the reconstituted Estonian Riigikogu.

On March 23, 1993, the Estonian legislature amended the citizenship law again, declaring that "now the country's citizens are those who were recognized as such by the time the existing law was in force; persons who are regarded as citizens by international treaties; persons born to at least one parent who was a citizen at the time of birth; and children found in Estonia whose citizenship of other countries cannot be established."[13] This amendment reinstates the condition from the original citizenship proposition that extended citizenship to individuals where only one parent is an Estonian citizen. Previously, this group was excluded from automatic citizenship.

In the summer of 1993 the Estonian legislature adopted a law on alien residents that threatened the legal status of Russian-speakers who had been born and raised in Estonia. The Law on Aliens required all noncitizens, regardless of how long they had lived in Estonia during the Soviet era, to apply for five-year residency permits. Former Soviet military personnel and KGB officers were excluded from applying for a residency permit. Furthermore, there were no guarantees that any application would be approved.

Russian-speakers were outraged by the new law, and the predominantly Russian towns of Narva and Sillamae embarked on a secessionist movement, calling for immediate autonomy. The referenda were held on July 16 and 17, 1993. More than 97% of those who took part in the Narva plebiscite voted for autonomy from Estonia, and 98.6% of the Sillamae voters, with 61% participation, supported territorial autonomy from greater Estonia.[14] The Estonian government declared the plebiscites illegal, finding that the Estonian constitution does not allow for autonomous territorial units.

Though Narva and Sillamae did not successfully achieve autonomy within Estonia, the political action pressured the government into softening its previous stance on resident aliens. Amendments to the Law on

---

[13] FBIS-SOV-93-055, p. 83.   [14] FBIS-SOV-93-140, pp. 78–79.

Aliens guaranteed that noncitizens living in Estonia prior to July 1990 would receive residency permits. And, with former Soviet passports expiring, the Estonian government developed a travel document called an "Alien Passport" that would allow noncitizens to travel freely and reenter Estonia without a visa.

On April 1, 1995 a new citizenship law went into effect in Estonia that provided minor changes. It changed the residency requirement for naturalization for individuals entering Estonia after April 1995 from two years to five years and spelled out rights and obligations for citizens under the Estonian constitution.

In the late 1990s, Estonia softened its stance toward its Russian-speaking minority. In July 1998, the Estonian Citizenship and Migration Board began to accept application for permanent residence permits.[15] This replaces the policy of only granting five-year residence permits. Furthermore, the Estonian legislature, on December 8, 1998 voted to liberalize requirements for naturalization.[16] The amendments to the naturalization law grant stateless children under fifteen who were born after February 26, 1992 eligibility for Estonian citizenship.[17] This legislation helped to bolster Estonia's chances for European Union membership and forestalled potential conflict with Russia of the type that plagued Latvia in 1998.

Latvia

Latvia's independence movement developed alongside Estonia's and also relied on the leadership of a popular front party, the Latvian Popular Front (PFL). The PFL developed in 1988 in support of perestroika and was not intended to supplant communist rule. Consider the following self-description: "The Latvian Popular Front, a mass sociopolitical organization of the republic, born out of the people's patriotic activity, is vigorously supporting and taking an active part in the radical restructuring of our society

---

[15] "Estonia Begins to Recognize its Noncitizens" *The Current Digest of the Post-Soviet Press* 50: 16.

[16] "Estonian Parliament Passes Amendments to Citizenship Law" RFE/RL *Newsline*, December 9, 1998.

[17] The new law details a naturalization mechanism where the eligible children's parents make the application on the child's behalf. The parents must also be stateless and legal residents of Estonia for at least five years. Opponents of the bill expressed fear that this process would not ensure that new applicants for citizenship would possess Estonian language fluency and argued that they should have to pass a language proficiency test.

in accordance with the principles laid down in the resolution of the 27th CPSU Congress and the 19th all-union party conference."[18] Thus, the Latvian Popular Front placed its organizational foundation squarely within the existing legal framework of the Soviet Union. The PFL posed no direct nationalist challenge to Russian-speakers in Latvia during its early years. Election results from the last Soviet election in Latvia in 1990 suggest that the movement received some Russian support. PFL candidates captured 139 out of 201 seats in the Latvian Supreme Soviet, a proportion greater than the share of ethnic Latvians in the republic.[19] These results were also echoed in Riga, a city that was 67% Russian-speaking where PFL candidates captured 31 of 69 seats. The Popular Front appealed to more than just Latvian nationalists with its call for an independent state.

The Latvian Popular Front led independent Latvia's initial foray into citizenship law making with poor results. Initially, prominent PFL leaders called for a variation on the "zero-option," where all permanent residents would be granted citizenship in the new state. For example, Andrejs Pantelejevs, the chairman of the Human Rights Commission in the parliament and Anatolijs Gorbunovs, the chairman of the legislature, called for a five-year residence and no language requirement for naturalization.[20]

Other politicians took more exclusionary postures. Visvaldis Lacis, the leader of the Latvian National Independence Movement, stated that Russians in Latvia were political "nobodies." He argued that Russians should possess social rights, but "they should have no more [political] rights" than he himself would have if he were to take a trip to Sweden."[21] This marked the dominant political stance in the Latvian debate over citizenship over the next couple of years.

The Latvian parliament adopted a resolution in October 1991 in its first attempt to develop a law governing citizenship and naturalization. The proposed law recognized that Latvia was a restored state and that its August 23, 1919 law on citizenship still existed. Naturalization would require sixteen years of residence for applicants who were neither interwar citizens nor direct descendants of a Latvian citizen. Additionally, applicants for citizenship would have to take an oath of loyalty to the Latvian constitution and pass a proficiency test in Latvian. The law was passed on

---

[18] FBIS-SOV-88-223.   [19] Lieven, *The Baltic Revolution* p. 148.
[20] Kolstoe, *Russians in the Former Soviet Republics* p. 123.
[21] Cited in Kolstoe, *Russians in the Former Soviet Republics* from "Vivaldis Lacis: 'Vy ne grazhdane vtorgo sorta, vy nikto'" *Sovetskoe Molodezh*, September 11, 1991.

its first reading in parliament but ultimately failed, for it did not receive the required second and third reading.

The October 1991 resolution never assumed the full force of law, for the Latvian parliament at the time, elected under the Soviet system, decided that only the reconstituted Saeima could rule on the passage of a citizenship and naturalization law. Furthermore, the resolution's procedures for naturalizations were delayed until the Saeima had adopted a policy. Thus, in the period immediately following independence, the actual guidelines for citizenship and naturalization were uncertain. This uncertainty created concern within Latvia's Russian-speaking community. Russians who traveled out of the country did not know whether or not they could obtain permission to return to Latvia or what their status within Latvia would be in the near future. What was clear, though, was that non-citizens – those who could not trace their roots to the interwar republic – would not be able to vote in the June 1993 elections.

In the 1993 elections, the Latvian Popular Front disappeared from the political scene. The party had splintered into smaller factions, and the only offshoot that managed to garner any seats was the moderate Democratic Center Party. The dominant political issue that directed the competing campaigns was the issue of citizenship. Who should have it? What process would noncitizens need to follow for naturalization? Five parties – the Latvian Way, the LNNK, the Latvian Farmer's Union, the Christian Democrats, and the Democratic Center party – favored some sort of residence requirement and language proficiency. The Latvian Way dominated the election and formed a coalition with the Farmer's Union.

In June 1994 the Saeima passed a citizenship and naturalization law that survived three readings in the legislature (the required number), but President Guntis Ulmanis returned the bill to the parliament for reconsideration. The bill possessed strict quotas that sparked vocal protest among the local Russian-speaking population and Russian politicians. The Council of Europe and the United States also pressured Ulmanis to reject the bill, favoring a softening of quota restrictions.

On August 11, 1994, Ulmanis signed into law a revised version of the citizenship bill that did not contain the strict numerical quotas of the previous version. Legal residents of Latvia who satisfy the following conditions can apply for naturalization:

- Have permanently resided in Latvia for at least five years, counting from May 4, 1990 or from the date of a permanent residence permit.

- Have a command of the Latvian language.
- Know the basic principles of the Latvian constitution.
- Know the national anthem and the history of Latvia.
- Have a legal source of income.
- Have taken an oath of loyalty to Latvia.
- Have officially renounced any previous citizenship.
- Individuals who served in foreign security forces or have been convicted of serious crimes cannot become naturalized citizens.

Additionally, the 1994 citizenship law limits who may apply for naturalization at any given time. This system of naturalization "windows" has sparked protest from the Russian Federation and Russian speakers in Latvia. During the first "window" for naturalization in 1996, only persons who were born in Latvia and between the ages of sixteen and twenty could apply for citizenship. In 1997, the window included those born in Latvia after 1972. The window system will not allow all resident aliens in Latvia to apply for naturalization until 2003.

Though this bill was approved by the OSCE and other international human rights organizations, it did not satisfy all Russian speakers in Latvia. Boris Tsilevich, an ethnic Russian member of parliament and a Popular Front activist, called Latvia's postindependence policies on citizenship and naturalization a "betrayal of those Russians who campaigned for Latvia's independence."[22] He claimed that the law unfairly retarded the opportunity for Russian speakers to obtain naturalization and placed arbitrary institutional obstacles in their way.

In the spring of 1998 the citizenship issue in Latvia reached a fever pitch. In March two rallies by elderly Russian demonstrators in Riga over low living standards and strict citizenship rules sparked a violent police response and a strong reaction from Moscow.[23] The Russian Federation Council expressed their support for the Russians living in Latvia by passing a nonbinding resolution that called for the Russian government to freeze

---

[22] From John Ginkel's interview with Boris Tsilevich on November 30, 1998.
[23] Press coverage of the rallies is well-reviewed in the RFE/RL *Newsline*. See especially, "Police Use Force to Disperse Demonstrators in Riga" March 4, 1998; "Russia, Latvia Spar Over Riga Police Action" March 6, 1998; Paul Goble, "Playing the Ethnic Card" March 10, 1998; "Russian-Speakers Rally Again in Riga" March 18, 1998; Paul Goble, "Trapped by Democracy?" March 18, 1998. The first rally occurred on March 3, 1998 and consisted of approximately 1,000 elderly Russians. The demonstration dispersed after police used batons to attack the protesters. The second rally on March 17, 1998 involved greater than 2,000 demonstrators and peacefully concluded of its own accord.

trade and impose economic sanctions against Latvia if "discrimination against the Russian-speaking population" continues.[24] These actions, along with pressure from the OSCE, led the Latvian parliament to consider softening its stance on naturalizing ethnic Russians.

On June 22, 1998, the Latvian parliament approved amendments to the citizenship law that offered three substantive changes: (1) citizenship would be extended to the children of noncitizens, at their parents' request, born after August 21, 1991; (2) the "naturalization windows" that restricted the number and timing of Russian applicants for citizenship would be abolished; and (3) language tests for applicants over the age of sixty-five would be simplified.[25] However, parliamentary deputies who opposed the measure, led by the nationalist Fatherland and Freedom Party, succeeded in delaying the promulgation of the new law until they could determine whether or not the public wanted to vote on the amendments via a referendum. This action required that 10% of eligible voters sign a petition in support of a popular referendum.[26] More than 224,000 signed the petition – far in excess of the required 131,000 – by the time of the August deadline, and a citizenship referendum was scheduled to take place alongside the October 3, 1998 parliamentary elections.[27]

The changes to the citizenship law barely passed. With two-thirds of the Latvian electorate participating, the amendments to the citizenship law passed by a vote of 53% in favor and 45% against.[28] Though the changes to the citizenship law passed by popular vote, Tsilevich still possesses concerns about ethnic relations in Latvia. He found the closeness of the referendum to be disturbing and feared that the result may not be an accurate reflection of political attitudes in the country due to the confused wording of the citizenship question.[29] The referendum read: "Do you want the law of 22 June 1998, 'The Amendments to the Citizenship Law,' to be repealed?" Thus, a vote of "no" actually expressed a desire to change the existing law on citizenship and naturalization. Still, the technical hurdles

---

[24] "Russian Federation Council Slams Latvia" RFE/RL *Newsline*, March 13, 1998.
[25] "Latvian Lawmakers Adopt Citizenship Law Amendments" RFE/RL *Newsline*, June 23, 1998.
[26] "Latvian Deputies Demand Delay in Publishing Amended Citizenship Law" RFE/RL *Newsline*, June 29, 1998.
[27] Jan Cleave, "Latvia to Hold Referendum on Citizenship Law Amendments" RFE/RL *Newsline*, August 25, 1998.
[28] The Baltic Times Staff, "Latvian Voters Say 'yes' to Amendments," *The Baltic Times*, October 8–14, 1998, pp. 1 and 9.
[29] From John Ginkel's interview with Boris Tsilevich on November 30, 1998.

for Russian residents to apply for Latvian citizenship have been lowered following the October referendum, and indicate that Latvia has softened its stance toward integrating its Russian population.

In both Estonia and Latvia, a similar pattern emerged. In the period immediately following independence, inclusive citizenship policy options were available. In Estonia, the first draft law was relatively tolerant; in Latvia, the proposals of Latvian Popular Front encouraged inclusion. However, these policies could not withstand democracy. Popular pressures forced a turn toward exclusion. In both states, though, citizenship policy softened after several years of confrontation. Thus, the Estonian and Latvian pattern can be summarized as (1) rejection of inclusion, (2) institution of exclusionary policies, and (3) softening of exclusionary policies. Lithuania would not follow this pattern.

Lithuania

Lithuanian legislators began to deal with issues of citizenship and naturalization before the republic's popular front party, Sajudis, ascended to power in the 1990 elections to the Lithuanian Supreme Soviet. The relatively homogenous Lithuanian legislature adopted citizenship guidelines for the Lithuanian Soviet Socialist Republic in November 1989. This republic-level law granted automatic citizenship to all persons who had been citizens prior to June 15, 1940 and their descendants living in Lithuania. It also provided automatic citizenship for permanent residents who had been born in Lithuania and those who could prove that one of their parents or grandparents had been born within the republic. Lithuanian residents who did not meet the criteria for automatic citizenship could become naturalized by signing a loyalty oath supporting the Lithuanian constitution and the republic's sovereignty.[30] Lithuanian citizenship was made still more inclusive in 1991 when the republic signed a treaty with Russia in July that extended citizenship to those who entered Lithuania after November 1989 but before the 1991 treaty. Importantly, there was no concomitant language requirement that non-Lithuanians needed to fulfill in order to obtain automatic citizenship as dictated by the 1989 law and the 1991 treaty.

For those desiring Lithuanian citizenship but not qualifying automatically under the 1989 law and the 1991 treaty, Lithuania developed a mech-

---

[30] Barrington, "The Domestic and International Consequences of Citizenship in the Soviet Successor States" p. 733.

anism for naturalization that was as difficult as that found in Estonia and Latvia. In order to become a naturalized Lithuanian citizen, the 1989 law held that the applicant needed to maintain permanent residence in Lithuania for ten years, prove proficiency in Lithuanian, possess a permanent source of legal income, and sign a loyalty oath to the constitution and republic.[31] However, this multilayered process did not provoke the outburst of anger that naturalization requirements in Estonia and Latvia caused, for the guidelines for automatic citizenship were so inclusive. Fewer than 10% of the population did not receive automatic citizenship during the two-year window of opportunity.

The Sajudis-led parliament that was elected in 1990, after the initial citizenship law had been passed but before independence, instituted a new citizenship law in December 1991, following the restoration of Lithuanian independence. The new law eliminated automatic citizenship for permanent residents but maintained the criterion for citizens of the interwar republic. Thus, residents who had not filed for automatic citizenship between 1989 and 1991 would be forced to go through the naturalization procedure if they desired Lithuanian citizenship.

Those seeking naturalization under the 1991 law faced a similar process that developed under the 1989 law, but some things were made more explicit. It was clearly determined that one may not hold dual citizenship with the Soviet Union, and proficiency in Lithuanian was codified according to both a spoken and written examination. Barrington points out, though, that the 1991 law provides a clause that allows the Lithuanian government to restrict citizenship later. The law states that "persons meeting the conditions specified in this Article shall be granted citizenship of the Republic of Lithuania taking into consideration the interests of the Republic of Lithuania."[32]

Despite its several twists and turns, the citizenship policies of Lithuania did not exhibit the process of its northern neighbors. Lithuania adopted an inclusive citizenship policy from the earliest days of the Baltic independence movement and has not backed down from this initial legislation despite having the opportunity to do so in December 1991 when the Sajudis-led legislature passed its first postindependence citizenship

---

[31] Ibid., p. 734.

[32] From the Law on Citizenship, Law of the Lithuanian Supreme Council, December 5, 1991. Unofficial translation, as cited in Barrington, "The Domestic and International Consequences of Citizenship in the Soviet Successor States."

legislation. Due to its basic inclusive nature, citizenship policy has not been the source of conflict as witnessed in Estonia and Latvia. However, Lithuania has not been entirely free of ethnic controversy. The primary friction has not been with Russians, but rather with Poles.

Lithuanians and Poles

Lithuanian actions toward its Polish minority have not been so tolerant. Snyder enumerates several instances of anti-Polish political action in Lithuania, stating that "ethnic Poles in Lithuania have come to believe, with some justification, that Lithuanian nationalists intend to force them to assimilate or emigrate."[33] According to 1989 population figures the Polish minority in Lithuania constitutes 7.0% of the population compared to a 9.4% share for the Russian minority in Lithuania.[34] Though they comprise a smaller percentage of the population than Russians, the Poles are more concentrated, making their influence greater in those regions. The Poles in Lithuania comprise a majority of the population in two counties (rayons), Vilnius and Salcininkai, and a large minority (28.8%) in Trakai.[35] Ethnic Russians are a majority in only one town, Visaginas (formerly Snieckus), where Lithuania's Iganalina nuclear power plant is located and staffed by Russian personnel.

There are several sources of friction between Lithuanians and Poles. First, Lithuanians believe that Poles threaten the integrity of the Lithuanian capital. Recall from Chapter 6 that Poles occupied Vilnius in the interwar period; the Soviets returned Lithuania's historic capital in 1939. Poles have deep historical and cultural claims in Vilnius. To take one example, Pilsudski, one of the most revered founders of the modern Polish state, is buried in Vilnius. Secondly, Lithuanians do not forget that the Salcininkai region declared autonomy in May 1989. Thirdly, and relatedly, Lithuanians remember that the Polish regions supported the August 1991 coup. The latter two events led to a perception of Poles as Soviet collaborators who took advantage of the Soviet era to become disproportionately powerful in Lithuania. Vardys and Sedaitis write:

[33] Tim Snyder, "National Myths and International Relations: Poland and Lithuania, 1989–1994" *East European Politics and Societies* 9 (1995): 323.

[34] Chauncy Harris, "The New Russian Minorities: A Statistical Overview" *Post-Soviet Geography* 34 (1993): 4.

[35] V. Stanley Vardys and Judith B. Sedaitis, *Lithuania: The Rebel Nation* (Boulder, CO: Westview Press, 1997).

Moscow kept control over Lithuanians by manipulating and improving the conditions of the Poles. Communist authorities supported some 250 Polish schools or educational programs, a republic-wide Polish daily, and several local publications as well as Polish TV and radio programs. They also monitored the appointment of Polish personnel in party and government structures.[36]

Following the failed coup in Moscow in August 1991, Lithuania dissolved the local governments of Vilnius and Salcininkai, the two largest centers of ethnic Poles in Lithuania. The Sajudis-led Lithuanian government regarded the Poles in these two regions as collaborators with the Moscow putsch and disbanded the local Polish councils in the Vilnius and Salcininkai districts and imposed direct central rule on them. Local rule was not returned to the two regions until elections in February 1993.

Further evidence of anti-Polish sentiment in Lithuania comes from the citizenship process. Though Lithuania adopted the "zero option" citizenship policy, whereby all permanent residents at the time of the citizenship law were granted Lithuanian citizenship, Poles have encountered difficulties. Polish applicants for citizenship have reported that they have been forced to accept Lithuanian versions of their name on official documents.[37] Vilnija, a Lithuanian nationalist group that finds support in parliament, publicly expresses its desire to assimilate ethnic Poles in Lithuania and claims that Polish names are nothing but warped versions of older Lithuanian names.[38] Institutional discrimination has also arisen in the school system. In September 1993, the Lithuanian parliament criticized a Polish-language teachers union for promoting Polish culture to the detriment of Lithuania.[39] Thus, it is not surprising to find that Polish-language schools in Polish-speaking areas must use Lithuanian-language textbooks.[40]

Assessment: Returning to the Puzzles

What explains the differences among Latvia, Estonia, and Lithuania in treatment of the Russian minority? Why would Lithuania adopt relatively

---

[36] Ibid., p. 214.   [37] Snyder, "National Myths and International Relations" p. 3.
[38] Ibid., p. 3.
[39] Michael Haxton, "The Poles of Lithuania," Minorities at Risk Project, 1994, (http://www.bsos.umd.edu/cidcm/mar/litpole.htm), p. 3.
[40] Konrad Niklewicz, "Twice Forgotten" *The Warsaw Voice* No. 17 (444), April 27, 1997, (http://www.warsawvoice.com.pl/Pl-iso/v444/neighbors.html), p. 2.

tolerant and inclusive policies toward its Russian minority and take more discriminatory actions toward Poles? Again, the explanatory merit of the four emotions can be judged in terms of target and description of process.

Hatred

The Hatred narrative holds that schemas arise during periods of structural upheaval. These schemas provide antagonistic roles. Applied to the post-1991 events, Hatred would hold that Balts consider Russians as an historical enemy. During the period of firm Soviet rule, this antagonistic role lay dormant, but awakened with the collapse of the Soviet Union. The realization (cognition) of Russian vulnerability and the possibility of change, combined with the freer speech produced by Glasnost, triggered Hatred schemas leading to an emotion that heightened the salience of vengeance against the Russian enemy. Past Soviet/Russian persecutions and deportations become daily fare on the television and in the press. The process cycles. With the arrival of independence, the first order of business, despite the appeals of some tolerant politicians, is to attack the political position of Russians, the historical enemy, in the most fundamental way possible – that is, to attack their rights as citizens.[41]

Does this story explain post-1991 variation? The previous chapters have argued against the existence of consistent historical roles among ethnic groups in the Baltics. However, the position of Russians might differ from that of Germans and Jews. Russians have been the one constant power, the one geographic omnipresence, a group that is almost never violently attacked. The problem is that Lithuanians would be expected to have developed an antagonistic and vengeful schema as much or more so than Estonians and Latvians, yet they have adopted the most tolerant stance. Soviet rule of the Baltic republics, instituted after the Molotov-Ribbentrop Pact, began with forced deportations that affected thousands. On June 14, 1941 more than 10,000 Estonians were taken from their homes, forced into cattle cars, and sent to Siberia.[42] In Latvia, Bilmanis estimates that more than 2% of the Latvian population was either deported or massa-

---

[41] The idea of cultural schema might also help explain the nonviolent actions of Balts. Historically, violent actions against the powerful Russians were implausible and ineffective; the role that evolves then becomes one involving more cunning and subtlety – one that would not produce automatic retaliation.

[42] Riina Kionka and Raivo Vetik, "Estonia and the Estonians" in Graham Smith, ed., The Nationalities Question in the Post-Soviet States (London: Longman, 1996).

154

cred between 1941 and 1942.[43] Deportations continued into the late 1940s. Lithuania, though, may have endured the most tremendous losses. Senn cites historical data stating that between 1940 and 1951, 200,000 to 240,000, between 10 and 12% of Lithuania's postwar population, was deported to Siberia and central Asia.[44] Given the record of deportations and population losses that Estonia, Latvia, and Lithuania endured following Soviet annexation of the Baltic republics, as well as experiences from the day of the Russian Empire, one could argue that each of the three newly independent Baltic states and their indigenous populations might have had similar historical materials that could lead to Hatred roles. This may be the case in Estonia and Latvia, but their action toward their Russian-speaking minority also begs the question: Why do we not see similar action in Lithuania?

The Lithuanian treatment of Poles adds to the weakness of the Hatred explanation. Why would Lithuanians carry a more antagonistic schema and set of roles toward Poles than Russians? This difference makes little cultural or historical sense. The perception of Poles also seems to have changed over the past few decades. Previously, it would seem, Poles were seen more as an "oppressor." Many of the more educated Poles of the interwar period left with the establishment of Lithuanian rule. Today, the Poles who remain are often considered "lower class." These shifting identities belie the story of Hatred.

In general, culturally based arguments do not seem able to explain this variation. There is little evidence that the "ancient" attitude of Lithuanians toward Russians is much more tolerant than that of the Estonians or Latvians. One commentator in 1990 went so far as to hold that Lithuanian intolerance toward minorities was a legitimate reason for slowing the rapid drive toward Lithuanian independence. In April of 1990, this editorialist wrote that while "the ugly character of Lithuanian nationalism should not be a reason to deny Lithuanian independence, it was a factor "that should not be overlooked, either. . . . We should take the concerns of the Russian and Polish minorities in Lithuania quite seriously. Lithuania's treatment of minorities is hardly reassuring."[45] However, the

---

[43] Alfred Bilmanis, *A History of Latvia* (Princeton, NJ: Princeton University Press, 1951).

[44] Alfred Erick Senn, *Lithuania Awakening* (Berkeley: University of California Press, 1990), p. 52.

[45] Benjamin Frankel and Brian D. Kux, "Recalling the Dark Past of Lithuanian Nationalism," *Los Angeles Times*, April, 29, 1990: M2.

reality has been that Lithuanians' behavior toward minorities has been reassuring, especially in comparison with some of the neighboring states. Furthermore, in the Latvian case, long-standing relationships between Russians and Latvians could not be characterized by "ancient hatred." It might be noted that Latvian and Russian workers had previously enjoyed good relations as well as political alliances against Baltic Germans earlier in the century. In sum, current variation in policy cannot be linked to historical-cultural variables.

Rage

The Rage narrative simply does not fit the post-1991 Baltic events. Rage is based on "lashing out" from general frustration, perhaps against substitute targets. The Baltic peoples could not be characterized as lashing out. Policies seemed to be developed in a calculating manner. The targets of institutional discrimination are direct. In Estonia and Latvia, Russians do pose a real demographic threat. Estonian and Latvian anti-Russian actions regarding citizenship are directly related to this demographic reality. Russians are not a living "inkblot" target. They are not accused of conspiracies, their image does not change to fit the problem at hand. Likewise, the Poles cannot be clearly described as a substitute target. They pose a concentrated demographic threat in certain regions. As mentioned above, Polish loyalty to the Soviet system in the late 1980s and during the 1991 coup cannot help but create some problematic relations between Poles and Lithuanians. The Poles may have good reasons not to trust Lithuanian rule, but the way the Soviet-Polish-Lithuanian triangular relationship has played out indicates direct and real conflicts rather than processes of cognitive distortion.

Resentment

Resentment predicts violence or discrimination against the group farthest up the hierarchy that is vulnerable to the effects of such action. Constraints come off, the vulnerability of ethnic groups becomes evident, emotion works to orient individuals to put the targeted group "in its proper place." In Estonia and Latvia, the target group was the Russian minority. As shown previously, Russians and Russified Balts occupied disproportionate numbers in the positions of force and authority. Furthermore, the very numbers of Russians residing in Estonian and Latvian cities made them a

156

threat to the dominance of the titular group. With violence not a realistic option, Latvians and Estonians reduced the group status position of Russians in the most blatant form available – stripping of citizenship. In Lithuania, Russians did not threaten status dominance of Lithuanians either in terms of positions of authority or in terms of total population. With the coming of independence, the issue of the status of Russians as a group was solved – they were unquestionably subordinate to Lithuanians. The only remaining status question concerned the Poles in the Vilnius and Salcininkai districts. Corresponding to the prediction of Resentment, these districts were targeted for discriminatory action. In addition to harrassment over citizenship and language polices, the Lithuanian state returned local rule only after two years of control by the central government. Lithuania's actions toward its Polish minority differs from Estonia's and Latvia's treatment of their Russian-speaking minorities, but the motivation in each of the cases bear a striking similarity. In each case, the titular nationality is reorganizing domains that had once been the province of an "unjustly" powerful ethnic group.

Resentment predicts the targeting patterns of the respective Baltic states. In several striking ways, Resentment also describes the overall process. First, Resentment hypothesizes that once dominance is established, continued attacks on the subordinated groups will cease and policy will soften. Indeed, this pattern can be observed in all three states.

Second, Resentment can help explain differences in citizenship policy even among the two exclusionary states. In Estonia, noncitizen permanent residents may participate in local elections. In Latvia they may not. When queried about this difference in policy between two states confronting similar problems, a member of the Latvian National Human Rights Office responded that this is due to the fact that Riga is a Russian city while Tallinn is largely Estonian in composition.[46] As a result of this policy,

---

[46] From John Ginkel's interview with Zinta Miezane, August 1997. Boris Tsilevich disputed this claim during a later interview and stated that Tallinn was also a Russian city. In the literature on the Baltics, there are conflicting data about the true demographic situation in the three Baltic capital cities. One of the more reliable reports, due to the quality of its sources, can be found in Jeff Chin and Robert Kaiser, *Russians as the New Minority: Ethnicity and Nationalism in the Soviet Successor States* (Boulder, CO: Westview Press, 1996), p. 95. Chinn and Kaiser present the following demographic information: Percent titular (1989): Vilnius, 50.5; Riga, 36.5; Tallinn, 47.5. Percent Russian (1989): Vilnius, 20.2; Riga, 47.3; Tallinn, 41.2. From this data, it is apparent that in Tallinn, though not a majority "Estonian" city, Estonians represent a plurality of the population. In Riga, ethnic Latvians are significantly outnumbered by the nontitular population.

following the May 1994 municipal elections, only four ethnic Russians were elected to Riga's sixty person city council. This is at odds with the fact that ethnic Russians make up better than 60% of Riga's population. In Estonia, where the population distribution favors ethnic Estonians, it does not matter that Russians can vote in local elections. In Latvia, though, it would be a symbolic blow if Russians were to control the nation's capital city.

Third, besides citizenship, the Estonians and Latvian regimes moved to decisively establish symbolic forms of group dominance in other realms. This process began even before independence was established. Distrust for the existing police forces in the Baltics led the popular front governments elected in 1990 and the post-independence governments to reform the Soviet-style militias. Estonia was the first of the Baltic republics to begin restructuring its police forces, after negotiating an agreement with the USSR Interior Minister to cede police control to republic oversight. Following this agreement, Estonian authorities targeted ethnic-Russian officers. The police in Estonia were predominantly Russian and the Estonian government in 1990 was unsure how they would behave when confronted with nationalist movements. In March 1991, the Estonian Supreme Soviet, led by popular front ministers, passed an Estonian language requirement that forced many former Russian militia members to leave the new police force. In addition, the new police unit was augmented by a home guard (*Kodukaitse*) of unarmed volunteers who were ethnic Estonians.

Similar steps were taken in Latvia. Though Latvia could not negotiate for separate republic-level control of its police forces before declaring independence – the Soviet Interior Minister who had signed the agreement with Estonia was replaced with a hardliner before Latvia could conclude its own agreement – it quickly reformed its own militia units at the first opportunity. And, like Estonia, Latvia developed a volunteer paramilitary home guard (*Zemessardze*) that was staffed only by Latvian citizens following independence. It was a 20,000 member force that augmented the official police forces and in some cases usurped its power.[47] Lithuania, too, during its independence drive developed a home guard staffed by volunteers, though its function was more symbolic than in the other two republics. Russians comprised less of the population in Lithuania, and the home guard was intended to provide a symbolic force

---

[47] Dreifelds, *Latvia in Transition* discusses the evolution of the Latvian Home Guard, p. 106.

158

that was distinct from the police and independent of any Moscow or Communist Party influence.

Latvia passed stringent language laws in 1992 that made Latvian a prerequisite for certain types of employment. The police is one of these occupations. It is uncertain, though, to what extent existing officers have been dismissed from service, for this would create pragmatic difficulties. However, to insure that the police will remain a Latvian domain, the 1994 citizenship law required that all applicants for police service be Latvian citizens possessing fluency in Latvian, thus over time the police will become completely Latvian. In all three new nation-states, steps have been taken to make sure that no predominately Russian unit will ever be in a position of armed authority over the eponymous people.

The 1992 law on languages affects more than just the composition of the police force. The law was designed to redress problems left over from an earlier language law in 1989 that was intended to allow people to choose Latvian or Russian when interacting with public officials. However, this law had little effect on changing language use in the civil service. The Latvian parliament passed a more stringent language law in 1992 that emphasized Latvian proficiency and provided for a state language inspectorate for enforcement. Public employees were required to pass a Latvian language exam at a level commensurate with their professional duties.[48]

Fourth, the events in post-Soviet Baltic states also seem to illustrate the relative weights of political status concerns and economic position, a central controversy attached to the Resentment argument. Consider the following description of the 1993 Press Ball in Riga, one of the highlights of the post-Communist 1993 social calendar:

To the strains of a pompous polonaise, independent Latvia's new elites paraded around the former Communist Party's congress hall, shiny new suits on their backs and in many cases, almost equally shiny wives and girlfriends on their arms. Almost without exception the politicians were Latvians, and the leading intellectual and cultural figures likewise; but the businessmen, many looking as if they had just climbed out of their tracksuits and knuckledusters, were overwhelmingly Russian and Russian-Jewish. For the moment, they are doing very well in Latvia, and more and more intelligent and determined young local Russians are rising to join their

---

[48] See Rasma Karklins, *Ethnopolitics and Transition to Democracy: The Collapse of the USSR and Latvia* (Baltimore, MD: Johns Hopkins University Press, 1994), pp. 153–57 for a discussion of language policy in Latvia.

ranks. So far, they have faced no serious obstacles in the economic sphere; and for that matter, for around $500 it is not difficult to buy Latvian citizenship from a corrupt official.[49]

To be sure, there was some consternation over the position of Russians and others in the field of business, but this emotion does not seem to compare to the passion aroused by the former Baltic world where one was forced to speak Russian and serve in the Soviet military. Here are the conditions for the general ethnic peace in the Baltics – the general populations of the eponymous peoples feel "masters of their own house" while the most ambitious individuals from other ethnic groups accept their new status, at least in Riga and Tallinn if not Narva, because they still retain an outlet for economic advancement, perhaps a better economic outlet than they could find in Mother Russia.

Fear

The version of Fear presented in Chapter 4 does not apply to the Baltic states. In that version, one ethnic group fears an attack by another ethnic group and so chooses to strike first. This story, based on the security dilemma, assumes two groups relatively equal in power. Obviously, in the Baltic, the titular peoples are no match for the Russians. However, the Fear story can be spun in a different and more convincing direction: The emotion that drives discriminatory action is not fear of physical attack, but rather fear of cultural extinction. Unless they defend themselves, unless they actively attack the position of the rival culture, small peoples may fade from the earth.

Here is a retelling of the Fear story. When two competing ethnic groups are relatively equal in terms of size and strength and each fears the potential cultural hegemony of the other, then the group that enjoys an initial structural advantage will exploit that position to engage a preemptive strike on the weaker group. As the population data in Table 7.1 indicate, the resident Russophone minorities in Estonia and Latvia are of nearly equal size to that of each nation's eponymous population. In Lithuania, the majority position of the titular majority was clear. Thus, it may seem reasonable to explain the presence of institutional ethnic conflict toward Russian speakers in Estonia and Latvia, versus the absence of such conflict in Lithuania, as a function of Fear.

[49] From Lieven, *The Baltic Revolution* p. xxvii.

The revised Fear story continues. Leaders of all three nations argued during the independence movements that their republics were threatened by two factors: environmental destruction and cultural annihilation.[50] At the time, many Russian residents supported independence and were mollified by claims that Estonia, Latvia, and Lithuania would support minority rights following independence. Once independence had been achieved in Estonia and Latvia, though, only the fear of environmental ravages seemed to have disappeared from the political agenda. Fear for the maintenance of Estonian and Latvian culture, its language and traditions, remained in the forefront of political debates. In Lithuania, in contrast, Sajudis leaders were true to their word and enacted liberal citizenship policies that allowed all legal Russian residents to become citizens, the "zero-option."

Fear predicts that the target of ethnic violence will be the group that is the biggest threat. In Estonia and Latvia, Russians may be perceived as a threat to the maintenance of the Estonian and Latvian languages. Polling data show that although most ethnic Estonians and Latvians speak Russian, only a small minority of ethnic Russians living in those two republics have bothered to learn the indigenous languages. Thus, Estonians and Latvians regard the language required in naturalization laws as a mechanism for ensuring the survival of their distinct cultural identities.

Furthermore, government officials in Estonia and Latvia tend to defend their actions on the grounds that they are merely attempting to protect, what have become, endangered cultures. For example, Tago Holsting, an Estonian foreign ministry official, succinctly states, "The only thing that we have that is our own is the language."[51] Consequently, language laws that have established Estonian and Latvian as the only state languages in their respective republics might be regarded as evidence that ethnic policy making in these two states is a function of fear, fear of a process of cultural winnowing should ethnic Russians constitute too large a portion of the population. The Forced Migration Project's report on human rights in Estonia and Latvia echoes this proposition.

---

[50] See Nils Muiznieks, "The Baltic Popular Movements and the Disintegration of the Soviet Union" (Unpublished Ph.D. dissertation: University of California, Berkeley, 1993) for an excellent discussion of the roles of cultural and environmental nationalism during the Baltic independence movements.

[51] Cited in Forced Migration Project, 1998. "Estonia and Latvia: Citizenship, Language and Conflict Prevention" The Open Society Institute, (http://www.soros.org/fmp2/html/baltics.htm.).

In Lithuania, where the relatively small number of Russians in the population do not pose a threat to Lithuanian culture, the Fear hypothesis would predict an absence of Lithuanian conflict directed toward Russians, which is indeed the case.

There are three reasons to question the cultural version of Fear. First, in contrast to Resentment, Fear would not predict a softening of policy if the populational percentages remained constant. Both Estonia and Latvia actively encouraged its Russian-speaking minority to emigrate. In Estonia, political leaders attempted to persuade Canada and Argentina to accept Russian speakers as immigrants.[52] In Latvia, the National Independence Movement Party (LNNK) publicly stated that there was a desirable ratio of Balts to non-Balts in Latvia, where non-Balts should comprise no more than 25% of the population.[53] And, former Prime Minister Birkavs also suggested that Latvia should encourage "voluntary re-emigration of Russian speakers to third countries."[54] To some extent these policies have worked; ethnic Estonians and ethnic Latvians comprise a greater proportion of their national population today than they did at the time of independence.[55] However, the changes in ethnic composition in Estonia and Latvia have not been so great as to argue that either country has less reason to fear for the maintenance of its own unique culture now than it did at the time of independence. The fact that Estonia and Latvia have softened, or are in the process of softening, their stances on citizenship and naturalization for Russian speakers despite the fact that each country still possesses a large population of non-Balts suggests that Fear is not the dominant emotion driving ethnic policy making in these two states.

Second, cultural Fear does not adequately explain the Lithuanian treatment of Poles. Snyder (1995) enumerates several instances of anti-Polish political action in Lithuania, stating that "ethnic Poles in Lithuania have come to believe, with some justification, that Lithuanian nationalists

---

[52] David Laitin, *Identity in Formation: The Russian Speaking Populations in the Near Abroad* (Ithaca, NY: Cornell University Press, 1998), p. 166.

[53] M. Opalski, B. Tsilevich, and P. Dutkiewicz, *Ethnic Conflict in the Baltic States: The Case of Latvia* (Kingston, Ontario: The Kashtan Press, 1994), p. 5.

[54] Ibid., p. 5. One Estonian politician stated for the record what might be assumed to be the unstated policy goal of a significant portion of his countrymen: "We hope that a third or so will become Estonian citizens, a third may remain here with Russian citizenship, and a third at least will leave," in Lieven, *The Baltic Revolution* p. 377.

[55] In Estonia the proportion of ethnic Estonians, mostly due to Russian emigration, has increased in the population, from 61.5% in 1989 to 64% in 1996; and in Latvia the titular population has increased from 52.0% to 55.1%.

intend to force them to assimilate or emigrate." Poles present no more a threat than Russians toward Lithuania, yet they are the target of institutional discrimination.

Third, and perhaps most crucially, the stated fear of cultural extinction cannot be taken at face value. The Baltic peoples are not small Eskimo tribes. Baltic languages are spoken in universities; novels and plays are written in Lithuanian, Latvian, and Estonian. Cultural Fear seems more likely a justification rather than a motivation. Certainly, the cultural version of Fear is more politically acceptable than any stated version of Resentment. In an interview in the Baltic Observer in 1992, the chairman of Latvian Way, Andrejs Panteljevs, discussed his opinion about ethnic relations in independent Latvia, "I see the concept of 'nationality' not as a matter of blood lines and descent, but rather of culture and language."[56] He stated that using this conception of nationality permits the use of citizenship laws as an integrating mechanism that protects Latvian culture while peacefully incorporating Russians into the Latvian community. This is the type of explanation that has predominated among politicians in the Baltics when discussing the issue of ethnic conflict and citizenship. This view communicates a sense that it is noble and just to protect one's culture, for ultimately it is the only defining marker of a unique ethnic group. Thus, politicians who favor exclusionary ethnic policies hope to avoid being tagged as racist or driven by vengeful impulses through reference to cultural Fear. While no politician would admit being driven by Resentment (perhaps they would not or could not admit this motivation to themselves), there is good reason to see ethnic policy in the Baltic states as an instrument to reorder the social hierarchy.

Summary

It is naïve to claim that all ethnic conflict that we observe in Estonia, Latvia, and Lithuania is attributable to just one type of emotional motivation. There exists a problem of overdetermination. Among some, ethnic hatred is surely present, and there are individuals in the Baltics who passionately fear for the maintenance of their cultures, afraid that such tiny countries will be enveloped in an ever homogenizing world.

However, notwithstanding this overdetermination, Resentment explains the greatest amount of variation in ethnic conflict in Estonia,

[56] *Baltic Observer*, 1992, p. 13.

Latvia, and Lithuania. It addresses the issue of Estonian and Latvian policies of exclusive citizenship and resolves why Lithuania forged a more inclusive citizenship procedure. Resentment also helps to explain why ethnic conflict in Lithuania targets the Polish minority as much or more as it does the Russian. And, the softening of rules of exclusion in Estonia and Latvia helps confirm that it is Resentment, not Fear, that drives ethnic conflict in the Baltic republics.

8

Across the Century

The previous three chapters have followed a similar form. After reviewing the relevant history of the preceding period, each has addressed ethnic conflict in a period of structural breakdown. In contrast to these chapters' more limited focus, this chapter looks at the century as a whole and makes more sweeping comparisons across historical eras. Despite the difference in scope, the general approach remains the same as in previous chapters. The first section makes three brief comparisons that generate a field of variation. The following section then assesses the ability of each emotional narrative to explain patterns within this field.

Comparisons

The Nature of Variation Looking Across All Periods

In looking across twentieth century Baltic history, one of the striking features of ethnic conflict in the region is the enormous variation in target. Consider each ethnic group in turn.

- Although the Baltic Germans possessed a dominant position since the medieval ages, only with the effects of modernization did they become targets, and even then action against them varied. Germans were targeted in 1905, but their significance as a focus of violence and discrimination is never strong afterward.
- Ukrainians attacked Poles in 1939 but not 1941; Lithuanians harassed Poles in the Vilnius region in 1941 and post-1991 periods.
- Jews have not been a constant prey. In 1941, Lithuanians attacked Jews in the Kaunas region and other Lithuanian regions; in the same

165

period, Latvians and Ukrainians in Poland B likewise acted against Jews. But Lithuanians and Latvians did not constantly or violently victimize Jews before 1941, they did not act against them when the constraints broke in 1905; Lithuanians did not launch a massive pogrom against Jews in Vilnius in June 1941; there is little evidence of mass actions against Jews in Belorussia and Estonia at that time; Ukrainians preferred to attack Polish landowners and Poles, not Jews, in 1939.

- Latvians and Estonians passed discriminatory citizenship laws against Russians in the post-1991 period, but Lithuanians did not.

Despite the overwhelming diversity in ethnic targets, some constants do emerge. For one prominent example, Balts have discriminated against Russians, but with a few minor exceptions, they do not engage in pogrom-like violence against Russians.[1] Less perceptibly, within the progression of ethnic violence and conflict Belorussians seem almost invisible, appearing neither as perpetrator nor as victim.

In the broader view, another phenomena that stands out is the shift from class to ethnic targets. In 1905, much of the violence was between peasants and landlords. Although not addressed in detail in the previous chapters, the fighting during the tail end of the First World War, could not be easily characterized as mass ethnic in character even though it helped create the Baltic nation-states.

Comparing Periods of Stability and Independence

Period Three, the interwar era, and Period Six, the post-1991 years, provide what is known in political science as a "similar case" comparison. In both periods, independent Baltic states were free to make policy without outside interference. Both periods were marked by relative stability. In both periods, a stable nation-state developed policies establishing the dom-

---

[1] Balts violently fought Soviet incorporation after the Second World War, but this fighting did not clearly "target" Russians. Many of the targets of assassination were native Baltic Communists or Communist collaborators. The fighting was largely defensive, not an attack on a particular ethnic group. See Roger Petersen, *Resistance and Rebellion: Lessons from Eastern Europe* (Cambridge: Cambridge University Press, 2001) for an extensive treatment of Baltic resistance to Soviet rule in 1944–50.

inance of the titular group. There were many changes between the two periods, but the basic story was similar in both.

Rogers Brubaker has described the interwar era as one of "nationalizing states" and lists seven defining characteristics: (1) the existence of a core nation; (2) the idea that the core nation legitimately "owns" the polity; (3) the belief that the core nation's aspirations are not sufficiently realized; (4) the idea that changes in language laws, economic and cultural policy, as well as efforts to attain demographic predominance, are necessary to establish the hegemony of the core nation; (5) the belief that remedial action is seen as necessary to make up for past discrimination against the nation when it was unable to promote its interests; (6) the idea that mobilization in state and nonstate organizations is necessary to promote state policies; and (7) the adoption of formal and informal practices to attain these objectives.[2] While Brubaker employs this list to describe interwar Poland, most of these criteria apply to Lithuania, Latvia, and Estonia as well. Emerging from a multinational empire, each of these states created state-funded, social-patriotic organizations to inculcate a sense of nationhood in the primarily rural population. In each of the Baltic states, as seen in the previous Lithuanian example, exclusionary cultural and economic policies gradually eclipsed some initial efforts at inclusion.

Significant differences separate the interwar and post-Communist eras. Demographically, Soviet Russians replaced Jews and Germans and the population became primarily urban. The economy was socialized and the society secularized. Yet, the similarities in ethnic policy are notable. As in the interwar years, most Balts in the post-Communist era believed that their national aspirations had not been realized under previous rule and that remedial efforts were necessary. Latvians and Estonians took action in language policy and have sought to thwart challenges to their demographic predominance. If anything, the desire and actions to establish the dominance of the core nation have been made more quickly in the post-1991 period than in the interwar era. In summary, Baltic states have instituted similar "nationalizing" policies in both eras of independence and stability. Notably, in neither period did the state encourage outright violence against any minority.

---

[2] I have paraphrased and shortened these seven points from Rogers Brubaker, *Nationalism Reframed: Nationhood and the National Question in the New Europe* (Cambridge: Cambridge University Press, 1996), pp. 83–84.

Comparing Periods of Upheaval and State Breakdown

There have been three periods of rapid structural change in the Baltics during this century. First came the collapse of empires wrought by the First World War (Period Two). Next came the period of occupations accompanying the Second World War (Period Four). Finally, the collapse of the Soviet system created a third swift and comprehensive change in the nature of authority (Period Six). Juxtaposing these three periods allows for comparison of ethnic violence across different periods of state breakdown. In the second period, empires that had lasted hundreds of years suddenly ceased to exist; in the fourth period, short-term occupation regimes came and went; in the sixth period, the Soviet system crumbled. How did ethnic relations differ across these different forms of collapse? Have there been common threads or readily observable differences?

Two features stand out. First, in comparison with the latter two periods, violence in Period Two carried a clearer and stronger class element. In the latter periods, violence and discrimination became unambiguously ethnic. Second, the most vicious ethnic violence ever to occur in the Baltics took place during Period Four, the time of occupations. In comparison, the reestablishment of independence in the post-1991 period was accomplished with a minimum of violence.

Assessment

Which of the four emotion-based narratives provides the best explanation of variation within this centurywide field?

Hatred

In light of these more general comparisons, the explanatory inadequacy of Hatred becomes even more apparent. The concept of Hatred is built on the existence of longstanding schemas that produce roles to guide and inform action. Structural change produces information precipitating a belief that an old, familiar conflict situation has again arisen. One recognizes the "ancient enemy" and the inherent negative characteristics of that foe. An emotion arises heightening the desire to act out a common role, often a role based on a story, a script, of group honor and vengeance. This desire, combined with the belief that constraints have been removed, motivates individual violence and discrimination.

The amount of target variation provides a severe challenge to this story. Despite similar structural breakdowns and changes, Jews, Poles, Russians, and Germans have taken turns as primary targets of Baltic action. In terms of the quality of the conflicts among Balts and minority populations, there is little that is "ancient" or even relatively constant. To take one example, Jews have been seen as possible allies (Period Two), as one group among many to be subordinated through policy (Period Three), as traitors to the state (Period Four), as basically irrelevant (Periods Five and Six). Likewise, relations among Balts and Germans and Poles on the other hand have witnessed twists and turns. One is hard pressed to discern consistent roles and proscriptions for action.

Two possible constants might exist in contrast to this general differentiation. One possible prescription seems to be "don't physically attack Russians." As seen in the last chapter, Baltic antipathy toward Russians can be palpable. Yet, there are very few instances of violence against Russian minority populations. A second possible prescription might concern Belorussians. As they don't seem to matter, inaction toward Belorussians is the prescribed behavior. While behavior toward Russians and Belorussians may possess a seemingly constant quality, this behavior does not seem tightly connected to historically formed or culturally embedded roles. The existence of a historical schema is not evident. Moreover, both Resentment and Fear, as instrumental emotions, would predict the observed patterns of interaction. Resentment predicts violence when it is useful and effective in bringing a rival group down the status hierarchy. Belorussians have never been in a dominant position, not even in relative terms, in Baltic hierarchies. Likewise, Resentment and Fear would not predict violence against Russians. Violence against the Russian minority might not be able to change their local status position – which is tied to their awesome numbers to the east – and might serve to precipitate a massive Russian counterattack. In the words of one Lithuanian while descending one of the crowded and elongated escalators of the Moscow subway, "When we Lithuanians are in Moscow we think only one thought – just how many are these Russians?"[3] Fear predicts violence when rival ethnic groups are of roughly equal power potentials. On this measure, Balts have never been equal to Russians or Belorussians. Being always weaker than Russians and always stronger than Belorussians, the logic of preemptive violence has

---

[3] Personal conversation with a Lithuanian in a Moscow subway.

not applied.[4] Along other lines as well, Hatred has little explanatory power. The emotion has little to say about why conflict might lose its economic overtones or why violence would be especially vicious in Period Four.

Fear

As just mentioned, the logic of Fear rests upon the existence of roughly equal power balances. While the concept may have a great amount of explanatory purchase regarding interstate wars, its merits explaining Baltic interethnic conflict are limited. The basic problem is obvious: The central players in Baltic conflict have seldom been battling on equal terms. Jews, most clearly, have never possessed threat potential; there has never been any reason to fear a physical attack from Jews. In regional terms Russians and Balts are not equal in power. The conflict among these groups has varied, but this variation does not seem related to physical threats. If ever there was a shifting power balance, it was occurring in the early 1990s. Then, the Russian garrisons were preparing to return to Russia. In order to prevent the growing power of titular peoples, Fear might have predicted that Russians act before the withdrawal of Soviet forces and before the development of Baltic power. However, such considerations did not appear to come into play. Conflict would play out in institutional forms; very few Russians feared for their physical safety.[5]

Rage

As a noninstrumental emotion, Rage is the most difficult to assess in any given case. As outlined in Chapter 4, Rage gains support when targets are clearly substitute rather than direct. The number of targets that could be clearly coded as substitute is not high. Violence among Balts, Poles, Ukrainians, and Russians seldom followed the story line of generalized or cumulative frustrations leading to a need to lash out.

---

[4] A possible exception might be the tail end of the First World War when the Baltic peoples acted against the weak emerging Soviet state.
[5] During some periods, "windows of opportunity" did open. For example, Ukrainians against Poles in 1939, Balts versus Germans in 1905. The existence of such windows of opportunity is only one element of the Fear argument, however. Another is that the perpetrators have a clear reason to fear attack by the target. On this point, the Polish-Ukrainian case might still hold, but not the Balt-German one.

The argument for Rage mainly rests with the instances when Jews were targeted. As previously discussed, no group in the region possessed an affinity with Jews. The conventional wisdom holds that violence against Jews cannot be explained without reference to a diffuse cultural anti-semitism underlying Eastern European culture (if not Christian culture as a whole). While Jews may not be targets in the Hatred sense, that is, there may be no consistent role or consistent prescription for action against Jews, they may more plausibly be targets in the Rage sense – living "inkblots" that serve as targets for a wide variety of occasions. A common story supporting this view goes as follows:

Ignace Paderewski, Poland's post-World War I premier was discussing the country's problems with Woodrow Wilson.
'If our demands are not met at the conference table,' he said, 'I can foresee serious trouble in my country. Why my people will be so irritated that many of them will go out and massacre the Jews.'
'And what will happen if your demands are granted?' asked President Wilson.
'Why my people will be so happy that they will get drunk and go out and mas-sacre the Jews.'[6]

Although conflict among other groups may be driven by realistic struggles over status, wealth, and power, Jews serve as the regional scapegoat when the Rage phenomenon is unleashed.

This section focuses on variation in conflict in the twentieth century Baltic region. Across the entire twentieth century, Lithuanians, Latvians, and Estonians only massively targeted Jews on one occasion – 1941.[7] As previously discussed, there were strong elements of the Rage narrative at work on this occasion. Yet even in this case, Jews were not targets in every city and region. The broader pattern of variation indicated that 1941 was not a simple story of frustration and the search for a scapegoat.

While there are undeniably unique elements to Jewish history in Eastern Europe, the Holocaust being chief among them, the analysis here indicates that Jews often shared the troubles of fellow minority groups. During the stable periods of nationalizing states, the dominant group dis-criminated against all other groups. Jews were not singled out. Certainly, prejudice against Jews existed in the Baltics. Jews, as elsewhere across

---

[6] J. Telushkin, *Jewish Humor* (New York: Morrow, 1992), p. 112, quoted in Jon Elster *Alchemies of the Mind: Rationality and the Emotions* (Cambridge: Cambridge University Press, 1999), p. 38.

[7] Collaboration with the Nazi regime is another matter. I have addressed that issue else-where. See Roger Petersen, *Resistance and Rebellion* Chapter 5.

Europe, were often considered greedy, collusionary, too powerful, disloyal. Without a doubt, in the personal lives of many prejudiced people, Jews represented a group worthy of hatred. However, in terms of mass-based violence or popular support for singling out one group for discriminatory action, the evidence does not support Rage and the scapegoating of a particular minority as a pervasive and driving force.

Resentment

Of the four emotion-based narratives, Resentment best explains broader Baltic patterns of ethnic conflict. Resentment is built on perceptions of ethnic hierarchy that develop with the new types of contact produced through modernization. Resentment would not be expected to operate until these new types of intergroup contact and comparison became regularized through universal education, conscription, and growth of state bureaucracy. Rather, premodern forms of conflict, such as disputes between landlords and peasants, would be expected more than conflict defined by struggles over ethnic group status.

Once perception of ethnic hierarchy has been established, Resentment predicts conflict among groups that are changing positions and no conflict against groups whose dominant or subordinate position is clear and unchangable. Within the broader picture, Resentment predicts the most conflict in times of status uncertainty and among groups whose positions on the hierarchy are most volatile and unstable. In fact, in the Baltics and Poland B most violent conflict has occurred among Lithuanians, Poles, Ukrainians, and Jews – all groups moving up and down the status ladder. Belorussians, the least modernized and occupants of a low level on any hierarchy, remained outside the fray. Russians, possessing a regional status unchangable through local violence, are the targets of discrimination, but are not targets of ethnic violence. Furthermore, when previously dominant groups come to occupy a stable, subordinate position on an ethnic hierarchy, action against them is predicted to soften. This phenomenon appears to have applied to both the Baltic Germans and Baltic Russians.

Once perception of ethnic hierarchy becomes a pervasive part of everyday life, regional majorities are likely to attempt to establish a dominant position. Simply put, ethnically conscious regional majorities are not likely to accept a subordinate position. This commonsense has played out in many areas of the modern and modernizing world – it is a basic corollary of Resentment. It is not surprising that the comparison of Periods Three and Six reveals very similar nationalizing policies. In both, a regional majority in control of the state apparatus passed an array of policies in language, bureaucratic hiring, and other areas that established the dominant position of the titular group.

Finally, Resentment provides some insight into the viciousness of Period Four. Resentment predicts that chances of violence are highest after a status reversal. Violence is the result of the emotional drive to "reverse a reversal." In order for this phenomenon to occur, two conditions have to be present – the perception of being on top of a hierachy and the experience of reversal. Period Four was the first time when these two conditions could have been present. The modernized and nationalized state produced the heady experience of being members of a dominant ethnic group. The Nazi and the Soviet occupation produced quick reversals. In 1941, the memory of independence and dominance was fresh – the day-to-day experience of *becoming* a member of a subordinate group was immediate and widespread. In 1991, the Baltic states had been under Soviet rule for forty-five years. Generations were raised with the realities of Soviet rule. The sense of correcting an unjust reversal was present, but it could not possibly be the burning issue it had been in the 1941 period.

Summary

This section has examined the history of Baltic ethnic conflict in the twentieth century. Four competing emotion-based theories have been compared in several ways. In a more narrow vein, the three preceding chapters examined puzzling variation within one period. Each story, Fear, Hatred, Resentment, and Rage, predicted differing processes and targets sets. With some exceptions, Resentment provided the clearest fit, especially in terms of target set. The present chapter has approached twentieth century ethnic conflict in the Baltics in a broader vein using comparison to identify overall patterns and repeating phenomena. Again, Resentment provides the most relevance in explaining the overall nature of ethnic conflict in the region.

Throughout the period, the one consistent thread was action by the rural majorities to gain predominance in the region where they lived. New regional majorities employed varied tactics to achieve this goal. Both violence and state policy have been tools. Targets changed depending on the ethnic hierarchy. However, beneath all this variation appeared one constant drive – a Lithuania for Lithuanians, a Latvia for Latvians, an Estonia for Estonians. And Resentment has served as the emotional motor for action underlying this drive.

The following chapters work to test the prevalence of Resentment in a wider arena. Again, this emotion-based narrative is pitted against its competitors in terms of providing answers for puzzling variation.

9

Czechoslovakia, 1848–1998

Beth Wilner

We have become poor, but we are not miserable; we quarrel, but our passions do not fly; we throw eggs but not grenades; we are willful, but not without will.

Pavel Tigrid, *Lidove noviny*, December 1991

The motivation for this chapter is the extraordinary change in ethnic group composition in Czechoslovakia over the past seventy years. When the First Czechoslovak Republic was formed in 1918, it was one of the most ethnically heterogeneous states in Europe. In fact, the Czechs held an absolute majority by only the slimmest of margins.[1] By 1987, however, the ethnic composition of Czechoslovakia had changed dramatically. While Czechs and Slovaks saw their percentage of the population increase during this seventy-year period, the Russian, German, and Hungarian populations watched their numbers decline (see Table 9.1). Moreover, the level of ethnic homogeneity that has evolved in the territories of the former Czechoslovakia seems even more stark when one separates the Czech Republic from Slovakia. The data in Table 9.2 clearly illustrate the level of demographic dominance achieved by Czechs and Slovaks in their respective republics at the start of the 1990s.

At the same time, the Czechoslovak national character has been hailed – or lamented, depending on the point of view – as tolerant and passive. In demonstrating tolerance, scholars tend to adopt a beneficent view; often they describe Czechoslovakia as having the longest functioning interwar democracy and as taking extra measures to protect its

---

[1] Stanislav Kirschbaum, *A History of Slovakia: The Struggle for Survival* (New York: St. Martin's Press, 1995).

Table 9.1. *Nationalities Living in the Territories of Czechoslovakia (percentage of total number of citizens)*

	Czechs	Slovaks	Russians	Germans	Magyars	Poles	Jews
1921[a]	52.5	15.1	0.8	24.7	5.1	0.8	1.3
1950[a]	67.9	26.3	0.6	1.3	3.0	0.6	NA
1961[b]	66.0	27.9	0.4	1.0	3.9	0.5	0.3
1970[b]	65.0	29.2	0.4	0.6	4.0	0.5	0.3
1980[c]	64.1	30.6	0.4	0.4	3.8	0.4	0.3
1987[d]	62.9	31.8	0.4	0.3	3.8	0.5	NA

[a] Source for the 1921 and 1950 census data is Vladimir Srb, 1967, *Demograficka prirucka*, Praha: Nakladatelstvi svoboda, p. 44.
[b] Information for the 1961 and 1970 census data is *Scitani lidu, domu a bytu k 1. prosinci 1970 v CSSR* (Dil 1), Praha: Federalni statisticky urad, p. 13.
[c] Source for the 1980 census is *Scitani lidu, domu a bytu*, Praha: Cesky statisticky urad, p. 88.
[d] Source for the 1987 census is Sharon Wolchik, 1991, *Czechoslovakia in Transition*, NY: Pinter Publishers, p. 186.

Table 9.2. *Nationalities Living in the Territories of the Czech Republic and Slovakia, 1991 (percentage of total number of citizens)*

	Czechs	Slovaks	Russians	Germans	Magyars	Poles	Others
Cz. Rep.	94.9	3.0	NA	0.5	0.2	0.6	0.9
Slovakia	1.1	85.6	0.1	0.1	11.0	NA	2.0

Source: Statisticka rocenka ceske a slovenske federativni republiky 1991, Praha: Statisticke a evid; encni vydavatelstvi tiskopisu, pp. 702–03.

minorities.[2] In terms of passivity, scholarly assessment has taken a more pejorative tone. Although Czechs did fight (and subsequently lost) the Battle of White Mountain in 1620 to maintain their independence from the Habsburgs, the general critique is that Czechs have been unwilling to act aggressively or passionately to defend their territory and interests. In short, Czechs and Slovaks may quarrel, but they do so without passion; they may fight, but they do so bloodlessly.

But if we juxtapose the demographic record with the cultural portrayal outlined above, one large paradoxical question looms: *How did the nation*

---

[2] Especially at the close of the First World War, historians generally agree that Czechoslovakia passed internal legislation above and beyond the existing international treaties as guarantees for minority rights.

portrayed as one of the most tolerant and impassionate in Europe end up with one of the most homogeneous populations on the continent? In asking this question, I counter traditional perspectives that implicitly define Czechoslovak culture and history as lacking violence or emotion. In particular, by examining the variation in forms of ethnic conflict within Czechoslovakia over time, I demonstrate how relations among and between ethnic groups there have been both violent and emotion laden. In this chapter, then, I illustrate how ethnic relations in Czechoslovakia have oscillated between tolerance, institutional discrimination, and outbursts of violence. Such an examination ultimately helps to explain the declining demographic diversity of the case.

Putting the Theory in Context: Some Introductory Comments

The application of the Fear/Hatred/Resentment/Rage hypotheses to the Czechoslovak case poses interesting challenges. First, as the following section will illustrate, the creation of explicit status hierarchies in this case is particularly difficult to define because the hierarchies have splintered and fused over time. For instance, until 1918 – and even somewhat after the close of WWI – the fact that the Czech lands and Slovakia were incorporated into different halves of the Austro-Hungarian Empire meant that there were two separate status hierarchies. These hierarchies coalesced until 1939, only to be split again under the control of Hitler. Thus, in the case at hand, it is not just the placement of ethnic groups on the hierarchy that shifts with each new political era, but also the very form of that hierarchy.

Structural Changes, Relevant Groups, and Variation in Action

With a few deviations, the history of the Czech and Slovak lands follows the periodization presented in the Introduction. The creation of status hierarchies occurred primarily under the period of Dual Rule – from 1867 to 1918 (Period One), an era of steady urbanization and improving literacy rates. As in the Baltic cases, rapid structural shocks first occurred with the end of the First World War (Period Two). The collapse of the Austro-Hungarian Empire – and the establishment of the First Republic in 1918 – in effect placed Germans and Hungarians in secondary status positions vis-à-vis Czechs and Slovaks. While the parliamentary democracy of the First Republic (Period Three) continued largely uninterrupted until the (puppet) independence of Slovakia in 1939, this event, the incorporation of the Czech lands into the Third Reich, and the ensuing war clearly present a second structural change. The third change occurs at the close of the Second World War (Period Four) with the Soviet "liberation" in 1948 (beginning Period Five). While the Soviet invasion of Prague twenty years later in 1968 would undoubtedly constitute a structural change in terms of Czechs and Slovaks, it did little to alter the relations between Czechs and Germans or Slovaks and Hungarians. Thus, the final structural shock to the Czechoslovak system is the removal of the communist government in the fall of 1989 (Period Six).

Within the broad contours of this structural progression, this chapter will examine both ethnic violence and the adoption of discriminatory institutions. Although almost all intergroup relations are discussed, the focus is the changing relationships among two sets of groups: (1) Germans and Czechs; and (2) Slovaks, Hungarians, and Czechs. For the former, the story is the long-term decline of Germans culminating in their expulsion in the aftermath of the Second World War. This story is not so straightforward – its twists and turns are used to generate variation for comparison of the emotion-based narratives. In the latter set, the key story is the slow rise of Slovaks ending in the formation of an independent nation-state in 1993. Again, this history provides interesting variation in target and timing. Both stories in combination work to answer the central puzzle of the chapter – what role have emotions played in the homogenization of the region?

The Emergence of Status Hierarchies: Ethnic Groups in the Czechoslovak Territories, 1848–1918

For two reasons, an understanding of the evolution of Czechoslovak politics and ethnic relations requires a brief examination of the incorporation of the Czechoslovak territories into the dual Austro-Hungarian monarchy. First, Czechs and Slovaks lived in different halves of the Austro-Hungarian Empire. The different experiences for Czechs and Slovaks, as well as Germans and Hungarians, during this period would leave an imprint on the emerging relationships between the national groups. Second, it was during this period of "Dual Rule" that perceptions of status hierarchies began to develop for each of the ethnic groups.

Beginnings of the Czech-German Puzzle

An examination of the development of status positions (and reactions to those positions) produces two simple questions regarding Czech-German relations that will be answered in subsequent sections. First, what accounts for the Czech tolerance of Germans (and other minorities) during the First Republic given their earlier subordination to Germans under imperial control? This tolerance stands in stark contrast to policies that arose in surrounding states during the period of nationalizing states (Period Three). Second, how can we explain the German atrocities toward Czechs in the late 1930s and early 1940s after they had been so well treated during the First Republic? While this first period appears relatively "quiet" in terms of ethnic conflict, I argue that the perceptions and emotions formed during this era had a dramatic impact on the nature of relations in successive time periods.

Although linked in some respects, the Austrian and Hungarian halves of the dual monarchy did not treat their minority subjects with the same degree of tolerance.[3] In contrast to the strict Magyarization policies to which the Slovaks were subjected, the Czechs under the Habsburgs were allowed some measure of local autonomy and a (small) voice in educational policy. For instance, although the region was under imperial control, Bohemia and Moravia were marked as independent administrative districts with the right and ability to make some municipal decisions. Seats on these councils were open for competition, and in the latter third of the century, Czechs were increasingly successful in winning seats to these local councils, as well as to the electoral curiae.[4] Moreover, in terms of local civil service positions, Czechs obtained more bureaucratic posts in Bohemia than Germans after the 1860s.

Language Rights and Administrative Posts   Although the Czechs were accorded some freedoms during part of the Habsburg reign, it is also undeniable that the Germans held a privileged position over Czechs in both political and economic terms. First, the ethnic distribution within the Habsburg Joint Army suggests a clear dominance by German speakers. As information in István Deák's book indicates, Czechs entered the Joint Army's military school in roughly equal numbers with German speakers:

---

[3] Owen Johnson, *Slovakia, 1918–1938: Education and the Making of a Nation* (New York: Columbia University Press, 1985); Kirschbaum, *A History of Slovakia* (New York: St. Martin's Press, 1985); Carol Skalnik Leff, *The Czech and Slovak Republics: Nation Versus State* (Boulder, CO: Westview Press, 1997); Hugh Seton-Watson, *Eastern Europe Between the Wars, 1918–1941* (New York: Harper & Row, 1967); Sharon Wolchik, *Czechoslovakia in Transition: Politics, Economics, & Society* (New York: Printer Publishers, 1991).

[4] Elizabeth Wiskemann, *Czechs and Germans* (London: Macmillan Press, 1967).

They formed 38.3% of the military student population compared to 36.9% for Germans.[5] But officer positions were overwhelmingly presented to the latter, with Germans holding almost 80% of the higher-level military positions and Czechs garnering fewer than 5.5%. Magyars, too, though comprising only 22% of the military school population, were rewarded in greater percentages than Czechs or Slovaks with officer positions, 7.6%. Slovaks held the smallest numbers of any ethnic group reported both in the military school population (0.0%) and in the distribution of officer positions (0.1%).

Furthermore, although German speakers were a minority within the Bohemian territory, they were a majority in terms of the larger Austrian empire:

There was no doubt that the Germans were the dominant nationality in the empire. . . . The designation of German as the basic language of administration and the requirement that instruction in the schools be in German afforded Germans an immense advantage [over other nationalities].[6]

Because German served as the language of "the army, the bureaucracy, the postal service, the railways, and of the overwhelming majority of industrial and commercial enterprises," Czechs were forced to both learn and function with German as their primary source of communication.[7] So, too, this implied that many Czechs needed to be educated in German schools so that they would receive appropriate training in the German language. Ultimately, this tactic of assimilation would become a tool of political survival for Czechs. Moreover, although Czechs held dominant political positions in Czech *local* government, Germans held a higher proportion of positions in the Viennese (Habsburg) administrative structure than Czechs. Of eighteen Ministers, thirteen were Germans and only one was a Czech; of the thirty-five secretaries of ministries, thirty were German and two were Czechs; of thirty-five vice secretaries of ministries, twenty-eight were

[5] István Deák, *Beyond Nationalism: A Social and Political History of the Habsburg Officer Corps, 1848–1918* (New York: Oxford University Press, 1990), p. 185. The data reported for Czechs includes all "Slav" nationalities – including Slovenes, Croats, and Serbs – although Czechs certainly formed the largest part of that group.
[6] Gregory Campbell, *Confrontation in Central Europe: Weimar Germany and Czechoslovakia* (Chicago: University of Chicago Press, 1975), p. 20.
[7] Jan Havrnek, "The Education of Czechs and Slovaks Under Foreign Domination, 1850–1918" in Janusz Tomiak et al., eds., *Comparative Studies on Governments and Non-Dominant Ethnic Groups in Europe, 1850–1940, Vol. I: Schooling, Educational Policy and Ethnic Identity* (New York: New York University Press, 1991), p. 244.

Table 9.3. *Median Rent per Household and Proportion of German Citizens in Ten Prague Census Wards in 1900 (the five richest and five poorest wards in Prague)*

District and Ward	Annual Rent (in crowns)	% German Citizens
1. Lower New Town, XXIV	790	24.0
2. Lower New Town, XXVI	705	29.8
3. Lower New Town, XXV	695	30.7
4. Upper New Town, XXIII	661	21.5
5. Vinohrady, X	656	27.8
6. Zizkov, VII	122	0.76
7. Zizkov, XI	118	0.79
8. Zizkov, IX	116	0.17
9. Smichov, VII	110	1.8
10. Smichov, IX	110	1.1

Source: Gary B. Cohen, *The Politics of Ethnic Survival: Germans in Prague* (Princeton, NJ: Princeton University Press, 1981), p. 114. Reprinted with permission of the author.

German and three were Czechs; of 295 positions in the Ministry of Finance, 224 were held by Germans and 24 by Czechs.[8] Thus, language concerns and poor representation in administrative positions overlapped: Lack of knowledge of the German language hindered the chances that a Czech would be selected for administrative service in the Viennese administrative structure in the first six decades of the nineteenth century.

Economic Status Economically speaking, Czech speakers tended to be less well off than German-speaking citizens through the turn of the century. If it is possible to extrapolate regional tendencies from relationships found in Prague, then it is clear that Germans living in Bohemia were to be found among the upper classes. As Table 9.3 indicates, Germans living in Prague tended to seek housing in the Old Town districts, historically a wealthy area in which to live, while avoiding the poorest areas of Prague, such as Smichov and ikov (historically an area in which Romany lived). Moreover, statistics outlining occupation by ethnicity indicate that by 1910, "German citizen residents of Prague and the inner suburbs as a whole had a significantly higher portion in the middle and upper economic strata than did the Czechs" (see

[8] See Elizabeth Wiskemann, *Czechs and Germans* (New York: St. Martin's Press, 1967), p. 62.

181

Table 9.3).[9] These facts suggest that German speakers were relatively well off vis-à-vis their Czech counterparts.

Land ownership also seemed to indicate that Czechs were being ill represented in the empire. In the last Austrian census before the turn of the century (1896), "peasant families in the Czech lands owned less than 300,000 hectares, approximately as much as was held there by only three noble families. Indeed, the 151 large landlords of the Czech lands, mostly German nobility, possessed nearly 1.5 million hectares."[10]

At least until the turn of the century, then, Germans living in Bohemia, Moravia, and Silesia found themselves in a privileged position vis-à-vis Czechs in both status and economic realms. This status differential, however, gradually weakened until the close of the war in 1918. For instance, the success of Czechs in obtaining local civil service positions mushroomed in the waning years of the empire; by the second year of the war, they held almost 90% of the civil service positions in Bohemia.[11] In addition, in the last two decades of the nineteenth century, half a million Czechs migrated to those areas previously dominated by Germans.[12] This migration affected the structure of relations between the two groups, so that

[b]y the end of the nineteenth century, the original social differentiation between a dominant German-speaking industrial and commercial bourgeois and a subordinate Czech lower middle class had largely disappeared in Bohemia, and survived only in some parts of Moravia and Silesia.[13]

These demographic changes, coupled with Czech victories in the local councils and electoral curiae, would have been effective in reducing the German dominance in Austrian and Bohemian politics. But in addition to

---

[9] Gary B. Cohen, *The Politics of Ethnic Survival: Germans in Prague* (Princeton, NJ: Princeton University Press, 1981), p. 121.

[10] Josef Anderle, "The First Republic, 1918–1938" in Hens Brisch and Ivan Volgyes, eds., *Czechoslovakia: The Heritage of Ages Past: Essays in memory of Josef Korbel* (Boulder, CO: East European Quarterly, 1979), p. 96.

[11] Campbell, *Confrontation in Central Europe* p. 22 and Wiskemann, *Czechs and Germans* pp. 61–62.

[12] Rogers Brubaker, "Aftermaths of Empire and the Unmixing of Peoples: Historical and Comparative Perspectives" *Ethnic and Racial Studies* 18(2) (1995): 189–218, see p. 195. Also see Campbell, *Confrontation in Central Europe*.

[13] Jiri Koralka, "Nationality Representation in Bohemia, Moravia, and Austrian Silesia, 1848–1914" in Geoffrey Alderman et al., eds., *Comparative Studies on Governments and Non-Dominant Ethnic Groups in Europe, 1850–1940, Vol. IV: Governments, Ethnic Groups and Political Representation* (New York: New York University Press, 1991).

these two factors, administrative revisions coming from the monarchs in Vienna added impetus to the declining position of Germans – and especially German liberals – in Bohemia and Austria.[14]

In the first half of the nineteenth century and through the Ausgleich, German-speaking inhabitants of the Czech lands were economically and politically better off than their Czech counterparts. However, as the First World War approached, Germans in the Czechoslovak territories were beginning to lose these advantaged positions. In terms of political office (both in Vienna and in Prague), German seats on administrative and electoral councils were lost to Czechs in a series of elections. So, too, because Czechs had become – out of necessity – more likely to be bilingual than Germans, they were increasingly chosen for bureaucratic positions in the imperial structure. In sum, the hierarchy that had given Germans dominance during the years of Austrian rule was beginning to be undermined on the eve of the new century.

Slovakia and Her Neighbors: The Slovak-Hungarian Puzzle

The Dual Compromise of 1867, which united the territories of the Austrian Empire with the "lands of the holy Hungarian crown," created a few joint Austro-Hungarian institutions and policies: a shared monarch; a common foreign affairs policy; a common defense policy; and a common finance ministry, which collected and distributed the budgets for defense and foreign affairs. But, on the whole, the two spheres of the empire retained separate social, economic, and political systems: "both halves of the empire had their own bicameral parliaments and separate domestic government, each with a prime minister at the head of a cabinet of ministers with individual portfolios . . . [and] their own territorial armies and autonomous financial administration."[15] Furthermore, the joint ministry was not permitted to intervene in the administration of policies of either government, unless the policies or acts emanated from common affairs. This unified-but-separate nature of the empire, then, meant that Slovaks were subject to the Hungarian Crown and its political tendencies. Those tendencies were much less liberal than the Austrian half, so Slovaks approached the First World War with a different set of political and economic experiences than their Czech counterparts. At the very least, the

[14] Cohen, *The Politics of Ethnic Survival* pp. 140–41.
[15] Jorg Hoensch, *A History of Modern Hungary* (New York: Longman Group, 1996), p. 17.

Table 9.4. *Nationality Distribution in the Hungarian Lands, 1867 (as percentage of the population)*

Hungarians	40.0
Germans	9.8
Slovaks	9.4
Rumanians	14.0
South Slavs	14.0
Ruthenes	2.3

Source: Jorg Hoensch, 1996, *A History of Modern Hungary*, New York: Longman Group, Ltd., p. 28.

numerical position of Slovaks within the Hungarian half of the Empire precluded an effective mobilization against the Crown (see Table 9.4).

Educational Policies and Language Rights

Several factors encouraged the development of Slovakia as an arm of Hungary, rather than as an independent territory or state. First, the mountainous structure of Slovakia facilitated a delineation along "the north-south direction and [restricted] east-west influences" and thus encouraged "its inclusion within old Hungary."[16] Furthermore, in the previous century transportation routes – notably the railways – were developed and built under Hungarian domination, lending a natural inclination for Slovakia to be more closely tied with Magyar policies and politics than with Austrian ones.[17] And, in contradiction to the Czech lands, Slovakia lacked independent administrative borders during this period. Instead, all matters within Slovakia, regardless of how minor, were ruled from Budapest and according to Hungarian policy. In short, although Slovakia was developing a national novement, which would counter Hungarian (and eventually, Czech) domination, it did not at this time have a viable, distinct political-territorial base from which to conduct the national movement.

Second, and even more important, as the "guardian" of Slovakia's future, Hungary was not nearly as generous in the formulation or application of minority rights as Austria. While Austria had been liberal in the

---

[16] Johnson, *Slovakia, 1918–1938* p. 17; C. A. Macartney, *Hungary and Her Successors: The Treaty of Trianon and its Consequences* (London: Oxford University Press, 1937).
[17] Johnson, *Slovakia, 1918–1938* p. 17.

design of its constitution and bill of rights, especially with regard to her national groups, the Hungarian half of the empire adopted much more conservative constitutional and electoral rights for minority groups. While this had permitted slight recognition of her national groups, Hungarian rulers "believed that neither collective rights for the nationalities nor the slightest degree of compromise on the question of administrative territorial independence were compatible with the idea of a Hungarian national state."[18] In short, the development of the Hungarian state overrode all concerns for any other state. To this end, a trio of Magyarization policies solidified the subordinate status position of Slovaks within Hungary: education, language laws, and censorship.[19]

In terms of the educational system, Magyar became a mandatory course for all students, even Slovak ones, while teachers at all state schools were required to learn (and teach in) Magyar. All three Slovak high schools were closed in the 1874–75 school year, and the number of Slovak elementary schools decreased from almost 2,000 in 1880 to 365 by the start of WWI.[20] The Elementary School Law of 1868 mandated schooling for all students between the ages of six and twelve and permitted instruction to continue in the language of the majority local population.[21] But the Magyar government increasingly believed that political assimilation would follow linguistic assimilation, and thus the regime forced the adoption of subsequent education laws (of 1879, 1883, and 1891), which all overrode the Minority Language Provision of 1868. Henceforth, students were compelled to learn Hungarian (and other classes *in* Hungarian) beginning in nursery school.[22]

One point that needs to be addressed is the fact that these Magyarization policies resulted in both a linguistic and demographic shift between 1867 and 1918. During this point in time, it became rational for Slovaks to adopt Hungarian as their citizenship and language, because there was no other way to obtain citizen or state rights. This "incentive" affected approximately 200,000 Slovaks:

---

[18] Hoensch, *A History of Modern Hungary* p. 30.
[19] Dia Lautenschlager, "Prior Regime Structure in Determining Nationalist Success – the Case of Slovak Independence," Paper presented at the 1994 Annual Meeting of the American Political Science Association, New York, September 1–4, 1994, p. 10.
[20] Lautenschlager, "Prior Regime Structure" p. 10; Macartney, *Hungary and Her Successors* p. 90.
[21] Hoensch, *A History of Modern Hungary* p. 30.   [22] Ibid.

Despite the pecking order imposed by Magyar national supremacy and the repression of the national minorities, Hungary offered reasonably good opportunities for development and a degree of security before the law to all the ethnic communities settled on its soil – provided they were prepared to respect the principle of the unity and indivisibility of the 'Hungarian political nation.'[23]

Thus, as many Slovak scholars have noted, it becomes very difficult to untangle statistical interpretations of nationality or language use during this period, since many Slovaks, *who would otherwise think of themselves as Slovak*, had assimilated into the Hungarian political culture as the only means for surviving. But what assimilation in this instance suggests, then, is that public identification as a Slovak – using the Slovak language or claiming Slovak citizenship – did not provide political or economic rewards. In fact, quite the opposite was true.

Censorship directed by Hungarian authorities toward Slovak cultural institutions and printed material further highlighted the status position of Slovaks under Austro-Hungarian rule. Founded in 1863 in Martin, Matica Slovenska was "devoted to raising the cultural level of the Slovak people."[24] It was first targeted by Hungarian authorities in 1875; once closed, its assets were taken over by Hungarian counterparts. After Matica Slovenska was closed, several other cultural institutions emerged in an attempt to fill the void, but none achieved the level of public recognition of Matica Slovenska. As for written Slovak material, however, in the form of newspapers and journals, the number of periodicals increased from eight to sixty-one in the last three decades before the outbreak of war.[25]

Administrative Powers

Compared to the Austrian government, the Hungarian crown retained a highly centralized political system, with county and local governments holding few powers.[26] For example, in the same year as the Compromise, the government passed regulations limiting the competencies of municipal councils, and by 1876 new civil service positions were created to supervise the compliance of national and county officials with the centralization policy.[27] In addition, non-Magyar nationalities were generally excluded from participation in government or suffrage – the Hungarian

---

[23] Ibid., pp. 35–36.   [24] Johnson, *Slovakia, 1918–1938* p. 37.
[25] Ibid., p. 38. Johnson relies on a survey taken by Matica Slovenska to reach these figures.
[26] Hoensch, *A History of Modern Hungary* p. 49.   [27] Ibid.

Table 9.5. *Distribution of Government Employees in Slovak Districts, 1874–1914*

(Language Spoken)	Magyar	German	Slovak
State Employees	1,733	32	2
County Employees	920	11	18
Municipal Employees	753	59	11
Public and District Notaries	1,080	20	33
Judges and Public Prosecutors	461	3	0
Lower Court Officials	805	13	10

Note: Macartney does acknowledge that statistics reporting this administrative ethnic distribution most likely refer to language spoken by the relevant person, rather than ethnic origin. Thus, while only two Slovak *speakers* held high-level state positions, additional ethnic Slovaks might have been classified under "Magyar" if they spoke the Magyar language.

Source: C. A. Macartney, 1937, *Hungary and Her Successors*, London: Oxford University Press, pp. 90–91.

parliamentary constitution concentrated on building a strong Magyar legislative body with little regard for the role of minorities in that legislature.[28] During this time, Slovaks were also increasingly successful at achieving places on town and city councils, as Czechs had been under Austrian rule, but they were less successful in winning seats to the parliament in Budapest. Three years later, the party reacted to these outcomes and adopted the strategy of not competing in the elections of 1881 at all. In addition, the party removed itself from Budapest "to settle quietly in Martin. Slovaks did not return to Hungarian political life until the 1896 campaign for Parliament, [and even then] not as the Slovak National Party."[29] Slovaks also held fewer than 10% of government/ministerial positions or university instructorships.[30] The figures in Table 9.5 are telling.

[28] Hans Kohn, *The Habsburg Empire, 1804–1918* (Princeton, NJ: Princeton University Press), p. 47.

[29] Johnson, *Slovakia, 1918–1938* p. 43.

[30] Bruce Pauley, *The Habsburg Legacy, 1867–1939* (New York: Holt, Rinehart, and Winston, 1972), p. 20.

Conclusions

There were several contradictory impulses affecting the course of Slovak status development from the nineteenth century through the First World War. On the one hand, Slovaks were increasing their political and national self-awareness, through the emergence of a distinct literary and liturgical language as developed by Ľudovit Stur. At the same time, although the Hungarian half of the monarchy closed many of the Slovak primary, secondary, and (all) university schools, the number of Slovak students attending these *levels* of education – albeit within Hungarian institutions – continued to increase throughout the years leading up to the First World War.[31] Similarly, the circulation of Slovak newspapers, journals, and books increased during the same period suggesting that "Slovak national awareness in Hungary was . . . increasing."[32] Finally, Slovaks were also beginning to hold an increasing number of important political positions, although only at the town level.[33]

These factors should not directly indicate that Slovakia was in any sort of privileged, or even satisfactory, position in the Hungarian half of the empire. Rather, as I have illustrated, counter to the emerging Slovak national movement was a set of influences that hindered a substantively strong and meaningful role for Slovaks within Hungary: few opportunities to speak Slovak, no chance for education in a distinctly Slovak institution, and no real political or economic power delegated to lower-level governmental institutions (where, ostensibly, Slovaks would be more likely to hold positions). What these competing factors suggest is that while Slovaks were undergoing assimilation at the hands of Hungary, they were becoming – as the twentieth century approached – increasingly aware of the possibility for Slovak nationhood.

The Interwar Years: Onset of Institutional Discrimination and Tolerance

The interwar period in Czechoslovak history presents two interesting facts. First, at the start of the period – essentially, with the close of the war

---

[31] Johnson, *Slovakia, 1918–1938* p. 16.   [32] Ibid.
[33] The extent to which these positions could be used to further Slovak national interests is not clear, since they did not have direct influence within the Hungarian political system.

and the signing of treaties to establish borders – the status hierarchies that had developed during Austro-Hungarian rule were reversed. The creation of the First Czechoslovak Republic in 1918 solidified a substantial shift in the alignment of power in the Czech lands. When Czechs claimed their dominance of parliamentary and ministerial positions in the new state, with a consequent adoption of Czech (rather than German) as the language of administrative and military function, Germans found themselves in a subordinate standing. Similarly, although it was much more difficult to do, Slovaks began to claim positions in the administrative and legislative system vis-à-vis Hungarians. Second, and unique to this case, after the reversal of status positions, it is generally recognized that Czechoslovakia did more for her minority ethnic groups than neighboring countries and more than was required under international law. Most historians claim, then, that what seems to be visible in the interwar years is tolerance rather than conflict.

Czechs and Germans

The collapse of the Austro-Hungarian Empire and the close of the war in 1918 solidified a change in the ethnic hierarchy between Czechs and Germans.

[T]he two groups had changed their political positions: that is, the Czechs having been non-dominant became dominant; the Germans having been dominant or, at least, having claimed a privileged status found themselves in the position of a non-dominant group.[34]

Moreover, even though the treatment and situation of German minority groups across the neighboring countries varied widely, it was still true that German minority groups held one thing in common: the loss of their previously dominant position in society and politics. Before 1914, Germans in Bohemia (as well as in Poland) "had been able to count themselves as members of the dominant national group, with all the resulting privileges and a corresponding conscious superiority, even if, in purely numerical terms, they were already a minority in their immediate

[34] Wolfgang Mitter, "German Schools in Czechoslovakia, 1918–1938" in Janusz Tomiak et al. eds., *Comparative Studies on Governments and Non-Dominant Ethnic Groups in Europe, 1850–1940, Vol. I: Schooling, Educational Policy and Ethnic Identity* (New York: New York University Press, 1991), p. 213.

Table 9.6. *Nationality of Citizens Living in the Czech Lands, 1921 and 1930 (in percentages)*

	1921	1930
Czechs	67.55	68.43
Slovaks	0.16	0.42
Germans	30.60	29.51
Hungarians	0.07	0.11

Source: Author's calculations from absolute numbers provided in *Scitani lidu v Republice Ceskoslovenske ze dne 15 unora 1921 (Dil 1)* and *Scitani lidu v Republice Ceskoslovenske ze dne 1 prosince 1930 (Dil 1)* as reported in Vladimir Srb, 1967, *Demograficka prirucka*, Praha: Nakladatelstvi svoboda, p. 45.

milieu."[35] Of course, after the Great War ended, this numerical minority (as outlined in Table 9.6) was translated into an institutionalized and realized minority *status*. Within the Czech lands, Germans were understandably not happy with this outcome, some stating overtly that "we were the first in Vienna and we do not want to take a back seat in Prague."[36] In short, "the Germans, reduced from the position of dominance to that of a minority, naturally resented the new setup."[37]

The Educational System, Language Rights, and Political Participation

The puzzle of Czech-German relations becomes even more compelling when one examines features of the First Republic. Although, as I will outline below, the wealthier Germans lost much of their landholdings under the First Republic, and although the German middle-class families had felt a relative decline in their economic standards (in relation to Czechs), the German social and political position in the Czech lands during this era was not as dire as in other countries. For instance, it is generally agreed that Czechoslovakia went much further than other post-

[35] Rudolf Jaworski, "The German Minorities in Poland and Czechoslovakia in the Interwar Period" in Paul Smith et al., eds., *Comparative Studies on Governments and Non-Dominant Ethnic Groups in Europe, 1850–1940, Vol. V: Ethnic Groups in International Relations* (New York: New York University Press, 1991), pp. 172–73.

[36] Karel Fremund and Vaclav Kral, *Lesson From History: Documents Concerning Nazi Policies for Germanisation and Extermination in Czechoslovakia* (Prague: Orbis, 1961), pp. 8–9.

[37] Robert Joseph Kerner, *Czechoslovakia* (Berkeley: University of California Press, 1945), p. 179.

empire countries in protecting minority rights. The Constitution of February 29, 1920, incorporated rights of national, religious, and racial minorities and Section VI "ensured full equality for all citizens and prohibited forced denationalization."[38] Moreover, as Seton-Watson has noted,

[a]s in the case of Poland, [Y]ugoslavia, and other reconstituted states which acquired territory from the enemy, Czechoslovakia was required by the Supreme Council to sign a special Minority Treaty. . . . But Czechoslovakia went a stage further, and simultaneous with her Constitution of 1920 adopted a Law of Nationalities which went considerably further than what was demanded of her. . . .[39]

Indeed, Germans living in Czechoslovakia were allowed to continue using German – especially at the local level – as a form of communication, they were allowed to form political parties and participate in the national government, and they reaped the benefits of a German educational system that remained fairly intact.[40]

In terms of language rights, the Language Law of February 29, 1920 declared Czechoslovak as the national language. However, there were provisions allowing the use of minority languages (as the *official* language) in districts where more than two thirds of the residents spoke that language (this affected approximately 2,225,000 Germans). Also, where more than 20% of the relevant population (but less than 66%) spoke the language, the minority language could be used in public instruction and official communications. In theory, then, affected citizens could use German, and officials would have to respond in German. Under all other conditions – namely, where less than 20% of the population spoke German – the citizens were forced to speak Czech. Only 130,000 Germans fell outside both parameters and were never allowed to speak German, except in private.[41]

With regard to education, the policies of the First Republic appear to have been especially lenient. For instance, the School Act of April 3, 1919, provided for the creation of German primary schools. This policy mandated that wherever the attendance of German children totaled more than

---

[38] Radomir Luza, *Transfer of the Sudeten Germans* (New York: New York University Press, 1964), p. 35.
[39] R. W. Seton-Watson, *A History of the Czechs and Slovaks* (Hamden, CT: Archon Books, 1965), p. 327.
[40] Mitter, "German Schools in Czechoslovakia, 1918–1938" p. 214.
[41] Radomir Luza, *Transfer of the Sudeten Germans* p. 36. The problem, of course, was that many more Czechs spoke German than vice versa (from the earlier links to Vienna). Thus, Germans had two years in which to learn Czech, or they would lose their local administrative jobs (Campbell, *Confrontation in Central Europe* p. 82).

Table 9.7. *Total Number of German Schools in the Czech Lands in the Interwar Years*

	1913–34[a]	1935–36[b]
Elementary Schools	2,407[c]	3,311
Higher Elementary Schools	258[c]	455
Secondary Schools	59	90
Specialist Schools	—	198
Technical Institutes	—	2
Universities	—	1
Other Schools	—	—

Note: [c] These numbers reflect private German schools as well: For basic elementary schools, there were seventy-three private German schools; of the higher elementary schools, sixteen were private.
Source: [a] Karl Gottfried Hugelmann, ed., 1934, *Das Nationalitatenrecht des alten Osterreich*, Vienna, as reported in Elizabeth Wiskemann, 1967, *Czechs and Germans*, London: Macmillan Press, p. 57.
[b] Radomir Luza, 1964, *The Transfer of the Sudeten Germans*, New York: New York University Press, p. 41.

forty, an elementary school was permitted to be formed. The outcome "provided the Germans with a higher percentage of national schools than they were entitled to proportionately," and in fact there were more schools per German students than had existed under the Habsburgs.[42] Table 9.7 illustrates the number of German schools at the onset of the First World War and in the middle of the interwar years.

In addition, during the First Republic, the number of German libraries increased from 458 with 282,255 volumes in 1920 to 3,570 libraries and over 2 million volumes in 1935. As one scholar remarks, "[e]ducation is perhaps the most important part of national culture, and there is ample evidence that the German educational system in the Republic was one of the most liberal and advanced in Europe and ensured the Germans free cultural development."[43]

Institutional Discrimination: Land and Industrial Reform Why did Germans perceive a reduction in status? Given that social and political indicators suggested that Germans were relatively well treated under the

[42] Radomir Luza, *Transfer of the Sudeten Germans* pp. 40–41.   [43] Ibid., p. 42.

First Republic, what other indicators might bolster the claim that they were, in fact, losing ground to Czechs? To begin, one of the first acts of the provisional parliament in the new Czechoslovak Republic was to reverse the underrepresentation of Czechs and Slovaks in landholdings. In late fall of 1918, the National Assembly seized all large estates for the sole purpose of carrying out a large-scale land reform. The Land Reform of 1919 "limited large estates to 150 hectares of arable land . . . and marked the released land (almost 32% of all land) for distribution among the [Czech] peasants . . . although some of the land was nationalized and operated by the state."[44] Compensation for the seized land was to be provided to previous owners, although members of the Habsburg family and all "citizens of an enemy state" were exempted from this compensation. Compensation was also not provided in equitable terms; owners were paid in Czechoslovak crowns, although at less than one sixth the market value of the property.

So, too, reform was carried out in the fields of industry and commerce. These amendments proceeded in a more piecemeal fashion than the land reform, and they included several types of reform, such as working hours and conditions, insurance, training, and unemployment support. But it was ownership control over the enterprises that affected the relationship between Czechs and Germans. To begin, many of the utilities and "essential services" were nationalized and run by the new Czechoslovak state. Railways, the telephone system, and postal services were taken over by the national government, while local utilities were to be managed at the municipal level. Private ownership was retained for the remainder of companies, but any enterprise owned by foreigners (and the majority of those "foreigners" were German) was forced to pass control to citizens or companies of Czechoslovak ethnicity.[45]

Conclusions Thus, by all accounts, and as described by Czech and German historians alike, minority policies in the interwar Czechoslovakia were more tolerant than those of other countries during the same time period. Why, then, were the Germans so unhappy with their lot in a "tolerant" Czechoslovakia? There are two answers to this question. First, even if these institutional forms of discrimination were relatively lax, it is nonetheless true that some German schools were closed that had been

---

[44] Anderle, "The First Republic" p. 97.   [45] Ibid., p. 97.

open under the Habsburgs; that Germans had to learn (many for the first time) how to speak Czech; and that the economic superiority of the Germans dwindled during this era, in particular during the world economic crises throughout the 1920s. Regardless of the intentions of the Czech policymakers, in the wake of ethnic unmixing with the collapse of the empire, the German minorities perceived these policies as both "systematically favouring Czechs in economic and cultural matters and aimed at weakening the ethnodemographic position of Germans."[46] From the *German* point of view, then, these policies were not perceived as tolerant.

But second, and more important, these institutional policies also gave German-speaking citizens information about their new status. In essence, the primary point of interest for the Germans was not the degree or content of discrimination in the language or educational policies; what mattered was the fact that they were subject to the policies in the first place. While it certainly is important that the Germans interpreted the policies as discriminatory, rather than liberal, it is also important that they perceived and resented the presence of any policies directed at them rather than from them.

Slovaks and Hungarians

As with the case of the Czech lands, Slovakia, too, experienced a dramatic reversal of powers with the creation of the First Czechoslovak Republic in 1918. Formerly at the mercy of the Hungarian half of the dual monarchy, Slovaks found themselves in a new and privileged position:

[i]t was not . . . until June 4, 1920, that the Treaty of Trianon stabilized the situation along the Slovak-Hungarian frontier and the long delay, . . . did much to exacerbate the relations of two peoples who had so dramatically changed places as upper and under dog.[47]

As a new minority within the Czechoslovak state, then, Hungarians enjoyed many of the same rights as Germans, particularly in language and educational terms. However, due to their smaller numbers, Hungarians were less likely to be able to take advantage of these rights (see Table 9.8). Because the Language Law granted rights based on numerical percentages

---

[46] Brubaker, "Aftermaths of Empire and the Unmixing of Peoples" p. 200.
[47] Seton-Watson, *A History of the Czechs and Slovaks* p. 324.

194

Table 9.8. *Nationality of Citizens Living in Slovakia,*
1921 and 1930 (in percentages)

	1921	1930
Czechs	2.40	3.66
Slovaks	65.07	67.70
Germans	4.86	4.70
Hungarians	21.68	17.61

Source: Author's calculations from absolute numbers provided in
Scitani lidu v Republice Ceskoslovenske ze dne 15 unora 1921 (Dil 1)
and *Scitani lidu v Republice Ceskoslovenske ze dne 1 prosince 1930*
(Dil 1) as reported in Vladimir Srb, 1967, *Demograficka prirucka,*
Praha: Nakladatelstvi svoboda, p. 46.

within given communities, Hungarians were not of sufficient number in
many communities to be able to speak their native tongue. Furthermore,
the Hungarian attempts to overtake parts of Slovakia in 1919 (which were
subsequently thwarted with the help of the Czech army) indicated an
unwillingness to see their status demoted to a secondary tier.

Although there was some initial armed conflict between the two groups,
as the Slovaks pushed the Hungarian army out of Slovakia, the situation
remained stable and similar to the German case throughout the interwar
era. Moreover, the position of Hungarians within the Republic seems to
have been somewhat beneath that of the Germans, since their smaller
numbers precluded them from enjoying educational and language rights to
the same degree as German speakers. At least one historian concurs with
this point of view, by arguing that Germans were incorporated into the
army and the civil service much more so than Hungarians, and they were
given a German university, while Hungarian higher education was nonexistent.[48] And yet, there was no systematic violent discrimination against
Hungarians between the two wars. This treatment of Hungarians in
Slovakia is notable when considered against their treatment after WWII.

Czechs and Slovaks

During the course of the First Republic, the Slovaks came to feel the same
way toward the Czechs as they had about Hungarians. Staffing in the

---

[48] Kalman Janics, *Czechoslovak Policy and the Hungarian Minority, 1945–1948* (New York:
Columbia University Press, 1982), p. 61.

administration, the designation of "Czechoslovak" as the official language (although no such language existed), and other matters of investment and pay provided sources for negative comparisons for the Slovaks, especially since the Slovaks had been promised equality in the new state.[49] In essence, although Slovaks were to be considered part of the majority group within the new Czechoslovakia, they were treated as if they were a minority group.

For example, at the close of the First World War, Hungarian administrators and Slovaks who had sympathized with the Hungarians were removed from their regional posts and forbidden to serve in the new government. In addition, Magyarization policies had produced only a very small intelligentsia in Slovakia, so that there was a shortage of available people for these positions. Moreover, the few Czechs who had served in the Vienna administration found few job possibilities when they came back to Prague, and thus the result was that many Czechs took over the positions in Bratislava.[50] While it has been debated whether Czechs came to serve in these positions for their own benefit or for altruistic reasons (to prevent Magyars from disrupting the new Slovak regime), it is acknowledged by both sides that Czechs filled these positions in substantial numbers, and their expected departure – to be replaced with native Slovaks – never occurred.[51]

Adding to the frustration over the lack of Slovak participation in regional administration was the discrepancy in employment opportunities in nonadministrative positions. The following data obtained from the 1925 Directorate of Railroads in Bratislava and Kosice illustrates that there was a clear delineation in labor structure within Slovakia:

of 5,134 engineers, 90% were Czech
of 12,355 "subordinate agents," 60% were Czech
of 16,025 manual workers, 30% were Czech

It is apparent that Slovaks held the lower-paying positions and lower-status jobs. Moreover, one historian has argued that "the Slovak peasantry rarely rose above the conditions of serfdom, (because) commerce and industry were overwhelmingly in Hungarian hands. Even after the establishment

---

[49] Leff, *The Czech and Slovak Republics*; Wolchik, *Czechoslovakia in Transition.*
[50] Katherine Day Wyatt and Joseph Mikus, *Slovakia, A Political History: 1918–1950* (Milwaukee: Marquette University Press, 1963).
[51] Seton-Watson, *A History of the Czechs and Slovaks*; Wyatt and Mikus, *Slovakia.*

of Czechoslovakia in 1918 this distribution of wealth and power changed little and then largely for the benefit of the Czech element."[52] Wyatt and Míkus echo this point by claiming that the continuous economic inequality between Czechs and Slovaks was neither the consequence of previous Magyarization policies nor the result of different topographical features between the two entities. Rather, the inequality in economic terms resulted from a "policy of pauperism" originating from Prague.[53]

Another measure of status for Slovaks within the new state, their role in central government, also indicated a disadvantaged position. Even twenty years after the close of the First World War, Slovaks were still poorly represented in the central administrative structure. At this time, the Slovaks represented 23% of the Czechoslovak population, and yet they held 1.7% of the total central administrative positions. According to Wyatt and Míkus, by 1939 Slovaks held only 60 of the 3,265 positions available in the ministries of the Czechoslovak state.[54] Similarly, out of the 224 parliamentary positions, only 1 Slovak was represented; only 3 of the possible 96 chief of state positions were staffed by Slovaks. In fact, in every administrative department – from post offices to agriculture, and from finance to public health – Slovaks held fewer than 12% of the total number of positions. And in all but 3 departments, they formed less than 5% of the available positions.[55]

Finally, the government in Prague created a special compensation figure, *slovenska vyhoda* (Slovak allowance), for those Czech civil servants located in Slovakia. The compensation provided them with residence and travel bonuses, and it created a situation whereby a "Slovak official of the 9th class earned 7,450 crowns, while his Czech colleague received 24,117 crowns for exactly the same work."[56] Finally, Czech civil servants got 30 crowns for each day they traveled or stayed in Slovakia (not actually living there), while Slovak civil servants traveling to Prague received nothing.

[52] Eric Roman, *Hungary and the Victor Powers, 1945–1950* (New York: St. Martin's Press, 1996), p. 102

[53] Wyatt and Míkus, *Slovakia* p. 34

[54] Katherine Wyatt and Joseph Míkus, *Slovakia, A Political History: 1918–1950*, (Milwaukee: Marquette University Press, 1963) pp. 38–39.

[55] The three exceptions were the ministry of justice, the ministry of unification (of which they still held only 11% of the total positions), and the presidency council.

[56] Wyatt and Míkus, *Slovakia* p. 36.

The Protectorate, the Slovak Republic, and the Second World War

For the young Czechoslovak state, several stunning structural changes occurred with the rise and expansion of the Nazi empire. First, under the guidelines of the 1938 Munich agreement, Germany directly incorporated a large portion of Czechoslovakia. Second, six months later, Hitler presented an ultimatum to the Slovaks: The Slovaks could become an independent, but subservient, state, or they could be thrashed by the German military. The Slovaks, under the leadership of Jozef Tiso, declared an independent Slovak Republic on March 14, 1939. The next day, the Germans occupied the western Czech provinces and set up the Protectorate of Bohemia and Moravia. Czechoslovakia ceased to exist. The event created new power relations and status reversals.

The Slovak Republic and its Aftermath

In 1944, 80,000 Slovaks would rise up against the Nazi occupation. In the meantime, however, the Slovak Republic commanded considerable support. Although the Slovak Republic's leadership had to act within the bounds set up by the Germans, it did have some leeway to act. Although seldom discussed, the new Slovak state did take action to redress the position of Czechs. Over 100,000 Czechs were expelled from Slovakia after the declaration of Slovak independence in 1939. On March 14, 1939, the Slovak Minister of the Interior ordered the expulsion of all Czech nationals from Slovakia ". . . as soon as possible, above all civil servants, while their property should be retained."[57] Thus Slovaks did quickly reorder the status hierarchy through removal of Czechs from positions of visible authority.

For two clear reasons, there would be no action against Hungarians during the war. First, most of the Hungarian-populated lands of Slovakia were ceded to Hungary in the Vienna Conference of 1938. This act gave over 10,000 square kilometers of land and 850,000 people (including 275,000 Slovaks) to Hungary.[58] With this redrawing of borders, the possibility of Hungarian dominance was eliminated. Second, given Germany's close relationship with Hungary, the Slovaks knew that actions against Hungarians would be restrained.

---

[57] Janics, *Czechoslovak Policy and the Hungarian Minority, 1945–1948* p. 48.
[58] Wyatt and Míkus, *Slovakia* p. 72.

With the end of the war, Czechoslovakia was reconstituted with its orig-inal borders. At one point, a small delegation of Czech and Slovak politi-cians arrived in Moscow to seek permission from Stalin to deport the remaining Germans and Hungarians from Czechoslovak territories. Accordingly, Stalin either agreed to or explicitly ordered the expulsion of two-thirds of the German and Hungarian populations; these numbers indicated an expulsion of two million Germans and 400,000 Hungarians.[59]

A few weeks later, Klement Gottwald made the intention to "solve" the minority problem through radical measures clear in his speech in Kosice, as did the Kosice Plan itself:

(1) Only those residents of Hungarian nationality will retain Czechoslovak citi-zenship who were anti-Fascist or who participated in the resistance movement for the liberation of Czechoslovakia or who were persecuted for their loyalty to the republic; (2) the Czechoslovak citizenship of all other Hungarian residents is with-drawn . . . ; (3) those persons of Hungarian nationality who have committed a crime against the republic . . . will be placed before a tribunal, deprived of their citizenship and forever expelled from the territory of the republic.

Thus, it was only at the close of the Second World War in 1945 that ". . . the Slovaks (would) at last have an opportunity to become dominant in their own country; their first agenda item was the purging of the Hungarian minority that once ruled them."[60] And purge they did through a series of decrees and legislative actions, which were aimed at removing Hungarians from Slovakia:

On May 25, 1945, all state employees of Hungarian nationality were dismissed without any right of compensation; the pensions of those who had retired were cut off. The Hungarian language was banned from official intercourse, even in the purely Hungarian parts of Slovakia. No telegram or even letter in the Hungarian language was delivered by the postal service. A decree of June 22 confiscated all landed property of 50 hectares or more owned by Hungarians; another one of July 22 sequestered all the cash and valuables kept by Hungarians in banks. A still later decree made all Hungarians who lost their citizenship liable to forced labor for reconstruction.[61]

No doubt some revenge motives against Hungarian collaborators were involved here, but the sweep of the legislation goes beyond revenge.

Finally, the postwar Slovak-German relationship should be mentioned. In stark contrast to the Czech lands, Slovaks committed no massive

---

[59] Roman, *Hungary and the Victor Powers, 1945–1950* p. 53.
[60] Ibid., p. 102. [61] Ibid., p. 104.

violence against the German population. The revolt of 1944 was politically oriented. On the whole, Slovaks were not obsessed with a "German problem" after the war.

Czechs and Germans

With the rise of Nazism and Hitler's incorporation of the Czech lands into the Third Reich on March 15, 1939, and the creation of the Protectorate, Germans were once again the dominant group in the region. Over 700,000 Czechs became subjects of Hitler and over 150,000 hectares were passed from Czech and Jewish hands to Sudeten Germans.[62] More barbaric were the numbers of Czechs killed in concentration camps – 300,000 – or deported to Germany – 600,000. So, too, in marked contrast to the Czech efforts to maintain a German educational system, the Germans ". . . closed all universities, executed the student leaders without sentencing them and sent 1,200 students to concentration camps."[63] In addition, two Czech villages, Lidice and Lezaky, were completely destroyed. All males were massacred, women and children were sent to concentration camps, and the villages themselves were set on fire and allowed to burn completely to the ground. This was supposedly in retaliation for the assassination of Heydrich.[64]

As the German armies retreated, Czechs went on a violent rampage against the German population in a number of localities. This violence was brutal, indiscriminate, and aimed to humiliate. As Norman Naimark sums up the actions of Czech militias:

These armed fighters drew few distinctions between anti-fascist Germans, plain farmers, or Henleinist sympathizers. In a paroxysm of violence that shocked even experienced Soviet tank commanders and political officers, Czechs beat up Germans, shot at them, forced them to do humiliating and life-threatening tasks and showed them no mercy. People were randomly killed, and villages were torched and burned to the ground. Germans were hung by their heels from trees, doused in petrol, and set on fire.[65]

---

[62] Elizabeth Wiskemann, *Germany's Eastern Neighbours: Problems Relating to the Oder-Neisse Line and the Czech Frontier Regions* (London: Oxford University Press, 1956), p. 51.

[63] Fremund and Kral, *Lesson From History* p. 15.

[64] Ibid., p. 17.

[65] Norman Naimark, *Fires of Hatred: Ethnic Cleansing in Twentieth Century Europe* (Cambridge, MA: Harvard University Press, 2001), p. 115.

One of the most famous incidents occurred at Usti nad Labem on July 31, 1945. After an explosion at a nearby factory, Czechs, suspecting sabotage, killed hundreds, if not thousands, of local Germans.[66] Women and children were thrown from a bridge.[67] On May 30, Czechs had attacked the German population of Brno, driving 30,000 out of their homes and beating them on their way to internment camps.[68] These actions were called "wildcat expulsions" because they were not grounded in any formal protocol or procedure. During the wildcat transfers, "mob action, beatings, lynchings, rapes, and general mistreatment on a large scale" forced more than three quarters of a million Germans to "flee their homes and farms often under appalling circumstances, and often with less than one hour's notice."[69]

Parallel to these evacuations were internments, which began the process of deportation for Germans or sent them to the interior as forced labor. Eventually, more formally recognized and sanctioned policies were established. On May 17, 1945, food rations to Germans were decreased to the amount that had been allotted to Jews during the Nazi occupation. German behavior was also severely restricted: They were forced to wear pieces of cloth on their arms that identified them as German; they had shopping curfews; and they were not permitted to ride on public buses.[70] In June of 1945, all German schools were closed, and property of the Sudeten Germans was seized without compensation. In addition, any German who had obtained citizenship of the Reich was stripped of his Czechoslovak citizenship, with little chance for regaining it.

Finally, in late August 1945, the steps for deportation began. Over one hundred camps were constructed for the majority of the expelled population, and the Czechoslovak army shipped 1,200 individuals per day into the hands of the allied authorities.[71] The Allied Control Council approved the transfer of 2.5 million Germans from Czechoslovakia in November, and with this approval the formal expulsions began on January 25, 1946. In this manner, the German problem would be solved.

---

[66] As in most such cases, the estimates exhibit a considerable range. See Ibid., p. 116.

[67] Alfred-Maurice de Zayas, *A Terrible Revenge: The Ethnic Cleansing of the East European Germans, 1944–1950* (New York: St. Martin's Press, 1986), p. 87. It should be noted that a plaque was placed on the Usti bridge in 1990 in remembrance of the victims of this massacre.

[68] Ibid., p. 86; also see Naimark, *Fires of Hatred* p. 119, and Ronald Smelser, "The Expulsion of the Sudeten Germans, 1945–1952" *Nationalities Papers* 24 (1996): 87.

[69] Smelser, "The Expulsion of the Sudeten Germans, 1945–1952" p. 86.

[70] Ibid., p. 87.   [71] Ibid.

Events in the Post-Communist Era

Although the German question was answered by elimination, the structural collapse of Communism has produced another round in the relationships among Slovaks and Hungarians. Since the collapse of the communist regime in November 1989, relations between and among Czechoslovakia's ethnic groups have once again been altered. Although the placement of Czechs, Germans, or Hungarians on the status hierarchy has not shifted since this point in time, the position of Slovaks has changed. With the division of the country into two separate and independent states on January 1, 1993, Slovaks gained a new position on their own hierarchy.

In contrast to generally dwindling Czech-German tensions, relations between Slovaks and Hungarians again turned conflictual with the collapse of Communism in 1989. The situation became dramatically worse after the dissolution of the Czech and Slovak Federal Republic (CSFR) on January 1, 1993, when Slovakia emerged as an independent state. The emergence of an independent Slovakia forced Hungarians into a new position: As a significant minority group within the former Czechoslovakia, Hungarians were – overnight – cast into the position of being the largest and most visible minority within the new Slovakia. As part of the old CSFR, Hungarians had been but a small percentage of the total population. But within a smaller Slovakia, Hungarians were and are a significantly greater percentage of the population. Thus, while their absolute numbers did not change on January 1, 1993, the relative numerical presence of Hungarians did change.

The change has not been without discrimination. Although Articles 33 and 34 of the Slovak Constitution give members of ethnic minorities "a guaranteed right to develop their own culture, of transmitting and receiving information in their mother tongue, of associating in ethnic associations, and to form and maintain educational and cultural institutions," these rights have not held up in practice. The Act on the State Language (1995) provided the first counter to these constitutional ideals, by declaring Slovak the official state language. The language act was approved by all parliamentary parties except the Hungarian Coalition – and the KDU, which abstained from voting – and declared that Slovak be used "in all spheres of life." This mandate of the act reversed an earlier law that had permitted minority languages to be used in official communication. Sanctions for violating the new law exist; violators will be fined by the

Ministry of Culture. The law has provoked more violent actions by Slovaks as well; since the campaign to adopt Slovak as the national language first emerged in the summer of 1990, Hungarian billboards and road signs were taken down or destroyed in the comingled areas of the state.

Summary and Assessment

Czechs and Germans

The history of Czech-German ethnic relations can be briefly summarized. Under the direction and control of the Austrian half of the Austro-Hungarian Empire, awareness of ethnicity rose in relatively tolerant circumstances. In the period preceding the First World War Czechs made some gains in both status and economics. In the newly formed Czechoslovakian state, Czechs established themselves as first among equals, but Germans suffered little of the outright discrimination witnessed by minorities in surrounding states. Despite the tolerance of the interwar Czechoslovak Republic, significant numbers of Germans did not come to terms with their new position and collaborated with the Germans after their occupation and annexation of the Sudetenland. As Smelser concludes, "from the Czech point of view, a sizable number of Sudeten Germans had either collaborated with, or passively accepted and profited from, the destruction of the first Czechoslovak Republic at the hands of the Hitler regime with its racist and pan-German ideology."[72] With the war's end, Czechs formed mobs and viciously attacked the German minority. With popular support, Czechs publicly humiliated the German population in a variety of ways. Finally, the regime engaged in massive deportation of its German citizens.

Is the emotions-based approach useful in understanding this sequence of events? Were there instances in which mass-based processes created a crystallization of ethnic identities and motivated one group to specifically target another for violence or discrimination? Clearly, Czech actions in the aftermath of the Second World War cannot be understood without reference to mass emotion. However, mass attitudes or emotions also lie at the base of two other puzzles in the progression of Czech-German relations: (1) What accounts for the tolerance of interwar Czech policies? Why so little action, in comparison with the Baltic states or Poland, in seeking

---

[72] Smelser, "The Expulsion of the Sudeten Germans, 1945–1952" p. 79.

clear Czech dominance? and (2) What accounts for the persistence of the German pursuit of dominance and their willingness to use violent and institutional means to regain a top position?

Fear has little explanatory power. It obviously cannot explain German actions against Czechs in the late 1930s and early 1940s. After annexation, Germans could not rationally anticipate any attack from the powerless Czech population. Nor is Fear relevant to Czech attacks against Germans in the immediate postwar period. With Western occupation and the defeat of the German war machine, Czechs no longer faced any physical threat from the German population. Hatred has little explanatory power. For the Czech-German relationship, no clear historical schema exists. Under Austro-Hungarian rule, Germans treated Czechs relatively well. Under interwar Czechoslovak rule, Germans also lived peacefully. The German actions against Czechs in the Nazi period, and the Czech actions against Germans in the war's aftermath, were deviations from the nature of previous interactions rather than any ritualized imitation of them.

Rage fits the Czech attacks against Germans in the postwar era. Rage sees a general or cumulative frustration leading to a general desire to lash out. The target of this lashing out can be either direct or substitute. The justification for the action need not be logical, it is committing the violence itself, and gaining some catharsis, that is essential. The Czech attacks at Usti nad Labem fit this narrative. Nazi rule involved a legion of various frustrations – economic, social, cultural. The emotion of Rage heightens a desire to lash out, but under German rule constraints force individuals to hold in their emotion. As the Germans leave, one more frustration occurs – an explosion at the local cable work. Although there is no evidence of sabotage, the belief quickly forms that the Germans are responsible. Germans are found. It does not matter that some are women and children, the desire to lash out against a target is too strong to let this inconvenient fact get in the way.

In this particular case, the violence seems to have possessed little of the symbolism of Resentment. It was the violence itself that was important, not putting the Germans in their place. In other incidents and policies in the Czech regions, the paths of Resentment and Rage appear to have intertwined to some extent. In a clear act of reversal, Germans were often forced to endure many of the same humiliations that they had previously inflicted on others. Yet, in the immediate days following the war, Czechs clearly aimed to go beyond humiliation and eliminate Germans once and for all. There was something wrong with Germans as a group in almost an innate sense. In the words of Jan Masaryk, "We are finished with the Germans in Czechoslovakia."

While Resentment may not fit Czech behavior, it does provide a good predictive and descriptive fit for German behavior. Resentment predicts that status reversals create the highest intensities of emotion. A structural change creates information that one's group is no longer in the dominant position. One's language is no longer the language of government; one needs to deal with members of other ethnic groups in positions of authority. Status concerns rise to the top of one's consciousness. A desire to regain a dominant status becomes a low-level obsession. When the possibility arises, compulsions to act on this desire drive violent actions or support for institutional discrimination. This story explains the German attitude toward the tolerant interwar regime. Resentment holds that humans can be motivated as much by status concerns, especially the loss of dominance, as by outright discrimination. Germans may have lived well in the interwar period, but individuals care about more than living well in absolute terms; relative status can drive behavior. Resentment helps explain local German support and participation after the Nazi annexation. The seizure of Czech lands was the first structural change since the status reversal after the collapse of empire in 1918; thus, it was the first opportunity for the Germans to reorder what they considered an unjust ethnic hierarchy. In addition, this analysis explains the reason for targeting Czechs more than Slovaks; Czechs were the only ethnic group that could be targeted by the Germans to reduce resentment.

This analysis begs comparison with the actions of German Balts. In the Baltic case, Germans slowly faded from dominance without a bitter struggle; in the Sudeten case, Germans continued to be a prominent force and appeared to wait for their chance to regain a dominant position. Recall the reaction of German Balts in the wake of the 1905 Revolution. As quoted, one German aristocrat returned to his burned estate "as a mere stranger, walking amidst the servants, still living untroubled on my estate, who watched me with mocking expressions."[73] The Sudeten Germans did not experience any such stark event that made them recalculate their social position. In this respect, Czech tolerance could perhaps be seen as counterproductive. Had the Czechs publically and vividly "put the Germans in their place," perhaps Germans would have come to accept a lower status

---

[73] John Hiden and Patrick Salmon, *The Baltic Nations and Europe: Estonia, Latvia, and Lithuania in the Twentieth Century* (London: Longman, 1994), p. 21.

position or would have left the new country. One could argue that violence and humiliation at least have the power to clarify social relations among peoples. In this particular case, such an argument would hold little power, however. Unlike the Baltic Germans, the Sudeten Germans formed a large, concentrated, and diverse population living across the border from their colinguists. Their position was more analogous to Russians in the post-Communist Baltic states. In both of these cases, the presence of a large powerful nation of ethnic brethren directly across the border changes the rules and alters the possibilities for reorienting group status relations.

The relevance of an emotions-based approach in explaining Czech behavior is not clear. Why didn't the Czechs more vigorously pursue clear dominance over other groups in the same fashion as the Lithuanians, or the Poles? Several factors come to mind: reciprocation for the relatively tolerant policies of the Austrian half of the Austro-Hungarian Empire, the personal influence and democratic ideology of Masaryk, the new state's geographic proximity and vulnerability to Germany. A host of relevant influences are at work here; emotions help explain the brutal actions of the Czechs after the frustrations of the war, but they are not the key to every puzzle.

Slovaks

The Slovak progression can be summarized as follows. A largely rural and underdeveloped people, Slovaks suffered complete subordination under the relatively harsh administration of the Hungarian half of the empire. In the interwar era, by all indicators the Slovaks continued to occupy a lower rung in the ethnic hierarchy of the new Czechoslovakian state. The Second World War provided the first opportunity for the Slovaks to establish their own state – and their own position of dominance. They did not let this opportunity go by. The Slovak puppet state immediately expelled 100,000 Czechs, specifically Czech civil servants. Hungary took care of the position of ethnic Hungarians in Slovakia through annexation. While the Slovak Republic's brief life ended with the demise of the Nazis, Slovaks were able to act against Hungarians in a variety of ways in the immediate postwar era. With the end of Communism and the breakup of Czechoslovakia a new Slovak state arose. Secession solved the Czech problem, but the Hungarians remained as a sizable minority. The Slovaks, through a series of language measures, once again sought clear status dominance.

Again, Fear has little relevance to this history. The Slovaks have not faced any serious physical threat. Rage also has little clear connection to the above progression; Slovaks have not gone on rampages against minorities. While historical antipathy toward Hungarians may exist, it is difficult to identify a historical schema that has created specific roles that guide action. The late development of Slovak national and ethnic consciousness also argues against Hatred schemas. Again, the story possessing the best overall fit is Resentment. Slovaks have sought status dominance when structural changes – the birth of the Slovak Republic, the end of the war and the reconstitution of Czechoslovakia, and the collapse of Communism – have allowed it. In all these instances, Slovaks have directed their actions toward the most relevant status target. In the Second World War, with Hungarians removed through territorial changes, Slovaks expelled 100,000 Czechs. In the post-Communist era, with Czechs removed through partition, the Slovaks engaged in restrictive language laws aimed toward Hungarians.

Like the Baltic cases, ethnic relations in the territories that formed Czechoslovakia have exhibited a great deal of variation. Some single events must be explained by idiosyncratic features of the area's history. However, the overall pattern contains features similar to the Baltic. Fear and "ancient hatred" would appear to have little relevance for either region. In both cases, Resentment provides an explanation of some puzzling targeting patterns. Resentment gives an answer to the general orientations and behaviors of Slovaks and Germans. If the Czechs are different, that fact might stem more from their development and geography rather than from their national character or lack of passion. Czechs exhibited their capacity for brutality and humiliation in the immediate postwar period.

In the end, a variety of actions were at play in the region – discrimination, deportation, partition, and genocide. But Resentment motivated individuals to participate in many of these actions. Resentment, combined with the Nazis' helping hand, helped create the homogeneous states that replaced one of the most heterogeneous states in Europe.

10

<hr style="height:4px; background:black;">

Yugoslavia

Twentieth century Eastern Europe has produced a multitude of cases of ethnic violence. Perhaps no case illustrates and examines the basic points of this project better than the collapse of Yugoslavia in the late 1980s and early 1990s. The bloody conflicts resulting from Yugoslavia's demise direct themselves toward both the micro and macro dimensions of this study.

First, there is the phenomenon of the essentialization of identities. Yugoslavia was a modern, complex society in social and economic realms. Ethnicity was only one of several forms of identification and often not the most important. Yet, as mentioned in the introductory chapter, neighbors often came to reduce each other to "enemy." Recall the quoted passage of Bringa from the first chapter: "the familiar person next door had been made into a depersonalized alien, a member of the enemy ranks." In 1989, the leading political science journal, *American Political Science Review*, published an article by Steven Burg and Michael Berbaum based on survey research. Focusing on the increasing numbers of those declaring themselves as "Yugoslav" on census forms, rather than some specific nationality, the authors, with some important qualifications, came to the following conclusion: "These findings support an interpretation of Yugoslav identity as evidence of diffuse support for the existence of a shared political community."[1] This shared political community would be violently ripped apart only two years later, replaced by homogenized nations.

[1] From the abstract of Steven L. Burg and Michael L. Berbaum, "Communty, Integration, and Stability in Multinational Yugoslavia" *American Political Science Review* 83(2) (1989): 535–54. For comparison, see two other articles published after the outbreak of conflict: Randy Hodson, Dusko Sekulic, and Garth Massey, "National Tolerance in the Former Yugoslavia" *American Journal of Sociology* 99(6) (1994): 1534–58; Dusko Sekulic, Garth Massey, and Randy Hodson, "Who Were the Yugoslavs? Failed Sources of a Common

Burg and Berbaum's finding can be juxtaposed with the following observation of Tim Judah, one of the foremost chroniclers of the Serbs' descent.
Regarding the beginning days of fighting, Judah writes:

Most men who found themselves on the Serbian side of the frontlines were mobilized whether they liked it or not, but there was also enthusiasm. Not only did
most genuinely believe they were waging a defensive war to prevent a 'new genocide' of the Serbian people but they were borne aloft by their early victories, intox-
icated with the joy of the military triumphs which they believed were their
generation's contribution to Serbian martial history. These were the illusions that
only gradually began to fade.[2]

Burg and Berbaum's survey research was well done and probably reflected
Yugoslav attitudes of shared political community in 1989. Judah's description of Serbian joy and intoxication at the destruction of that shared political community only two or three years later is also probably accurate.
What is needed is an explanation of this transformation. Survey research,
no matter how well done, can only reflect answers to questions within
the context in which they were asked. In Yugoslavia, this context changed
quickly and radically in a matter of months. In turn, as argued throughout this work, rapid structural change produced new information and
beliefs. Critically, emotions resulted in direct actions that could not have
been predicted from previously held attitudes. In the study of ethnic conflict, emotional mechanisms are often more important than knowledge of
attitudes.

These emotional mechanisms help us explain actions taken during rapid
transformations in a way that survey research cannot. Tens of thousands
of individuals participated in violence and attended mass rallies supporting nationalist and exclusionary causes. What drove these actions? Were
the same mechanisms seen in previous chapters at work in Yugoslavia? Did
Resentment play the same role? In the opening pages of this book, Richard
Holbrooke, echoing a common opinion, attributed Bosnia's postwar

Identity in the Former Yugoslavia" *American Sociological Review* 59 (1994): 83–97. The
former article, using data collected by the Consortium of Social Research Institutes of
Yugoslavia in 1989 and 1990, supported the modernization thesis that diversity and
increased intergroup contact led to greater tolerance in Yugoslavia. For a more complex
view of the contact hypothesis using American data, see H. D. Forbes, *Ethnic Conflict: Commerce, Culture, and the Contact Hypothesis* (New Haven, CT: Yale University Press, 1997).
This volume is the most extensive recent treatment of the contact hypothesis.

[2] Tim Judah, *The Serbs: History, Myth and the Destruction of Yugoslavia* (New Haven, CT: Yale
University Press, 1997), p. 297.

problems to the existence of evil influences: "the forces of darkness – separatists, racists, war criminals, and crooks – are still there, continuing their efforts to keep the people in the dark ages."[3] Is it true that evil leaders manipulated masses of Yugoslavs or did broader forces produce the motivation to fight, humiliate, and harass? Why didn't modernity prevent the barbarity?

The recent Yugoslav violence also plays into the larger macro story underlying this book. In the last decade of the twentieth century, Yugoslavia fragmented into no less than eight functionally autonomous entities. Slovenia, Croatia, and Macedonia retained their borders from the time when they were socialist republics. Bosnia-Hercegovina, while internationally recognized as a single state, in reality broke into separate Muslim, Serbian, and Croatian zones. Serbia, Montenegro, and Voyvodina, three former federal units demographically dominated by Serbs, formed a new Yugoslavia. Kosovo, a NATO protectorate at the time of this writing, officially remained in the new Yugoslavia, but only officially. In sum, the majority of people in each sizable territory of land of the former Yugoslavia, with few exceptions, had gained political power. Moreover, demographic homogenization accompanied political consolidation in almost every case. At the time of this writing, only a small percentage of the refugees had returned to mixed areas in Bosnia, Croats had cleansed 200,000 Serbs from Krajina, and Kosovar Albanians were in the process of eliminating Serbs, Gypsies, and other minorities from Kosovo. In large part, this book is about regional homogenization through violence and discrimination. Yugoslavia is a prime case. It is also a case that challenges Gellner's macro story. Language does not lie at the base of the various Yugoslav wars – Serbs, Croats, and Muslims all spoke Serbo-Croatian. Nor does the timing fit Gellner's theory. The Yugoslav state, for the most part, was already industrialized; the structural changes required by modernization, the catalyst for Gellner, had already run their course in Yugoslavia by the late 1980s.

Furthermore, the Yugoslav case provides rich material for testing competing conventional wisdoms. Scholars rail against Hatred as an uninformed, journalistic, conventional wisdom. In opposition, the bulk of the academic community has developed a counterconventional wisdom. A composite goes something like the following. Yugoslavians lived peacefully and prosperously for decades. A system of institutional checks, balances, and vetoes facilitated the smooth functioning of the system. Ethnic prob-

---

[3] *The New York Times* September 14, 1999.

lems and even ethnic consciousness faded with the onset of modernity. Then economic problems, exacerbated by excessive borrowing and the insensitivities of the international financial world, emerged to destroy the system's equilibrium. Furthermore, the breakdown of the Soviet system, the collapse of Communism throughout Eastern Europe, and the end of the Cold War removed the ideological underpinnings and rationale of continued one-party rule. Communist elites needed to find a new justification for power – nationalism was the most effective choice. Using their control over the media, the Communist-turned-nationalist elites dredged up bloody histories and told lies in an effort to permeate their constituencies with fear. This fear, due to the dynamics of the security dilemma, became self-fulfilling. With all groups organizing and arming, prudence and lack of credible commitments created the incentives for preemptive strikes. In essence, individuals were motivated to participate in the elites' program by Fear. This story, or parts of it, can be found in the work of Russell Hardin, Barry Weingast, Barry Posen (as discussed in the section on Fear), Susan Woodward, Victor Gagnon, Misha Glenny, and others.

This scholarly conventional wisdom, like the views of Holbrooke, concentrates on immediate responses of agents to medium-term events and processes. This chapter confronts this approach by first looking at the long term through a brief examination of the whole of Yugoslavia's history. Secondly, the book's basic method is employed – the application of the four emotions-based narratives to specific puzzles of a more fine-grained nature. After presenting the historical material, the chapter addresses three such puzzles: (1) What explains the outbreak of the Croatian War in 1991?; (2) What explains Bosnian Croatian, as well as Bosnian Serb, violence and discrimination against Muslims in Bosnia?; and (3) What explains Serbian participation and tacit mass approval in the expulsion of over a million Albanians in Kosovo? One explanatory caveat: The emotions-based approach cannot provide a complete answer for these questions, perhaps no approach could. Milosevic's politics drives much of the story. However, a concentration on emotional mechanisms will shed light on one of the most fundamental, and least understood, pieces of the puzzle – the role of individual motivations.

Background

The main axis of Yugoslav politics has always rotated around the relationship between Croats and Serbs; centralization of power has usually been the main battlefield. The question of federalism versus unitarism dominated the first Constituent Assembly of 1920. The issue arose again in the restructuring of the state in 1929, 1939, in the late 1960s, and finally, and decisively, in the late 1980s. As Ivo Banac has summarized: "Indeed, despite dictatorships and attempts at democratic renewal, occupations and wars, revolutions and social changes, after 1921 hardly any new elements were introduced in the set pattern of South Slavic interactions."[4]

From the beginning, Resentment has driven individual Croatians, although the reasons differ from those in Gellner's story. In Gellner's story of Ruritania, or at least in the version told here, slow structural changes associated with modernization and the growth of the state bring rural populations into contact with an intrusive state dominated by an ethnic and linguistic "other." Beliefs form regarding the injustice of this state of affairs. In turn, Resentment results and fuels actions to establish the status dominance of the majority population. While Resentment can form from other phenomena, this general trajectory helps explain the prevalence of this emotion in Eastern Europe. The Baltic cases provided some support for this theory. When considering Yugoslavia, however, the story has a different starting point and runs a different course. Formed from the debris of the First World War and the Balkan Wars, the Kingdom of Serbs, Croats, and Slovenes (as the state was called until 1929 when it was renamed Yugoslavia), combined peoples that had already developed a political consciousness. While the broad contours of Gellner's story have some applicability for Muslims, Macedonians, and perhaps Slovenians, they are not much help in analyzing the main axis of Yugoslav politics – that is, the Serb-Croat relationship. From the earliest years, these two groups have battled over the essential nature of the state. Beliefs about the justice of power and status relationships did not emerge from a slow structual process, but were there from the beginning.

For many Serbs, the first Yugoslavia was an extension of the Serbian state. One-fifth of the Serbian nation had perished during the First World War. For Serbs, this sacrifice helped liberate their fellow south Slavs. Serbs expected a measure of gratitude as well as the right to build the new state upon the government, bureaucracy, and military of prewar Serbia. For Serbs, it was only natural that the king of the new state would come from the Serbian dynasty. Combined with an ideology of a unitary state and cen-

[4] Ivo Banac, *The National Question in Yugoslavia: Origins, History, Politics* (Ithaca, NY: Cornell University Press, 1984), p. 415.

tralized governance, this reliance on the foundations of the prewar Serbian state was a recipe for Serbian dominance.[5] The following figures illustrate the extent of interwar Serbian dominance in high status positions.[6] On the eve of the Second World War, 161 of 165 Yugoslav generals were Serbian, 2 were Croats and 2 Slovene. These numbers are even more astounding when it is taken into account that Croats comprised 15% of the Austro-Hungarian Empire's generals and admirals. Moreover, these figures were not about to radically change as 1,300 of 1,500 military cadets were Serbs. Serbian dominance among senior permanent functionaries was nearly as pronounced. In 1939, Serbs held all 13 positions in the Office of the Premier, 30 of 31 in the Royal Court, 113 of 127 in the Ministry of the Interior, 180 of 219 in the Ministry of Foreign Affairs, 150 of 156 in the Ministry of Education, 116 of 137 in the Justice Ministry, 15 of 26 in the Transportation Ministry, and 196 of 200 in the State Mortgage Bank. In short, Serbs controlled all visible levers of force and power. By all indicators, Serbs dominated the status hierarchy of the interwar state.

The new day-to-day practices of the new state often exacerbated Croatian antipathies. As Serbian gendarmes and military personnel replaced that of Austro-Hungary, Serbian police administrative techniques replaced those of their predecessor. One difference concerned corporal punishment. Croatians had been free of physical penalties since 1869, now fifty years later the new state reimposed such punishment through the institution of Serbian law.[7] Croatians saw their ethnic brethren being beaten by new Serb police and they responded with name calling and other actions exhibiting disrespect for Serbian traditions. Sometimes, the Serb police responded in kind by forcing Croatians to participate in acts repugnant to Croatian ethnic sensibilities. In one such event, occurring in January 1921, Serbian gendarmes in Topusko went from house to house forcing Croatian peasants to strip naked and kiss a picture of Nikola Pasic, the Serbian unitarist political leader, while repeating that Pasic's picture was "God the Father."[8]

---

[5] Ivo Banac embeds his analysis of the founding of the Yugoslav state and its subsequent nationality problems in the differences among national ideologies. See *The National Question in Yugoslavia*. He comes back to this theme in "The Fearful Asymmetry of War: The Causes and Consequences of Yugoslavia's Demise" *Daedalus* 121(2) (1992): 141–75.

[6] All of these figures are from Joseph Rothschild, *East Central Europe Between the Two World Wars* (Seattle: University of Washington Press, 1974), pp. 278–79.

[7] Banac, *The National Question* p. 148.   [8] Ibid., p. 129.

Having lived as second class citizens under Austro-Hungary, Croats were not ready to accept a similar status under the less-developed Serbs. Joseph Rothschild sums up the relationship between Serbs and Croats when they were first joined in the interwar state:

[T]he former subjects of the late "Central European" Habsburg Empire considered themselves more advanced, in terms of all such cultural and socioeconomic criteria, than the "Balkan" Serbs to the south, by whom they were politically dominated to their lasting ire. The Serbs of the prewar Serbian Kingdom, in turn, repudiated the cultural pretensions of the northerners and dismissed their political legacies as Austrophile, formalistic, and irresponsible. They viewed themselves as "doers" and these others as "carpers."[9]

For Croats and Serbs, perceptions of status were inherent in the new state. Croatians transferred their previous resentments to the new relationship.

Furthermore, Croatians brought their previous political organization into the new system. In 1904, Stjepan Radic, along with his brother Ante, founded the Croatian Peasant Party which rapidly emerged as the leading force for Croatian rights as well as agrarian interests. It is not surprising that Croats rebelled against the intrusions of the new state almost from the beginning. From September 4 to September 24, 1920, Croatian peasants rose in revolt against the new state's policy on draft animal registration.[10] On the surface, the policy appeared relatively harmless. The new state, like Austro-Hungary before it, registered draft animals, horses and oxen, to tow military equipment in the event of war. Unlike the Austro-Hungarian regime, the new Yugoslav state, extending the laws of the prewar Serbian state, branded the animals. Croat peasants did not fully understand the need for this new procedure and also may have feared reduced values on animals branded as rejects. It was one of the first intrusions of the new state into Croatian social and economic life – and it was met with violent resistance. In dozens of villages, peasants disarmed or attacked local authorities. In many instances, participants burned the images of King Petar and Regent Aleksander; in some cases, attempts were made to set up new local government. The military finally put down the revolt, but only after at least two dozen peasants and authorities lost their

---

[9] Rothschild, *East Central Europe* p. 209.
[10] A description of the 1920 Croat peasant rebellion can be found in Banac, *The National Question* pp. 248–60.

lives. Thousands of Croatians, in the very beginning years of the state, were protesting state intrusion over a relatively trivial issue.[11]

Several reorganizations of the state attempted to solve the Croatian problem. In 1925, King Alexander granted substantial autonomy to Croatians. In 1929, shortly after the assassination of Radic on the floor of Parliament, King Alexander attempted to change the very ethnic consciousness of the country by creating new administrative units cutting across historical and ethnic boundaries. These units were called banovinas, an ancient Croatian term, to pacify Croats; they were named after rivers to avoid any ethnic or national favoritism. No Serbian and Croatian national symbols were to have connection to the government. In 1939, after the rise of the Ustasha, a Croatian political and terrorist organization that managed to assassinate King Alexander in 1934, Prince (Regent) Paul again recognized Croatian authority in the form of the Sporazum. This agreement ceded to Zagreb a variety of budgetary and administrative powers. After signing the reform, the Prince Regent visited Zagreb, the first time the Royal House had paid a visit there in over ten years.

The Sporazum did not go far enough for many radicalized Croatian nationalists, thousands of whom participated in the genocidal Nazi puppet regime under Ante Pavelic.[12] The goals and achievements of the Ustasha regime are well known: a particular solution to the Serbian problem (one-third to be killed, one-third deported, and one-third converted);[13] tens

---

[11] For further discussion of anti-Serb protests in 1918, see Hannes Grandits and Christian Promitzer, "'Former Comrades' at War: Historical Perspectives on 'Ethnic Cleansing' in Croatia" in Joel M. Halpern and David A. Kideckel, eds., *Neighbors at War: Anthropological Perspectives on Yugoslav Ethnicity, Culture, and History* (University Park, PA: Pennsylvania State University Press, 2000), pp. 132–33.

[12] Most commentators see the sadism of the Ustasha regime as a historical aberration. See Christopher Bennett, *Yugoslavia's Bloody Collapse: Causes, Course and Consequence* (New York: New York University Press, 1995), pp. 43–46 for a discussion. Tim Judah, in his Serb-centered account, agrees: "Between 1918 and 1941 many Croats resented Serbian domination in the new Yugoslav state and welcomed the birth of the NDH, but there was no reason for Serbs or the vast majority of Croats for that matter to have any inkling of the fanatical hatred that was about to be unleashed by the Ustasha. Whereas there had been a long history of bloodshed between Serbs and Muslims and Serbs and Albanians, the genocidal wave unleashed by the Ustashas in 1941 was an aberration and a break with history (*The Serbs* p. 125)." As the reader will note as follows, my interpretation concurs with Judah's. The majority of Croats were driven by Resentment, not Hatred, although the most active participants probably conformed to a variety of hatred. The main point, however, is that this widespread well of Resentment allowed this virulent hatred to flourish.

[13] Reported statement of Mile Budak, the NDH Minister of Education, June 22, 1941.

and perhaps hundreds of thousands of Serbs, Jews, and Gypsies killed at the Jasenovac death camp;[14] countless massacres, many of a primitive and horrific nature.[15] The populations of whole villages were driven into barns or the local Orthodox church where they proceeded to be burned to death.[16] So many corpses had been thrown into the Naretva River that the government paid peasants a bounty for each body pulled out of the water.[17] Furthermore, the Ustasha lacked a coherent ideology. As Aleksa Djilas sums up: "The Ustashas combined modern totalitarianism with primitive traditions of rebellion and revenge. They were terrorists first. Fascism came only later, and it was never fully absorbed, let alone developed."[18]

The immediate postwar years provided the longest respite in the Croatian struggle for recognition. There were several reasons for this lull. First, the most virulent Croatian nationalists were physically eliminated. Croatians following the retreating German army into Austria were turned back by the British to Yugoslavia, where they usually met death. The leader of the Croatian Catholic Church, Archbishop Stepinac, was convicted of being a war criminal and sentenced to sixteen years in prison in 1946.[19] Many Serbian nationalists also suffered a cruel end. Draza Mihailovic, the

[14] Franjo Tudjman puts the number killed in all camps at only 56,639. Scholarly sources and Nazi officials usually put the figures much higher. Aleksa Djilas succinctly summarizes the debate over numbers killed in *The Contested Country: Yugoslav Unity and Communist Revolution 1919–1953* (Cambridge, MA: Harvard University Press, 1991), pp. 125–27. Ivo Banac, however, argues that the Ustasha crimes have been greatly exaggerated and supports a figure of 60,000 to 80,000. See "The Fearful Asymmetries of War," pp. 153–55. Bennett, citing the figures of Vladimir Zerjavic, supports a figure of 85,000. See *Yugoslavia's Bloody Collapse* p. 46.

[15] As Bishop Misic wrote to Archbishop Stepinac: "Men are captured like animals, they are slaughtered, murdered, living men are thrown off cliffs." For a more extended passage from this letter, see Judah, *The Serbs* p. 127. German reports support the views of Bishop Misic. See Paul Hehn, *The German Struggle Against Yugoslav Guerrillas in World War II: German Counter-Insurgency in Yugoslavia, 1941–1943* (Boulder, CO: East European Quarterly, distributed by Columbia University Press, 1979).

[16] An early example occurred in Glina on August 5, 1941.

[17] Jonathan Steinberg, *All or Nothing: The Axis and the Holocaust 1941–1943* (London: Routledge, 1990), p. 272, note 59. Steinberg also notes that the German Army felt the Croatians were too brutal and unrestrained. Steinberg cites German reports claiming that "the Ustasha have gone raging mad." See Steinberg 272, note 57.

[18] Aleksa Djilas, *The Contested Country* p. 124.

[19] Archbishop Stepinac's actual complicity is a matter of impassioned debate. See Sabrina Ramet, *Balkan Babel: The Disintegration of Yugoslavia from the Death of Tito to Ethnic War* (Boulder, CO: Westview Press, 1996), pp. 140–43 for a concise review of his trial.

leader of the nationalist Chetniks, was captured and eventually executed in July of 1946. The highly publicized trials of Mihailovic and others allowed the Communists to muzzle all forms of nationalist rhetoric. By connecting prewar political leaders to Mihailovic, the Communists could taint opposition as reactionary and fascist. Fearing this tactic, prewar leaders with any nationalist credentials shrunk from public life or attempted to recreate their image as Yugoslavs or Partisans. Often overlooked, Stalinist hardliners, led by secret police chief Aleksandar Rankovic, directed the Yugoslav Communists in the immediate postwar years. This centralized organization exercised brutal control without the least hesitation. Following Soviet nationality policy, republics were nationalist in form, but socialist, meaning controlled by a centralized party, in content.[20]

Twenty years after the war had ended, the nationalist form began to take on real and troublesome content. The first two decades of Communist rule witnessed dramatically uneven economic development. The richer north increased the gap with the poorer south. At the same time, the practice of enterprise self-management eroded the Party's grip over day-to-day economic and social life. The Brioni Plenum of 1966 marked a significant change in the Yugoslav system. The Party was still in command but now the locus of its power would be regional rather than federal. Given local economic autonomy, strong political bosses emerged at lower levels. Also at the Brioni Plenum, the hardline Rankovic, then vice president of Yugoslavia and the highest ranking Serb Communist, was stripped of all his powers including control of the secret police. The ouster of Rankovic, the most powerful opponent of political decentralization, combined with economic reform, unleashed centrifugal forces including a renewal of Croatian nationalism.

By 1969, the taboo on nationalist speech in Croatia was no longer in effect. The opinion that Croatia had become an exploited nation became commonplace. The official press regularly published such claims. A 1969 article written by the head of the Croatian Literary Society, Peter Segedin,

---

[20] Stevan Pavlowitch sums up the Yugoslav version of Communist nationality policy that emerged in the immediate postwar years: "It substituted ideological integration for ethnic integration, capping federalism with a unitarism of power and ideology. Ethnic pluralism and federal forms were meant as lightning conductors for national emotions until Communism had managed to do away with them." See *The Improbable Survivor: Yugoslavia and its Problems, 1918–1988* (Columbus: Ohio State University Press, 1988), p. 71.

and published in the bimonthly *Kolo*, illustrated the nature and range of Croatian grievances.[21]

1. Croats are treated as illegal residents in their own country.
2. Croatian interests are subordinate to the interests of Serbia.
3. To feel Croatian under the current circumstances is to be worthy of pity.
4. To lose one's language is to lose one's ethnic identity.
5. The Croatian nation has, by various nefarious means, been portrayed as criminal.
6. Croatia is still being equated with the Ustashe.
7. Belgrade is attempting to assimilate the Croats, that is, to Serbianize Croatia.
8. Croatia has become a "no-man's land."
9. Croatia has lost everything essential to the preservation of its culture.
10. The Serbs have a definite program designed to assimilate Croatian youth and to cause the Croatian nation to disappear without a trace.

Matica Hrvatska, the most influential Croatian social organization, came to propose the following new first amendment to the Croatian constitution:

SR Croatia is the national state of the Croatian nation. National sovereignty – one indivisible, inalienable, and imperishable – belongs, in SR Croatia, to the Croatian nation and it realizes it through deputies and by direct expressions of its will.

In the Croatian Communist Party, now riven by factionalism as to how far to press demands, anti-Tito slogans could be heard at Party meetings. In support for the Party faction fighting for Croatian autonomy, students initiated a series of strikes in November of 1971. Thirty-thousand students participated.[22]

After considering the deployment of troops, Tito decided on wholesale removals from the Croatian Party. The resulting purge was massive. Fifty-thousand members of the Croatian League of Communists lost their party cards; up to five thousand were imprisoned; fifty-thousand students were

---

[21] Sabrina Ramet provides this summary in *Nationalism and Federalism in Yugoslavia 1962–1991* (Bloomington: University of Indiana Press, 1984), p. 106. She in turn is citing the summary of Stipe Suvar in *Nacionalno and nacionalisticko* (Split: Marksisticki Centar, 1974), pp. 332–34.

[22] Ibid., pp. 128–29.

identified as "class enemies."[23] The imprisoned included Franjo Tudjman, who would emerge later as independent Croatia's first president. With the use of the Party's repressive power, Yugoslav politics regained equilibrium. Tito employed a mixed strategy to try to retain it. On the one hand, the purges and imprisonments decapitated the nationalist threat. Furthermore, publication of any nationalist rhetoric was banned until the early 1980s, after Tito's death. On the other hand, Tito conceded ever-increasing autonomy to the republics. To pacify Croatia, Tito first gave in to specific economic demands such as allowing the republic to retain a higher percentage of tourism earnings. Soon, decentralization entered the political arena, most dramatically in the form of the 1974 constitution. This document attempted to solve the national problem by granting maximal autonomy to each republic and creating extensive veto powers over federal initiatives.[24] In effect, any major decision required unanimous consent. In a move that many believe helped speed Yugoslavia's destruction, the autonomous regions of Voyvodina and Kosovo, located within the boundaries of the Serbian Socialist Republic, gained powers nearly equal to those of the socialist republics. Kosovo and Voyvodina could veto Serbian Republic initiatives but the Serbian republic could not veto the initiatives of these internal federal units. Undoing this relationship became one of Milosevic's earliest, and most popular, political moves.

Until the late 1970s, the question of Croatian autonomy, closely related to the issue of decentralization, dominated Yugoslav political conflict. The Croat-Serb dynamic fueled the problems at the state's inception, drove the attempts at reform in 1929 and 1939, provoked the most horrific and murderous wartime events, and propelled the movement toward decentralization that culminated in the 1974 constitution. By the 1970s, however, the Croatian problem, and more importantly the attempts to solve it, began to catalyze other nationality problems. The Croatians' demands for higher autonomy led Muslims, both slavic Muslims and Albanians, to seek greater ethnic power as well. Rankovic had subscribed to the theory that Bosnia's Muslims were in reality Serbs who had converted through force or opportunity during Ottoman rule; he was adamantly opposed to granting any significant recognition to this collectivity. Within a few years of his demise,

---

[23] Ibid., p. 202.
[24] See Robert Hayden, *Blueprints for a House Divided: The Constitutional Logic of the Yugoslav Conflicts* (Ann Arbor: University of Michigan Press, 1999) for a discussion of the 1974 constitution (pp. 49–52) and Yugoslav constitutions in general.

Tito declared that Muslims must be recognized as a nation. In 1971, the option of declaring oneself an ethnic Muslim on the census form first became available. Wanting to show their strength, nationalist agitators urged individuals to declare themselves "Muslim, in the ethnic sense." The campaign was apparently successful given the nearly 1.5 million who so registered. In the late 1970s, Muslim religious observance increased, reversing the previous long-term trend.[25] By 1983, Yugoslavian authorities uncovered illegal Muslim organizations tied to Islamic groups abroad. Eleven members were sentenced to lengthy prison terms, among them was Alija Izetbegovic who would go on to become Bosnia's first president.

Rankovic's distaste for Albanians is well known. His removal precipitated revelations of the extent of state repression of Albanians. In 1968, riots broke out in Kosovo. Violence left thirty-seven injured and one dead.[26] The events were marked by a call for an independent university in Pristina and the first open demands for republican status. Tito's regime responded in a consistent fashion: On the one hand, the protest leaders received five-year prison sentences and the demand for republic status was unequivocally rejected; on the other hand, the regime created an independent university in Pristina and allowed the Albanian flag to be displayed alongside that of Yugoslavia. Perhaps most crucially, the regime began to promote significant numbers of Albanians into positions of political authority. Tito's repressive one-party regime again kept short-term order by combining suppression of the most obvious nationalist challenges with a more quiet devolution of authority.[27] Clearly, this strategy could not work forever. For the Kosovo problem, it did not work at all.

Above all, Serbs did not tolerate the rapid Albanization of positions of authority. The percentage of Albanian employees in the social sector rose from 58.2% in 1974 to 83% in 1978 and to 92% in 1980. The figures for Serb employment for the same years show a decline from 31% to 9.3% to 5%.[28] In essence, Serbs went from gross overrepresentation to underrepresentation in a matter of six years. Perhaps Serbs found the change in the Party and police forces to be even more grating. By 1981, Albanians made up approximately two-thirds of the League of Communists in Kosovo and

---

[25] Ramet, *Nationalism and Federalism* p. 185.   [26] Ibid., pp. 190–91.
[27] In the words of Ramet, "(T)he Kosovo case exemplifies conflict accomodation as practiced in communist Yugoslavia: jail the troublemakers but grant their nondisintegrative demands." *Nationalism and Federalism* p. 192.
[28] Ibid., pp. 192–93.

three-fourths of the police.[29] Serbs often complained that Albanian police discriminated against them. Whether this is true or not as historian Noel Malcolm sums up, "No doubt there were cases where Serbs and Montenegrins came under pressure from Albanian-speaking officials and policemen, and found it a new and unpleasant experience."[30]

Despite this status reversal, and the changes of the 1974 Yugoslav Constitution, Albanians continued to protest. Nationalist riots beginning at the University of Pristina shook the Yugoslav state in March and April of 1981.[31] Spreading throughout every sizable town in Kosovo, thousands of demonstrators, some armed, clashed with police resulting in significant numbers of dead and wounded as well as thousands imprisoned.[32] The unrest never abated. Anti-Serb graffitti, violence at sports events, bombings, and physical attacks became relatively commonplace.[33] Although perhaps not the primary cause, these events helped propel the exodus of thousands of Serbs and Montenegrins from Kosovo.[34]

By the early 1980s, a vicious Serbian backlash, both in Kosovo and Serbia proper, arose in response to the events in Kosovo.[35] A wide range

---

[29] Noel Malcolm, *Kosovo: A Short History* (New York: New York University Press, 1999), p. 326

[30] Ibid., p. 326.

[31] See Julie Mertus, *Kosovo: How Myths and Truths Started a War* (Berkeley: University of California Press, 1999), pp. 17–93 for an extensive look at the 1981 student demonstrations that includes a discussion of the perceptions of that event as well as interviews of participants.

[32] There are various figures regarding the numbers of casualties and imprisonments. Malcolm, citing the Yugoslav political journal, *NIN*, put the number of those given substantial prison sentences at 1,200 and those jailed for three months or less at 3,000 (*Kosovo* p. 335). Ramet, in *Nationalism and Federalism* (p. 196), cites reports of 1,000 killed. Pavlowitch gives a figure of 1,600 prison sentences (*The Improbable Survivor* p. 86). All commentators agree that the protests were massive and marked a new era in Kosovo. Mertus notes that changes occurred at the personal level as well as the political level: "According to both Kosovo Serbs and Albanians, 1981 was the year in which many previously harmonious relationships between members of different groups grew sour or broke off completely" *Kosovo* p. 41.

[33] Steven Burg, "Elite Conflict in Post-Tito Yugoslavia" *Soviet Studies* 38(2) (1986): p. 171. Ramet states, "Arson, sabotage, terrorism, and pamphleteering became, overnight, a way of life in Kosovo" *Nationalism* p. 197. Mertus, among others, warns against exaggerating the extent of this violence and shows how several incidents evolved into powerful myths serving to drive ethnic conflict and mistrust.

[34] Politicians, as well as academics, have debated the relative weights of safety factors versus economic factors in producing this flight. See Mertus, *Kosovo* pp. 41–42, for commentary.

[35] See Branka Magas, *The Destruction of Yugoslavia: Tracking the Break-up, 1980–1992* (London: Verso, 1993), pp. 195–97 for a concise summary.

221

of Serbs accused Albanians of promoting the intimidation and violence against Serbs as part of a plan of "genocide." In Kosovo, the Kosovo Committee of Serbs and Montenegrins formed to protest Albanian actions and call for the institution of military rule. They made trips to Belgrade to appeal to the government and supporters in the Serbian capital, but were rebuffed by officials. Their mission, however, was soon adopted by a wide ranging group of Serbian intellectuals. On January 21, 1986, a collection of 216 Belgrade intellectuals connected with the Serbian Academy of Sciences sent a document to both the Serbian and Yugoslav assemblies lamenting the treatment and abandonment of Kosovo's Serbs. It appealed to the assemblies to respond to the petition of the Kosovo Serbs and implied that ignoring their demands would be no less than an act of treason complicit in genocide. The document went further, though. It painted Serbia as the constant victim of Tito's policies, especially those embodied in the 1974 Constitution. At several points, Serbia's victimization is framed in even broader historical terms. The Memorandum, as it came to be popularly known, is exemplified by the following excerpt:[36]

No nation willingly gives up its right to exist and the Serb nation is not and will not be an exception.

In the last twenty years, 200,000 people have been moved out of Kosovo and Metohija, more than 700 settlements have been ethnically 'purged,' the emigration is continuing with unabated force, Kosovo and Metohija are becoming 'ethnically pure,' the aggression is crossing the borders of the Province.

The political condemnation of the Petition has therefore moved us, the undersigned, to turn to public opinion with an appeal to support its demands for a radical change in the situation in Kosovo and Metohija. Political reason insists that emergency sessions of the assemblies of SFRJ and SR Serbia should be convened to consider the Petition of Serbs from Kosovo and undertake immediate and effective measures to put an end to this chronicle of one long, destructive genocide on European territory. As is known from historical science, from still unextinguished memory, the expulsion of the Serb people from Kosovo and Metohija has already been going on for three centuries. Only the protectors of the tyrants have changed: the Ottoman Empire, the Habsburg Monarchy, Fascist Italy, and Nazi Germany have been replaced by the Albanian state and the ruling institutions of Kosovo. In place of forced Islamization and Fascism there is Stalinized chauvinism. The only novelty is the fusion of tribal hatred and genocide masked by Marxism.

The methods have remained the same: The old poles now carry new heads.

The supporters of this document cannot be easily caricatured as conservative hardliners cynically adopting nationalism to hold on to their job.

---

[36] Magas, *The Destruction of Yugoslavia*, reprints the Memorandum on pp. 49–52.

Dobrica Cosic, who played a major role in the drafting of the Memorandum, had been expelled from the Party presidency for voicing similar sentiments as far back as the late 1960s. Signers of the document included Zaga Golubovic, Mihailo Markovic, and Ljuba Tadic, three former editors of the journal *Praxis*. In a letter defending their actions, these liberal intellectuals reiterated the historical litany of the Memorandum:

First, there is a century-old history of national conflict in Kosovo, a series of acts of aggression and counter-aggression, of acts of violence and bloody revenge – a story of true horror. It is only human to feel sympathy 'under the veil of ignorance' for the smaller Albanian people. But the little David had the upper hand most of the time because it was amply supported by overwhelming allies: the Islamic Ottoman Empire during five centuries until 1912, Austria-Hungary which occupied the entire territory during World War One; fascist Italy and Germany which did the same during World War Two; the Soviet Union and China after 1948; eventually a dominating anti-Serbian coalition in Yugoslavia itself over the last twenty years.[37]

This letter broke all the taboos against nationalist rhetoric. In response, Ivan Stambolic, the President of Serbia at the time, vehemently attacked the Memorandum. In a speech, at Belgrade University, Stambolic declared: "The so-called Memorandum is not new. It is the old chauvinist concern for the fate of the Serbian cause with the well-known formula that Serbs will win the wars but lose the peace."[38] However, these attacks did not resonate. Unlike the aftermath of previous nationalist outbursts, authorities brought no formal charges against the authors. How could the Party arrest anyone for saying what most Serbs believed?[39] Despite the power and presence of antinationalist Serbian reformers, Stambolic, and those with similar views, would soon be forced off the stage.

Slobodan Milosevic built his career as a faceless bureaucrat. In 1987, he vaulted to leadership on the issue of Kosovo. Although he had made his

---

[37] This letter is reproduced in Magas, Ibid., pp. 55–61. Numerous treatments of the Memorandum's significance exist. For one brief summary, see Norman Cigar, "The Serbo-Croatian War, 1991" in Stephan G. Mestrovic, ed., *Genocide After Emotion: The Postemotional Balkan War* (London: Routlege, 1996), pp. 51–90. The Memorandum is discussed on pages 55–58. Susan Woodward discusses the Memorandum in "Diaspora, or the Dangers of Disunification? Putting the Serbian Model into Perspective" in Michael Mandelbaum, ed., *The New European Diasporas: National Minorities and Conflict in Eastern Europe* (New York: Council of Foreign Relations, 2000), pp. 193–95.

[38] From Mertus, *Kosovo* pp. 140–41.

[39] This is Mertus' conclusion (p. 141), as well as my own.

nationalist sympathies known earlier,[40] Milosevic firmly established his public image as defender of the Serbian people one night in late April of 1987. After a clash between Serbian demonstrators and predominately Albanian Kosovar police, Milosevic was reported to declare, "No one shall beat these people." Regardless of the real context of his statement, the phrase was taken as a guarantee that Albanians would not be allowed to persecute Serbs under his watch. The crowd exploded with chants of "Slobo! Slobo!" As Malcolm has described, "With a skill which he had never displayed before, Milosevic made an eloquent extempore speech in defense of the sacred rights of the Serbs. From that day, his nature as a politician changed; it was as if a powerful new drug had entered his veins."[41] Stambolic was gone by the end of the year; Milosevic assumed the reins of the Communist Party.

The rise of Milosevic inevitably awakened Croat-Serb tensions. From the Serbian nationalist standpoint now championed by Milosevic, solving the Kosovo problem would require reducing its autonomy and thus effectively recentralizing the Yugoslav federal system. As in the earliest days of the state, as in 1929 and 1939, as in the late 1960s, the question of unitarism versus federalism came to dominate Yugoslavia's politics. This time, however, the issue arose in combination with economic crises, massive foreign debts,[42] and a collapse of ideology. Milosevic was neither King Alexander nor Tito. His most powerful tool was not the army, secret police, or the Party, but rather his capacity to generate intimidating mass rallies ("the antibureaucratic revolution"). While Milosevic's goal was a recentralization of the state, his strategy could only work to enhance the centrifugal tendencies of the Yugoslav political system. Employing mass demonstrations, Milosevic ousted the leaderships of Kosovo and Voyvodina, the autonomous republics within Serbia, as well as that of Montenegro. In each case, Milosevic installed his own loyal clients. As each of the eight federal units basically controlled one vote in the post-1974 federal system, Milosevic now commanded four of eight votes and could block any moves toward reform not to his liking. At this point, it was

---

[40] At the Party meeting in Kragujevac in December of 1986, Milosevic had called for the unification of Serbia. Malcolm claims that is the only instance where he betrayed any nationalistic impulse before April 1987. See Malcolm, *Kosovo* p. 426, note 17.

[41] Ibid., pp. 341–42.

[42] On the economic crisis and the role of foreign debt, see Susan Woodward, *Socialist Unemployment: The Political Economy of Yugoslavia 1945–1990* (Princeton, NJ: Princeton University Press, 1995).

possible that some form of confederation might have saved Yugoslavia. But given the nature of Milosevic and his nationalist and hardline supporters, the chances for confederation were slim. Soon, only two viable options remained: conceding to recentralization or opting for independence.

Slovenia was the first out. Due in part to its ethnic homogeneity, Slovenia left with relatively little bloodshed. The crucial case, as always, was Croatia. Croatia's secession, addressed below, led to massive bloodshed. It also made the secession of Bosnia, and its subsequent warfare, an inevitability. In turn, these wars led to Serbia's international isolation and internal enervation. By the late 1990s, Kosovar Albanians were successfully controlling swaths of Kosovo. The Serbs' brutal crackdown and expulsions led to NATO's intervention and eventually to the de facto autonomy of Kosovo.

This historical gloss is necessarily selective in its choice of events and details. However, it has aimed to illustrate the depth and recurrence of several of Yugoslavia's ethnic dilemmas. First and foremost, Croatians have always had a problem with Serbian authority. I will return to this issue in the very next section. Secondly, as the reader might have noted, Bosnia and the Muslims did not play such a major role in this historical progression. Thirdly, Kosovo has been a long-term problem. This wound in the Yugoslav system was open and bitter since the late 1960s, well before the rise of Milosevic. These three points are essential to understanding the three specific puzzles addressed below in chronological order.

Puzzle 1: What Accounts for the Outbreak and Severity of the Croatian-Serbian War?

The Fear narrative holds that a structural change, such as the breakdown of a state, produces information that leads to the belief that one is in danger. The emotion heightens sensitivity to signals regarding that danger. One is more likely to think in terms of a worst case scenario; the violent, rather than the cooperative, elements of interethnic history come to the fore. Very suddenly, one's neighbor is reidentified as one's enemy. The basic premise of the security dilemma operates: The defensive actions of another group are perceived as threatening. One acts on a combination of emotion and belief. The individual becomes motivated to participate in a preemptive strike against the other group.

Not surprisingly, those scholars favoring a version of the Fear story employ the Croatian-Serbian War as their exemplar. Barry Posen applies the security dilemma to ethnic conflict in a straightforward manner. He describes Croatian thinking in the following manner:

Having lived in a pre- and postwar Yugoslavia dominated by Serbs, the Croats had reason to suspect that the demise of the Yugoslav Communist Party would be followed by a Serbian bid for hegemony. In 1971, the Croatian Communist Party had been purged of leaders who had favored greater autonomy. In addition, the historical record of the Serbs during the past 200 years is one of regular efforts to establish an ever larger centralized Serbian national state on the Balkan peninsula. Thus, Croats had sufficient reason to fear Serbs. . . .

From the military point of view, the Croats probably would have been better off postponing their secession until after they had made additional military preparations. However, their experience in 1971, the more recent political developments, and the military preparations of the Yugoslav army probably convinced them that the Serbs were about to strike and that the Croatian leadership would be rounded up and imprisoned or killed if they did not act quickly.[43]

Other scholars are more focused on the Croatian fears engendered more specifically by Slobodan Milosevic and his policies. Barry Weingast and Rui deFigueiredo go so far to state, "From the perspectives of Croatians at large, they viewed they had a madman next door, gaining control over a largely Serbian army."[44] The Serbs, especially those in the Krajina region, are seen as thinking along similar lines. In most accounts, Serbs were reluctant to engage in any conflict with their Croat neighbors but were forced into action by the presence and strategies of outside Serb extremists. In Krajina, relations were fine until the Spring of 1991 when, as an emotion-based approach predicts, a rapid polarization occurred.[45] Based on actions of the recently elected Tudjman government (discussed below) and the propaganda and presence of Serbian nationalist paramilitary groups (led by Milan Martic),

---

[43] Barry Posen, "The Security Dilemma and Ethnic Conflict and Ethnic Conflict" in Michael E. Brown, ed., *Ethnic Conflict and International Security* (Princeton, NJ: Princeton University Press, 1993), p. 161.

[44] Rui deFigueiredo and Barry Weingast, "The Rationality of Fear: Political Opportunism and Ethnic Conflict" paper presented at the Political Economy meetings, San Francisco, February, 1997.

[45] See the descriptions in Misha Glenny, *The Fall of Yugoslavia: The Third Balkan War* (London: Penguin Books, 1992); James Fearon, "Commitment Problems and the Spread of Ethnic Conflict" in David Lake and Donald Rothchild, eds., *The International Spread of Ethnic Conflict: Fear, Diffusion, Escalation*; Ejub Stitkovac, "Croatia: The First War" in Jasminka Udovicki and James Ridgeway, eds., *Burn This House: The Making and Unmaking of Yugoslavia* (Durham, NC: Duke University Press, 1997), pp. 153–73.

Serbs in Krajina began to panic. Ejub Stitkovac, a journalist, recalls the following exchange with a Serbian friend:

"You journalists are nuts," he said. "Instead of staying in Belgrade where you are safe, you come here, where the lid's about to blow off. Don't you feel it in the air? Catch the first train back. Later you might not be able to get out." He told me that the Croats were preparing to massacre the Serbs; the local Croatian Democratic Union (HDZ) was drawing up a list of Serbs to be shot. "We'll have to take to the woods again and fight. The army is our big hope, but it's falling apart. Nobody can expect Croatian officers to fight against Croats. The Generals will go over to Tudjman, and us here, we'll be sitting ducks." My Serbian friend took off into the woods two days later. He became known by his war name, Struja (Electric).[46]

Here is Fear. Individuals feeling something in the air, sensing life-threatening dangers, believing that the enemy has one's name on a death list, fleeing to the woods. Here is how ordinary individuals are motivated to become nationalist fighters with names like Electric.

There is no need to belabor the motivations of average Serbs and Croatians in areas like Krajina. I accept that individuals were motivated by the general outlines of the Fear narrative and that elites and their paramilitaries were instrumental in setting this process in motion. However, there are some elements of the Croatian-Serbian War that go beyond Fear, especially its security dilemma form. The security dilemma shows how the structural condition of anarchy can create conflict even when both sides have benign intentions. With the lack of a sovereign, security and survival become paramount. In this situation, prudence dictates that the other side's efforts be seen as threatening, as offensive rather than defensive; prudence calls for matching actions that can lead to spiraling dynamics and preemptive strikes. There is nothing in the security dilemma, or the Fear narrative, however, that can explain clearly provocative actions. If one is driven by Fear, the goal is to defend oneself or perhaps to reconcile differences.

With this fact in mind, consider the following actions taken by the Croatian government that was popularly elected in April 1990:

- In July 1990, the sahovnica, the traditional red and white checkerboard symbol of Croatia, replaced the red star emblem of the Yugoslav flag. Serbs identify the sahovnica with the Ustasha state of the Second World War.

---

[46] Stitkovac, *Croatia* pp. 153–54.

- Streets and public places named for World War Two victims were renamed for figures associated with the pro-Hitler Pavelic regime.
- In December of 1990, the constitutional status of the Croatian Serbian minority was downgraded from "constituent nation" to "national minority."[47]
- In early 1991, Serbs were expunged from the police force, from educational and medical institutions, and even some private firms. In effect, Serbs were eliminated from almost all day-to-day positions of dominance.

As was well known by the electorate, Tudjman had written a revisionist history of Croatia during the Second World War. In his book, *Bespuca*, Tudjman argued that the number of victims at the Jasenovac death camp was only a fraction of the commonly reported number. During his campaign, Tudjman stated that the wartime Independent State of Croatia "was also an expression of the historical aspirations of the Croatian People."[48] As Susan Woodward has summed up, "In contemporary Croatia, Tudjman's regime institutionalized an exclusionary, *jus sanguinis*, ethnic concept of the Croatian nation, and made it clear that Serbs, in particular, were no longer welcome, even in their ancestral home."[49]

Some might argue that these actions were unintelligent or insensitive actions to take at that particular moment; perhaps the voters were uninformed of the nature and the intentions of Tudjman and his HDZ Party.[50] There is a far more plausible interpretation: Croatians, leaders and mass alike, knew that these actions were provocations. Croatians knew that they were likely to escalate conflict, but they didn't care. Significant numbers of Croats desired clear symbolic signs of dominance over Serbs, they wanted Serbs eliminated from day-to-day positions of authority. Contrary to the Fear story, individuals were willing to take on enhanced risks of conflict and war to live in a state in which their group would establish status dominance. In the critical period of flux, Croats were motivated as much by Resentment as by Fear. Structural collapse provided an opportunity to

---

[47] See Hayden, *Blueprints for a House Divided* pp. 69–71 for a discussion of the Croatian Constitution of December 1990.

[48] Ibid., p. 155.   [49] Woodward, "Diaspora, or the Dangers of Disunification?" p. 200.

[50] Slaven Letica provides an apologetic view of these actions in "The Genesis of the Current Balkan War" in Stephan G. Mestrovic, ed., *Genocide After Emotion: The Postemotional Balkan War* (London: Routlege, 1996), pp. 91–112. See especially pages 100 and forward for an analysis totally counter to the one presented here.

reorder status relations. They voted and supported candidates and organizations that would eliminate Serb overrepresentation in the police and political institutions once and for all; they supported symbolic changes establishing Croat dominance. They were driven to these actions by emotions that overrode knowledge and beliefs of the incumbent risks.

Analysis

On August 4, 1995, the Croatian army, with the blessing of the United States,[51] brutally cleansed Krajina of its Serbian population. Two hundred thousand Serbs fled from the region. Croats shelled civilian areas; Croat police guided Serbs quickly across the border.[52] Thirty-eight thousand homes were destroyed. The Helsinki Human Rights Committee estimated that six thousand Serbs disappeared during the operation.[53]

With Serbs abandoned by Milosevic and left defenseless, the savage cleansing operation of Krajina does not fit the Fear story. However, the nature of this action also does not fit the Resentment story. Resentment does not call for cleansing a population, only "putting them back in their place." Cleansing, the act of getting rid of a group entirely, suggests that perpetrators see something wrong with the group itself – some perceived defect. This quality, as discussed earlier, is definitive of hatred. This connection naturally leads us to the question of whether the Hatred narrative applies to the Croatian War. Did structural change activate a ritualized schema that informed and motivated individual action?

As Ivo Banac has argued, "after 1921 hardly any new elements were introduced in the set pattern of South Slavic interactions."[54] In 1920–21, Croatians reacted against the imposition of authority from the "culturally backward" Serbs; the reforms of 1939 attempted to alleviate Croatian

[51] As Richard Holbrooke reports in *To End a War* (New York: The Modern Library, 1999) a member of his staff, apparently recognizing the brutality of the Croatian assault, wrote the following note to Holbrooke concerning the Croatians: "We 'hired' these guys to be our junkyard dogs because we were desperate. We need to try to 'control' them. But this is no time to get squeamish about things. This is the first time the Serb wave has been reversed. That is essential for us to get stability, so we can get out." p. 73.

[52] See Robert Hayden, "Schindler's Fate: Genocide, Ethnic Cleansing, and Population Transfers" *Slavic Review* 55(4) (1996): 727–48.

[53] Ibid., pp. 167–68. Also see Yves Heller, "How Croatia Reclaimed its Accursed Land" *Guardian Weekly* 31 (1996).

[54] Ivo Banac, *The National Question in Yugoslavia: Origins, History, Politics* (Ithaca, NY: Cornell University Press, 1984), p. 415.

bitterness through decentralization; in the Second World War, the Ustasha regime engaged in cleansing; in 1971, Croatians again engaged in efforts to decrease centralized, and Serbian, influence. Seen in this light, the Croatian secession of 1991 is just one more round, one more effort at breaking free from an unwanted "big brother." For many Croatians, the Serbs have always played the same role in a constant schema: a culturally backward people attempting to establish dominance through centralization of political institutions. The Croatian self-image is of the unjustly dominated Central European who, through the misfortune of history and geography, was forced to live with Serbians and the even more backward Albanians and Macedonians. To summarize in broadest terms, the history of Croatians in Yugoslavia is one of repeating (ritualized?) Resentment. It would seem that for this case, Resentment and Hatred merge into one phenomena.

Although there are clear elements of schema and ritual in the Croat-Serb relationship, the Hatred narrative remains problematic. While a schema and roles exist, it is not clear that they work to inform or motivate any specific action. In both the Second World War and in 1995, significant numbers of Croats engaged in or supported ethnic cleansing. In the interwar, 1971, and late Communist eras, Croatians used political channels to seek greater autonomy. While a stereotyped role of the Serbs may have always been present, at least latently, in the Croatian political consciousness, it is not clear whether a script capable of directing Croatian action has ever been present.

In the quotation above, Barry Posen wrote that "the historical record of the Serbs during the past 200 years is one of regular efforts to establish an ever larger centralized Serbian national state on the Balkan peninsula. Thus, Croats had sufficient reason to fear Serbs." However, one needs to ask whether Croats actually *feared* physical attack and subjugation by Serbs or just deeply *resented* the subordination that a centralized Serbian state might produce. Both the Fear and Resentment narratives produce a coherent explanation of the events that brought on the twenty thousand deaths of the Croatian War. Elements of Hatred, schema, and roles, are also present. Following the lines of Taylor's argument mentioned in the chapter on Resentment, one might make an argument that elite Resentment helped produce mass Fear. I would simply conclude by stating that the Serb-Croat war was overdetermined. The collapse of the state was bound to set both the Fear and Resentment processes into motion. The policies of Milosevic and Tudjman inflamed the situation and guaranteed that carnage would result. Whether another set of leaders could have prevented the slide is a subject of debate. As one scholar of Croatian history has concluded, "Croatia is better off as an independent state. The 'marriage' with Serbia was flawed from the beginning."[55] Given the widespread nature of this opinion, it is little wonder that leaders trying to keep Yugoslavia together failed to effectively counter Tudjman.

Puzzle 2: What Explains Bosnian Croatian, as well as Bosnian Serb, Violence and Discrimination against Muslims in Bosnia?

Bosnia witnessed horrendous killing and humiliation. While final death and rape counts remain a matter of speculation, their scale cannot be disputed. The general outline of the war and the actions of Serbs are well known. Between late 1990 and early 1992, Serbian militias under the direction of Radovan Karadzic began a buildup in conjunction with the Yugoslav Army. On December 20, 1991, Bosnian President Alija Izetbegovic asked the European community to recognize Bosnia. Bosnian Serbs followed with their own declaration creating the Serbian Republic of Bosnia-Hercegovina. On January 9, 1992, Bosnian Serbs declared independence; on March 3, the Izetbegovic government proclaimed Bosnia an independent state. A situation of multiple sovereignty came into being. War followed with Serbs, aided by Milosevic's regime and the Yugoslav army, gaining control over 70% of Bosnia's territory. By the end of the summer of 1992, thousands of Bosnian civilians had been killed and perhaps two million left homeless.[56] A series of peace conferences (the Vance-Owen plan, the European Union Plan of 1994) failed to effectively end the fighting. Mass murders, the most heinous occurring at Srebrenica in July 1995, took place before the eyes of UN peacekeepers.[57] Finally, the development of Bosnian and Croatian military forces began to change the balance of forces on the ground. As noted previously, Milosevic

---

[55] From Elinor Desplatovic, "The Roots of the War in Croatia" in Joel M. Halpern and David A. Kideckel, eds., *Neighbors at War: Anthropological Perspectives on Yugoslav Ethnicity, Culture, and History* (University Park, PA: Pennsylvania State University Press, 2000), p. 101.

[56] Sabrina Ramet provides this figure in *Balkan Babel: The Disintegration of Yugoslavia from the Death of Tito to Ethnic War* (Boulder, CO: Westview, 1996), p. 248. She also provides a number of fifty thousand killed in this period.

[57] On Srebrenica, see Jan Willem Honig and Norbert Both, *Srebrenica: Record of a War Crime* (New York: Penguin Books, 1996).

abandoned Krajina in August 1995, beginning a retreat of the Serbs. Milosevic, prodded by Western bombing, was forced to the negotiating table. The Dayton Accord (signed on November 22, 1995) stabilized Bosnia by creating a state of two "entities" – the Bosnian Muslim-Croat Federation (comprising 51% of the former republic) and Republika Srpska (the remaining 49%). Sabrina Ramet has produced figures of 200,000 dead by December 1994, 2.7 million refugees, 20,000 to 50,000 women raped.[58] More reliable figures put the number dead in the tens of thousands and the number of Bosnian refugees lower, but in any event, the numbers are staggering, especially for late twentieth century Europe.

While Serbian atrocities have been well publicized, Croatian aggression in the Bosnian War has not. Croatian actions against Muslims have, at several junctures, closely resembled those of Serbs. I will argue that Resentment has helped motivate the anti-Muslim actions of both Croatians and Serbs. For a minority of both Bosnian Croats and Serbs, primarily those living in rural areas, the emergence of a new state in which Muslims would potentially become the dominant political group was certainly distasteful, if not repugnant. In the view of both Serbian and Croatian perpetrators, Muslims are simply not a group worthy of dominant status. For an active minority, violence and discrimination against these unworthy pretenders was justifiable.

Events

In the free and fair elections of 1990, the vast majority of Croats voted for the nationalist Croatian Democratic Union (HDZ) rather than for a nonnational alternative.[59] In fact, with the imminent collapse of the federal state, all three communities voted for their respective national party. Led by the ultranationalist Mate Boban, Croatians proclaimed the independent republic of Herceg-Bosna on July 3, 1992. It is entirely conceivable that

---

[58] Ramet, *Balkan Babel* p. 267. For a far lower estimate, see George Kenney, "The Bosnian Calculation" *The New York Times Magazine*, April 23, 1995. Kenney, formerly of the U.S. State Department, puts the figure at 25,000 to 60,000.

[59] For concise overviews of the beginning years of the conflict, see Robert Hayden, "The Partition of Bosnia and Hercegovina, 1990–1993" *Radio Free Europe/Radio Liberty Research Report* 2(22) (1993). Also see Susan Woodward, *Balkan Tragedy*, the ninth and tenth chapters; Jasminka Udovicki and Ejub Stitkovac, "Bosnia and Hercegovina: The Second War" in Jasminka Udovicki and James Ridgeway, eds., *Burn This House: The Making and Unmaking of Yugoslavia* (Durham, NC: Duke University Press, 1997); Sabrina Ramet, *Balkan Babel*, the twelfth chapter.

the Serbs, despite their overwhelming advantage in weaponry, could have been defeated by a combined Croat-Muslim effort.[60] After one year, the Bosnian government fielded 120,000–150,000 troops; the well-equipped Croatian Defense Council commanded 25,000–30,000 men. In opposition, the Serbian forces consisted of 70,000–90,000 soldiers – not nearly enough to fight and supply multiple fronts.[61] Had the Croatian Defense Council and Bosnian government coordinated their actions, the Serbs would have had to concentrate their forces and reduce their territorial ambitions. Instead, Croatians attacked Bosnian Muslim positions early on. In early 1993, Croats attacked Muslims in Gornji Vakuf. In the spring Croats launched offensives against Vitez and Mostar at the same time as Serbs assaulted Gorazde in Eastern Bosnia. Of these targets, the Croats most strongly coveted Mostar which they considered the capital of Hercegovina. The nature of the Croatian actions in Mostar closely resembles those of the Serbs in Muslim areas. Croats bombarded Muslim sections of the city in much the same manner as Serbs shelled Sarajevo. As Misha Glenny writes, "The Croats proved that they were as willing as the Serbs to perpetrate atrocities against Muslim civilians. At the height of the fighting in the Hercegovinian capital, Mostar, UN observers registered up to 1,000 Croat shells a day fired at the eastern, Muslim side of the city."[62] Residents were left without food and water. As Robert Donia and John Fine summarize: "The Croatian-Bosnian fighting in 1993 was among the war's bitterest, accompanied by vicious campaigns of ethnic cleansing by both sides."[63] In some contested areas, masked Croats went house to house finding and often killing Muslims. Thousands of Muslim men were imprisoned in underground tunnels near Mostar.[64] By the fall of 1993, Mostar had become separated into two ethnically homogenized districts divided by the Neretva River.

Notably, Serbs and Croats cooperated with one another in the early stages of the war. Boban and the Bosnian Serb leader Radovan Karadzic

---

[60] See James B. Steinberg, "Turning Points in Bosnia and the West" in Zalmay M. Khalilzad, ed., Lessons from Bosnia (RAND report CF-113-AF, 1993). Steinberg's statement is based on his conversation with Martin Spegelj, a Croatian Army General.

[61] Ibid., pp. 12–13.

[62] Misha Glenny, The Balkans: Nationalism, War and the Great Powers (New York: Viking, 2000), p. 641.

[63] Robert J. Donia and John V. A. Fine, Bosnia and Hercegovina: A Tradition Betrayed (New York: Columbia University Press, 1994), p. 252.

[64] Udovicki and Stitkovac, "Bosnia and Hercegovina" see pp. 18–19 for an extended description of Herceg-Bosna.

had met on May 7, 1992 in Graz, Austria to discuss their mutual goal of Bosnian partition (Croats and the Bosnian government had signed an Agreement on Friendship and Cooperation in May as well). In the summer of 1992, Croatian forces rented artillery from the Serbs that would later be used to attack Bosnian government forces. Throughout the conflict, Croatians sold oil and other essentials to Serbs.[65] In June of 1993, Croats and Serbs had ceased fighting each other allowing the Croatians to make gains against Bosnian positions. Tudjman and Milosevic met on June 16th to discuss the partition of Bosnia.

In November of 1995, the warring sides, represented by Tudjman, Izetbegovic, and Milosevic, signed the Dayton Accord, brokered by the United States under the leadership of Richard Holbrooke. The agreement called for a federation of two political entities – Republika Srpska (49% of the territory) and the Muslim-Croat Federation (receiving 51%). The accord called for Herceg-Bosna to disappear by January 1996. Four years later, the Herceg-Bosna had little connection with Bosnian government. Residents of the territory voted in Croatian elections, watched Croatian television, used the Croatian *kuna* as currency, and began political rallies with the Croatian national anthem.[66] Bosnian Croatians held seats in the Croatian Parliament. Perhaps most telling, the region had its own ethnically homogeneous police and paramilitary – the Croat Defense Council – who wore the insignia of the "Croatian Republic of Herceg-Bosna." Concerning Mostar, internationally brokered efforts at reconciliation and reintegration occurred even sooner. Local officials signed a Memorandum of Understanding on June 10, 1994 aimed at reunifying Mostar. Yet, as in the region as a whole, little progress was made. In a 1994 report, Tadeusz Mazowiecki described continued Croatian actions toward Mostar's remaining Muslims as a policy of "soft ethnic cleansing," combining continuous harassment with occasional assaults and attacks. The mayor of east Mostar has noted the continued Croatian obstruction of reconciliation efforts and emphasizes that Croatian intransigence over police jurisdictions makes any move toward reunification of the city impossible.[67] As late as 1997, Croats expelled five hundred Muslims from Jajce.[68]

---

[65] Glenny, *The Balkans* p. 645.
[66] Gordon Bardos, "The Bosnian Cold War: Politics, Society, and International Engagement after Dayton" *The Harriman Review* 11(3) (1999): 1–26.
[67] Safet Orucevic, "Mostar: Europe's Failure" *Bosnia Report* April–June, 1996. Orucevic was Mayor of East Mostar.
[68] Bardos, The Bosnian Cold War p. 20.

In the immediate post-Dayton years, the Bosnian government has adopted a strategy of trying to weave Croatians into the Federation. For example, Muslim politicians have proposed integrating the armed forces. Despite a Muslim population four times that of Croatians, Muslim politicians have supported equal representation in Federation institutions. In return, Croatians have proposed new political arrangements that would produce even further separation of Croats and Muslims. Various Croatian initiatives have called for new monoethnic cantons and municipalities with Croatian educational, judicial, revenue and police control.[69] The words of Kresimir Zubak, the Croatian member of the joint Bosnian-Hercegovinian presidency, are illustrative:

The Dayton solutions for the Croats in Bosnia-Hercegovina are relatively favorable: The problem is the fact that we are in a Federation with a partner with whom we are not satisfied. We feel their attempts at domination. We are aware of their attempts to revise Dayton in order to create some type of unitary Bosnia-Hercegovina, which today is no longer possible and will not be for a long time.[70]

It should be noted that Zubak was the replacement for Mate Boban. Zubak was chosen because he was seen as a "pliable politician more acceptable to Western diplomats."[71]

In summary, despite the current existence of a Muslim-Croat Federation, in the recent past a sizable number of Croatians have participated in acts of violence against Muslims similar to those committed by their Serb counterparts. Moreover, Croatians cooperated with Serbs in attempting to dismember Bosnia. Although international politics and balance of power considerations have worked to make Croats and Muslims partners in a political federation, this arrangement has conspicuously never instituted any form of Muslim authority over Croatians. Despite the Muslim-Croat Federation, or perhaps because of it, Bosnian Croats have exhibited more positive views toward Serbs than Muslims in recent survey research.[72] Several years after Dayton, all visible day-to-day signs of authority in Croatian-controlled territory – police positions, currency, license plates, postage stamps – were Croatian, rather than Bosnian. The Serbs of Republika Srpska have likewise shown little desire to accept

[69] Ibid., p. 21.
[70] Quotation from interview with Kresimir Zubak, *Globus* January 2, 1998, p. 19.
[71] Donia and Fine, *Bosnia and Hercegovina* p. 271.
[72] See various works by Kjell Magnusson.

the authority of the Bosnian government in the immediate post-Dayton years.

Analysis

As in Croatia, the Fear narrative can be applied to many individual actions in Bosnian localities after the breakdown of Yugoslavia. With central authority disintegrating and all ethnic groups arming, security considerations became paramount. This being said, there are several aspects of the Bosnian conflict that simply do not fit Fear. First of all, any version of Fear stressing Milosevic and the Serbs as genocidal maniacs does not fit. Fear predicts action against the strongest threat. At the beginning of the war, the Serbs, with weapons from the Yugoslav National Army, were clearly the greatest military threat. Extending the logic of the international relations theory underlying the narrative, Fear would predict balancing and cooperation among Croats and Bosnian forces. Instead, Serb and Croat leaders made deals to divide up Bosnia. At the mass level, Croatian forces appeared to have few qualms about cleansing and bombarding Muslim localities. Local Croatians clearly targeted mosques and other Muslim cultural symbols. Furthermore, the Fear narrative has little to say about the Croatian unwillingness to unify the day-to-day functioning of the Muslim-Croat Federation. Why no imperative to coalesce against the continued threat posed by Milosevic's regime in the years after Dayton?

Hatred likewise carries little explanatory weight. Despite commonly heard claims of "ancient hatred," there are few historical precedents for Croat-Muslim interethnic violence.[73] Bosnia has often witnessed violence, but the targets have been Ottoman and Austro-Hungarian overlords rather than other ethnic groups. The important exception to this overall nonviolent ethnic history is the substantial killing that occurred during the Second World War. While it is true that some groups of the 1990s have adopted the names and rhetoric of World War Two predecessors, the conduct of the fighting in the 1940s was so diffuse that it could not produce the coherent roles and scripts that define Hatred. In effect, three different conflicts played out in Yugoslavia during the Second World War – the fight against German and Italian occupiers, the political battle between

---

[73] An emphatic attack on Bosnian "ancient hatred" can be found in Donia and Fine, *Bosnia and Hercegovina.*

Communists and Chetniks, and interethnic violence among various groups. The respective historical legacies of these three contests vary across regions as well as across group relationships. Serbs, especially those in the Krajina region, might be seen as forming a sustained cultural code from the Croatian-Ustasha elimination of Serbs, with special meaning attached to Jasenovac. In this case, the ethnic aspects of the Second World War left a clear and powerful residue. But for Serb-Muslim relations, no such clarity exists. While Jasenovac provides a lasting symbol of Croatian threat, no such symbol can be attached to the Muslims. On the one hand, Muslims served in a Croatian-organized S.S. division. In Eastern Hercegovina, Muslim collaborators killed Serbs and Serbs retaliated.[74] Later in the war, in contrast, significant numbers of Muslims joined the Partisans in fighting against the Ustasha. In both the Ustasha and the Partisans, the Muslims played a supporting role. While historical memories of Muslim collaboration no doubt colored later Serbian views, the war years did not create roles that could coherently provide directions for action in the 1990s. In the 1990s, Serbs created a bogeyman of Muslim fundamentalism. Nationalist rhetoric played up an international Islamic threat. The use of this particular propaganda and imagery has little historical precedent.[75]

Discussion of pre-1991 Bosnia usually centers on its unusual degree of tolerance, its lack of day-to-day visible ethnic hierarchies, and its rates of ethnic intermarriage. Few scholars place much explanatory weight on the motivations of local participants because they assume that malignant emotions could not have risen out of this pacific ethnic environment. The blame must be fully and squarely placed on outsiders and their political designs which served to initiate the Fear sequence. While there is something to be said for this view, I would argue that the similarity in Croat and Serb actions, as well as Serb-Croat cooperation, suggests something more: Both Croats and Serbs found the possibility of Muslims occupying a superior position on an ethnic hierarchy unnatural and distasteful. In other words, Resentment, as well as Fear, motivated perpetrators.

---

[74] Donia and Fine, *Bosnia and Hercegovina* p. 142.

[75] Michael Sells, in *The Bridge Betrayed: Religion and Genocide in Bosnia* (Berkeley: University of California Press, 1998) argues that both Serbs and Croats attacked Muslims from Christoslavism – the belief that Slavs are by nature Christians and those that convert (the Bosnian Muslims) are Judas figures worthy of elimination. Sells describes how rituals and roles relating to the passion of Christ can be appropriated to justify violence against outside groups. Sells' theory would fit Hatred, I believe.

Most scholars fail to consider Resentment because they concentrate too much on Sarajevo and Bosnian urban life.[76] The present study, on the other hand, concerns the motivations of perpetrators – who in Bosnia came in large part from *rural* areas. First of all, perception of ethnic consciousness differed across city and country. While Sarajevans may have barely known their ethnic background in the prewar era, residents of the countyside did. As Tone Bringa states in her anthropological study: "While in the village people of different ethnoreligious backgrounds would live side by side and often have close friendships, they would rarely intermarry. In some neighborhoods they would not even live side by side and would know little about each other. And while some families would have a long tradition of friendship across ethnoreligious communities others would not."[77]

Secondly, mobilization of rural communities differs from urban ones. The strong personal networks able to catalyze communities for rebellion are more likely to be present. Among Serbs, relations among god-families (*cumovi*) provide communication and social norms conducive to armed organization. Commenting on Serbian nationalism, Sabrina Ramet holds that social memory in the countryside differs from its urban counterpart.[78] Rural Serbs and Croats were more likely to see Muslims as the heirs of Ottoman occupation – a system in which non-Muslims seldom owned land and lived as second-class citizens. In the simpler and more traditional rural areas, survivors of the atrocities of the Second World War and their descendants maintained both networks and active memories. Ramet concludes:

But there is a world of difference between a national movement founded on urban mobilization (even if it manipulates the symbols and mythologies of the countryside, in its own distorted mirror) and a national movement based, to a great extent, on rural mobilization. From the standpoint of the potential for chauvinist excesses, for the suspension of any notions of tolerance and for excesses of violence, the latter, rural mobilization, is, as Eugen Weber has noted, the more dangerous.[79]

---

[76] There are some notable exceptions. See, for example, Eric D. Gordy, *The Culture of Power in Serbia: Nationalism and the Destruction of Alternatives* (University Park, PA: University of Pennsylvania Press, 1999) and John B. Allcock, "Rural Resentment and the Break-up of Yugoslavia" paper presented at the American Association for the Advancement of Slavic Studies, St. Louis, Missouri, November 18–21, 1999.

[77] Tone Bringa, *Being Muslim the Bosnian Way: Identity and Community in a Central Bosnian Village* (Princeton, NJ: Princeton University Press, 1995), p. 4.

[78] Sabrina Ramet, "Nationalism and the Idiocy of the Countryside: the Case of Serbia" *Ethnic and Racial Studies* 19(1) (1996): 70–87.

[79] Ramet, "Nationalism and the Idiocy of the Countryside" p. 85.

Third, Bosnia's Serb and Croatian residents had realistic reasons to anticipate status reduction in the new state. In 1970, Izetbegovic wrote *The Islamic Declaration: A Programme of the Islamisation of Muslims and Muslim Peoples.* This work stated that the "attainment of the Islamic order is a sacrosanct goal which cannot be overridden by any vote."[80] In 1990, Izetbegovic's political party – the Party of Democratic Action (SDA) – became the first openly Islamic party in post-Second World War Yugoslavia.[81] While the SDA did not openly seek a program of dominance, some of its statements regarding the "take-over" of power certainly appeared to embrace such a position. As Xavier Bougarel has summarized:

(T)he political project of the SDA has always revolved around three main goals: the sovereignty of the Bosnian Muslim nation, the independence and territorial integrity of Bosnia-Hercegovina and the territorial autonomy of Sandjak. Together, these three objectives comprise what could be called the 'greater Muslim' project of the SDA: a state composed of Bosnia-Hercegovina and Sandjak, in which the Muslims would be the majority, and the Serbs and Croats would be reduced to national minorities.[82]

In its effort to establish a Muslim majority status, the SDA urged Muslim participation in the 1991 census with the slogan "On our numbers depend our rights." Some Serbs and Croats likely saw more than "rights" as a Muslim goal. With the historical baggage of the Ottoman Empire and the political victory of an Islamically defined and oriented political party, Serbs and Croats foresaw the unpleasant possibility of political subordination to an ethnic group that wasn't even recognized as a nation until 1968.[83]

While outsiders may have instigated much of Bosnia's violence, Resentment drove many locals to join in or look the other way. Keeping in mind that the goal here is to explain the motivations of primarily rural Serbs and Croats in Bosnia-Hercegovina, the Resentment narrative produces the

---

[80] Aleksandar Pavkovic, "Anticipating the Disintegration: Nationalisms in the Former Yugoslavia, 1980–1990" *Nationalities Papers* 25(3) (1997): 427–40. Quote is from p. 435.

[81] For an overview of Bosnian Islam in the 1990s, see Xavier Bougarel, "Cultural Identity or Political Ideology? Bosnian Islam Since 1990" Paper presented for the Annual Convention of the Association for the Study of Nationalities, Columbia University, New York, April 15–17, 1999.

[82] Bougarel, p. 12.

[83] Pavkovic, "Anticipating the Disintegration: Nationalisms in the Former Yugoslavia, 1980–1990" summarizes, "In this context, the affirmation of an Islamic religiously-defined identity in politics was viewed, by many Serbs and Croats, as a drive towards renewed political and economic dominance of the Muslims over the other nations in Bosnia-Hercegovina" on p. 436.

following sequence. There was little support for secession among Serbs and Croats in Bosnia-Hercegovina until the breakup of the state appeared imminent. At that point, however, abundant information indicated that a reversal of status was imminent. Serbs and Croats were exposed to the Slovenian and Croatian examples, the background of Izetbegovic and the SDA, and propaganda from Belgrade and Zagreb. In the grip of emotion, one essentializes identities. Who are the Muslims? They are a group formed from religious conversion and collaboration with the Ottomans, tainted with collaboration in the Second World War, and not even recognized as a nation until 1968. To be below this weak group was a humiliation. Emotion made formerly unthinkable actions now possible. Previously, the ethnicity of one's neighbor was of little consequence, but now events had imbued ethnicity with status connotations. Muslims became objectified in a way that legitimated violence or at least passivity. This Resentment sequence may have played out most prominently among male, rural Serbs and Croats in areas like western Hercegovina, but they are exactly the perpetrators whose actions must be explained.

In Bosnia, the urban-rural dichotomy is central to the activation of emotion. For rural Serbs and Croats, the effeminate Sarajevans could be an object of contempt. Certainly, for many Sarajevans, the rural dwellers, or *Seljaci*, were an object of derision. Consider the following passage from Sarajevan Zlatko Dizdarevic's published war journal. He laments the loss of friends and that:

... we dug ourselves the same grave because we didn't know how, or didn't want, to defy the hicks from the woods when we should have. We kept telling jokes at their expense, while they came down from the hills, dragging one another, hating us because we knew about soap and water, about washing our feet and wearing clean socks.[84]

Westerners may wonder how Serbs sat in the mountains around Sarajevo sending in shell after shell against a defenseless population. But the "hicks from the woods" knew the contempt that the cosmopolitans had for them. With the collapse of Yugoslavia, and the possible creation of a Muslim-centered Bosnian state, ethnic markers attached to urban ones. Sarajevan targets were now urban Muslims trying to establish status dominance. For the "hicks," Sarajevans deserved what they got.

[84] Zlatko Dizdarevic, *Sarajevo: A War Journal* (New York: Henry Holt and Company, 1994), pp. 111–12.

Russell Hardin has interpreted the rural Serbs' actions against Sarajevo as mainly a matter of ignorance. In Hardin's interpretation, Serbian elites wishing to retain power created a myth of Islamic jihad. The rural Bosnian Serbs, living in the ignorance of country life, formed sincere beliefs that jihad will threaten their lives and so are motivated to action by these distorted beliefs. As Hardin writes:

The mobilizers of ethnicity want ignorance first and foremost. They want woefully restricted horizons in order to induce the lowest denominator of the epistemological comforts of the ethnic home, in order to induce blinkered loyalty. Evidently, they find people who fit their mold more readily in rural areas than in cities. Ignorance and urbanity have gone to war, and urbanity has been the instant loser in Yugoslavia.[85]

After describing some of the precise targeting of specific Muslim religious and cultural institutions, Hardin continues:

They specifically wish to destroy anything that smacks of Muslim community just as they wish to destroy anything that smacks of cosmopolitan transcendance of narrow community.

Hardin's view echoes that of the urban Muslims who also saw the rural Serbs as ignorant: Elites produce skewed information and myth that in turn produce distorted beliefs within an ignorant mass. Hardin's rational choice account relies upon a well of massive ignorance.

The alternative theory of Resentment assumes no ignorance at all. Resentment assumes that individuals are hypersensitive to interactions that place them in a subordinate position, especially if they are unaccustomed to such situations. In a new Bosnian state, especially one founded on the conceptions of Alia Izetbegovic, Serbs were going to occupy a secondary position on the ethnic hierarchy. It was particularly galling that such a weak people, the urban people with little martial tradition, a people who had previously been pushed down the ethnic hierarchy, would now be in a position superior to Serbs, the group that had been, at the very least, first among equals. While mimicing their leaders' warnings of jihad, the rural Bosnian Serbs, well aware of the cosmopolitans' views of their inferiority, loaded their cannons and targeted another mosque to put the urban Muslims in their place. By destroying mosques, rural Bosnian Serbs were doing what their urban forerunners had done in the previous century. After

---

[85] Russell Hardin, *One for All: The Logic of Group Conflict* (Princeton, NJ: Princeton University Press, 1995), p. 162.

the liberation of Belgrade from the Ottomans in 1806, Serbs methodically destroyed all signs of Ottoman dominance, including mosques. Today in Belgrade, only one mosque from that period exists.[86]

Croatian shelling of Mostar, and its mosques, resembled that of Sarajevo, and for the same reasons. Muslims had stepped out of place; they deserved what they were getting. In the post-Dayton years, despite the internationally brokered Muslim-Croat Federation, Croats, like the Serbs, have been unwilling to accept any Muslim authority and blocked it at every turn. The reason that Croat actions often mirrored those of Serbs is that both held disdain for the Muslims and the possibility of their attaining a status they did not deserve. Although Serbs and Croats could kill one another in other arenas, this common view, and the Resentment that followed it, created the possibilities for cooperation on actions against Muslims. On Bosnia, Tudjman and Milosevic, like Boban and Karadzic, held common views on a Muslim state. So did many other Serbs and Croats, especially numbers of Serbs and Croats living in the Bosnian-Hercegovinian countryside who joined outside instigators.

Puzzle 3: What Explains Serbian Participation and Tacit Mass Approval in the Expulsion of More Than One Million Albanians in Kosovo?

On March 24, 1999, NATO began bombing Yugoslavia. In response, the Milosevic regime initiated a program to expel the majority of Kosovo's Albanian population. By early May, the U.S. State Department reported that over 90% of all Kosovo's Albanians had been driven from their homes – 900,000 across borders and 500,000 displaced within Kosovo. In all, five hundred villages were emptied and destroyed.[87] Furthermore, killings and humiliations occurred during the operation. While the various motivations of the Milosevic regime, NATO, and the United States are still a matter of debate, a few things are clear concerning this ethnic cleansing operation.

First, a significant and diverse number of Serbs participated in the expulsions. Refugee accounts tell of masked terrorists and outsiders, but

---

[86] See Andrei Simic, "Nationalism as Folk Ideology" in Joel M. Halpern and David A. Kideckel, eds., *Neighbors at War: Anthropological Perspectives on Yugoslav Ethnicity, Culture, and History* (University Park, PA: Pennsylvania State University Press, 2000), p. 112.

[87] These figures are from John Kifner, "How Serb Forces Purged One Million Albanians" *The New York Times*, May 29, 1999.

they also mention local people and neighbors. All varieties of Serb/ Yugoslav security forces were involved: the regular army, the Special Police, private paramilitary groups, armed units of the Interior Ministry, and local police and volunteers. There are few reports indicating that these various forces had trouble working together during this operation.

Second, Serbs stripped Albanians of all proof of Yugoslav citizenship including not only identity papers but also license plates. The apparent purpose was to deny Albanians clear legal means to return and claim property and citizenship.

Third, the Serbs, despite early reports to the contrary, murdered a relatively small number of Albanians. The first official estimates put the number killed at 44,000. Then the figures were progressively halved to 22,000 and then 11,000. This last figure is still probably too high. For instance, Spanish forensic experts were told to expect 2,000 cadavers and mass graves in their assigned zone in northern Kosovo. They found only 187 bodies in individual graves.[88] Contrary to expectations, no mass of dead were found in Kosovo's mines. In comparison, Serbian forces killed more than 7,000 Muslims in the Bosnian town of Srebrenica alone. Serbs committed a violent expulsion of Albanians from Kosovo, but they did not commit genocide.

Fourth, there is little evidence that any sizable number of Serbs felt or feel remorse or shame at the Kosovo cleansing operation. Some speculated that if Serbs knew what was being done in their name they would vigorously protest. However, given the numbers of residents in Serbia proper with family and personal connections to Kosovo Serbs, it is difficult to believe that Serbs were ignorant of what was going on in Kosovo. Milosevic has always faced opposition in Serbia. At times, it appeared that the opposition might even bring down his regime. During the bombing, however, Serbs defiantly stood on bridges with targets strapped on their backs. After Milosevic signed the peace accord that brought NATO troops into Kosovo, popular criticism focused on losing the territory rather than any crimes that may have been committed there.

Fifth, although there is a large number of Albanians living in Belgrade, there is little evidence that Albanians became targets of violence during the period of bombing and expulsion.

The events concerning Kosovo in the spring of 1999 can be briefly summarized: A large and diverse number of Serbs, both from Serbia proper

---

[88] From the article by Pablo Ordaz, *El Pais*, September 23, 1999.

and from Kosovo, participated in a popularly (if tacitly) supported and coordinated effort to expel massive numbers of Albanians from Kosovo and strip them of the necessary means to return. How can this phenomenon be explained? Up to this point in the book, Hatred has not been found to be the most plausible explanatory sequence for any question. Hatred, I will argue, fits the Serb expulsion of Albanian Kosovars very well. After reviewing Hatred and applying it to Serbian participation in March 1999, I will compare its fit with the Fear, Resentment, and Rage alternatives.

Hatred produces the following story and predictions: Structural changes such as the collapse of the center eliminate constraints and produce an opportunity to commit aggression against other groups. The target of ethnic violence will be the group that has frequently been attacked with similar justification over a lengthy time period. If the target has not been a long-hated or frequently attacked ethnic group, or if the target is attacked with a completely new justification, then Hatred is not supported. Hatred is based on the existence of a cultural schema that motivates individual action. The conception of Hatred as a schema relies on four crucial elements. The schema must contain a constant and negative representation of the innate nature of the opposing ethnic group. The schema should provide a script specifying roles and the nature of action. The justification for action should remain the same across historical periods. Finally, the acts of violence and humiliation should possess ritualistic qualities. Of all the cases considered in this manuscript, the conflict in Kosovo comes closest to meeting these criteria, as a brief history of the region indicates.

The March 1999 mass expulsions were the fourth instance of ethnic cleansing in Kosovo during the twentieth century. In each case, the goal was a demographic transformation of Kosovo. The participants in this contest, both active and passive, appear to know the rules in this game and act accordingly. The first wave of expulsion and flight came when Serbians and Montenegrins ended Ottoman control over Kosovo with the campaigns of the 1912–13 Balkan War. The 1913 Carnegie Endowment report describes the Serbian advance into Kosovo in the following fashion:

Houses and whole villages reduced to ashes, unarmed and innocent populations massacred *en masse*, incredible acts of violence, pillage and brutality of every kind – such were the means which were employed and are still being employed by the Serbo-Montenegrin soldiery, with a view to the entire transformation of the ethnic character of regions inhabited exclusively by Albanians.

244

We thus arrive at the second characteristic feature of the Balkan wars, a feature which is a necessary correlative of the first. Since the population of the countries about to be occupied knew, by tradition, instinct and experience, what they had to expect from the armies of the enemy and from the neighboring countries from which these armies belonged, they did not await their arrival, but fled. Thus, generally speaking, the army of the enemy found on its way nothing but villages which were either half deserted or entirely abandoned. . . . All along the railways interminable trains of carts drawn by oxen followed one another; behind them came emigrant families and, in the neighborhoods of the big towns, bodies of refugees were found encamped.[89]

Leon Trotsky was a correspondent covering the Balkan wars for the Ukrainian newspaper *Kievskaia Mysl*. Trotsky was convinced that a demographic project lay at the root of the atrocities he witnessed: "The Serbs in Old Serbia, in their national endeavour to correct data in the ethnographical statistics that are not quite favourable to them, are engaged quite simply in systematic extermination of the Muslim population."[90] Helping to facilitate this brutality, a generation of anti-Albanian writings helped to reduce Albanians to a set of dehumanized stereotypes. Dr. Vladan Djordjevic, a Serbian statesman and public health specialist, held that Albanians possessed "prehuman" physical traits and no significant history.[91] Not surprisingly, the historic myth of Kosovo held a powerful sway over the events. Many Serbs consider Kosovo the cradle of Serbian civilization. The Serbian defeat in Kosovo in 1389 is perhaps the most celebrated event in Serbian history. For over five hundred years, the Turks had occupied the heart of historic Serbia. In 1912–13, Serbs were taking it back. King Petar came to Kosovo to perform a candle-lighting ceremony to mark the return of Serbs. Finally, Serbs had avenged Kosovo. The only problem was the fact that few Serbs lived in the historic heart of Serbia.

A second wave of violence occurred in 1918–19. During the First World War, Serbs were forced to evacuate the region in 1915 leaving it to Austro-Hungarian control. When the Serbs returned, their entrance was even more brutal than in the Balkan Wars. They killed 800 in the Djakovica

---

[89] Carnegie Endowment for International Peace, *The Other Balkan Wars: A 1913 Carnegie Endowment Inquiry in Retrospect* (Washington, DC: Carnegie Endowment for Peace, 1993), p. 151.

[90] Quoted by Malcolm, *Kosovo* p. 253.

[91] Ivo Banac, *The National Question in Yugoslavia* pp. 293–94. The Serbian debate over the nature and historical origins of Albanians is far more complex than this racial stereotyping, as Banac discusses at greater length. However, I wish to emphasize here the Serbian idea that Albanians innately hold negative traits.

region and destroyed villages in the Rugova Gorge.[92] Italian figures put the numbers of January and February 1919 at 6,040 killed and 3,873 houses destroyed.[93] Again, Albanians fled, some to the high ground and some south to Shkoder. The reconquest of the region introduced an era of official policies aimed at transforming the ethnic numbers of Kosovo. Authorities closed schools using the Albanian language, underreported the Albanian population by 50% in the 1921 census, and most crucially, began programs aimed at Albanian emigration and Serb colonization.[94] In some counties, the government restricted Albanian landholdings to amounts insufficient for subsistence.[95] A treaty with Turkey provided an outlet for emigration for these beleaguered peasants. On the other side of the equation, the government ceded over 57,000 acres to 17,679 Serbian families from Montenegro, Lika, and Hercegovina in an effort to increase Serbian numbers in the territory.[96] The Yugoslav government even enlisted international help in fostering the removal of Albanians. In 1935, Turkey agreed to take 200,000 "Turks." In 1938, the Serbs offered Turkey 15,000 dinars for each family they would take and Turkey agreed to take 40,000 families at a price of 500 Turkish pounds per family. This transfer was supposed to take place over a multiyear period stretching from 1939–44, but was prevented by the outbreak of the Second World War.[97] The Serbs had a serious program to expel massive numbers of Albanians during the interwar years. The colonization program, despite the emigration of tens of thousands,[98] failed to significantly change the ethnic imbalance in Kosovo. But the dream continued. Vaso Cubrilovic, a respected historian, wrote in a March 7, 1937 government memorandum entitled "The Expulsion of the Albanians": "It is impossible to repel the Albanians just by gradual colonization. . . . The only possiblity and method is the brutal power of a well-organized state. . . . We have already stressed that for us the only efficient way is the mass deportation of Albanians out of their triangle."[99]

The third wave of interethnic violence occurred during the Second World War, but this time the direction of expulsions was reversed. Accord-

---

[92] Banac, *The National Question* p. 298.   [93] Malcolm, *Kosovo* p. 272.
[94] Ibid., pp. 298–300.   [95] Ibid., p. 285; Banac, *The National Question* p. 301.
[96] Banac, *The National Question* pp. 299–300.
[97] For more details, see Malcolm, *Kosovo* pp. 283–85.
[98] Malcolm, *Kosovo* p. 286 puts the total figure at 90,000 to 150,000 from 1918–1941.
[99] Dusan Necak, "Historical Elements for Understanding the 'Yugoslav Question'" in *Yugoslavia, the Former and Future: Reflections by Scholars from the Region* (Washington: The Brookings Institution, 1995), p. 24.

ing to German reports, forty thousand Serbs were driven out of Kosovo during Italian and German occupation of the region.[100] Serbs would remember, and inflate, these numbers in later decades. The introduction of a Communist state and media control sent open discussion of the Kosovo problem underground. Yet it still remained in latent form. Dobrica Cosic, a top Communist official, was dismissed from the Central Committee for his criticisms of Kosovo. The heightened autonomy created by the 1974 constitution brought more rumblings. By the 1980s, Kosovo emerged as the major grievance of Serbian intellectuals. Dimitrije Bogdanovic's *A Book about Kosovo*, published in 1985, openly accused Kosovo Albanians of seeking a policy of Albanian ethnic purity. Similar books followed. Recall from the previously quoted section of the memorandum how Serbian intellectuals saw the situation in Kosovo: "First, there is a century-old history of national conflict in Kosovo. . . . But the little David had the upper hand most of the time because it was amply supported by overwhelming allies: the Islamic Ottoman Empire during five centuries until 1912; Austria-Hungary which occupied the entire territory during World War One; fascist Italy and Germany which did the same during World War Two; the Soviet Union and China after 1948; eventually a dominating anti-Serbian coalition in Yugoslavia itself over the last twenty years."

This passage illustrates the elements of a cultural schema at work. Albanians have consistently persecuted Serbs with the help of outside powers – the Ottomans for five centuries, the Austro-Hungarians in World War One, the fascist powers in World War Two, the Soviets in the immediate postwar. Now, again in the post-war period, Albanians have combined with anti-Serb peoples of Yugoslavia to drive Serbs out of Kosovo, to commit genocide against Serbs. By 1990, these political deficiencies had been translated into racial terms, innate deficiencies justifying, and defining, hatred. As Julie Mertus writes, "Kosovo was not merely a place where things happened that could be subject to political manipulation. Kosovo was an abstraction, a set of national myths in the popular imagination. Over time, the nationalism became racialized, that is, difference was framed in terms of perceived physical differences in skin, noses, ears, IQ, sexuality. . . . Accused in the past of being culturally inferior, Albanians increasingly were depicted as genetically inferior as well. This is racism of the purest sort."[101]

[100] Malcolm, *Kosovo* p. 305.   [101] Mertus, *Kosovo* p. 8.

On the eve of the March 1999 cleansing of Kosovo, a cultural schema was in place capable of motivating participation and producing callousness toward Albanian suffering. This schema contained roles: Albanians as persecutors in league with outside powers; Serbs as victims, a persecuted minority in the cradle of their own culture. These roles took on an innate, racialized quality definitive of hatred. This schema provided a script for action: mass expulsion (not genocide) of the Albanian population. This schema provided a consistent justification for committing or tolerating atrocities: Saving Kosovo could only be accomplished by radical demographic changes. Albanians had driven out Serbs; Serbs would drive out Albanians. These were the rules, both sides knew them.

With this background, Hatred can now be applied to the puzzle at hand. What explains Serbian participation and tacit mass approval in the expulsion of more than one million Albanians in Kosovo? Structural changes produced information and beliefs that triggered the activation of a cultural schema. The Kosovo Albanians were playing their traditional role by collaborating with outside protectors, this time the West and NATO. Serbs were again persecuted, demographically overwhelmed, and driven out of their historic cradle by the actions of the newly formed KLA. The script specified action. With the removal of observers and the beginning of NATO bombing, Serbs had little to lose in carrying out their historically consistent solution: mass expulsion. Albanians, as in previous times, streamed to safety in the wake of Serbian terror. While it is debatable whether the violence and humiliations during the expulsion contained ritualistic qualities, the terror, the burning of houses, the flight of refugees all had their precedence in previous episodes. These actions apparently produced little moral outrage among perpetrators and Serb civilians. For outside observers, the action was one of the most inhumane in Europe since the end of the Second World War. For many Serbs, under the sway of Hatred, the mass expulsions could not generate any feelings of compassion or guilt. The historical schema created an aura of something like common sense concerning the purge. It was something that was bad, but somehow justifiable.

Alternative Explanations

Rage would posit that Albanians serve as a scapegoat for Serbian frustrations. Serbs see in Kosovo Albanians what they want to see – rapists, thieves, women as baby factories. After the losses in Croatia and Bosnia and the terrible economy, Serbs felt some relief in violence and humiliation against Albanians. Two types of evidence argue against Rage. First, there are many Albanians living in Belgrade and other locations in Serbia, but they did not come under attack. There is something specific to Albanians in Kosovo. Second, the form of the Serb action must be addressed. Why massive expulsions? Hatred has an answer for both of these issues; Rage does not. History produced roles and actions specific to Kosovo. Albanians living in Kosovo were not "inkblots." Serbian imagery of Kosovar Albanians as an unjust majority worthy of expulsion was consistent over the course of decades.

Resentment tells a story based on observable changes in status indicators. Such a change did occur, but in the 1970s. As outlined above, Albanians gained both a new constitutional status and control over the police and the bureaucracies in the 1970s. Serbs had retaken these positions in the 1980s. In September 1990, for instance, two hundred Albanian judges' district and public attorneys were sacked and replaced with Serbs.[102] Serb police constantly harassed Albanians with no fear of repercussions. After the dissolution of the old Yugoslav state, army units moved into Kosovo from Macedonia. A long list of other features of Kosovo life could be mentioned but suffice it to say that in terms of day-to-day experience, the Albanians were unquestionably a subordinated people by the early 1990s. No status reversal precipitated the timing or nature of Serb actions in 1999.

The most plausible contender to Hatred is Fear. The Kosovo Liberation Army had emerged from nowhere to effectively attack Serbs. The KLA killed many Serbs, many of them police, in fighting during the previous year. It was realistic to believe that the KLA might grow stronger over time. Certainly, given the high birth rates of Kosovar Albanians, the demographic imbalance would only grow worse over time. Serbs, both elites and the general population, sensed a window of opportunity, and aimed a decisive blow against the population – the support base of the KLA. For most Serb individuals, the terror and the suffering of the Albanian refugees was unfortunate but the fear of future battles with a strong KLA made it excusable.

Although there were certainly military and defensive reasons for Serb actions, Hatred possesses more power for the events of spring 1999. First,

---

[102] Hugh Poulton and Miranda Vickers, "The Kosovo Albanians: Ethnic Confrontation with the Slav State" in Hugh Poulton and Suha Taji-Farouki, eds., *Muslim Identity and the Balkan State* (New York: New York University Press, 1997), pp. 158–59.

Hatred would seem to better predict the nature of the action. Fear might predict the cleansing of the areas around KLA strongholds, but not the mass expulsion of the majority of Albanians in the entire region. This project, as well as its widespread brutality, goes beyond anything defensive. Hatred places the mass expulsions in a historical context in which a complete purge of Albanians has become a sort of common sense. Fear does not explain why individuals not in direct danger (those living in Belgrade for instance) would support such a project. Finally, the Serbian obsession with Kosovo is so consistent, striking, and ubiquitous that its power to form a cultural schema seems difficult to question.

Summary

Taken together, the answers to the three puzzles highlight the diverse motivations that drove perpetrators and supporters during the collapse of Yugoslavia and the resulting conflicts. Hatred pervaded Serbian actions in the expulsions of Albanians from Kosovo; Resentment toward Muslims appears to have helped drive Croatian and Serbian actions in Bosnia; Fear and Resentment mixed to create the carnage of the Croatian War. These findings suggest that "Yugoslavia" cannot be considered a single case but rather a set of related cases created or at least exacerbated by varying emotions. Yet, these Yugoslav cases do provide for a few general conclusions.

First, the cases emphatically demonstrate that history matters. Such a statement may seem banal, but many, if not most, political science treatments of the Yugoslav violence stress recent elite manipulations or the situational dynamics of Fear and the security dilemma. The treatment above shows that Croatian actions in the early 1990s are the most recent manifestation of historic resentments. Serbs participating in the clearing of Kosovo in 1999 were motivated by a deeply embedded cultural schema which helped produce a devaluation of Albanian life and a "common sense" for a policy of mass expulsion. Neither the Croatian case nor the Kosovo puzzle can be fully understood outside of their broad historical contexts.

Second, the chapter has reinforced the previous chapters' findings of the power and pervasiveness of Resentment. Croats resented Serbian status dominance since the inception of the state in the days after World War One. Many Croats and Serbs could not easily accept the status equality or inferiority with Muslims that would have accompanied the formation of a Bosnian state. Although not the primary cause of the March

1999 events, Kosovo Serbs could not tolerate the status reversals of the 1970s. The fact that history matters and Resentment is a powerful force might seem to suggest support for Ernest Gellner's theory and its implicit mechanisms. In fact, the Yugoslav cases do not offer such support. Gellner envisioned the march of industrialization as almost mechanically producing the need for language rationalization. Modernization and language policy would naturally provoke resentments and the drive for new nations. In Yugoslavia, the Resentment sequence had little to do with language dynamics. Croats resented Serbs, and Serbs and Croats resented Muslims – but all three groups spoke the same language. Gellner saw modernization as the driving force behind the rise of nationalism and its intendant emotions. Yet, in Yugoslavia the emotions motivating conflict cannot be directly connected to modernization. Croatians were more economically advanced than the Serbs. Their self-image as a more modern and western people than the Serbs helped fuel their antagonism toward Serbs. In contrast, in Bosnia the rural Serbs and Croats were economically backward in comparison to their counterparts in Sarajevo, but they had little trouble in shelling the Bosnian capitals and its mosques. The larger point is that the status reversals and status inconsistencies driving Resentment need not be connected to any mechanical process. Resentment can arise out of the development and resentments of Ruritanians, but it may arise in a host of other situations as well.

The importance of history also provides insight into the relationship between the elite and the mass. If history is important, then it will serve as a constraint on the strategies of elites. Elite attempts at manipulation will fail if they do not resonate with historical experience. The elite versus mass question is, in most cases, a matter of degree. Certainly, charismatic leaders can organize and motivate populations with their ideas; of course, elites can use the control of the media to distort information and manipulate numbers of people. But there is no reason to assume that elites always constrain and manipulate masses rather than the other way around. Many times it is impossible to determine who is leading whom.

One look at the leaders of some nationalist movements is enough to cast doubt on elite-led arguments focusing on charisma. For example, consider the rise of the virulently nationalist and violent post-Communist Serbian movement. Slobodan Milosevic was a faceless bureaucrat in the banking system for most of his political life. He transformed into a charismatic leader only after going to Kosovo and proclaiming that no one has the right to beat Serbs. Who provided the charisma, Milosevic himself or the masses of Serbs who possessed a well of hatred against Albanians? Other regional Serbian leaders were little different. It would be hard to find a Lenin or Ho Chi Minh among this motley crew.

Radovan Karadzic is often seen as an evil, manipulative elite who has led many well-intentioned but badly informed individuals down a path to destruction. As an indicted war criminal, he is assigned much of the blame for the thousands of deaths and rapes occurring in Bosnia. However, it is difficult to see how this bad poet, average psychiatrist, and convicted embezzler could become a leader so easily if he did not tie into some existing motivational force among Bosnian Serbs. Vladimir Srebrov, one of Karadzic's former friends from his early days in Sarajevo, provides an interesting insight helpful to understanding Karadzic's success:

> What was interesting about Radovan Karadzic is that he was into the style of flower children and he had long hair and dressed in groovy clothes, and so on. However, that was only his appearance on the outside, inside he remained what he always was – a peasant who came to the big city. Look at his collections of poetry. In them you'll find a peasant's big hatred of an urban center. You can find a man who's a city killer, and who's ready to destroy anything belonging to the life of the city.

Bosnian Serbs would indeed rain shells upon Sarajevo after Izetbegovic declared an independent Bosnia. The question here is whether Karadzic led them (duped them?) into this action or whether he simply presided over actions that many Serbs of similar background were already inclined to do. Where should the emphasis be placed?

I have used the example of Karadzic for another reason. In addition to the question of elite versus mass, the present study challenges the view of the nature of the mass actor in Eastern European ethnic conflict. In the Karadzic example just mentioned, as in the general Eastern European history in the other cases, the actors in many periods are the rural inhabitants or their modernized/modernizing offspring. Commonly, this social element is seen as a Marxian "bag of potatoes," as possessing a strong desire for the "epistemological comforts of home" as living in the "idiocy of rural life" – a group prone to pettiness or jealousy, simple and uninformed. The approach here dramatically differs. It treats this group, the majority throughout most of twentieth century Eastern Europe, as complex and intelligent. Complex in that they often pursued multiple goals – security, status, wealth. Complex in that they were both rational and emotional. Complex in that they were capable of self-sacrifice, benign and malign motivations, and, sometimes, terrible violence. Under different conditions and different political-structural situations, Karadzic was at one point a flower child poet, at another a corrupt bureaucrat, at still another an indicted war criminal. However, if we are to believe his friend quoted previously, he always maintained the emotional baggage of his rural Montenegrin roots. Karadzic is certainly a complex character mixing predictable characteristics of his ethnic and social background into his actions in a structurally changing present. The nationalist murderer lies hidden, but rapid political change brings out powerful and emotional motivations to commit acts that were unimaginable just a brief time before. For this study, Karadzic is not an exceptional person, but rather a vivid exemplar.

11

Conclusion

People hate. They resent the authority of ethnically different others. They can find themselves in situations in which they fear for their lives and the lives of their families. No one denies that these emotions exist, but few have tried to systematically link them to ethnic conflict. This work has treated these emotions as central to four narratives of social processes leading to ethnic violence and discrimination. Because individual intentions and motivations are difficult to discern and sometimes contradictory, leading scholars of revolution and political violence have chosen not to pursue them as a central object of study.[1] While it may be difficult to study these elements of ethnic conflict, motivation poses a major puzzle for many of the violent outbursts and ethnic cleansings of Eastern Europe. In these events, significant numbers of individuals participated or tacitly supported brutal actions against a relatively defenseless people. Despite the difficulties and ambiguities in the study of emotion and motivation, this phenomenon demands an answer. The present work contributes to the literature on ethnic conflict by identifying four emotion-based paths to ethnic conflict and systematically comparing their abilities to explain variation within limited puzzles and across broad historical sweeps. What have we learned through this exercise?

Summary of Findings

First, one of the most widely accepted theories of political science, Fear, is not very helpful in explaining ethnic violence in the majority of cases

---

[1] See Tilly's discussion in "Revolutions and Collective Violence" in F. I. Greenstein and N. W. Polsby, eds., *Handbook of Political Science: Macropolitical Theory* (Reading, MA: Addison-Wesley, 1975), pp. 483–555.

found in Eastern Europe. Based on the logic of the security dilemma, Fear provides a coherent and straightforward explanation, but one that is applicable to only a minority of cases. The structural conditions that define the security dilemma and Fear simply were not present in most of the cases here. While Krajina Serbs and all Bosnian groups may have been driven by Fear, other emotions were also apparent. Croatian provocations of the then powerful Serb regime have no place in the Fear narrative; neither do the similar Croatian and Serb actions and atrocities versus Muslims. Fear does not explain the Baltic puzzles of 1905, the pattern of interwar discrimination, the variation witnessed in the 1939–41 period, nor the difference in Baltic policies after the collapse of Communism. Fear does not help explain German actions in Czechoslovakia nor the Czech postwar expulsions. In short, individuals in Eastern Europe have been very capable of attacking and denigrating their ethnically different neighbors in the absence of threat.

Second, this work challenges two major conventional wisdoms concerning Hatred, or "ancient hatred." In opposition to the popular journalistic conventional wisdom, "ancient hatreds" do not seem to drive many cases. Only one case, the Serbian expulsion of Albanians in Kosovo, possesses an excellent fit. The cases show that social relationships have usually varied over time – members of other ethnic groups have been seen as allies at one point and enemies at another. During outbreaks of violence, the targets have often changed accordingly. The changes in targets of violence, as well as in justification and the nature of action, argues against Hatred. As defined here, the process is based on the existence of a constant, if usually latent, script capable of generating roles and actions. Few such scripts could be identified in the case material here.

On the other hand, this work argues against the academic conventional wisdom that dismisses Hatred out of hand. Powerful cultural schemas do exist and can motivate individual action; history's images and symbols can affect behavior. Twentieth century Eastern Europe, however, has witnessed a fluidity of social interaction that has constantly created new experiences and images. The establishment of a coherent and specific schema is unlikely given the rapid changes produced by industrialization, births and deaths of empire and ideology, and multiple wars and occupations. Yet, as argued, a schema defined by a script, roles, and well-known justifications guided Serbian actions during the mass expulsions of Albanians from Kosovo. While ethnic identity is usually in flux, some elements may harden and become the foundations for the cultural schemas of Hatred.

255

The cases demonstrated little support for Rage, at least as a complete and coherent narrative, capable of explaining variation in ethnic violence. Elements of the Rage narrative, however, appeared within the cases. Certainly, some measure of frenzy and vehemence were behind the violent actions witnessed in the preceding chapters. Rage fits the Czech anti-German pogroms of the immediate postwar period. Rage is a strong competitor in the 1941 Baltic and Poland B cases. However, as far as coherently linking changes in the social and political environment, intervening mechanisms, and observed overall patterns in targets, Rage generally failed to present a convincing alternative to the instrumental narratives. In the conflicts between Czechs and Germans, Slovaks and Hungarians, and Serbs and Albanians, as well as among Croats and Serbs and Muslims, and among the peoples of the Baltic, the instrumental narratives explained more variation in ethnic violence and discrimination.

Among the four emotion-based paths to violence oulined here, Resentment provides the best descriptive and predictive fit. With Resentment, structural changes produce new day-to-day experiences of dominance and subordination. These experiences provide information regarding ethnic status hierarchy – which groups are on top and which are on the bottom. Beliefs form about the justice of this hierarchy. The belief that one's group is in an unjust position leads to the emotion of resentment and, in turn, the desire to act to rearrange the hierarchy. Resentment predicts that the ethnic target will be the group perceived as farthest up the ethnic status hierarchy that can be most surely subordinated through ethnic/national violence. Resentment combines the feeling that status relations are unjust with the belief that something can be done about it. Whether Resentment produces violence or not depends in large part on the intensity of the emotion. Four hypotheses about intensity were developed in the third chapter:

1. Status reversal creates the highest intensity of Resentment and produces the highest liklihood of *violent* conflict. Status reversal results when a more regionally powerful group in an established hierarchy is dislodged from its position and placed below a less powerful group.
2. When Resentment develops from gradually changing perceptions created by slower structural processes such as modernization, the emotion is less intense and the conflict is most likely to develop in nonviolent institutional forms.
3. If the hierarchy among groups is not clearly established, *cooperation* among them is likely, at least until a hierarchy is formed.

4. If in the period immediately dislodging the empirical or occupying regime the remaining groups are of relatively equal status and power, then *cooperation* is more likely.

Underlying all of these intensity-related hypotheses is the degree of clarity and strength of perception of ethnic hierarchy. Reversals of established hierarchies are more likely to breed Resentment than hierarchies in the process of formation. Resentment is less likely to emerge to prevent cooperation if the ethnic hierarchies are unclear or if no group has reason to feel itself entitled to dominant status.

With the exception of (4), the empirical puzzles at the center of each substantive chapter provide evidence to confirm these hypotheses. In the cases of Baltic states and Poland B, the interwar years worked to create widely established and deeply held perceptions of ethnic status hierarchy. Along the lines of Resentment, the nature of the changes in that hierarchy predicted the variation in ethnic targets that occurred in the shifting occupations of the Second World War. Resentment provides an answer for why Lithuanians assaulted Jews in Kaunas but not Vilnius, why Ukrainians attacked Poles in 1939 and Jews in 1941, why Belorussians and Russians are seldom targeted. Resentment helps us make sense of the nature of the action – the targeting of community symbols and the acts of humiliation. In the Czechoslovakian territories, Resentment does not yield answers to all events but furnishes an explanation for why Slovaks expelled Czechs during the Second World War but passed language laws detrimental to Hungarians in the post-Communist period. Resentment suggests why Germans were unhappy with their situation in interwar Czechoslovakia. However, Resentment has little to say about interwar Czech tolerance toward Germans, or their violent attacks on Germans in the immediate postwar period. For the Yugoslav puzzles, Resentment appears at the root of Croatian actions toward Serbs; it helps explains the similarity in actions of Croats and Serbs toward Bosnian Muslims. However, Fear and Hatred also possess explanatory power for the violence that occurred during the collapse of the former Yugoslavia. In sum, Resentment provides an answer to most, but by no means all, of the puzzles presented by the empirical chapters.

Resentment also helps explain the broader contours of Eastern European ethnic politics. In one sense, Resentment supplies a plausible micromechanism driving Gellner's Ruritanians toward nationhood in the era of modernizing empires. Resentment also seems to furnish the microlevel

257

motivations fueling the interwar consolidation of titular group dominance (Poland for Poles, Latvia for Latvians) in the nationalizing states described by Rogers Brubaker. Building on the conclusions of the Yugoslavia chapter, I will argue, though, that the empirical material as a whole suggests something different, something beyond the theories of Gellner and Brubaker.

In Gellner's view, the passion underlying nationalism resulted from modernization. Requiring a single language for efficiency, the machinery of the industrialized state inevitably produced noncongruence between an individual's culture, embodied almost exclusively in language, and the broader environment. As he clarified in later writings, Gellner stated:

Modern life *is* contact with bureaucrats: shop assistants, railway clerks, etc., etc. It is this which pushes people into nationalism, into the need for the congruence between their own 'culture' (the idiom in which they can express themselves and understand others) and that of the extensive and interconnected bureaucracies which constitute their social environment. Non-congruence is not merely an inconvenience or a disadvantage: it means perpetual humiliation. . . . The passion is not a means to some end, it is a reaction to an intolerable situation, to a constant jarring in the activity which is by far the most important thing in life – contact and communication with fellow human beings.[2]

In response to their day-to-day humiliation, the resulting passion motivated individuals to do whatever it took to create linguistic congruence in their own efficient modern state. Shop assistants and railway clerks would still speak one language, but, as common sense or justice dictated, it would be the language of the territorial majority. Drawing out the implications of this argument, when language congruence is in place, the humiliation ends and the passion recedes.

The passions and humiliations identified by Gellner resonate with the Resentment narrative. Gellner's story describes the Baltic and Slovak experience especially well. Taken as a whole, however, the substantive chapters suggest that Gellner is describing only one subset of Resentment. Language, the basis of Gellner's argument, is only one daily marker of subordination and humiliation; other markers can also produce Resentment's passion. The Yugoslavian cases provide ample evidence. Serbs, Croats, and

---

[2] From Ernest Gellner, "Reply to Critics" in John A. Hall and I. C. Jarvie, eds., *The Social Philosophy of Ernest Gellner* (Amsterdam: Rodopi, 1996), pp. 625–87. Passage is from p. 626. John Hall discusses this text in the "Introduction" in John A. Hall, ed., *The State of the Nation: Ernest Gellner and the Theory of Nationalism* (Cambridge: Cambridge University Press, 1998), p. 11.

Muslims all spoke Serbo-Croatian, yet as the last chapter has argued, Resentment rose through symbolic politics. Croatians expelled Serbs from most positions of political authority and resurrected Croatian nationalist symbols, almost taunting the Serbs. Some Croats and Serbs, especially those living in rural areas, found the possibility of residing in a Muslim-dominated state humiliating. In contrast to Gellner, Yugoslavian Resentment did not possess a mechanical quality, it developed in different ways depending on the historical, cultural, and economic backgrounds of the region and the set of ethnic groups residing there. In Croatia, the seeds of Resentment were planted at the very inception of the state. Croats, as former residents of the Austro-Hungarian Empire, perceived themselves as culturally and economically more advanced than their Serbian "big brothers." Serbs, as the masters of their own prewar state, perceived themselves as superior to the Croatians. The implementation of Serbian administrative policies, the branding policy for example, and the gross overrepresentation of Serbs in the interwar state, established early on a set of structures, information, and beliefs that would repeatedly set the stage for the formation of Resentment. Bosnia's ethnic relations have not exhibited anything like the constancy of Croatia's. The first Yugoslavia – the Kingdom of Serbs, Croats, and Slovenes – did not recognize Muslims as an equal people. Many Serbs and Croats saw Tito's creation of a Bosnian Socialist Republic as a way to reduce Croatian and Serbian power by scattering their numbers across republic boundaries. Given this background, as well as the legacy of the Ottoman Empire, significant numbers of Serbs and Croats would not tolerate the prospect of living in a Bosnian state as second-hand citizens. The possibility of this status change transformed the nature of interethnic relations in Bosnia.

Why Has Resentment Been so Prevalent in Eastern Europe in the Twentieth Century?

Is there something special about Eastern European mentality or culture? Is it because Eastern Europe serves as a faultline for the "clash of civilizations"?[3] A review of the links of Figure 2.1 helps address this question. Resentment describes a process linking structure to information, information to belief, belief to emotion, and emotion and belief to action. A

---

[3] See Samuel Huntington, "The Clash of Civilizations," *Foreign Affairs* 72(3) (1993): 22–49.

review of each of these links shows why and how Eastern European history and politics have created strong links at each point of this chain.

Structure and Information   Few areas of the world have ever witnessed rapid structural changes in the manner of Eastern Europe in the twentieth century. In massive numbers, illiterate peasants learned to read and moved to the cities. With the collapse of the empire, these former peasants and sons of peasants became masters of their own house. In the words of Istvan Deak (also quoted earlier): "The establishment of Eastern European nation-states has been the most spectacular change on the European continent in the last 150-odd years, and the only one to prove lasting."[4] When given the chance, the interwar governments created grossly skewed proportions in the military and bureaucracies. Consider again some examples cited earlier: Toward the end of interwar Yugoslavia, Serbs held 161 of 165 generalships in the army and 150 of 156 positions in the Ministry of Education; in the latter years of interwar Czechoslovakia, Slovaks, although comprising 23% of the population, held only 1.7% of positions in the central administration; in interwar Lithuania, Jews and other minorities held few positions of authority after the 1926 coup. These figures represent the type of information produced by the structural changes of the third period, the interwar era. Resentment is based on the perception of ethnic status hierarchy. The intensity of the emotion relates to the strength of ethnic hierarchy. Given these figures from the tail end of the third period, it is hard to see how the newly literate and urbanizing ethnic groups could help but develop a strong sense of ethnic hierarchy. It is worth recalling the experience described by a Lithuanian Jew during the Soviet occupation of 1940–41: "Every Jew held his head high. If he met a Lithuanian on the sidewalk, the Lithuanian would step off the curb to let him by. Before the Russians came, it had been just the reverse." In interwar and wartime Eastern Europe, the simple act of walking down the street could be an experience imbued with ethnic dominance. In some cases, the rise of the peasants and their pursuit of status dominance created this situation. In other cases, the political or economic development at the time of formation created skewed numbers in the positions of power. Across every case in this book, however, the structural processes of mod-

---

[4] Istvan Deak, "The Rise and Triumph of the East European Nation-States" *In Depth: A Journal for Values in Public Policy* 2 (1992): 77–95.

ernization and state formation helped create a mentality permeated by status consciousness.

Furthermore, few regions of the world ever witnessed the rapid structural upheavals seen in Eastern Europe from 1939 to the late 1940s. Consider Lithuania. In the course of a few years, Lithuania went from independence, to Soviet occupation, to German occupation, to Soviet reoccupation. Czechoslovakia saw partition of the Sudetenland, followed by German occupation, followed by quasi-independence, followed by Soviet control. In 1939, Yugoslavia was struggling with new decentralized political structures (recall the 1939 Sporazum). In 1940, the Germans, Italians, Hungarians, and Bulgarians, along with the newly formed Independent State of Croatia, occupied and partitioned the Yugoslav state. After a partisan and civil war, a new federated socialist state composed of six republic-level units was born. During this era, structural upheavals reversed established interwar hierarchies. The result was the gruesome violence described in previous chapters. Again, the Soviet and German occupation policies provided experiences (information) that reinforced consciousness of ethnic status hierarchy (given the racist theories and racial hierarchies of the Nazis, this effect is hardly surprising).

The postwar system of federated socialist republics were political forms that maintained consciousness of group status. In Czechoslovakia, the relationship between the Czech and Slovak halves of the federation were a continual matter of debate. In Yugoslavia, the Croats and Slovenes asked why they should fund the southern republics. These federations were not designed to quell ethnic consciousness. Rather, their explicit ethnic form came to breed information used in ethnic comparison. Indeed, in retrospect the informational qualities and mobilizational potential of these ethnically federated structures seems more important than the fact that these systems sometimes reduced ethnic gaps in education or income.

In sum, the types of structural change seen in Eastern Europe – rapid modernization, collapse of empire, multiple occupations by brutal regimes, formation of ethnically federated states – produced information and experiences (including the episodes of violence and humiliation) that created and maintained perception of ethnic status hierarchy.

Information and Beliefs   Resentment posits a straightforward progression from structural change to information and then a second step from information to beliefs that ethnic status orderings are unjust and offensive. Culture, ideology, or elite persuasion could alter the interpretation or

appraisal of information. For instance, two cultures, one religiously oriented and the other secular, might form different beliefs regarding the
justice of ethnically skewed bureaucracies. The local moral order is a "cognitive repertoire of the community" informing one of the range of appropriate attitudes.[5]

Despite these possibilities, the case material demonstrates more similarities than differences in the linkage of information to belief. Few
regional majorities failed to form the belief that demographic dominance
should be reflected in numerical dominance in positions of authority.
Almost all of these regional majorities negatively reacted to rapid reversals of those numbers. This lack of variation is not surprising given the
blatancy of the information. Consider the numbers mentioned above. How
could Croats fail to develop a belief that the gross Serb overrepresentation in the military constituted unjust dominance? How could Slovaks,
holding a number of administrative positions that was just one thirteenth
of their populational percentage, fail to form a belief that they were a subordinated ethnic group?

Secondly, state formation involves symbol formation. New states
require flags, insignia, the renaming of streets, the rewriting of history
texts. These symbols provide a cheap and quick way to establish group
dominance and they can serve as badges of ranked order. I can remember
crossing the border between Lithuania and Latvia in the summer of 1992,
in the early days of Latvian independence. The Latvian border guards,
youth wearing new uniforms, were determined to go through the process
of having everyone get off of the bus, have luggage searched, and carefully
check documentation. Their function was symbolic more than anything
else – to demonstrate that they were an independent country. In Weber's
famous dictum, statehood is defined by a monopoly of force. In general in
Eastern Europe, nation-statehood is defined by the monopoly of force
primarily by one national group. Through their ability to force people
to leave the bus, through their right and practice of searching luggage,
through their presence with uniforms and guns, Latvians were establishing dominance that helped define the new political entity as a Latvian
nation-state.

Thirdly, new states change language laws. Following Gellner, language
is the most powerful marker of status dominance. Across the century,

---

[5] See Rom Harre, "An Outline of the Social Constructionist Viewpoint" in Rom Harre, ed.,
The Social Construction of Emotions (New York: Basil Blackwell, 1986).

emerging East European nation-states have passed laws establishing language dominance of the titular group. Slovakia, Latvia, and Estonia, for example, passed laws that clearly established the subordinate position of minority languages.

Finally, violence is another blatant form of information that is largely immune to cultural nuances.

In sum, the prevalence of Resentment in Eastern Europe has resulted in large part from the blatant nature of information. Undoubtedly, culture and ideology can impact belief formation. Elite persuasion and framing can alter mass beliefs. In Eastern Europe, however, these forces could not significantly influence the appraisal and interpretation of gross imbalances in the visible positions of authority, the symbols of statehood, the imposition of language laws, and the brutal acts of violence and humiliation. The majority of people would interpret the imbalances, symbols, language laws, and violence as clear indications of a status hierarchy and clear evidence of the position of their own group within that hierarchy.

Beliefs and Emotion   Resentment holds that a belief that one's group is unjustly subordinated will trigger an emotion that heightens the saliency of status concerns. One feels compelled to act against the unjustly dominant groups as a way of changing the imbalance, or putting the other group "in its place." Why did a belief in unjust group hierarchy so consistently lead to the emotion of resentment in Eastern Europe?

This question raises the issue of culture. As in the previous link, culture can affect how beliefs translate into emotions.[6] A similar belief may initiate a strong emotional reaction in one culture, while the same belief may cause a weaker, or different, emotion in another. Was there something specific to twentieth century Eastern European culture that served to frequently translate the belief of unjust hierarchy into such intense emotion?

The substantive chapters do suggest at least one specific area in which culture intervenes between belief and intensity of emotion. The belief that one was subordinate to Jews, rather than other ethnic groups, appears to have created an especially intense emotion of resentment. Recall Jan Gross's description of how Poles reacted to the sight of Jews in the Soviet administration: "It is a reflection of how unseemly, how jarring, how

---

[6] One of the most convincing studies of the link between culture and emotion is Richard E. Nisbett and Dov Cohen, *Culture of Honor: The Psychology of Violence in the South* (Boulder, CO: Westview Press, 1996).

offensive it was to see a Jew in a position of authority." The quoted passage of the Lithuanian writer recalling the role of Jews in the 1940–41 Soviet occupation mirrors this reaction: "They interfered in everything and told everyone how to live. Jewish agitators flooded the villages. They called upon the peasants to begin the sowing or the reaping. The people were silent and bit their tongues. But as soon as the agitators left, the people began to spit in rage: Of what value is the advice of a person who had never in his life held a scythe in his own hands, who had never pushed a plow in his life." While any minority group that advances far up the status ladder during an occupation will likely be the target of Resentment, the fact that Jews were that group in 1940–41 led to an especially strong emotion, an exceptionally obsessive drive to act to use violence to put the group "in its place." Historically, Eastern Europeans, as indicated by the previous quote, saw Jews as a foreign element unconnected to the land, an urban and effeminate group.

But is there an identifiable regional cultural influence on emotion formation? This question is obviously beyond the scope of this project. However, one must ask in how many modern or modernizing societies does such a belief *not* elicit resentment? Donald Horowitz's passage describing the developing world comes to mind: "Everywhere the word *domination* (emphasis in original) was heard. Everywhere it was equated with political control. Everywhere it was a question of who were 'the real owners of the country' and of who would rule over whom." The psychological research cited in the fourth chapter suggests that one of the fundamental underpinnings of Resentment, the desire for esteem, is part of human nature.[7] While perhaps less ingrained, a second key element of Resentment assumes that human beings easily and naturally identify with the experience of their groups. Emotions may be socially constructed to a great degree, but they are not infinitely malleable. Some emotions may have been "hard-wired" to some degree during sociobiological evolution. Eventually, biological research may provide solid answers to whether the need for self-esteem and the individual identification with groups are part of the human genetic constitution. The substantive material here, though, does little to discount such a conjecture.

---

[7] For a particularly relevant recent source see Albert Somit and Steven Petersen, *Darwinism, Dominance, and Democracy: The Biological Bases of Authoritarianism* (Westport, CT: Praeger, 1997). See especially the discussion in Chapter 5, "Dominance and Hierarchy."

Emotion and Action   The final link in Resentment's chain connects the emotion-produced desire to "put groups in their place" to violence and punitive or discriminatory laws. It is important to note that these actions result from both the desire to commit them and the belief that punishment can be avoided. While emotion heightens certain desires and creates compulsions to act, individuals will not completely ignore dangers and penalties. Even the most resentment-filled individual may be deterred. Resentment has led to violence in Eastern Europe partly because constraints on behavior have collapsed so often. The two world wars and their brutality created situations of near anarchy seldom seen in this century. The regional collapse of empires and states also eliminated deterrents to violence (witness Bosnia).

Summary of Resentment   In retrospect, it is hardly surprising that Resentment has been the motor for ethnic conflict in twentieth century Eastern Europe. Modernization brought the rural, regional majorities in contact with the ethnically foreign cities in their midst. The collapse of empires created the opportunity for the emergence of nation-states and the pursuit of nationalizing agendas. The Second World War brought multiple occupations and status reversals and rereversals. Individuals witnessed rapid changes in the states they lived in and the symbols around them. Ethnically based federations arose and disintegrated. The entire century was punctuated with periods of near anarchy when the most emotionally driven were relatively free to act on their desires. Modern Eastern European history has been a recipe for Resentment.

Caveat

As discussed in the introduction, Fear, Hatred, Resentment, and Rage are parsimonious narratives created for comparison with each other. Each narrative links a micromechanism to macrostructural changes. Clearly, ethnic violence is a complicated manner and any approach seeking parsimony will leave out many important elements. Seeking a century-wide sweep, this book has left out much of the politics of ethnic violence.

   To be sure, specific political decisions have been discussed in the cases. For example, while the Yugoslav chapter dismissed the effects of charisma, it did include many of the policies of Tito and the Yugoslav Communist Party that eventually led to Resentment. As argued, Yugoslav Resentment has, in major part, stemmed from the nature of the formation of the state (creating the template for Croatian Resentment against Serbs) and the reforming of the state as a socialist federation. Without the mobilization potential and symbolic significance of republic-level government, the Bosnian events may not have taken the course they did. If Tito and the Communists had not created a Bosnian Republic in the wake of the Second World War, it is unlikely that modernization would have produced a Muslim-led drive for a Bosnian state. Certainly, in contrast to Gellner, language incongruence would never have furnished the passion needed for such a movement. Some of the more specific policies also had an impact. Tito played the ethnic issue both ways – he jailed nationalists who broke certain taboos (Tudjman and Izetbegovic, for example) but pacified ethnic groups through territorial and cultural concessions. It was a balancing act that could be sustained in a powerful one-party state, but a strategy that produced embittered ethnic entrepreneurs and mobilizational capabilities to bring down a weakened state. This policy was not directly related to macrostructural changes of language and modernization. Industrialization may have exacerbated the situation by increasing the intrusiveness of the government and creating federal investment strategies that pitted one republic against another. But specific historical and political features did have a major part in producing the status inconsistencies and status reversals underlying Resentment in Bosnia.

Politics can also matter when sequences of emotions open up opportunities for leaders to exploit. In the Croatian case, for example, Resentment, Fear, and possibly Hatred, were all present. Barry Posen's security dilemma argument outlined earlier actually mixes Fear and Hatred. The breakdown of the state and the introduction of emerging anarchy sets Fear into motion, but Hatred schemas possessing threatening roles and scripts may then arise as well. Some leaders will have incentives to make sure that the Hatred schemas come to the fore. As posited by the Hatred narrative here, these schemas will only be effective if they have historical resonance and they may emerge without leadership or manipulation. In contrast, other scholars view leaders as being able to largely create new schemas, or at least creatively manipulate old ones. Elite ability to manipulate history is an important issue, but also an empirical one.[8] Either way, however, leaders and politics may come into play given this sequence of emotions.

---

[8] Stuart Kaufman's work is perhaps the most sophisticated treatment of this question. Kaufman, concentrating on a form of hatred, distinguishes between elite-led and mass-led paths to ethnic violence. He tests his theory on several cases from regions from the former Soviet Union. See Stuart Kaufman, *Modern Hatreds: The Symbolic Politics of Ethnic War* (Ithaca, NY: Cornell University Press, 2001).

Politics and leadership do matter. But politics must be played within the constraints that history and structure provide. This statement leads into a discussion of the politics of prevention.

Lessons for Prevention of Ethnic Violence

A major implication of this book is that ethnic violence is very difficult to prevent. A review of Fear, Hatred, and Resentment shows why this is so.

Fear, Hatred, Resentment, and Rage are all plausible explanations of ethnic violence. For each, a different set of preventions would apply. One reason why social scientists tend to favor the Fear argument is that it holds out the best chances for successful intervention. If the structure of the security dilemma is producing Fear, then steps could be taken to reduce the military vulnerabilities of groups. In effect, outsiders considering intervention can act to close windows of opportunity either through transferring armaments to threatened groups or sending in peacekeeping troops. These solutions, though, are not easy to implement. Above all, states are reluctant to send troops into these situations. Furthermore, if states do develop policies to intervene, ethnic groups will have incentives to avoid serious negotiations with their opponents and try to accomplish their own narrow goals by enticing international intervention. The Kosovo Liberation Army, to take one example, chose to escalate violence in order to heighten chances of Western intervention. At the time of this writing, Kosovo is a NATO protectorate largely cleansed of Serbs and other minorities while elements of the KLA are destabilizing neighboring Macedonia. Kosovo illustrates the complexities of intervention.

This book also provides a warning against the tendency to place too much emphasis on countering the structural logic of Fear. The lesson here is to avoid the temptation to see Fear as the most common path to ethnic conflict in the modern world. Simply changing the military potentials that underlie the security dilemma will help in some cases, but the prevalence of Resentment points out that the basis of conflict is often wider than the nature of threat. Fear helped drive the bloody outcomes in Croatia and Bosnia, but so did the Resentment that propelled the Tudjman regime to power. As was argued, Resentment also helps explain similar Croatian and Serbian attacks on Bosnian Muslims.

Stopping Hatred is very difficult. It is not clear how much deeply embedded and latent cultural schemas can be changed. Certainly, education and fair renditions of history might help in some cases. Education and a freer and better press may have helped to counter the myths, gross exaggerations of persecution, and talk of Albanian genocide against Serbs that inflamed the Kosovo conflict. Yet, at the base of that conflict lay a history, not a mythology, peppered with mass expulsions. The scripts and roles played by Serbs during the 1999 expulsions had roots based more in repetitions during the twentieth century than the 1389 battle that most commentators usually mention. This schema cannot be easily changed. Serbs could easily be mobilized to participate in brutal actions in Kosovo (as compared to mobilization against Slovenia). Outsiders could have deterred Serbs from the policy of expulsion, but, given the Serbs' widely held schema, they were unlikely to persuade the Serbian population that it was an inhuman act worthy of world contempt. Efforts to "educate" the Serbs would have been counterproductive. Fortunately, the book has shown that Hatred is rare.

The major finding of this book is the ubiquity of Resentment. Can there be interventions within this path? The possibilities for intervention can be discussed by going through the Resentment narrative link by link.

Structural Preventions

Structural changes may prevent the process from ever beginning. Two structural programs come to mind. Partition, possibly accompanied by population transfers, can obviously eliminate the basis for Resentment. Homogeneous states have no ethnic status hierarchies. Partition will prevent daily interactions (and status reversals) among ordered groups, the starting point of Resentment. A retrospective look at the course of Eastern Europe, makes homogenizing policies not look so bad. Do we really want a million Germans in the Sudetenland again? Does anybody really think the breakup of Czechoslovakia was a tragedy? If Kosovo Albanians and Serbs never live together again, is that such a loss given their history?

Achieving homogeneity, though, is a drastic process usually involving massive human suffering. Furthermore, partition will create a myriad of other problems, especially if significant minorities remain. It may be true that Eastern Europe has been homogenized and will no longer see Resentment the way it once did. This being said, the genocides and mass expulsions that created this homogeneity are hardly examples of prevention. In large part, this book is a testimony to the misery, suffering, and carnage created by Eastern Europe's homogenizing history. Peaceful partition does have its advocates, and debate on this issue will continue.[9] As with the interventions involved with preventing Fear, this book provides no easy answer to this controversy.

Federalism is a clear alternative to partition. By granting autonomy, especially cultural and linguistic autonomy, societal features of dominance and subordination are dulled. Each ethnic group, while not the master of its own house, can at least be the master of one of the rooms. Twentieth century Eastern European experience and history does not offer much support for the longevity or peacefulness of federations. All three federations in the region – Yugoslavia, Czechoslovakia, the USSR – collapsed. Despite the claims of those extolling the virtues of postwar Yugoslavia, the Yugoslav experience provides real doubts as to the effectiveness of federation. Even the smallest differences could provide the sparks for simmering resentments. Croatians, for example, bristled at the overrepresentation of Serbs in the Communist Party in Croatia. And, as I have argued, the change in status of a group like the Muslims brought out emotional responses by active segments of both Croatians and Serbs. Although highly autonomous and relatively prosperous under the former federation, the Slovenians today do not seem to lament the death of Yugoslavia.

Information

State policy on information could retard the development of Resentment. Information in the premodern period was limited. The illiterate, immobile, and isolated peasants of the premodern era in Eastern Europe had little opportunity or information to form beliefs about hierarchies or their unjustness. They may have occasionally killed their landlords, but they did not experience ethnic resentments. Ethnic ignorance could lead to ethnic bliss. Today, many states do not publish figures on the ethnic composition of the police force or officer corps. Perhaps, if these numbers were unavailable, ethnicity itself would be harder to talk and think about.

It is doubtful that either institutional or societal ignorance can be a viable policy in the twentieth century. As formulated here, Resentment is

---

[9] Recent proponents of partition plans include Chaim Kaufmann, "Possible and Impossible Solutions to Ethnic Civil Wars" *International Security* 20(4) (1996): 136–75 and John Mearsheimer and Steven Van Evera, "When Peace Means War" *The New Republic* December, 1995. Also see Robert Hayden, "Schindler's Fate: Genocide, Ethnic Cleansing, and Population Transfers" *Slavic Review* 55(4) (1996): 727–48. One recent opponent of partition is Radha Kumar, *Divide and Fall: Bosnia in the Annals of Partition* (London: Verso, 1997).

based on the actual day-to-day experiences of subordination. Restriction of information by the state will not change this experience; in fact, it is likely that overestimations of outgroup dominance would result. Furthermore, purposeful ignorance is hardly a normatively appealing policy.

Beliefs

In the Resentment progression, beliefs reside between information and emotion. Elites are often seen as framing events in ways that provoke and inflame violent resentments. However, it is possible that elites could use persuasion and reason at this juncture to shape more benign beliefs. For example, while many commentators admit that there may be a kernel of truth in Serbian complaints regarding underrepresentation and the form of the 1974 constitution, they see the belief in Serbian "victimhood" as largely a creation of demagogues like Milosevic and Karadzic. Some argue that if there were better outlets of information, more opportunities to hear voices of reason and moderation, alternative beliefs would form.[10] To a great extent, this book presents a counterargument to elite-based arguments and the view that ethnic conflict is the result of "the forces of darkness – separatists, racists, war criminals, and crooks" [see page 1]. If beliefs are almost infinitely malleable and arise out of elite discourse, then the entire conception of Resentment and the other structurally based emotional processes must be rejected. The empirical material, the recurring patterns and outcomes, suggest the opposite, however. Discourse, at least to a considerable extent, follows large scale structural change at least as much as it shapes it.

Action

While it is extremely difficult to stop structural changes and the information, beliefs, and emotions that flow from them, it may be somewhat more possible to deter actions. The members of Group X may come to want to commit violence against Group Y. Emotion heightens the desire to do so. However, at least for the instrumental Fear, Hatred, and Resentment, emotion does not lead to insanity or even gross forms of irrationality. Outsiders can hold perpetrators responsible by threatening economic and

---

[10] For an analysis of this argument, see Jack Snyder and Karen Ballentine, "Nationalism and the Marketplace of Ideas" *International Security* 21 (1996): 5–40.

political sanctions. Such threats will not stop all forms of emotion-based ethnic violence, or perhaps most of them. But it may be the best that outsiders can do.

Final Thoughts

There is a clear need in the social sciences to study the role of emotion. As the theoretical sections point out, emotions underlie a host of existing approaches. It is difficult to study emotions and almost impossible to measure them. But they are too important to be ignored.

In particular, social scientists need to examine the role of group status and related emotions. I doubt that resentment, in some form, will cease to play a major role in political and social life. Anyone who has experienced the emotion knows its power. Jackie Robinson is considered one of America's greatest heroes. In the face of constant harassment, he persevered to become baseball's first African-American major league player. Despite daily taunting by opposing teams, Robinson refrained from retaliation. Beneath this restraint, as Robinson would write, a violent passion sometimes simmered:

What a glorious, cleansing thing it would be to let go. To hell with the image of the patient black freak I was supposed to create. I could throw down my bat, stride over to the Phillies dugout, grab one of those white sons of bitches and smash his teeth in with my despised black fist.

Robinson reacted to harassment with emotion that heightened a desire for violent action, a release of fury that would be "a glorious, cleansing thing." Human nature provides a capacity for an emotion capable of motivating violence toward ethnically distinct others. This capacity existed in Jackie Robinson whose number prominently hangs in honor from every major league baseball stadium in America. It clearly existed in Robinson's white tormentors. It existed in the Eastern Europeans described in this book. It will continue to exist in a host of societies around the world. Unfortunately, it is unlikely that most human beings will be able to exercise the restraint and self-control of Jackie Robinson.

Bibliography

Abelson, Robert P. 1996. "The Secret Existence of Expressive Behavior." In Jeffrey Friedman, ed., *The Rational Choice Controversy: Economic Models of Political Behavior Reconsidered*, pp. 25–36. New Haven, CT: Yale University Press.

Ackerman, Nathan and Marie Jahoda. 1950. *Anti-Semitism: An Emotional Disorder*. New York: Harper.

Adorno, Theodor W., E. Frenkel-Brunswik, D. J. Levinson, and R. N. Sanford. 1950. *The Authoritarian Personality*. New York: Harper.

Allcock, John B. 1999. "Rural *Ressentiment* and the Break-up of Yugoslavia." Paper presented at the American Association for the Advancement of Slavic Studies. November 18–21, 1999, St. Louis, Missouri.

Allport, Gordon. 1954. *The Nature of Prejudice*. Cambridge, MA: Addison-Wesley Publishing Co.

1955. *The Resolution of Intergroup Tensions: A Critical Appraisal of Methods*. New York: National Conferences of Christians and Jews.

"An Open Response to the Editorial Board of the *Los Angeles Times*." Lithuanian Research and Studies Center of Chicago.

Anderle, Josef. 1979. "The First Republic, 1918–1938." In Hans Brisch and Ivan Volgyes, eds., *Czechoslovakia: The Heritage of Ages Past: Essays in Memory of Josef Korbel*. Boulder, CO: East European Quarterly, distributed by Columbia University Press.

Anderson, Benedict. 1991. *Imagined Communities: Reflections on the Origin and Spread of Nationalism*. London: Verso.

Andric, Ivo. 1992. "Letter from 1920." In Celia Hawkesworth, ed., *The Damned Yard and Other Stories*, pp. 107–20. London: Forest Books.

Arad, Yitzak. 1980. *Ghetto in Flames: The Struggle and Destruction of the Jews in Vilna in the Holocaust*. Jerusalem: Ahva Cooperative Printing Press.

Armon-Jones, Claire. 1986. "The Social Functions of Emotion." In Rom Harre, ed., *The Social Construction of Emotions*, pp. 57–82. New York: Basil Blackwell.

1986. "The Thesis of Constructionism." In Rom Harre, ed., *The Social Construction of Emotions*, pp. 32–56. New York: Basil Blackwell.

273

Armstrong, John A. 1992. "The Ethnic Scene in the Soviet Union: The View of the Dictatorship." In Rachel Denber, ed., *The Soviet Nationality Reader.* Boulder, CO: Westview Press.

Arnold, Magda B. 1960. *Emotion and Personality.* New York: Columbia University Press.

Banac, Ivo. 1984. *The National Question in Yugoslavia: Origins, History, Politics.* Ithaca, NY: Cornell University Press.

1992. "The Fearful Asymmetry of War: The Causes and Consequences of Yugoslavia's Demise." *Daedalus* 121: 141–75.

Banfield, Edward. 1990. *The Unheavenly City Revisited.* Boston: Little, Brown and Company.

Bardos, Gordon. 1999. "The Bosnian Cold War: Politics, Society, and International Engagement after Dayton." *The Harriman Review* 11: 1–26.

2001. "Balkan History, Madeleine's War, and NATO's Kosovo." *The Harriman Review* 13(1–2): 36–51.

Barrington, Lowell. 1995. "The Domestic and International Consequences of Citizenship in the Soviet Successor States." *Europe-Asia Studies* 47: 731–63.

Bartoszewski, Wladyslaw. 1986. "Polish-Jewish Relations in Occupied Poland, 1939–1945." In Chimen Abramsky, Maciej Jachimczyk, and Antony Polonsky, eds., *The Jews in Poland*, pp. 147–60. Oxford: Basil Blackwell.

Becker, E. 1971. *The Birth and Death of Meaning.* London: Penguin Books.

Beissinger, Mark. 1998. "Nationalisms that Bark and Nationalisms that Bite: Ernest Gellner and the Substantiation of Nations." In John A. Hall, ed., *The State of the Nation: Ernest Gellner and the Theory of Nationalism*, pp. 169–90. Cambridge: Cambridge University Press.

Benes, Vaclav L. 1973. "Czechoslovak Democracy and Its Problems, 1918–1920." In Victor S. Mamatey and Radomir Luza, eds., *A History of the Czechoslovak Republic, 1918–1948*, pp. 39–98. Princeton, NJ: Princeton University Press.

Bennett, Christopher. 1995. *Yugoslavia's Bloody Collapse: Causes, Course and Consequences.* New York: New York University Press.

Benz, Ernst. 1990. *Die Revolutionen von 1905 in den Ostseeprovinzen Russlands.* Mainz: Johanes-Gutenberg Universitat.

Berkowitz, Leonard. 1989. "Frustration-Aggression Hypothesis: Examination and Reformulation." *Psychological Bulletin* 106: 59–73.

Berlin, Isaiah. 1969. *Four Essays on Liberty.* Oxford: Oxford University Press.

Billig, Michael. 1976. *Social Psychology and Intergroup Relations.* London: Academic Press.

Bilmanis, Alfred. 1951. *A History of Latvia.* Princeton, NJ: Princeton University Press.

Bloom, William. 1990. *Personal Identity, National Identity, and International Relations.* Cambridge: Cambridge University Press.

Bollerup, Soren Rinder and Christian Dons Christensen. 1997. *Nationalism in Eastern Europe: Causes and Consequences of the National Revivals and Conflicts in Late-Twentieth Century Eastern Europe.* New York: St. Martin's Press.

Bougarel, Xavier. 1999. "Cultural Identity or Political Ideology? Bosnian Islam Since 1990." Paper presented for the Annual Convention of the Association for the Study of Nationalities. Columbia University. New York, April 15–17, 1999.

Bowen, John and Roger Petersen. 1999. "Introduction." In John Bowen and Roger Petersen, eds., *Critical Comparisons in Politics and Culture*, pp. 1–20. Cambridge: Cambridge University Press.

Bradley, John F. N. 1991. *Politics in Czechoslovakia, 1945–1990.* New York: Columbia University.

Brewer, Marilyn. 1991. "The Social Self: On Being the Same and Different at the Same Time." *Personality and Social Psychology Bulletin* 7(5): 475–82.

Bringa, Tone. 1995. *Being Muslim the Bosnian Way: Identity and Community in a Central Bosnian Village.* Princeton, NJ: Princeton University Press.

Brubaker, Rogers. 1995. "Aftermaths of Empire and the Unmixing of Peoples: Historical and Comparative Perspectives." *Ethnic and Racial Studies* 18(2): 189–218.

1996. *Nationalism Reframed: Nationhood and the National Question in the New Europe.* Cambridge: Cambridge University Press.

Budreckis, Algirdas Martin. 1968. *The Lithuanian National Revolt of 1941.* Boston: Lithuania Encyclopedia Press.

Burant, Stephen R. and Voytek Zubek. 1993. "Eastern Europe's Old Memory and New Realities: Resurrecting the Polish-Lithuanian Union." *East European Politics and Societies* 7: 370–93.

Burg, Steven. 1986. "Elite Conflict in Post-Tito Yugoslavia." *Soviet Studies* 38: 171.

Burg, Steven and Michael Berbaum. 1989. "Community, Integration, and Stability in Multinational Yugoslavia." *American Political Science Review* 83(2): 535–54.

Burg, Steven and Paul Shoup. 1999. *The War in Bosnia-Herzegovina: Ethnic Conflict and International Intervention.* New York: M. E. Sharpe.

Calhoun, Cheshire. 1984. "Cognitive Emotions?" In Cheshire Calhoun and Robert C. Solomon, eds., *What Is an Emotion: Classical Readings in Philosophical Psychology.* New York: Oxford University Press.

Campbell, F. Gregory. 1975. *Confrontation in Central Europe: Weimar Germany and Czechoslovakia.* Chicago: University of Chicago Press.

Carnegie Endowment for International Peace. 1993. *The Other Balkan Wars.* Including a reprint of Carnegie Endowment for Peace. 1914. *Report of the International Commission to Inquire into the Causes and Conduct of the Balkan Wars.* Washington: Carnegie Endowment for Peace, Division of Intercourse and Education, Publication No. 4.

Chinn, Jeff and Lise A. Truex. 1996. "The Question of Citizenship in the Baltics." *Journal of Democracy* 7: 133–47.

Clark, Alan. 1965. *Barbarossa: The Russian-German Conflict.* New York: Quill.

Cleave, Jan. 1998. "Latvia to Hold Referendum on Citizenship Law Amendments." *RFE/RL Newsline* August 25, 1998.

Coakley, John. 1990. "National Minorities and the Government of Divided Societies: A Comparative Analysis of Some European Evidence." *European Journal of Political Research* 18: 437–56.

Cohen, Gary. 1981. *The Politics of Ethnic Survival: Germans in Prague.* Princeton, NJ: Princeton University Press.

Connor, Walker. 1994. *Ethnonationalism: The Quest for Understanding*. Princeton, NJ: Princeton University Press.

Czechoslovak Ministry of Foreign Affairs. 1941. *Two Years of German Oppression in Czechoslovakia*. Prague: Department of Information.

Danjoux, Olivier. 1998. "Citizenship, Baltic Style. The Legacy and the Scruples." Paper presented at the Association for the Advancement of Baltic Studies meeting. Bloomington, Indiana. June, 1998.

Davies, James C. 1962. "Toward a Theory of Revolution." *American Sociological Review* 6(1): 5–19.

Davies, Norman and Antony Polonsky. 1991. "Introduction." In Norman Davies and Antony Polansky, eds., *Jews in Eastern Poland and the USSR, 1939–1946*, pp. 1–59. New York: St. Martin's Press.

Daxner, Igor. 1961. *L'udactvo pred narodnym sudom*. Bratislava: Slovenska Academia.

Deak, Istvan. 1992. "The Rise and Triumph of the East European Nation-State." *In Depth: A Journal for Values in Public Policy* 2: 77–95.

DeFigueiredo, Rui and Barry Weingast. 1997. "The Rationality of Fear: Political Opportunism and Ethnic Conflict." Paper presented at the Political Economy meetings. San Francisco, California. February, 1997.

Dershowitz, Alan. 1992. *Contrary to Popular Opinion*. New York: Pharos Books.

DeSousa, Ronald. 1987. *The Rationality of Emotion*. Cambridge, MA: MIT Press.

de Zayas, Alfred-Maurice. 1986. *A Terrible Revenge: The Ethnic Cleansing of the East European Germans, 1944–1950*. New York: St. Martin's Press.

Ditmer, Lowell. 1977. "Political Culture and Political Symbolism: Toward a Theoretical Synthesis." *World Politics* 29(July): 552–83.

Djilas, Aleksa. 1991. *The Contested Country: Yugoslav Unity and Communist Revolution, 1919–1953*. Cambridge, MA: Harvard University Press.

Djilas, Milovan. 1958. *Land without Justice*. New York: Harcourt, Brace, and Co.

1962. *Conversations with Stalin*. New York: Harcourt, Brace & World.

Dizdarevic, Zlatko. 1994. *Sarajevo: A War Journal*. New York: Henry Holt and Company.

Dollard, John, L. Doob, N. Miller, O. Mowrer, and R. Sears. 1939. *Frustration and Aggression*. New Haven, CT: Yale University Press.

Donia, Robert J. and John V. A. Fine. 1994. *Bosnia and Hercegovina: A Tradition Betrayed*. New York: Columbia University Press.

Douglas, Tom. 1995. *Scapegoats: Transferring Blame*. London: Routledge.

Dreifelds, Juris. 1977. "Latvian National Demands and Group Conciousness Since 1959." In George W. Simmonds, ed., *Nationalism in the USSR and Eastern Europe in the Era of Brezhnev and Kosygin*, pp. 136–56. Detroit, MI: University of Detroit Press.

1996. *Latvia in Transition*. Cambridge: Cambridge University Press.

Duff, Sheila Grant. 1970. *A German Protectorate: The Czechs Under Nazi Rule*. London: Frank Cass & Co., Ltd.

"Eastern Europe." *East European Jewish Affairs* 25(1): 49–72.

Einsatzgruppe A. 1941. Report of October 15, 1941, YVA, 0-51/57-1.

Ekman, Paul. 1992. *Telling Lies*. New York: Norton.

Bibliography

Elster, Jon. 1999. *Alchemies of the Mind: Rationality and the Emotions*. Cambridge: Cambridge University Press.

1996. "Rationality and the Emotions." *The Economic Journal* 106: 1386–88.

1993. *Political Psychology*. Cambridge: Cambridge University Press.

1989. *The Cement of Society*. Cambridge: Cambridge University Press.

1989. *Nuts and Bolts for the Social Sciences*. Cambridge: Cambridge University Press.

1983. *Sour Grapes: Studies in the Subversion of Rationality*. Cambridge: Cambridge University Press.

Enzensberger, Hans Magnus. 1993. *Civil Wars: From L.A. to Bosnia*. New York: The New Press.

"Estonia Begins to Recognize its Noncitizens." *The Current Digest of the Post Soviet Press* 50: 16, 28.

"Estonian Parliament Passes Amendments to Citizenship Law," *RFE/RL Newsline*, December 9, 1998.

Ezergailis, Andrew. 1996. "Latvia." In David S. Wyman, ed., *The World Reacts to the Holocaust*, pp. 354–87. Baltimore, MD: Johns Hopkins University Press.

Fanon, Frantz. 1961. *Wretched of the Earth*. Paris: Maspero.

FBIS-SOV-88-223.

FBIS-SOV-92-059, p. 80.

FBIS-SOV-92-059, p. 81.

FBIS-SOV-93-055, p. 83.

FBIS-SOV-93-140, pp. 78–79.

Fearon, James D. 1998. "Commitment Problems and the Spread of Ethnic Conflict." In David Lake and Donald Rothchild, eds., *The International Spread of Ethnic Conflict: Fear, Diffusion, Escalation*, pp. 107–26. Princeton, NJ: Princeton University Press.

1996. "Ethnic War as a Commitment Problem." In David Lake and Donald Rothchild, eds., *Ethnic Fears and Global Engagement*. LaJolla, CA: Institute on Global Conflict and Cooperation, University of California, San Diego.

1995. "Rationalist Explanations of War." *International Organization* 49: 379–414.

Fein, Helen. 1979. *Accounting for Genocide: National Responses and Jewish Victimization During the Holocaust*. New York: The Free Press.

Festinger, Leon. 1954. "A Theory of Social Comparison Processes." *Human Relations* 7: 117–40.

Fitzpatrick, Sheila. 1992. *The Cultural Front: Power and Culture in Revolutionary Russia*. Ithaca, NY: Cornell University Press.

Forbes, H. D. 1997. *Ethnic Conflict: Commerce, Culture, and the Contact Hypothesis*. New Haven, CT: Yale University Press.

Forced Migration Project. 1998. "Estonia and Latvia: Citizenship, Language and Conflict Prevention." The Open Society Institute. http://www.soros.org/fmp2/html/baltics.htm.

Frankel, Benjamin and Brian D. Kux. 1990. "Recalling the Dark Past of Lithuanian Nationalism." *Los Angeles Times* (April 29): M2.

Franks, David D. and Viktor Gecas. 1992. "Current Issues in Emotion Studies and Introduction to Chapters." In David D. Franks and Viktor Gecas, eds., *Social Perspectives on Emotion*, pp. 3–24. Greenwich, CT: JAI Press.

Fremund, Karel and Vaclav Kral. 1961. *Lesson From History: Documents Concerning Nazi Policies for Germanisation and Extermination in Czechoslovakia.* Prague: Orbis.

Frijda, Nico H. 1994. "Les Talionis: On Vengeance." In Stephanie H. M. van Goozen, Nanne E. Van de Poll, and Joseph A. Sergeant, eds., *Emotions: Essays on Emotion Theory,* pp. 263–90. Hillsdale, NJ: Lawrence Erlbaum Associates.

1987. *The Emotions.* Cambridge: Cambridge University Press.

Frome, Frieda. 1988. *Some Dare to Dream: Frieda Frome's Escape From Lithuania.* Ames: Iowa University Press.

Gagnon, V. P. 1994. "Serbia's Road to War." *Journal of Democracy* 5 (April): 117–31.

1995. "Ethnic Nationalism and International Conflict: The Case of Serbia." *International Security* 19: 130–66.

Gellner, Ernest. 1983. *Nations and Nationalism.* Ithaca, NY: Cornell University Press.

1996. "Reply to Critics." In John A. Hall and I. C. Jarvie, eds., *The Social Philosophy of Ernest Gellner,* pp. 623–86. Amsterdam: Rodopi.

Gerrits, Andre. 1995. "Antisemitism and Anti-Communism: The Myth of 'Judeo Communism' in Eastern Europe." *East European Jewish Affairs* 25(1): 49–72.

Gilbert, Martin. 1972. *Atlas of Russian History.* Great Britain: Dorset Press.

Gilmore, Al-Tony. 1975. *Bad Nigger! The National Impact of Jack Johnson.* Port Washington, NJ: Kennikat Press.

Girnius, Saulius. 1991. "The Lithuanian Citizenship Law." Radio Liberty Research Report. September 19, 1991.

Gitelman, Zvi, ed. 1997. *Bitter Legacy: Confronting the Holocaust in the USSR.* Bloomington: Indiana University Press.

Glenny, Misha. 1992. *The Fall of Yugoslavia: The Third Balkan War.* New York: Penguin Books.

2000. *The Balkans: Nationalism, War and the Great Powers, 1804–1999.* New York: Viking.

Goble, Paul. 1998. "Playing the Ethnic Card." *RFE/RL Newsline.* March 10, 1998.

1998. "Trapped by Democracy." *RFE/RL Newsline.* March 18, 1998.

Goffman, Erving. 1963. *Stigma: Notes on the Management of Spoiled Identity.* Engelwood Cliffs, NJ: Prentice Hall.

Goldhagen, Daniel Jonah. 1996. *Hitler's Willing Executioners: Ordinary Germans and the Holocaust.* New York: Alfred A. Knopf.

1999. *New Republic* May 17, 1999.

Gordon, Harry. 1992. *The Shadow of Death: The Holocaust in Lithuania.* Lexington: The University Press of Kentucky.

Gordy, Eric D. 1999. *The Culture of Power in Serbia: Nationalism and the Destruction of Alternatives.* University Park, PA: Pennsylvania State University Press.

Graham, Malbone W. 1940a. "Constitutional and Political Structure." In Robert J. Kerner, ed., *Czechoslovakia,* pp. 106–36. Cambridge: Cambridge University Press.

1940b. "Parties and Politics." In Robert J. Kerner, ed., *Czechoslovakia,* pp. 137–90. Cambridge: Cambridge University Press.

Bibliography

Green, Donald P. and Ian Shapiro. 1994. *Pathologies of Rational Choice Theory: A Critique of Applications in Political Science*. New Haven, CT: Yale University Press.

Greenfeld, Liah. 1992. *Nationalism: Five Roads to Modernity*. Cambridge, MA: Harvard University Press.

Gross, Jan T. 2001. *Neighbors: The Destruction of the Jewish Community in Jedwabne, Poland*. Princeton, NJ: Princeton University Press.

1993. "The Jewish Community in the Soviet-Annexed Territories on the Eve of the Holocaust: A Social Scientist's View." In Lucjan Dobroszycki and Jeffrey Gurock, eds., *The Holocaust in the Soviet Union*, pp. 155–71. New York: M. E. Sharpe.

1991. "The Sovietization of Western Ukraine and Western Byelorussia." In Norman Davies and Antony Polonsky, eds., *Jews in Eastern Poland and the USSR, 1939–1946*, pp. 60–76. New York: St. Martin's Press.

1986. "Polish-Jewish Relations During the War: An Interpretation." *European Journal of Sociology* 27: 199–214.

Gurr, Ted. 1970. *Why Men Rebel*. Princeton, NJ: Princeton University Press.

Hall, John A. 1998. "Introduction." In John A. Hall, ed., *The State of the Nation: Ernest Gellner and the Theory of Nationalism*, pp. 1–19. Cambridge: Cambridge University Press.

Hardin, Russell. 1995. *One for All: The Logic of Group Conflict*. Princeton, NJ: Princeton University Press.

Harre, Rom. 1986. "An Outline of the Social Constructionist Viewpoint." In Rom Harre, ed., *The Social Construction of Emotions*, pp. 2–14. New York: Basil Blackwell.

Harris, Chauncy. 1993. "The New Russian Minorities: A Statistical Overview." *Post-Soviet Geography* 34: 1–27.

Havrnek, Jan. 1990. "The Education of Czechs and Slovaks Under Foreign Domination, 1850–1918." In Janusz Tomiak et al., eds., *Comparative Studies on Governments and Non-Dominant Ethnic Groups in Europe, 1850–1940, Vol. I: Schooling, Educational Policy and Ethnic Identity*. New York: New York University Press.

Haxton, Michael. 1994. "The Poles of Lithuania." *Minorities at Risk Project*. http://www.bsos.umd.edu/cidcm/mar/litpole.htm.

Hayden, Robert. 1999. *Blueprints for a House Divided: The Constitutional Logic of the Yugoslav Conflicts*. Ann Arbor: The University of Michigan Press.

1996. "Schindler's Fate: Genocide, Ethnic Cleansing, and Population Transfers." *Slavic Review* 55(4): 727–48.

1993. "The Partition of Bosnia and Hercegovina, 1990–1993," Radio Free Europe/Radio Liberty Research Report, 2 (No. 22) May 1993.

Hebb, D. O., and W. R. Thompson. 1968. "Emotion and Society." In Leon Bramson and George Goethals, eds., *War: Studies From Psychology, Sociology, and Anthropology*, pp. 45–64. New York: Basic Books.

Hecker, Hans. 1994. *Die Deutschen im Russischen Reich, in der Sowjetunion und ihren Nachfolgestaaten*. Koln: Verlag Wissenschaft und Politik Claus-Peter von Nottbeck.

Hedstrom, Peter and Richard Swedberg, eds. 1998. *Social Mechanisms: An Analytical Approach to Social Theory.* Cambridge: Cambridge University Press.

Hehn, Paul. 1979. *The German Struggle against Yugoslav Guerrillas in World War II: German Counter-Insurgency in Yugoslavia 1941–1943.* Boulder, CO: East European Quarterly (Distributed by Columbia University Press).

Heller, Yves. 1996. "How Croatia Reclaimed its Accursed Land." *Guardian Weekly* 31 March 1996.

Hiden, John and Patrick Salmon. 1994. *The Baltic States and Europe: Estonia, Latvia, and Lithuania in the Twentieth Century.* London: Longman.

Hobbes, Thomas. 1963. *Leviathan.* New York: Meridian Books.

Hobsbawm, Eric. 1990. *Nations and Nationalism since the 1780s: Programme, Myth, Reality.* Cambridge: Cambridge University Press.

Hodson, Randy, Dusko Sekulic, and Garth Massey. 1994. "National Tolerance in the Former Yugoslavia." *American Journal of Sociology* 99(6): 1534–58.

Hoensch, Jorg. 1996. *A History of Modern Hungary.* New York: Longman Group.

Holbrooke, Richard. 1999. *To End a War.* New York: The Modern Library.

Honig, Jan Willem and Norbert Both. 1996. *Srebrenica: Record of a War Crime.* New York, NY: Penguin Books.

Horowitz, Donald. 2001. *The Deadly Ethnic Riot.* Berkeley: University of California Press.

1998. "Structure and Strategy in Ethnic Conflict." Paper presented for the Annual World Bank Conference on Development Economics, Washington DC, April 20–21, 1998.

1985. *Ethnic Groups in Conflict.* Berkeley: University of California Press.

1973. "Direct, Displaced, and Cumulative Ethnic Aggression." *Comparative Politics* 6(1): 1–16.

Hroch, Miroslav. 1985. *Social Preconditions of National Revival in Europe: A Comparative Analysis of the Social Composition of Patriotic Groups Among the Smaller European Nations.* Cambridge: Cambridge University Press.

1996. "Nationalism and National Movements: Comparing the Past and the Present of Central and Eastern Europe." *Nations and Nationalism* 2(11): 35–44.

Hugelmann, Karl Gottfried, ed. 1934. *Das Nationalitatenrecht des alten Osterreichs.* Vienna: W. Branmuller, Univeritats-Verlagsbuch handlung.

Huntington, Samuel. 1993. "The Clash of Civilizations." *Foreign Affairs* 72(3): 22–49.

Ignatieff, Michael. 1993. *Blood and Belonging: Journey into the New Nationalism.* New York: Noonday Press.

Janics, Kelman. 1982. *Czechoslovak Policy and the Hungarian Minority, 1945–1948.* New York: Columbia University Press.

Jaworski, Rudolf. 1991. "The German Minorities in Poland and Czechoslovakia in the Interwar Period." In Paul Smith et al., eds., *Comparative Studies on Governments and Non-Dominant Ethnic Groups in Europe, 1850–1940, Vol. V: Ethnic Groups in International Relations.* New York: New York University Press.

Jelinek, Yeshayahu. 1983. *The Lust for Power: Nationalism, Slovakia, and the Communists, 1918–1948.* New York: Columbia University Press.

Bibliography

Jervis, Robert. 1976. *Perception and Misperception in International Politics*. Princeton, NJ: Princeton University Press.

1978. "Cooperation Under the Security Dilemma." *World Politics* 2: 167–213.

Johnson, Owen. 1985. *Slovakia, 1918–1938: Education and the Making of a Nation*. New York: Columbia University Press.

Jubulis, Mark. 1997. *Nationalism and Ethnic Relations in Latvia's Transition from Communism: Citizenship and Language in the Post-Soviet Nation State*. Unpublished Ph.D dissertation. University of Notre Dame, South Bend, Indiana.

Judah, Tim. 1997. *The Serbs: History, Myth, and the Destruction of Yugoslavia*. New Haven, CT: Yale University Press.

Kaplan, Robert. 1993. *Balkan Ghosts: A Journey Through History*. London: Papermac.

Kappeler, Andreas, et al. 1987. *Die Deutschen im Russischen Reich und im Sowjetstaat*. Koln: Markus Verlag.

Karklins, Rasma. 1994. *Ethnopolitics and Transition to Democracy: The Collapse of the USSR and Latvia*. Baltimore, MD: Johns Hopkins University Press.

Kaufman, Stuart. 1996. "Spiraling to Ethnic War." *International Security* 21(2): 108–38.

Kaufmann, Chaim. 1996. "Possible and Impossible Solutions to Ethnic Civil Wars." *International Security* 20(4): 136–75.

Kellas, James G. 1991. *The Politics of Nationalism and Ethnicity*. New York: St. Martin's Press.

Kenney, George. 1995. "The Bosnian Calculation." *The New York Times Magazine*, April 23, 1995.

Kerner, Robert Joseph. 1945. *Czechoslovakia*. Berkeley: University of California Press.

Kifner, John. 1999. "How Serb Forces Purged One Million Albanians." *The New York Times*, May 29, 1999.

Kionka, Riina and Raivo Vetik. 1996. "Estonia and the Estonians." In Graham Smith, ed. *The Nationalities Question in the Post-Soviet States*, pp. 129–46. London: Longman.

Kiraly, Bela K. and Nandor F. Dreisziger, eds. 1985. *War and Society in East Central Europe: East Central European Society in World War I*. Boulder, CO: Social Science Monographs, distributed by Columbia University Press.

Kirschbaum, Stanislav J. 1995. *A History of Slovakia: The Struggle for Survival*. New York: St. Martin's Press.

Kohn, Hans. 1940. "The Historical Roots of Czech Democracy." In Robert J. Kerner, ed., *Czechoslovakia*. Cambridge: Cambridge University Press.

1961. *The Habsburg Empire, 1804–1918*. Princeton, NJ: Van Nostrand.

Kolitz, Zvi. 1993. "The Physical and Metaphysical Dimensions of the Extermination of the Jews in Lithuania." In Lucjan Dobroszycki and Jeffrey Gurock, eds., *The Holocaust in the Soviet Union*, pp. 195–204. New York: M. E. Sharpe.

Kolstoe, Paul. 1995. *Russians in the Former Soviet Republics*. London: Hurst and Company.

Koralka, Jiri. 1991. "Nationality Representation in Bohemia, Moravia, and Austrian Silesia, 1848–1914." In Geoffrey Alderman et al., eds., *Comparative*

281

Studies on Governments and Non-Dominant Ethnic Groups in Europe, 1850–1940, Vol. IV: Governments, Ethnic Groups and Political Representation. New York: New York University Press.

Korzec, Pawel, and Jean-Charles Szurek. "Jews and Poles under Soviet Occupation (1939–1941): Conflicting Interests." In Antony Polonsky, ed., *From Shtetl to Socialism: Studies from Polin*, pp. 385–406. London and Washington: Littman Library of Jewish Civilization.

Kumar, Radha, 1997. *Divide and Fall?: Bosnia in the Annals of Partition.* London: Verso.

Laitin, David D. 1998. *Identity in Formation: The Russian-Speaking Populations in the Near Abroad.* Ithaca, NY: Cornell University Press.

1998. "Nationalism and Language: A Post-Soviet Perspective." In John A. Hall, ed., *The State of the Nation: Ernest Gellner and the Theory of Nationalism,* pp. 135–57. Cambridge: Cambridge University Press.

1991. "The National Uprisings in the Soviet Union." *World Politics* 44: 137–77.

Lake, David A. and Donald Rothchild. 1996. "Containing Fear: The Origins and Management of Ethnic Conflict." *International Security* 21: 41–75.

Laqueur, Walter. 1996. *Fascism: Past, Present, Future.* Oxford: Oxford University Press.

"Latvian Lawmakers Adopt Citizenship Amendments." *RFE/RL Newsline.* June 23, 1998.

"Latvian Deputies Demand Delay in Publishing Amended Citizenship Law." *RFE/RL Newsline.* June 29, 1998.

Latvija Demografijas Gadagramata (Demographic Yearbook of Latvia). 1995. Riga: Latvijas Republikas Valsts Statistikas Komiteja.

Lautenschlager, Dia. "Prior Regime Structures in Determining Nationalist Success: The Case of Slovak Independence." Paper presented at the 1994 Annual Meeting of the American Political Science Association, The New York Hilton, September 1–4, 1994.

Law of the Lithuanian Supreme Council. 1991. *Law on Citizenship.* December 5, 1991.

Leff, Carol Skalnik. 1988. *National Conflict in Czechoslovakia.* Princeton, NJ: Princeton University Press.

1997. *The Czech and Slovak Republics: Nation Versus State.* Boulder, CO: Westview Press.

Levin, Dov. 1980. "Jews in the Lithuanian Establishment." *Soviet Jewish Affairs* 10: 21–37.

1987. "The Jews and the Socio-Economic Sovietization of Lithuania, 1940–41." *Soviet Jewish Affairs* 17: 17–30.

Soviet Jewish Affairs 10: 39–51. "The Jews and the Election Campaigns in Lithuania, 1940–41."

Levita, Roman and Mikhail Loiberg. 1994. "The Empire and the Russians." In Vladimir Shlpentokh, Munir Sendich, and Emil Payin, eds. *The New Russian Diaspora: Russian Minorities in the Former Soviet Republics.* Armonk, NY: M. E. Sharpe.

Bibliography

Lieven, Anatol. 1993. *The Baltic Revolution: Estonia, Latvia, Lithuania, and the Path to Independence*. New Haven, CT: Yale University Press.

"Lithuania Starts to Wipe Out Convictions for War Crimes." *The New York Times*, September 5, 1991.

Luza, Radomir. 1964. *Transfer of the Sudeten Germans*. New York: New York University Press.

Maas, Peter. 1996. *Love Thy Neighbor: A Story of War*. New York: Alfred A. Knopf.

Macartney, C. A. 1937. *Hungary and Her Successors: The Treaty of Trianon and Its Consequences, 1919–1937*. London: Oxford University Press.

Magas, Branka. 1993. *The Destruction of Yugoslavia: Tracking the Break-up, 1980–1992*. London: Verso.

Malanowski, Jan. 1991. "Sociological Aspects of the Annexation of Poland's Eastern Provinces to the USSR in 1939–41." In Keith Sword, ed., *The Soviet Takeover of the Polish Eastern Provinces, 1939–41*, pp. 71–85. New York: St. Martin's Press.

Malcolm, Noel. 1999. *Kosovo: A Short History*. New York: New York University Press.

Mamatey, Victor S. and Radomir Luza, eds. 1973. *A History of the Czechoslovak Republic, 1918–1948*. Princeton, NJ: Princeton University Press.

Mason, T. David. 1994. "The Ethnic Dimension of Civil Violence in the Post Cold War Era: Structural Configurations and Rational Choices." Paper presented at the Annual Meeting of the American Political Science Association, New York, September 1–4, 1994.

Mayer, Arno. 1988. *Why Did the Heavens Not Darken?: The Final Solution in History*. New York: Pantheon Books.

Mead, George Herbert. 1934. *Mind, Self, and Society*. Chicago: University of Chicago Press.

Mearsheimer, John and Stephen Van Evera. 1995. "When Peace Means War." *New Republic*, December 1995, Vol. 213: 16–21.

Mendelsohn, Ezra. 1983. *The Jews of East Central Europe Between the World Wars*. Bloomington: Indiana University Press.

Mertus, Julie. 1999. *Kosovo: How Myths and Truths Started a War*. Berkeley: University of California Press.

Mestrovic, Stjepan, ed. 1996. *Genocide after Emotion: The Postemotional Balkan War*. London: Routledge.

Míkus, Joseph. 1977. *Slovakia and the Slovaks*. Washington: Three Continents Press.

Mishell, Walter. 1988. *Kaddish for Kovno: Life and Death in a Lithuanian Village, 1941–1945*. Chicago: Chicago Review Press.

Misiunas, Romuald J. and Rein Taagepera. 1983. *The Baltic States: Years of Dependence, 1940–1990*. Berkeley: University of California Press.

Mitter, Wolfgang. 1990. "German Schools in Czechoslovakia, 1918–1938." In Janusz Tomiak et al., eds., *Comparative Studies on Governments and Non-Dominant Ethnic Groups in Europe, 1850–1940, Vol. I: Schooling, Educational Policy and Ethnic Identity*. New York: New York University Press.

Mouzelis, Nicos. 1998. "Ernest Gellner's Theory of Nationalism: Some Definitional and Methodological Issues." In John A. Hall, ed., *The State of the Nation: Ernest Gellner and the Theory of Nationalism*, pp. 158–65. Cambridge: Cambridge University Press.

Mueller, John. 2000. "The Banality of 'Ethnic War.'" *International Security* 25(1): 42–70.

Muiznieks, Nils. 1993. *The Baltic Popular Movements and the Disintegration of the Soviet Union*. Unpublished Ph.D. dissertation. University of California, Berkeley.

Muller, Edmund and Karl Dieter Opp. 1986. "Rational Choice and Rebellious Collective Action." *American Political Science Review* 80: 472–87.

Naimark, Norman M. 2001. *Fires of Hatred: Ethnic Cleansing in Twentieth Century Europe*. Cambridge, MA: Harvard University Press.

Necak, Dusan. 1995. "Historical Elements for Understanding the 'Yugoslav Question.'" In Payam Akhavan and Robert Howse, eds., *Yugoslavia, the Former and the Future: Reflections by Scholars from the Region*, pp. 13–28. Washington, DC: The Brookings Institution.

Niklewicz, Konrad. 1997. "Twice Forgotten." *The Warsaw Voice* No. 17(444) April 27, 1997. http://www.warsawvoice.com.pl/Pl- iso/v444/neighbors.html.

Nisbett, Richard E. and Dov Cohen. 1996. *Culture of Honor: The Psychology of Violence in the South*. Boulder, CO: Westview Press.

Olson, David. 1994. "The Sundered State: Federalism and Parliament in Czechoslovakia." In Thomas F. Remington, ed., *Parliaments in Transition*, pp. 97–123. Boulder, CO: Westview Press.

Opalski, M., B. Tsilevich, and P. Dutkiewicz. 1994. *Ethnic Conflict in the Baltic States: The Case of Latvia*. Kingston, Ontario: The Kashtan Press.

Ordaz, Pablo. 1999. *El Pais*. September 23, 1999.

Orucevic, Safet. "Mostar: Europe's Failure." *Bosnia Report*, April–June 1996.

Ortner, Sherry B. 1990. "Patterns of History: Cultural Schemas in the Foundings of Sherpa Religious Institutions." In Emiko Ohnuki-Tierney, ed., *Culture Through Time: Anthropological Approaches*. Stanford, CA: Stanford University Press.

Ortony, Andrew, Gerald Clore, and Allan Collins. 1988. *The Cognitive Structure of Emotions*. Cambridge: Cambridge University Press.

Parming, Tonu. 1982. "Population and Ethnicity as Intervening Variables in the 1905/1917 Revolutions in the Russian Baltic Provinces." In Gert von Pistohlkors et al., eds., *Die Baltischen Provinzen Russlands Zwischen den Revolutionen von 1905 und 1917*, pp. 1–19. Koln: Bohlau Verlag.

Pauley, Bruce F. 1972. *The Habsburg Legacy, 1867–1939*. New York: Holt, Rinehart and Winston.

Pavkovic, Aleksander. 1997. "Anticipating the Disintegration: Nationalisms in the Former Yugoslavia, 1980–1990." *Nationalities Papers* 25: 427–40.

Pavlowitch, Stevan. 1988. *The Improbable Survivor: Yugoslavia and its Problems, 1918–1988*. Columbus: Ohio State University Press.

Petersen, Roger. 1999. "Structure and Mechanism in Comparisons." In John Bowen and Roger Petersen, eds., *Critical Comparisons in Politics and Culture*, pp. 61–77. Cambridge: Cambridge University Press.

2000. *Resistance and Rebellion: Lessons from Eastern Europe.* Cambridge: Cambridge University Press.

Petrovic, Ruza. 1992. "The National Composition of Yugoslav's Population, 1991." *Yugoslav Survey*, No. 1, 1992.

"Police Use Force to Disperse Demonstrators in Riga." *RFE/RL Newsline.* March 4, 1998.

Posen, Barry R. 1993. "The Security Dilemma and Ethnic Conflict." *Survival* 35: 27–47.

Poulton, Hugh and Miranda Vickers. 1997. "The Kosovo Albanians: Ethnic Confrontation with the Slavic State." In Hugh Poulton and Suha Taji Farouki, eds., *Muslim Identity and the Balkan State*, pp. 139–69. New York: New York University Press.

Pratto, Felicia, James Sidanius, Lisa M. Stallworth, and B. F. Malle. 1994. "Social Dominance Orientation: A Personality Variable Predicting Social and Political Attitudes." *Journal of Personality and Social Psychology* 67: 741–63.

Prunskis, Juozas. 1979. *Lithuania's Jews and the Holocaust.* Chicago: Lithuanian American Council.

Ramet, Sabrina. 1996. *Balkan Babel: The Disintegration of Yugoslavia from the Death of Tito to Ethnic War.* Boulder, CO: Westview Press.

1996. "Nationalism and the 'Idiocy' of the Countryside: The Case of Serbia." *Ethnic and Racial Studies* 19: 70–87.

1992. *Nationalism and Federalism in Yugoslavia, 1962–1991.* Bloomington: University of Indiana Press.

Rauch, George von. 1974. *The Baltic States: The Years of Independence.* Trans. Gerald Onn. Berkeley: University of California Press.

Raun, Toivo U. 1982. "Estonian Social and Political Thought." In Gert von Pistohlkors et al., eds., *Die Baltischen Provinzen Russlands Zwischen den Revolutionen von 1905 und 1917.* Koln: Bohlau Verlag.

1994. "Ethnic Relations and Conflict in the Baltic States." In W. Raymond Duncan and G. Paul Holman, Jr., eds., *Ethnic Nationalism and Regional Conflict: The Former Soviet Union and Yugoslavia.* Boulder, CO: Westview Press.

Reynolds, Vernon, Vincent Fagler and Ian Vine. 1986. *The Sociobiology of Ethnocentrism: Evolutionary Dimensions of Xenophobia.* Athens: University of Georgia Press.

Roman, Eric. 1996. *Hungary and the Victor Powers, 1945–1950.* New York: St. Martin's Press.

Rose, Richard. 1997. "New Baltic Barometer III: A Survey Study." *Studies in Public Policy Number 284.* Glasgow, Scotland: Centre for the Study of Public Policy.

Rosenthal, A. M. 1991. "Absolutions for Killers." *Los Angeles Times*, September 10: A19.

Rothschild, Joseph. 1974. *East Central Europe Between the Two World Wars.* Seattle: University of Washington Press.

Roucek, Joseph S. 1940. "Czechoslovakia and Her Minorities." In Robert J. Kerner, ed., *Czechoslovakia*, pp. 171–92. Cambridge: Cambridge University Press.

Rubinstein, Richard. 1990. "Modernization and the Politics of Extermination." In Michael Berenbaum, ed., *A Mosaic of Victims: Non-Jews Persecuted and Murdered by the Nazis*, pp. 3–19. New York: New York University Press.

"Russia, Latvia Spar Over Riga Police Action." *RFE/RL Newsline*. March 6, 1998.

"Russian Federation Council Slams Latvia." *RFE/RL Newsline*. March 13, 1998.

Salert, Barbara. 1976. *Revolutions and Revolutionaries*. New York: Elsevier.

Sardamov, Ivelin. 1999. "Ethnic Warriors: Ethnicity and Genocide in the Balkans." Paper presented at the Fourth Annual Convention of the Association for the Study of Nationalities, Columbia University, New York, April 15–17, 1999.

Scheff, Thomas J. 1994. *Bloody Revenge: Emotions, Nationalism, and War*. Boulder, CO: Westview Press.

Schneider, Gertrude. 1993. "The Two Ghettos in Riga, Latvia, 1941–1943." In Lucjan Dobroszycki and Jeffrey Gurock, eds., *The Holocaust in the Soviet Union*. New York: M. E. Sharpe.

Schofield, Norman. 2000. "Constitutional Political Economy: On the Possibility of Combining Rational Choice Theory and Comparative Politics." *Annual Review of Political Science* 3: 277–303.

Scott, James C. 1990. *Domination and the Arts of Resistance*. New Haven, CT: Yale University Press.

Sekulic, Dusko, Garth Massey, and Randy Hodson. 1994. "Who Were the Yugoslavs? Failed Sources of Common Identity in the Former Yugoslavia." *American Sociological Review* 59: 83–97.

Seeburger, Francis F. 1992. "Blind Sight and Brute Feeling: The Divorce of Cognition From Emotion." *Social Perspectives on Emotion* 1: 47–60.

Sells, Michael A. 1998. *The Bridge Betrayed: Religion and Genocide in Bosnia*. Berkeley: University of California Press.

Senn, Alfred Erich. 1990. *Lithuania Awakening*. Berkeley: University of California Press.

Seton-Watson, Hugh. 1967. *Eastern Europe Between the Wars, 1918–1941*. New York: Harper & Row.

Seton-Watson, R.W. 1965. *A History of the Czechs and Slovaks*. Hamden, CT: Archon Books.

Sewell, William. 1992. "A Theory of Structure: Duality, Agency, and Transformation." *American Journal of Sociology* 98: 1–29.

Shelley, Louise I. 1996. *Policing Soviet Society: The Evolution of State Control*. New York: Routledge.

Shner-Neshamit, Sara. 1997. "Jewish-Lithuanian Relations during World War II: History and Rhetoric." In Zvi Gitelman, ed., *Bitter Legacy: Confront the Holocaust in the USSR*, pp. 167–84. Bloomington: Indiana University Press.

Shtromas, Aleksandras. 1994. "The Baltic States as Soviet Republics: Tensions and Contradictions." In Graham Smith, ed., *The Baltic States: The National Self-Determination of Estonia, Latvia and Lithuania*, pp. 86–117. New York: St. Martin's Press.

Bibliography

Siann, Gerda. 1985. *Accounting for Aggression: Perspectives on Aggression and Violence.* Boston: Allen and Unwin.

Sidanius, James. 1993. "The Psychology of Group Conflict and the Dynamic of Oppression: A Social Dominance Perspective." In Shanto Iyengar and William J. McGuire, eds., *Explorations in Political Psychology*, pp. 183–219. Durham, NC: Duke University Press.

Sidanius, James and Felicia Pratto. 1999. *Social Dominance: An Intergroup Theory of Social Hierarchy and Oppression.* Cambridge: Cambridge University Press.

Sidanius, James, Felicia Pratto, and Diana Brief. 1995. "Group Dominance and the Political Psychology of Gender: A Cross-Cultural Comparison." *Political Psychology* 16(2): 381–96.

Siekierski, Maciej. 1991. "The Jews in Soviet Occupied Eastern Poland at the End of 1939: Numbers and Distribution." In Norman Davies and Antony Polonsky, ed., *Jews in Eastern Poland and the USSR, 1939–1946*, pp. 110–15. New York: St. Martin's Press.

Slapnicka, Helmut. 1993. "Majorities and Minorities in an Inverted Position: Czechoslovakia, 1918–1939." In Sergij Vilfan et al., eds., *Comparative Studies on Governments and Non-Dominant Ethnic Groups in Europe, 1850–1940, Vol. III: Ethnic Groups and Language Rights.* New York: New York University Press.

Smelser, Ronald. 1996. "The Expulsion of the Sudeten Germans, 1945–1952." *Nationalities Papers* 24(1): 79–92.

Smith, Graham, Aadne Aasland, and Richard Mole. 1994. "Statehood, Ethnic Relations and Citizenship." In Graham Smith, ed. *The Baltic States: The National Self-Determination of Estonia, Latvia and Lithuania.* New York: St. Martin's Press.

Snyder, Jack and Karen Ballentine. 1996. "Nationalism and the Marketplace of Ideas." *International Security* 21: 5–40.

Snyder, Tim. 1995. "National Myths and International Relations: Poland and Lithuania 1989–1990." *East European Politics and Societies* 9: 317–44. Information Access reprint.

Somit, Albert and Steven A. Peterson. 1997. *Darwinism, Dominance, and Democracy: Biological Bases of Authoritarianism.* Westport, CT: Praeger.

Srb, Vladimir. 1967. *Demografika prirucka.* Praha: Nakladatelstvi svoboda.

1996. "Asimilace a p eklaneninarodnosti obyvatelstva eskoslovensku ve sv tle scitani lidu 1950–1991." *Demografie* 38(3): 158.

Stanek, Tomas. 1991. *Odsun Nemcu z eskoslovensko, 1945–1947.* Praha: Nase vojsko.

Statistical Yearbook of the Czech and Slovak Federal Republic. 1991.

Steinberg, James B. 1993. "Turning Points in Bosnia and the West." In Zalmay M. Khalilzad, ed., *Lessons from Bosnia.* Rand Report CF-112-AF.

Steinberg, Jonathan. 1990. *All or Nothing: The Axis and the Holocaust 1941–1943.* London: Routledge.

Stern, Paul. 1995. "Why Do Individuals Sacrifice for Their Nations?" *Political Psychology* 16: 217–36.

Sternell, Zeev. 1994. *The Birth of Fascist Ideology.* Princeton, NJ: Princeton University Press.

287

Stinchcombe, Arthur. 1991. "On the Conditions of Fruitfulness of Theorizing about Mechanisms in Social Science." *Philosophy of the Social Sciences* 21: 367–88.

Stitkovac, Ejub. 1997. "Croatia: The First War." In Jasminka Udovicki and James Ridgeway, eds., *Burn This House: The Making and Unmaking of Yugoslavia*, pp. 153–73. Durham, NC: Duke University Press.

Subtelny, Orest. 1988. *Ukraine: A History*. Toronto: University of Toronto Press.

Suhl, Yuri. 1967. *They Fought Back: The Story of the Jewish Resistance in Nazi Europe*. New York: Crown Publishers.

Suvar, Stipe. 1974. *Nacionalno and nacionalisticko*. Split: Marksisticki Centar.

Taagepera, Rein. 1993. *Estonia's Return to Independence*. Boulder, CO: Westview Press.

Tajfel. H. 1981. "Social Stereotypes and Social Groups." In J. C. Turner and H. Giles, eds., *Intergroup Behaviour*. Oxford: Blackwell.

Taylor, Charles. 1998. "Nationalism and Modernity." In John A. Hall, ed., *The State of the Nation: Ernest Gellner and the Theory of Nationalism*, pp. 191–218. Cambridge: Cambridge University Press.

Telushkin, J. 1992. *Jewish Humor*. New York: Morrow.

The Baltic Observer, November 26–December 2, 1992, p. 13.

The Baltic Times Staff. 1998. "Latvian Voters Say "yes" to Amendments." *The Baltic Times*, October 8–14.

Tigrid, Pavel. 1991. *Lidove noviny*. Czech Republic, Prague.

Tilly, Charles. 1975. "Revolutions and Collective Violence." In F. I. Greenstein and N. W. Polsby, eds., *Handbook of Political Science: Macropolitical Theory*, pp. 483–555. Reading, MA: Addison-Wesley.

Todd, Emmanuel. 1994. *Le Destin des Immigres B Assimilation et segregation dan les democraties occidentales*. Paris: Seuil.

Tory, Abraham. 1990. *Surviving the Holocaust: the Kovno Ghetto Diary*. Cambridge: Harvard University Press.

Tuskenis, Edvardas, ed. 1999. *Lithuania in European Politics: The Years of the First Republic, 1918–1940*. New York: St. Martin's Press.

Udovicki, Jasminka and Ejub Stitkovac. 1997. "Bosnia and Hercegovina: The Second War." In Jasminka Udovicki and James Ridgeway, eds., *Burn This House: The Making and Unmaking of Yugoslavia*, pp. 174–214. Durham, NC: Duke University Press.

van den Berghe, Pierre. 1981. *The Ethnic Phenomenon*. New York: Elsevier.

van der Dennen, John M. G. 1986. "Ethnocentrism and In-group/Out-group Differentiation: A Review and Interpretation of the Literature." In Vernon Reynolds, Vincent Fagler, and Ian Vine, eds., *The Sociobiology of Ethnocentrism: Evolutionary Dimensions of Xenophobia*, pp. 1–47. Athens: University of Georgia Press.

Vardys, V. Stanley and Judith B. Sedaitis. 1997. *Lithuania: The Rebel Nation*. Boulder, CO: Westview Press.

Venclova, Tomas. 1989. "Jews and Lithuanians." *Cross Currents* 8: 55–73.

Bibliography

"Vicvaldis Lacis: 'Vy ne grazhdane vtofgo sorta, vy niktoí.'" *Sovetskaia Molodezh,* September 11, 1991.

Volkan, Vamik D. 1987. "Psychoanalytic Aspects of Ethnic Conflicts." In Joseph Montville, ed., *Conflict and Peacemaking in Multiethnic Societies,* pp. 81–92. Lexington, MA: Lexington Books.

Von Rauch, Georg. 1974. *The Baltic States: The Years of Independence 1917–1940.* New York: St. Martin's Press.

Weingast, Barry. 1994. "Constructing Trust: The Political and Economic Roots of Ethnic and Regional Conflict." Unpublished manuscript.

Weiss, Aharon. 1991. "Some Economic and Social Problems of the Jews of Eastern Galicia in the Period of Soviet Rule (1939–1941)." In Norman Davies and Antony Polonsky, eds., *Jews in Eastern Poland and the USSR, 1939–1946,* pp. 77–109. New York: St. Martin's Press.

West, Rebecca. 1995. *Black Lamb and Grey Falcon: A Journey Through Yugoslavia.* New York: Penguin Books.

Wightman, Gordon. 1995. "The Development of the Party System and the Break-up of Czechoslovakia." In Gordon Wightman, ed., *Party Formation in East-Central Europe,* pp. 59–78. Brookfield, VT: Edward Elgar.

Wilhelm, Hans-Heinrich. 1997. "Inventing the Holocaust for Latvia: New Research." In Zvi Gitelman, ed., *Bitter Legacy: Confronting the Holocaust in the USSR,* pp. 104–22. Bloomington: Indiana University Press.

Wiskeman, Elizabeth. 1956. *Germany's Eastern Neighbours: Problems Relating to the Oder-Neisse Line and the Czech Frontier Regions.* London: Oxford University Press.

———. 1967. *Czechs and Germans.* London: Macmillan Press.

Wittram, Reinhard. 1973. *Baltische Geschichte.* Darmstadt: Wissenschaftliche Buchgesellschaft.

Wolchik, Sharon. 1991. *Czechoslovakia in Transition: Politics, Economics, & Society.* New York: Pinter Publishers.

Woodward, Susan. 2000. "Diaspora, or the Dangers of Disunification? Putting the 'Serbian Model' into Perspective." In Michael Mandelbaum, ed., *The New European Diasporas: National Minorities and Conflict in Eastern Europe,* pp. 159–213. New York: Council on Foreign Relations Press.

———. 1995. *Socialist Unemployment: The Political Economy of Yugoslavia 1945–1990.* Princeton, NJ: Princeton University Press.

Wyatt, Katherine Day and Joseph Míkus. 1963. *Slovakia, A Political History: 1918–1950.* Milwaukee, WI: Marquette University Press.

Ycikas, Sima. 1997. "Lithuanian-Jewish Relations in the Shadow of the Holocaust." In Zvi Gitelman, ed., *Bitter Legacy: Confronting the Holocaust in the USSR,* pp. 185–213. Bloomington: Indiana University Press.

Young-Bruehl, Elizabeth. 1996. *The Anatomy of Prejudices.* Cambridge, MA: Harvard University Press.

Zaprudnik, Jan. 1993. *Belarus: At a Crossroads in History.* Boulder, CO: Westview Press.

Zbikowski, Andrzej. 1993. "Local Anti-Jewish Pogroms in the Occupied Territories of Eastern Poland, June–July 1941." In Lucjan Dobroszycki and Jeffrey Gurock, eds., *The Holocaust in the Soviet Union*, pp. 173–79. Armonk, NY: M. E. Sharpe.

Zenner, Walter P. 1987. "Middleman Minorities and Genocide." In Isidor Walliman and Michael N. Dobkowski, eds., *Genocide and the Modern Age: Etiology and Case Studies of Mass Death*, pp. 253–81. New York: Greenwood Press.

Zubac, Kresimir. 1998. *Globus*. January 2.

Zuvintas, A. 1989. "An Open Letter to Tomas Venclova." *Cross Currents* 8: 62–67.

Index

Adorno, Theodore, 77
Albanians, 13, 230, 243, 246, 256
  in Kosovo, 210–11, 219–24, 242–51,
  255, 268
  see also Kosovo
Alexander, King, 215, 224
anarchy, 68, 70–1, 74, 95, 98, 99, 101,
  104, 119, 227, 265
"ancient hatreds." *see* Hatred
Andric, Ivo, 6, 67–8
antisemitism, 113, 115, 116, 118, 130,
  132, 134, 171–2
Argentina, 162
attribution. *see* Rage and target
  selection
Austria, 179, 182–4, 206
  see also Vienna Conference
Austro-Hungarian Empire, 54, 120,
  176–80, 189, 193, 203–4, 206,
  213–14, 222–3, 236, 245, 247, 259
  Dual Compromise, 183

Balkan Wars, 65, 212, 244–5
Baltic Germans, 87–94, 165, 172,
  205–6
  see also Germans
Banac, Ivo, 212, 229
Barbarossa, 85, 95, 98, 99, 101, 112,
  113, 114, 128
Belorussia, 101, 111, 112, 166, 169,
  172

Belorussians, 10, 101, 103, 111, 119,
  121, 125, 129, 257
Bespuca. *see* Tudjman, Franjo
Boban, Mate, 232, 233, 235, 242
Bogdanovic, Dimitrije, 247
Bosnia-Hercegovina, 67–8, 83, 209–
  10, 225, 231–42, 259, 265–
  7
  Bosnian Muslim-Croat Federation,
  232, 234–6, 242
  Croatian Democratic Union
  (HDZ), 232
  Herceg-Bosna, 232, 234
  Party of Democratic Action (SDA),
  239–40
  see also Croats, Bosnian Muslims,
  Serbs
Bosnian Muslim-Croat Federation. *see*
  Bosnia-Hercegovina
Bosnian Muslims, 13, 83, 210, 211–12,
  219–20, 225, 232–9, 255–7, 259,
  266–7, 269
Bringa, Tone, 7, 203, 238
Brioni Plenum, 217
Britain, 216
Bristol School, 46–8
Broz, Josef. *see* Tito
Brubaker, Rogers, 9, 58–60, 167,
  258
Byelorussia. *see* Belorussia
Byelorussians. *see* Belorussians

291